DREAMers and the Choreography of Protest

RECENT TITLES IN
OXFORD STUDIES IN CULTURE AND POLITICS
Clifford Bob and James M. Jasper, General Editors

Political Voice
Protest, Democracy, and Marginalised Groups
Aidan McGarry

Flexible Authoritarianism
Cultivating Ambition and Loyalty in Russia
Anna Schwenck

Base Towns
Local Contestation of the U.S. Military in Korea and Japan
Claudia Junghyun Kim

The Return of the Native
Can Liberalism Safeguard Us Against Nativism?
Jan Willem Duyvendak and Josip Kešić
with Timothy Stacy

Rally 'round the Flag
The Search for National Honor and Respect in Times of Crisis
Yuval Feinstein

Gains and Losses
How Protestors Win and Lose
James M. Jasper, Luke Elliott-Negri, Isaac Jabola-Carolus, Marc Kagan, Jessica Mahlbacher, Manès Weisskircher, and Anna Zhelnina

The Silk Road
Connecting Histories and Futures
Tim Winter

Unconventional Combat
Intersectional Action in the Veterans' Peace Movement
Michael A. Messner

Discursive Turns and Critical Junctures
Debating Citizenship after the Charlie Hebdo Attacks
Donatella della Porta, Pietro Castelli Gattinara, Konstantinos Eleftheriadis, and Andrea Felicetti

Democracy Reloaded
Inside Spain's Political Laboratory from 15-M to Podemos
Cristina Flesher Fominaya

Public Characters
The Politics of Reputation and Blame
James M. Jasper, Michael P. Young, and Elke Zuern

Empire's Legacy
Roots of a Far-Right Affinity in Contemporary France
John W.P. Veugelers

Situational Breakdowns
Understanding Protest Violence and other Surprising Outcomes
Anne Nassauer

Democratic Practice
Origins of the Iberian Divide in Political Inclusion
Robert M. Fishman

Contentious Rituals
Parading the Nation in Northern Ireland
Jonathan S. Blake

Contradictions of Democracy
Vigilantism and Rights in Post-Apartheid South Africa
Nicholas Rush Smith

Plausible Legality
Legal Culture and Political Imperative in the Global War on Terror
Rebecca Sanders

Legacies and Memories in Movements
Justice and Democracy in Southern Europe
Donatella della Porta, Massimiliano Andretta, Tiago Fernandes, Eduardo Romanos, and Markos Vogiatzoglou

DREAMers and the Choreography of Protest

MICHAEL P. YOUNG

OXFORD
UNIVERSITY PRESS

Oxford University Press is a department of the University of Oxford. It furthers
the University's objective of excellence in research, scholarship, and education
by publishing worldwide. Oxford is a registered trade mark of Oxford University
Press in the UK and certain other countries.

Published in the United States of America by Oxford University Press
198 Madison Avenue, New York, NY 10016, United States of America.

© Oxford University Press 2024

All rights reserved. No part of this publication may be reproduced, stored in
a retrieval system, or transmitted, in any form or by any means, without the
prior permission in writing of Oxford University Press, or as expressly permitted
by law, by license, or under terms agreed with the appropriate reproduction
rights organization. Inquiries concerning reproduction outside the scope of the
above should be sent to the Rights Department, Oxford University Press, at the
address above.

You must not circulate this work in any other form
and you must impose this same condition on any acquirer.

Library of Congress Cataloging-in-Publication Data
Names: Young, Michael P., author.
Title: DREAMers and the choreography of protest / Michael P. Young.
Description: New York : Oxford University Press, [2024] |
Series: Oxford studies in culture and politics |
Includes bibliographical references and index.
Identifiers: LCCN 2024017120 (print) | LCCN 2024017121 (ebook) |
ISBN 9780197608197 (paperback) | ISBN 9780197608180 (hardback) |
ISBN 9780197608210 (epub)
Subjects: LCSH: Noncitizens—Political activity—United States. |
Immigrant youth—Civil rights—United States. | Immigrant youth—Legal status,
laws, etc.—United States. | Immigrant youth—Political activity—United
States. | Social justice—United States. | Youth protest
movements—United States. | Illegal immigration—United States.
Classification: LCC JV6477 .Y68 2024 (print) | LCC JV6477 (ebook) |
DDC 323.3/291208350973—dc23/eng/20240509
LC record available at https://lccn.loc.gov/2024017120
LC ebook record available at https://lccn.loc.gov/2024017121

DOI: 10.1093/oso/9780197608180.001.0001

For my parents, Jennie Murphy and Bill Young, who always backed me with love and affirmation.

Contents

Preface: "There's No Movement" ix

Introduction: "To Speak In Its Name": Movement Reification
and Radicalization 1

1. Conjuring the DREAMer 7

2. Campus DREAMers 35

3. DreamACTivist.org 69

4. 2010, Act I: "The Dream is Coming" 101

5. 2010, Act II: Noodles 2.0 138

6. 2011: NIYA and the Bad Dreamers 181

7. 2012 and 2013: Infiltrators and Coyotes 222

Conclusion: On the Mysteries of Movements and Radicalization 250

Acknowledgments 263
Appendix: Methods and Data 265
Notes 267
Bibliography 289
Index 297

Preface

"There's No Movement"

Southside of San Antonio, Texas: September 18, 2013

Laura Barberena and I arrive at Felipe Vargas's family home to interview Mohammad Abdollahi. We have two dozen interviews with DREAMers under our belt and have heard much about Mohammad. Mo was one of the three DREAMers arrested at the sit-in at Senator John McCain's Tucson office in the spring of 2010. He organized the sit-in of DREAMers on Capitol Hill later that summer, devised the infiltration of an immigrant detention center in Florida in 2012, and planned the border crossing of the Dream 9 at Nogales just two months earlier. Some told us he was single-handedly radicalizing the migrant rights movement. Some described him as brilliant but dangerously reckless. Some said he was evil. All agreed he was some kind of genius.

Preparing for the interview, my first Google search of his name yielded a *Daily Kos* post: "Mohammad Abdollahi: Says F Obama & Go Suck United We Dream's D." Written by a "Dose of Tequila," the article is one of many character attacks in the blogosphere and on social media directed not just at Mo, but also at Prerna Lal, Lizbeth Mateo, and a few other DREAMers associated with the National Immigrant Youth Alliance (NIYA).[1] These online attacks, penned by avowed immigrant rights advocates, charge NIYA leaders with reverse racism and treason to the cause. They link these activists to the far right or the far left, and sometimes incoherently to both. NIYA is either working in league with nativists to undermine the immigrant rights movement by tainting it with extremism *or* with undermining US sovereignty by espousing a far left open-borders ideology. The Dose of Tequila article is typical. It presents no analysis of why Mo had gone rogue, but it is replete with angry posts ripped from his Facebook and Twitter accounts that appear racist and intended to damage the cause for immigration reform.[2]

A few weeks earlier, we interviewed Gaby Pacheco, possibly the most famous of all DREAMers. In the gulf between moderate and radical undocumented youth activists, Gaby and Mo occupy distant positions. She described an ugly fight with Mo during a sit-in at Senator John McCain's Washington, DC, office.[3] Gaby's words still ring in my head as I sit down for the interview with Mo: "He yelled at me 'you manipulating bitch!'"[4]

Felipe greets us warmly at the front door. Mo and Benito Deal are busy working on their laptops at the kitchen table. Felipe and Benito, along with the lawyer David Bennion, are among the very few US citizens with whom NIYA will work. Mo appears restless. He is eager to get on the road. It is the second time Felipe has hosted Laura and I for an interview. The first was in the summer of 2012, when I interviewed him in Van Ormy on the southwest outskirts of San Antonio, TX. He audio recorded our interview. I thought it a little odd at the time. "NIYA folks love to record all their interactions," Gaby Pacheco told us later. Felipe was frank and unguarded in the interview. He took us seriously that day and squirreled away in the back of his head a plan to steer our research. It hinged on getting us to interview Mo. But "Mo does not like to do interviews."[5]

Felipe sprung the interview on Mo only a few hours before we arrived. He does not look pleased as we sit down. Laura sets up her lights, camera, and microphones as Mo talks on the phone answering questions and giving directions. I hear for the first time his rapid, somewhat pressured, pattern of speech when he is at work. I catch a glimpse of his ability to jump with lightning speed from one task to the next. The interview takes place in an open living room and dining space of a ranch-style house. Felipe sits just off camera on a couch behind and to the right of Mo. Some minutes into the interview, Benito stops working on his laptop and moves from the kitchen table to another couch, just to the left of me. All the activity in the room comes to a halt as they listen to Mo speak for over two hours.

The interview starts poorly.[6] Mo asks me to rephrase my questions several times: "You'll have to be more specific." The interview continues in this balky way for a bit with Mo answering questions reluctantly and tersely. I start with biographical questions about his family and childhood. After giving some bare facts about where his family immigrated from, Iran; when, 1989; and the immigration status of his siblings and parents, a complex but not unusual mix of citizen, legal resident, and undocumented; he moves me along firmly: "I don't like talking about my family. I understand if you need some background, but I don't want to talk about my family."

Further into the interview, after parrying most of my biographical questions, Mo changes his tone and begins to draw out his answers and steer the conversation. I get the sense that he has resigned himself to a long interview and decided that if he must sit through this tediousness, he might as well teach these people something. But I suspect Laura and I are not his main audience. Mo, it seems to me, is speaking for the benefit of Felipe and Benito.

Mo speaks frankly about his interactions with advocates for the DREAM Act and immigration reform. When I ask him about the 2010 sit-in at McCain's Washington, DC, office and his interaction with Gaby, he does not sugar coat it. "She came out of McCain's office and I called her a manipulative bitch." He explains why. "The only point of that whole action was to get Gaby Pacheco, the superstar DREAMer from the Trail of Dreams . . . ." Felipe, off camera, interrupts with "You mean Trail of Tears." It's a nasty inside joke. In the early months of 2010, Felipe had driven equipment for Gaby and the other participants of the "Trail" as they walked from Miami, FL, to Washington, DC. Mo laughs and continues: "The *only* point was to get Gaby arrested and have all the DREAMers who loved her to flood the Hill with phone calls. So, when she emerged from McCain's office leaving the others to get arrested, I blew up at her." His unapologetic account of attacking Gaby for her failure to execute his plan to exploit her as a DREAMer idol is breathtaking. Mo tells me, matter-of-factly, "I mainly act out of anger. It's my main motivation for most of what I do." I do not doubt him.

I am taken aback by this brutal honesty of using DREAMers for purely strategic purposes, and his frequent use of terms rejected by most immigrant rights advocates: "illegals," "self-deport," "anchor baby." But most surprising is Mo's response to a question Laura asks as the interview is winding down: "How do DREAMers fit in the larger immigrant rights movement?" Mo rejects the premise of the question. "I don't think there's a movement," he says:

> What is happening right now for immigration reform, gathering petition signatures, you know, doing movie screenings, is the exact same strategy that happened two years before, two years before that, two years before that. There is really no growth there. I think a lot of folks are just here to get foundation money and for me that's not an authentic movement. A real movement comes, is led by people who are most oppressed and most affected, and then it disappears.

He was not always so cynical.

Mo did once believe in the existence of a movement—back in what he refers jokingly as "the good all days," before he knew what the "big orgs were up to." These big nonprofit organizations boasted of a powerful immigration reform movement and the importance of DREAMer activism for its success. This movement pitch from the "big orgs" turned Mo into a founding organizer of United We Dream. A year into working alongside nonprofit organizations for the DREAM Act, he came to believe that these "allies" used the "movement" to "pimp" DREAMers like him. The movement, Mo insists in our interview, is fake, a ruse designed by nonprofits to deceive undocumented immigrants and to exploit them to win foundation grant money. The charge against the nonprofits I have heard before, but I balk at his wholesale rejection of any movement.

The interview ends. Laura and I are packing up when Mo asks us if we want to observe NIYA's upcoming Laredo campaign. He describes it as a "legal coyote" action.

La Casa del Migrante Nazareth, Nuevo Laredo: Last Week of September 2013

In the middle of the week, the DREAMers start to arrive at the Catholic shelter for migrants, one of a network run by Scalabrinian missionaries throughout Mexico. They arrive from the four corners of Mexico—Mexicali, Monterey, Guadalajara, D.F., Queretaro, Quintana Roo—and one from Peru. Some fly into the border city but most arrive by bus. The priest running the shelter provides the group with a meeting room for their preparations for Monday's action. By the weekend, they number thirty. Late on Saturday, the priest closes the shelter to new migrants to ensure the DREAMers' safety. The shelter is a magnet for extortion by cartel members trying to monopolize the traffic of unauthorized migrants across the border, and there are rumors that the Zetas who control the Nuevo Laredo corridor know about Monday's action.

Laura and I are the only outside observers for the days leading up to the action. The DREAMers tell us different stories of how they got to this point, but they share a common goal: to return home.[7] Some were deported to Mexico. Some followed deported parents, some left to be with dying relatives, and some just thought their future might be brighter in a country that acknowledges them as citizens. Most of them are very young: the majority in their early- to -mid-twenties, a few are minors, and a couple are just over thirty. From the roof of the shelter, they can see the Rio Grande, and, on the other side, Texas. They are gay, straight, jocks, nerds, junior ROTC, evangelical, Catholic, atheist—all raised in the United States, all undocumented, and all trapped on the wrong side of the border.

For three days they sit in workshops led by Benito Deal. They role-play what will happen on Monday. They tell their life stories to each other. They worry, cry, laugh, and bond. Monday morning, they embrace in a circle and take turns jumping into the center to address the group. They voice their fears, their hopes, and they speak about how they have changed over the last few days in the shelter. They use the word love freely. As the morning wanes, a dozen reporters arrive to cover the action. The group waits for a shuttle bus and a van to transport them to the central plaza.

Laura and I pile into Felipe Vargas's car along with two DREAMers and Steve Pavey, a photographer and anthropologist, and leave the shelter ahead of the group. Benito stays with the rest of the DREAMers waiting for transportation. For the next few hours, Felipe and Benito stay in constant contact with the undocumented organizers of the action on the US side of the border. Felipe's car is a 2001 Chevy Impala he calls the War Pony. We head west through the residential neighborhood of the shelter. We pass well-kept homes sprinkled among run-down and abandoned houses and empty lots strewn with garbage. Stray dogs roam the streets. Men in groups of three and four hanging on the corners eye us as we drive past. Felipe, not knowing exactly where he is going, feels his way to the downtown plaza. He drives effortlessly, nudging the overloaded War Pony to coasting speed, adjusting smoothly to the ebb and flow of traffic, and avoiding potholes. The car's old suspension moans under our weight and gives out an occasional screech of metal-on-metal over broken stretches of road. We approach the downtown area. Most of the stores are shuttered, abandoned to the still raging drug war. Felipe is talking nonstop. It is comforting until we pass the central plaza and he says menacingly: "This is where they shot the mayor, and where the Zetas brought the decapitated heads." One of the DREAMers says, "I should have gone to the bathroom."

We find parking a couple of blocks away from the plaza and walk back. There we wait for what seems like an eternity for the rest of the group. An hour in, a few allied members of the Rio Grande Community of DREAMers arrive. They have just crossed over on foot from Laredo, Texas. The two DREAMers with us are relieved by their presence—a welcome sign that they are almost home. At long last a small bus and van arrive from the shelter. The group clusters in the park and dons graduation caps and gowns—the DREAMer uniform. Television reporters set up their cameras and start broadcasting. Passersby stop and watch. Benito assembles the group in a line—they have grown to thirty-four over the last two days. He puts the most fearless in the front, middle, and back of the line to build a column that will not break. One last check, Benito touches each one on their shoulders and looks them in their eyes for a long moment, saying not a word. And they are ready.

Four pesos in hand, they walk around the northern edge of the plaza and one block north to the pedestrian "Bridge #1" joining the two Laredos. Two of the youngest DREAMers, both teenagers, say goodbye to their father. The family hugs and cries. The youngest is distraught. Her will to cross unravels. She turns back to her father. He wishes her on. Her older sister takes her hand and gently pulls her toward the group. They all file through the entrance of the bridge paying the four-peso toll. Blasé Mexican soldiers stand-by letting them pass without a word, barely a glance.

They get halfway across the bridge when the chants begin. In a call and response, DREAMers and allies gathered on the US side chant, "UNDOCUMENTED"; and the crossers respond, "UNAFRAID." US Border Patrol in boats under the bridge gun their engines drowning out the chants. A flash of fear spreads through the column, but only for a moment. The chants from the US side grow louder and steel their nerves. The crowd calls out one-by-one the names of the returnees: "When Rocio comes under attack, what do we do? STAND UP, FIGHT BACK! When Alberto comes under attack, what do we do? STAND UP, FIGHT BACK!"

They arrive at the point of entry. Border Patrol agents stop them. Their lawyer, David Bennion, pulling a small hand truck, presents three boxes of papers filled with legal petitions and supporting documentation asking for humanitarian patrol for each of them. The chants continue. They stand for half an hour, maybe more, in the Texas heat as David negotiates with the agents, and then they file into US custody. NIYA calls the action the Dream 30.

It is a brilliant act of civil disobedience—as audacious as any in the history of American social movements. It is the culmination of four years of escalating activism blazed by an activist network of undocumented youth. Two months earlier, NIYA crossed the Dream 9 from Mexico into Arizona at Nogales. All nine, including veteran NIYA activists Lizbeth Mateo and Marco Saavedra, gained successful re-entry and release into the United States. The

Dream 30 aims to prove that this was no fluke. The action stakes a claim for the right of return for deported DREAMers. I watch the Dream 30 file into US custody. I believe I am witnessing the cutting-edge of a growing migrant rights movement.[8] But I can't quite shake Mo's insistence, just days before in San Antonio: "there's no movement." Standing on the border between the two Laredos, watching DREAMers return home, I think we are at the beginning of something powerful. In fact we are at its end.

Introduction

"To Speak In Its Name": Movement Reification and Radicalization

I took Mo's claim that day in San Antonio that there did not exist "an authentic movement" as something of a taunt. Was Mo, a wickedly intuitive thinker, having a go with a sociologist who had come to interview him about his role in the migrant rights movement? Was he feeding me the sour fruit of his failed struggle for leadership and recognition in that movement? Or did he understand something important that I was missing? This book is largely the result of my trying to square his claim with protests on the ground that seemed to me to be contouring a radical and dynamic migrant rights movement—actions that included the DREAM 30 border crossing I had just witnessed.

The empirical analysis I present in the following chapters challenges and confirms aspects of Mo's claim. These chapters cover a decade of collective actions organized by undocumented youth. They chronicle how a relatively small network of activists almost single-handedly radicalized a social movement. But to understand how this happened, Mo's claim that there was no movement must be taken seriously. If this "no-movement" claim is contradicted by the very actions organized by National Immigrant Youth Alliance (NIYA) and emulated by other organizations, the activists who pulled off these influential protests managed to do so precisely because they believed there was no real movement.

Defending the claim that there *was* a social movement turns out to be a slippery intellectual task. It is not simply a matter of finding evidence to answer an empirical question. Sociologists are not in agreement about what social movements are. It is not much of an exaggeration to say that no one knows what a movement is. Many scholars have decided to simply jettison the term, and all the fuzzy thinking associated with it, for alternatives like "contentious politics" or "challengers."[1]

We often see social movements where they do not exist. We extend the movement label to tidily gather up a wide range of collective actions and protests that appear to advance a cause for or against social change. We turn otherwise unconnected acts, carried out by varied organizations and social networks, into a movement with a unitary character. Having tidied up the mess of disparate actions, we conflate certain organizations and social networks with this unified characterization of a movement and make the organizations and networks stand in for *the* movement. We then, in turn, credit this unitary character with collective actions that this hypostatized actor could have ever pulled off. Charles Tilly and Alberto Melucci, two giants in the sociology of social movements who followed very different empirical and theoretical approaches, both warned analysts against these errors of *reification* when trying to explain social movements.[2]

Without reading a lick of social movement theory, Mo and fellow radical DREAMers became convinced that a reified immigration reform movement promoted by a network of nonprofit organizations served to hide what was or, more importantly, was not happening in the fight to defend undocumented immigrants against state violence. They came to this conclusion as they battled for agency with the citizen "allies" directing these "big orgs" championing immigration reform. When I first interviewed Mo, he was angry and finished with these allies and their boasted claims about "the movement." From his perspective, there had been many opportunities for "real growth," for "authentic movement," over the previous four years. The "fake" movement publicized by large nonprofit organizations had blinded undocumented activists to these openings. He was done with all talk of movement. Ironically, at the very time I interviewed him in San Antonio, there were real signs of movement life and growth in the audacious agency of DREAMers radicalized by their angry rejection of the reified claims of movement by nonprofit professionals.

Over the next two years, as I interviewed NIYA members, studied their past actions, and observed their border crossing actions and detention center infiltrations in 2013 and 2014, I slowly came to this interpretation: While these young activists rejected what they saw as a reified immigrant rights movement and their role in it as fetishized DREAMers, they remained caught up in a bruising love–hate struggle with this role, and they were still looking over their shoulders as they choreographed defiant protests to see if "the movement" was following them. This backward glance, at the movement they denied existed, guided them as they exploited their DREAMer image in a series of creative and escalating direct actions. This psychologically fraught dynamic inspired a series of increasingly audacious masterstrokes of protest, and a newly dynamic movement *was* following their lead.

By launching community pressure campaigns to stop deportations in 2008 and 2009, by initiating acts of civil disobedience leading to the arrest of undocumented immigrants in 2010, by using DREAMers to purposefully get in and then out of deportation proceedings in 2011, by infiltrating immigrant detention centers in 2012 to spring jailed immigrants facing deportation, by targeting the Democrats and the President in organized sit-ins at "Obama for America" campaign offices in swing states in 2012, and by working as "coyote DREAMers" to bring deported immigrants back to the United States in 2013 and 2014, the undocu-activists of NIYA led a radical edge of a movement that cut a discernible arc.

Rejecting the immigrant rights movement as fake fueled NIYA's escalating protests. In turn, this escalation gave life to and radicalized a movement they rejected—a movement these radical DREAMers could not forget or forgive for how it had deceived, used, and hurt them. Other collective actors imitated and learned from NIYA's escalating protests. Although I did not realize it as I observed the NIYA border-crossing action in Laredo, this movement was very near its end. Mo was wrong, then, to claim a movement did not exist, but he was very soon to be right.

Grasping the significance of pivotal moments in the history of a social movement is hard. It requires cutting through the layers-upon-layers of movement hypostatization constructed by varied and competing actors, as particular constructions of the movement trigger alternative and competing constructions of the movement. It requires getting deep into the weeds of this recursive dynamic of mythmaking and movement-building. From a detached, sociological view, movements are not unitary actors. Heeding the counsel of Melucci or Tilly not to reify them, movements are not things, but reticulated concatenations of collective actions and actors gleaned through an analytical lens.[3] This detached analytical perspective is useful, for my present purpose, not because it brings into focus the real migrant rights movement. Rather, it provides a means to untangle the competing narratives and characterizations of "the movement" that animate all social movements in a reflexive age.

The following analytical approach, useful only as a brief and provisional guide, provides some hold from which to begin to untangle conflicting claims made by advocates about the immigrant or migrant rights movement and its pivotal moments. This approach focuses on collective acts that seek to (1) challenge restrictive (im)migration policies and enforcement at the federal, state, and local level; (2) defend or expand the political, legal, and economic rights of (im)migrants, documented and undocumented; and (3) protect (im)migrants' sense of dignity and respect in interaction with US citizens and institutions. Under this analytical lens, the following "social movement" comes roughly into view. An explosion of interrelated but uncoordinated demonstrations in the spring of 2006 mark a first, mass burst of movement. This first phase of movement stalls within a year. It clearly picks up again in 2010—primarily with protests resisting Arizona's anti-immigrant law SB 1070 and actions championing the DREAM Act, abating once again after a year. In terms of levels of collective action, the movement appears to fall somewhat into abeyance from 2011 into early 2012, but a proliferation of new and varied forms of actions at the local and state level marks this as a creative period of protest. These innovative direct actions accelerate in number into and through 2013, shifting to increasingly target federal policies, and then fall off again, indefinitely, in 2014.[4]

For half a decade, the actions of undocumented youth associated with NIYA constituted the radical cutting edge of this social movement, anticipating and shaping its pace, form, and targets.[5] To explain this accomplishment, a sociological skepticism of reifying movements no longer helps. Reifying social movements may be bad "analytical" social science, but it is irresistible, and maybe indispensable, for those who *make* movement. Francesca Polletta's narrative theory of the revitalization of the civil rights movement by the students behind the Student Nonviolent Coordinating Committee (SNCC) brilliantly illuminates this point.[6]

In the chapters to follow, I explain how interpretive and interactive conflicts amongst activist over reifications of the movement and movement actors revitalized and radicalized protests for migrant rights. I chronicle how nonprofit professionals proposed a legal, categorical distinction that interpolated the DREAMer and then used the exceptional student hailed by this abstraction as a fetishized character to steer the movement for immigration reform. Fights between undocumented youth and with their allies over the meaning of "the movement" and the characterization of its leading collective actor, the DREAMer, inspired new lines of protest. Breaking the spell of its fetishism, a faction of undocumented youth instrumentalized the DREAMer character to challenge the authority of their former allies. Leveraging the public influence of the DREAMer, they unleashed a series of audacious actions of civil disobedience to challenge their erstwhile nonprofit patrons. As a demystified weapon in the hands of radical undocumented youth, the DREAMer opened opportunities not only to challenge the nonprofit movement for immigration reform, but also federal policies and practices governing the policing of migrants. These chapters show how reification operated as deceit, revelation, and avatar, inspiring a choreography of protest that radicalized a movement.

Richard Sennett, in a forward to Alain Touraine's magisterial *The Voice and the Eye*, described the book as "seeking a choreography of conflict." Through social protests, Touraine argued, movements create new social forms and cultural orientations. Social movements are the creative force in "society's self-production." Contentious interpretive struggles over a movement's character shape this protean power to remake society. Sennett puts it best: "part of the life of a social movement is the effort to say what it is, to see its contours in order to speak in its name."[7] Touraine reserved a special role for sociologists in this interpretive work, but activists also seek the contours of a movement. They, too, struggle to speak for it. And they frequently fight amongst themselves in this effort.

Unlike sociologists, activists can directly shape a movement's contours through the collective actions they coordinate. Activists interpret what a movement is, in no small part, through the form, force, pace, and sequence of the protests they imagine and struggle to execute. The movement they imagine—and fight for—takes form through their choreography of protest. This choreography, in turn, is shaped by their struggle against rival activists and competing reifications of the movement. In this contentious effort to speak in the movement's name, the creative clash of new and challenging forms of protest shapes the contours of the inchoate social movement and articulates a name for it, albeit a contested one.[8] That, at least, is how it happened in the radicalization of the struggle for migrant rights in the United States from 2008 to 2014.

***

This book is based on fifty-seven interviews with undocumented youth activists, extensive archival research of their online activities, and years of ethnographic study.[9]

I hope readers with little or no interest in abstract social movement theory will find in the seven chapters to follow a compelling history of the events and activists behind the DREAMer radicalization of the migrant rights movement. While I do draw links to social movement theory in these empirical chapters, I do so only lightly, and in a way that hopefully does not distract from the historical narrative.

Chapter 1 provides a history of the creation of the "DREAM-ACT student" at the hands of the nonprofit professional advocates of immigration reform and the news media. Chapter 2 traces the early organizing of undocumented youth on college campuses and their interaction with nonprofit organizations. It tracks youth organizers from Texas, Florida, and California. Chapter 3 focuses on the online network of undocumented youth who created DreamACTivist.org. It chronicles the early engagement of this network with the politics of the DREAM Act, the convening of United We Dream, and that organization's first year of operation. Chapter 4 chronicles the first half of the 2010 fight to pass the DREAM Act. It covers in detail the organizing behind the first acts of civil disobedience by undocumented youth. Chapter 5 traces the second half of 2010, with its escalation of direct actions, a growing split between moderate and radical DREAMers, and the final Senate vote on the DREAM Act. Chapter 6 follows the establishment of the National Immigrant Youth Alliance in 2011. It explains the genesis of NIYA's strategy of using the arrest of DREAMers to escalate protests, and how activists hit on the idea that they could organize inside detention centers. The last chapter outlines the logic of this final escalation by tracking NIYA actions from 2012 into 2014, chronicling detention center infiltrations and border crossing actions. In the concluding chapter, I return to the abstract theme of movement reification and radicalization in the choreography of protest.

1
Conjuring the DREAMer

When the DREAMers burst onto the political scene in 2010, Gaby Pacheco was the most famous of them all. A founding member of one of the first organizations of undocumented students in the nation, Gaby was at the time the most influential member of a relatively small number of "DREAM elders"—undocumented activists who could convey a history of the "movement" to the thousands of DREAMers rallying to the cause. When I interviewed Gaby a few years after those momentous events, she told me a funny origin story of the DREAMers. It casts their birth as premature, almost accidental, and, perhaps presaging parental disavowal.

"In 1999," Gaby says, "that's when they come up with the idea of the DREAM Act." The story, she insists, starts with "Republicans in states like Texas and Utah" brainstorming about legislation to "deal with undocumented students who are going through the system but not graduating." These discussions percolate up to Washington policymakers and "then this person from NILC," Gaby pauses and laughs, "or was it MALDEF? If I confuse the two, they'll fight. You don't know how it is!" She can't remember, but she's clear that "he used the Cuban Adjustment Act as a model and still has the floppy disk with all the information"—evidence of "the original idea," proof of paternity.[1]

This inchoate idea for legislation to adjust the immigration status of undocumented students becomes a political football. "MALDEF and NILC start fighting for the thing. That's when Josh Bernstein comes into the picture. He's working with Senator Orin Hatch." Gaby adds, "Josh was not part of the original discussion." As Josh is wordsmithing the legal language for what would become the DREAM Act, "US Representative Luis Gutiérrez jumps the gun!" He thinks, "this is the perfect issue and submits the bill before it was finished." "So," Gaby continues, "now you have, in 2001, the introduction of the DREAM Act and it starts this national debate."

The debate is not, at first, exactly national, but it does soon catch the attention of undocumented students like Gaby, who recognize themselves as its subject and feel called or hailed. As Gaby says, "this debate starts bringing people together, because you actually had legislation that was *about us*. We needed to fight for it." Although these early fighters are few and scattered across the nation, they do not go unseen. "The people in DC," Gaby says, "were like, 'oh, these are the perfect poster children to move this legislation forward. Let's train them!'" I ask Gaby who were these people in Washington, DC. The directors at NILC? "Yes," but Gaby adds a qualification, "well, everybody, because they're all the same, they just have different names: CCC, NILC, SEIU...."

Gaby was one of these poster children. Not a child, but a young college student, she organized an undocumented student group in Florida before the policy professionals in Washington, DC, fully recognized the power of the subjects they had conjured by their legislative craft. Gaby's origin story of the DREAMer expresses an unease shared by many of the early undocumented youth activists about the origins of this fight and their role in it. There was something a little dodgy about the start of it all. As best as Gaby could suss out, an unfinished piece of legislation, drafted by competing nonprofit professionals and jumped on too quickly by an overly ambitious politician, offered undocumented youth like her the best chance to adjust their immigration status.

The DREAM Act was more than just about them. It in no small part constituted them as political subjects with a fighting chance to win citizenship and, more immediately, to go to college and to fend off threats of deportation. As glimpsed in her account of these early years, undocumented youth did not initiate or direct this fight for their own lives. Their campaign was largely commanded by the "people in DC" who provided them with an (mis)education in the politics of immigration reform and managed their early activism. Thrown into a bewildering and intimidating arena of national politics, these young activists quite sensibly reified a complex organizational network of DREAM Act champions: "They're all the same, they just have different names." But their impressions of a unified world of nonprofit professionals and politicians operating behind a curtain trying to manage them and the politics of immigration reform were not baseless.

This chapter provides a historical look behind this curtain. Drawing on archival records, it tracks the work of the nonprofit organizations that championed the DREAM Act up to 2007, the year when these organizations first brought together a national network of undocumented students. The chapters to follow then pick up this history from the perspective of undocumented youth.

Nonprofits, Foundations, and the Immigration Field

In the early days, DREAMers owed their national level organizing and political education to the directors and staffers of the National Immigration Law Center (NILC) and the Center for Community Change (CCC). They are two very different nonprofits, both in organizational form and substantive work. NILC is an organization of immigration lawyers and CCC is an organization that trains community organizers to expand their capacities. Their material support, however, comes from similar funders, and they interact within a shared nonprofit network of advocacy for migrants and immigrants. NILC and CCC are an integral part of what funders refer to as a nonprofit "immigration field."

This "field" emerged in the early 1980s and expanded steadily over the next three decades. It is one small part of a larger "voluntary sector" that has exploded in size in the United States since the middle of the twentieth century. In the early 1970s, sociologists John McCarthy and Mayer Zald observed that the private foundations and nonprofit organizations of this sector were transforming the nature of activism in the United States. The dramatic growth of foundation asset funds was funneling money into social movements. And this funding was changing the organizational morphology and substantive concerns of movements. It was driving a professionalization of social movement organizations and their managers across the sector.

A half-century ago, McCarthy and Zald recognized that an expert world of foundation funding and nonprofit management was simultaneously increasing the available resources for social movements and domesticating their causes. From the professional command posts of private foundations and large nonprofits, "movement entrepreneurs" tended to "take a rather jaundiced view of social movement organizations with publicly stated radical goals."[2]

Much of the scholarly work building on McCarthy and Zald's insights on the nexus between nonprofits and movements focuses on the activist's dilemma of material resource dependency. Material resources furnished by nonprofits and foundations can empower movements by enhancing their capacity to mobilize support, but these same resources can ensnare movements by constraining and co-opting their causes. In these materialist approaches, movements are specified as distinct social phenomenon from the foundations and nonprofits that resource them. The interaction between the distinct phenomena is seen as sequential: an already formed movement, albeit often inchoate, raises public consciousness around a cause and stirs action; then nonprofit organizations move to support the movement with grants won from foundations. As this support flows to the movement, it reshapes the cause. But recent work on the nonprofit movement nexus suggests more nuanced dynamics.

Newer work calls attention to how professional organizations can frame new political issues, create new social identities, and even generate social movements from the grasstops down. Stark examples of this movement manufacturing come from sociologist Edward T. Walker's research on consultants working for corporations and professional interest groups. Walker reveals that "behind the curtain" of many seemingly grassroots mobilizations is a world of "backstage" professional policy elites framing the political issues for curated audiences in the service of managing a political environment for corporate and interest group clients. As this chapter documents, the DREAM Act advocacy of nonprofits shares a strong family resemblance to the practices of the "grassroots consultants" hired by corporations—undoubtedly because the domains of nonprofit and for-profit professionals overlap.[3]

Professionals directing NILC and CCC profoundly shaped the activism of undocumented youth. Their ultimate influence stemmed less from the material resources they mobilized on behalf of undocumented youth than from the unintended consequence of the categorical distinction they drew among immigrants as they tried to steer policy reform. Critical to the unintended outcome of these efforts was how undocumented youth imagined unforeseen possibilities in the cultural space created by the symbolic projects of nonprofit professionals. This chapter tracks two of these symbolic projects: the making of the DREAMer and the myth-building around a massive immigration reform movement. These twin cultural projects were part of larger efforts by nonprofit professionals and allied politicians to manage both the institutional politics of immigration reform and the unruly contentious politics over migrant rights.

According to most accounts, NILC's Director of Federal Policy, Josh Bernstein, was primarily responsible for the form and substance of the "Development, Relief, and Education for Alien Minors Act." First introduced to the Senate in 2001 by Orin Hatch, the DREAM Act amended a 1996 immigration act "to permit States to determine State residency for higher education purposes and to authorize the cancellation of removal and adjustment of status of certain alien college-bound students who are long-term United

States residents." In effect, the act proposed repealing the denial of eligibility from higher education benefits and granting temporary legal status and a pathway to permanent residency and citizenship for a particular category of undocumented immigrants. Over the next decade, the DREAM Act's legal language on eligibility would change, but not so much as to efface its original categorization of its subject. Across these changes it sought to carve out relief for college-bound undocumented youth who had spent much of their childhood in the United States. In its ugly legal language, the bill offered protection for a special category of "illegal aliens." Eligibility depended on "if the alien demonstrates that":

- the alien has not, at the time of application, attained the age of 21;
- the alien, at the time of application, is attending an institution of higher education in the United States;
- the alien was physically present in the United States on the date of the enactment of this Act and has been physically present in the United States for a continuous period of not less than five years immediately preceding the date of enactment of this Act;
- the alien has been a person of good moral character during such period.

Age requirements would change with subsequent re-introductions of the bill, but being young remained a primary category of eligibility, as did having lived in the United States for several years as a child. Required educational achievements would also change in different iterations, but eligibility remained tied to being a college student or being college bound. And the requirement of being a person of good moral character would become more judicial over time, specifying legal transgressions that would make someone ineligible. However, the DREAM Act remained symbolically and categorically designated for youth who followed the rules and obeyed authority. With these categories of eligibility, the DREAM Act was attempting a discriminating intervention in immigration law on behalf of children who had done nothing wrong in following their families to the United States, excelled at school, followed the rules, and faced a bright future—if only for their vexed immigration status.[4]

NILC's advocacy for undocumented students started decades before the legal crafting of the DREAM Act. NILC started as the "Aliens' Rights Project" in 1977 under the Legal Aid Foundation of Los Angeles (LAFLA). At the time, LAFLA was one of a few legal aid projects to receive funding from the federal government's Legal Services Corporation (LSC) to work on immigrant rights. In 1979, the project formally separated from LAFLA to form a national legal support center operating under a new name, the National Center for Immigrants' Rights. The center opened with two attorneys and an operating budget of around $150,000. Its budget was almost entirely dependent on LSC funds.

The center gained national attention as a legal advocate for undocumented youth with the 1982 Supreme Court decision in *Plyler v. Doe*. In this case, the center, working with the Mexican American Legal Defense and Educational Fund (MALDEF), challenged a Texas law denying undocumented children free access to primary and secondary school education. By the early 1990s, and renamed the National Immigrant Law Center, the organization employed six attorneys and five support staff members, with an operating budget around $750,000. LSC funding covered less than one-half of the organization's expenses, with grants from private foundations making up the remainder. By the early 2000s, NILC's annual expenses exceeded $1.5 million dollars, with almost all its revenue coming from private foundations.[5]

NILC's growth as a legal advocate for immigrants coincided with the development of a specialized field of immigrant and refugee advocacy organized by liberal nonprofit organizations and private foundations. From the early 1980s to the 2000s, NILC's organizational growth, increased private funding, and evolving legal work as a national legal aid society for immigrants tracked the development of this specialized nonprofit field. The single most important funder for the field was the Ford Foundation.

A Ford Foundation initiative to fund an "institutional infrastructure" for nonprofit organizations protecting immigrant rights started in the early 1980s. The Ford Foundation was, at the time, going through a difficult period of reorganization. Economic stagflation forced the foundation to downsize its staff, cut projects, and reconsider its missions. Directors questioned the wisdom of the traditional social development model that guided its earlier international work. Human rights became a new focus as Ford Foundation leadership responded to criticism that its past grants intended to fuel agricultural gains and manufacturing growth only served to enrich corrupt elites, further economic inequality, and weaken political institutions in the Global South. As human rights became more central to its mission, the foundation started to break down the divisions between its international and domestic work. The refugee crisis that emerged in Southeast Asia after the US withdrawal from Vietnam punctuated the need to view international and domestic projects as interconnected. As did the passage of the 1980 Refugee Act and a sharp increase in the flows of Central American, Cuban, and Haitian refugees.

In this context, Frank Sutton, Deputy Vice President of Ford's International Division, wrote a paper requesting $500,000 to launch an immigration program that looked beyond particular refugee crises toward "long-term solutions." Sutton's boss "needled" him "for writing a fifty-page paper for such a tiny request." But this "tiny" grant turned out to be just a down payment on a much larger investment made by the Ford Foundation over the next two decades to support nonprofit organizations working with immigrants. Diana Morris, one of the hires to lead the new Ford program, described their mandate: "We had been tasked with helping support the emergence of an immigration field."[6]

NILC was an early beneficiary of the Ford Foundation's immigration initiative. Its LSC funding disappeared under the Reagan administration, but foundation grants sustained the organization's work. Another major Ford Foundation beneficiary was the National Immigration Forum (NIF). Launched in 1982 with a start-up grant of $300,000 from the foundation, the NIF brought together "over 100 national and community organizations." From its outset, the NIF was closely connected to the International Ladies' Garment Worker's Union (ILGWU), signaling an important shift in organized labor's role in immigration politics. For labor union organizers in the garment industry and the service sector, support of immigrant rights and open immigration policies aligned with the interests of their members. The influence of these unions started to break down the traditional restrictionist position on immigration held by American labor. By the 2000s, UNITE HERE!, an organizational outgrowth of the ILGWU's merger with other garment unions, and the Service Employee International Union (SEIU) joined with the nonprofits in the immigration field to form a coalition pushing for immigration reform.[7]

Other Ford Foundation grantees active in nonprofit immigration field included MALDEF and the National Council of La Raza (NCLR)—two organizations with long funding histories with the Ford Foundation extending well before the emergence of this field. Also included were newer regional and state-level immigrant rights organizations: nonprofits such as the Coalition for Humane Immigrant Rights of Los Angeles (CHIRLA), the New York Immigration Coalition (NYIC), Massachusetts Immigrant and Refugee Advocacy Coalition (MIRA), Illinois Coalition for Immigrant and Refugee

Rights (ICIRR), and the Florida Immigrant Coalition (FLIC). Many of these state organizations would work with NILC and CCC in the mid-2000s to organize undocumented youth at the state and national level.

The organizations populating this immigration field developed interlocking directorates. Directors involved in DREAM Act advocacy moved between key organizations within the field. Josh Bernstein, NILC's Director of Federal Policy for fourteen years, moved in 2009 to become SEIU's Director of Immigration. Frank Sharry, National Director of NIF for eighteen years, moved in 2008 to form America's Voice, a new media outlet for the field, and was replaced by Ali Noorani, who had been director of MIRA, an organization Frank Sharry helped found in 1986. Undocumented youth interacting with nonprofits in the field picked up on these directorate interlocks. They quickly understood that behind the many immigrant rights organizations there was a relatively tight network of professionals. As Gaby Pacheco quipped: "They are all the same. They just have different names."

Policy and the Nonprofit Immigration Field

The Immigration Reform and Control Act (IRCA) of 1986 profoundly shaped this emerging nonprofit field. In response to IRCA's amnesty provisions, considerable foundation money, much of it from the Ford Foundation, flowed to support organizations working to adjust the status of the millions of undocumented immigrants. NILC, as well as many other nonprofits in the field, received grants to provide training and education on the provisions in IRCA that opened a pathway to citizenship for undocumented immigrants.

The immigration field grew in organizational strength as a result, but it proved a weak counterforce to the nativist backlash that ensued. The political winds shifted quickly after IRCA. As millions of immigrants moved to legalize their status under the law, economic integration between Mexico and the United States fueled new migrant flows. Through the 1990s the population of undocumented immigrants living in the United States increased to levels well above those before the passage of IRCA and was met with a wave of anti-immigrant sentiment that swept across the nation's two political parties.

Nativist organizations were poised to steer this growing public sentiment against immigrants because they had been working for over a decade through what political scientist Alfonso Gonzales calls a "state-civil society" nexus to stoke it. An organized counter to the Ford Foundation-funded immigration field, this nativist field was led by a series of organizations formed by John Tanton, including the Federation for American Immigration Reform (FAIR), founded in 1979, and its affiliate, the Center for Immigration Studies (CIS), founded in 1985, and a host of others including Numbers USA, English First, and the American Immigration Control Foundation. Seeded by money from the Pioneer Fund and the Scaife Foundation, this network of advocacy groups launched a strategy to block and roll back immigration that their leaders came to refer to as "attrition through enforcement."[8] The impact of this strategy is evident in over a quarter-century of anti-immigration policies. At the state level these policies extend from the passage of Proposition 187 in California in 1994 and SB 1070 in Arizona in 2010 to Operation Lone Star in Texas in 2022. At the national level, a most significant victory in the strategy came early under the Clinton administration with the passage of the Illegal Immigration Reform and Immigration Responsibility Act (IIRIRA) in 1996.[9]

With IIRIRA, the leaders of the nonprofit the immigration field compromised long-standing positions conceding that increased control of unauthorized immigration was necessary. As Frank Sharry, director of NIF at the time, recalled, "we didn't think we could turn the restrictionist tide, couldn't stop the reform juggernaut, and it looked like something close to zero immigration was on the verge of being enacted."[10] Sharry's fear was not unfounded. Political scientist Aristide Zolberg argues in *A Nation by Design* that it is surprising that the doors to *all* immigration were not shut given the political climate of the time: "there was widespread agreement on the need to deter illegal immigration, with only some of the Latino national organizations holding out in the name of civil liberties." As they fought to keep the "front door" of legal immigration open, liberal policy experts conceded to the politically popular crack down on undocumented immigration through the "back door."

Both political parties played to the anti-immigrant sentiments of the time, supporting bipartisan legislation to close the back door to future migrants and to kick out "illegals" already inside the country. The Clinton administration signed two acts in addition to IIRIRA that created still greater insecurity for immigrants and their communities across America: the Personal Responsibility and Work Opportunity Act (PROWRA) and the Antiterrorism and Effective Death Penalty Act (AEDPA). Together, all three laws advanced the nativist strategy of attrition through enforcement. PRWORA aimed to reduce immigrant use of public assistance programs.[11] AEDPA removed a number of the existing legal processes available to immigrants who were facing deportation, making it far easier for the government to detain and deport. IIRIRA removed judicial review of a wide range of Immigration and Naturalization Service (INS) decisions, considerably enhancing the powers of the executive branch over the courts. It established an "expanded and retroactive definition of deportable offenses" and procedures for "expedited removal" at all US ports of entry. It removed from the "discretionary power" of judges "to grant relief from or suspend deportation" for legal immigrants with criminal records or for undocumented immigrants who had strong family and community ties in the United States. Further, it established mandatory multi-year and lifetime bars of admissibility to undocumented immigrants caught re-entering the United States.[12] Title V of Section 505 of IIRIRA targeted undocumented youth to restrict their access to postsecondary education benefits. Most government officials at the state level interpreted this section of the law as making undocumented students ineligible for in-state tuition rates at public universities.[13]

These bipartisan policies to punish immigrants took effect just as the implementation of North American Free Trade Agreement (NAFTA) accelerated economic integration between Mexico and the United States. Capital investments in rural Mexico displaced millions of people tied to agricultural work. The bifurcation of the labor market in the United States increased the demand for labor at the bottom-rung of the occupational ladder. This political and economic mix of policies affecting immigration was incoherent and contradictory.[14] New laws aimed at getting tough on immigration served more to trap unauthorized migrants and their growing families inside the United States than to block new immigrants. Earlier moves to criminalize immigration under IRCA and to militarize the border had already reduced the cycle of return migration. Enhanced border militarization and more severe penalties for those caught re-entering under IIRIRA choked off the regular flows of worker migration back and forth between the two countries. Immigrants kept coming but now along the more dangerous routes of the Southwest wilderness and with the intention of settling.[15] Through the late 1990s and into the new century, the population of undocumented immigrants continued to grow. And as families increasingly looked to settle permanently, immigrant communities appeared in places well beyond the traditional destination states of past migration.[16]

The DREAM of a New Millennium

With the ink on Clinton-era legislation barely dry, some politicians from both parties saw future electoral and economic costs to the continued packaging of anti-immigrant policies for nativist consumption. Demographic forces ensured an expanding electoral power for immigrant communities. With George W. Bush's election, some predicted the political pendulum was poised to swing back against these anti-immigrant policies. For the GOP supporters of this view, Bush's victory argued for a charm offensive with socially conservative Latino voters that included a softening on immigration. Bush's success with Latino voters in Texas and his rapport with Vicente Fox, the first post-Industrial Revolutionary Party (PRI) leader of Mexico, suggested that the party could benefit from distancing itself from nativist policies.

The professionals directing the nonprofit organizations in the immigration field also anticipated a popular countermovement to this nativism. After playing defense for much of the 1990s, these directors were buoyed by the forceful entry of a new funder to the nonprofit immigration field. George Soros's foundation, the Open Society Institute, provided new grant money to support immigrant rights. Soros committed $50 million to the field over five years. His gift was reportedly prompted by a *New York Times* article about how new legislation under Clinton had cut off benefits to impoverished immigrant families with permanent residency. Soros's money flowed first and foremost to service provisions but also to "social justice" campaigns. Money from other foundations followed and new grants totaling in the hundreds of millions of dollars flowed to long-favored grantees like NILC *and* to a new arrival to the field—the Center for Community Change (CCC).[17]

It was in this rarified air of elected officials gauging shifting political winds and nonprofit professionals eyeing new flows of foundation money that NILC's Josh Bernstein penned (or revised) the first version of the DREAM Act. As with most pro-immigration policies before it, the bill moved quietly through the legislative process. It followed the well-traveled path of immigration politics, "where," in the words of Zolberg, "small and well-organized groups intensively interested in a policy develop close working relationships with officials responsible for it, largely outside of public view and with little outside interference."[18] Many longstanding supporters of the DREAM Act say it would have passed in the fall of 2001 but for the terrorist attacks of 9/11.

The attacks on 9/11 wrecked many political agendas. By the time politicians got back to work on business unrelated to terrorism, nativist organizations had drafted on the political winds of war to further their attrition-through-enforcement strategy. Incredibly, they succeeded in framing unauthorized migration across the border with Mexico as a new front in the war on terror. The militarization of the Mexican border and internal policing of the unlawful presence of immigrants were folded into the anti-terrorist campaign of the new Department of Homeland Security (DHS).

The budget for border patrol and internal immigration control swelled with the administrative reorganization of federal agencies after 9/11. The new agency for Immigration and Customs Enforcement (ICE) organized under DHS became the largest law enforcement agency in the federal government. ICE expanded federal cooperation with state and local policing departments under the 287(g) program established by IIRIRA and under a new Bush program, Secure Communities. The 287(g) program authorized the federal government "to enter into agreements with state and local law enforcement agencies, permitting designated officers to perform immigration law enforcement functions... under the supervision of" federal immigration authorities.[19] The newer and more impactful Secure Communities program linked federal databases to local jails to process biometric data and flag undocumented immigrants for removal. With this stepped-up coordination between federal and local law enforcement, the number of deported undocumented immigrants increased under Clinton and then skyrocketed under Bush.

In this post-9/11 climate of increasing risks of detention and deportation for immigrants, the DREAM Act was re-introduced multiple times in the Senate and House as a standalone bill or an attachment to an omnibus bill. The original act was modified to concede ground to popular restrictionist positions, but its core categorical distinction—offering protection to kids who had done nothing wrong in following their families to the United States, excelled at school, and followed the rules—remained mostly intact. It fell short of passage in 2003 and again in 2005, but it continued to attract bipartisan support in the House and Senate.[20] Despite these legislative losses, liberal policy experts in Washington considered this piece of legislation as a strategic first step in a larger effort to push back against anti-immigrant policies and move toward a more comprehensive plan of immigration reform. At mid-decade, there was a general agreement amongst these experts that wider immigration reform had to start with incremental goals like the DREAM Act.[21]

Concurrent with the developing national politics around the DREAM Act, advocates for undocumented students at the state level drafted complementary pieces of legislation to allow undocumented youth to continue their public education from secondary to tertiary schools. These state laws sought a workaround of Title V of Section 505 of IIRIRA, opening access to postsecondary education benefits for undocumented youth residing in the state. The first law providing undocumented youth "in-state" tuition at public colleges and universities passed in Texas in 2001. California followed suit the next year.[22] By the end of 2005, six other states had joined them. As the legislative battles unfolded for the DREAM Act at the national levels and for in-state tuition at the state level, a DREAMer narrative took shape in the media.

The Emergence of the DREAMer Narrative

The outlines of the DREAMer narrative appeared in the print media as early as 2002. These reports gradually crystallized into a stock story. The narrative centered around a rather generic, flat character drawn by the categorical distinctions determining eligibility for relief under the DREAM Act. Media profiles consistently highlighted the youth, innocence, smarts, and virtue of their subjects. And across these characteristics they painted them as passive victims.[23] Nonprofits curated some of these stories for the press, but most came from journalists looking for human interest stories to put a face to the stakes behind legislative battles over the DREAM Act or in-state tuition bills. Even as social and political contexts changed, the narrative remained surprisingly stable with only slight changes at the margins and occasional biographical plot twists. Two decades later, this narrative continues to appear regularly in the news.

The stabilizing element in the narrative is the DREAMer character. This character is not referred to as a "Dreamer" until 2009, but their American dream is front-and-center from the very first media report. The stock story typically opens with a short vignette of an exceptional student with limitless potential stymied by their immigration status. The story is always about a student. It highlights the student's outstanding academic achievements, extra-curricular activities, and civic participation. The stock characters are honor students, winners of science competitions, varsity athletes, and tireless volunteers.

The story refers to the student's "illegal" immigration—typically occurring at a very young age and initiated by their parent(s). These accounts of illegal immigration to America vary: some DREAMers overstay a visa, some cross the desert in the dead of night, and some suddenly find themselves in America illegally because of the mistake of a family lawyer. In all instances it is emphasized that the student was not responsible for breaking the law. The student is portrayed as innocent, and even a victim, of their illegal immigration status. Victimhood is often emphasized, and this extends beyond their illegal coming. Disabled and abandoned children feature in early newspaper accounts. These stories work to disassociate undocumented youth eligible for the DREAM Act from the images of dangerous, freeloading illegal immigrants that populate the moral panics of nativists. The stories also implicitly rob the undocumented students of any agency in their own migration stories. The students are characterized as passive victims. If the undocumented student is quoted in the story, which is not always the case, they sound all-American and often apologetic for their illegal status. They only ask for an opportunity to give back to the one country they love. In their heart and mind, they are American and what they can give back to her country is framed as great.

The "newsworthy" reason for providing the vignette of this innocent and exemplary student is some current political maneuvering around the federal DREAM Act or in-state tuition policies for undocumented students. The story informs the reader that the (federal or state-level) DREAM Act would realize the dreams of these exemplary but star-crossed students. It is typical in these stories that only the first name of the gifted student is given. Because their life is legally precarious and their families must live in the shadows of society, these stories grant their subjects anonymity. Occasionally, the story is about a student who is threatened by deportation, and it explains how the DREAM Act would not just realize their dreams but save them from deportation to a foreign country with which they do not identify or even remember.

Josh Bernstein from NILC is regularly quoted in these stories, speaking to the basic decency embodied in the DREAM Act. The following example from a *Los Angeles Times* article is typical:

> "A lot of immigration issues are contentious. This one has not been. I guess it's because, how can you really be against these kids?" said Bernstein. The

legislation "speaks to a value, that every individual should be treated on their own merits.... It corrects a flaw in immigration law, which is not to recognize the good works of these particular kids."[24]

For journalistic balance, usually toward the end of the piece, a countervailing argument from a member of FAIR or CIS is included, most often Ira Mehlman or Mark Kirkovian. Their argument attacks the DREAM Act as legal amnesty for illegals, an encouragement for chain migration, and a reward for law breakers.

A very early example of this type of story appeared in July 2002 in an issue of the *Lowell Sun*, a regional Massachusetts newspaper with a modest circulation. It begins as a report on a lobbying visit: "Sam and a group of other students drove, no green card means no airplane, to Washington, D.C. this week in an attempt to talk with their senators about the importance of the DREAM Act." But the piece quickly shifts to the heart of the matter. "This is Sam's story":

> Sam's name has been changed to protect his identity. Nowadays, the government is trying to crack down on illegal immigrants, he says. On the way into a restaurant, he holds open the door with his hand, balancing himself on metal crutches. A cup in one hand, grasping onto his support with the other, he pushes himself through the entryway. His legs were taken by polio. From ages 3 to 12, he lived in a hospital miles away from his parents. His family couldn't afford to visit him. He only saw his mother and father at New Year's Day and once during the summer. When he got out of the hospital, things weren't much better. Disabled people in his country had no future, no work, no money, no prospects.

The story explains that Sam and his family came to the United States on a visa and when it ran out, they simply stayed. America is now Sam's home, and he is devoted to it:

> "I study very hard in school. I want to be legal here so I can work for this country," says the 20-year-old. Sam loves pizza. And hot dogs. And the Red Sox. He got all A's on his last report card. He got perfect scores in his math class. He volunteered at the Pollard Memorial Library after school. Does he want to go to college? "Yeah, I do," he says in his soft voice. "That's my dream. Because I want to have a better life."[25]

Another early DREAMer narrative featured the story of Danny King Cairo. It was a pure victim story and it appeared more than once in newspaper articles that same summer. Senator Orrin Hatch of Utah, an original sponsor of the DREAM Act, first told Danny's story from the floor of the US Senate. Danny's mom brought him illegally to this country when he was six years old. She abandoned him when he was eight. Danny was raised by foster parents in Utah. Against all odds, he excelled in school. Quoting his adoptive father, Hatch described Danny as "exactly what our country needs more of. He is a natural born leader with charisma and intelligence and a drive that will take him wherever he wants to go. But this will not be possible if Danny is unable to obtain permanent residency."[26] Hatch presented Danny as an example of someone who would benefit from the DREAM Act and as someone who clearly should not be punished for the "sins" of his parents. Danny's story differs from most early DREAMer narratives in that it reveals his full identity. His story gained considerable attention in Utah, but it did not spread much beyond that state.

The first story to gain national attention followed on the heels of Danny's story. It stemmed from a profile of Jesus Apodaca, published in August 2002 in *The Denver Post*.[27] It describes how this model student, a graduate with honors from Aurora High School in Denver and admitted to the University of Colorado at Boulder, faced insurmountable economic roadblocks to continuing his education because of his immigration status. Jesus came to the United States at age 12 and thrived in Denver public schools. Now, even with graduation accolades and admission to the state's flagship university, his dreams are coming to an end. The story uses Jesus's plight to raise the political question of whether or not Colorado should follow states like Texas and California in offering in-state tuition to students like Jesus.

Unlike Sam's story from Lowell, the piece does not protect Jesus's identity or that of his family. Unlike Danny Cairo King's story in Utah, Jesus's story triggered a political attack against him. The story stirred heated national attention when Representative Tom Tancredo of Colorado, a leader of the nativist Right in the US Congress, responded to the article by calling on INS to act on the unlawful presence of Jesus and his family. *The Denver Post* reported Tancredo's actions as a call to deport Jesus. Senator Ben Nighthorse Campbell of Colorado kept the Jesus Apodaca story in the headlines by responding to Tancredo's attacks with a personal bill to protect Jesus. The media storm around Jesus Apodaca made him the first public DREAMer, *avante la lettre*.

After the Jesus Apodaca story, the threat of deportation became an important feature of the DREAMer narrative. A year later, *The Denver Post* published another piece about two brothers from Sanford:

> Growing up in this little town on the southern Colorado border, Eduardo and Edgar Garcia led an all-American life. They starred in school plays and hit Little League homers. In their final years of high school, they lettered in basketball, football and wrestling. The brothers knew they were in the country illegally, because they can remember their mother recounting how she sneaked Edgar, the younger of the two, across the border on her shoulders when he was 3. But amid sports practice and going out with girls, they didn't give it much thought. After a police stop in late September—when neither could produce a driver's license or proof of citizenship—it did. Pulled over for a broken taillight at 6:30 on a Friday morning, they were in the border city of Ciudad Juarez four days later, wearing the same work clothes they were arrested in.[28]

The article is remarkable and unusual in its account of the collective, yet frustrated, will of the conservative residents of Sanford to undo the fast train of legal action leading to the Garcia brothers' deportation. Their story fits a common moralizing frame in the narrative that undocumented youth should not be punished for an illegal border crossing that they only know about from the stories they are told by their family.

The Garcia brothers' story is also exemplary of the DREAMer narrative in highlighting the unimpeachable Americanness of the brothers. The story of Sam in the *Lowell Sun* made this same claim with his love of hot dogs and the Red Sox. A story from the *San Bernardino Sun*, reporting on the struggles of an undocumented "Cal State Bernardino freshman," follows the archetype with its opening lines:

> She was smuggled to the United States at age 7, but is a typical American teenager in many ways. She listens to hip-hop and Jessica Simpson, sings in the church choir, plays the piano and gives out Thanksgiving baskets to needy families. Spanish is her first language, but she speaks English with no hint of an accent. But her undocumented status makes her an outsider in the eyes of the government.[29]

Most undocumented students appear in newspapers only under their first name or a pseudonym, and, in either case, only once. These media accounts provide glimpses of a rather flat DREAMer character. It could not really be otherwise. A more rounded characterization was near impossible without exposing the subject and their family to the risk of deportation. In 2005, the story of Marie Gonzalez broke this mold.

Center for Community Change and the "We Are Marie" Campaign

When Marie Gonzalez's story became national news, she and her family were already in deportation proceedings. Marie was five years old when her family moved to the United States from Costa Rica in 1991. The family settled in Jefferson City, MO. A decade later, Marie was a model student at Helias High, with dreams of law school. Marvin Gonzalez, her father, was working as a courier for the then-Missouri Governor Bob Holden. The Gonzalez family had put down deep roots in their Midwestern community. And then, in the summer of 2002, their American life started to unravel. An anonymous tip to a local newspaper led to an article about the "illegal immigrant" working for the governor. Holden's office fired Marvin and soon thereafter DHS started deportation proceedings against the family.

Her parents' time in the United States ran out in the summer of 2005, but Marie was not deported. Defended in the court of public opinion, the case to stop her deportation won out. Marie actively participated in her own defense. She spoke compellingly in public about her plight, and she made lobbying visits to politicians organized by NILC and CCC. As the media chronicled Marie's case—the deportation of her parents, her painful separation from them, and the stay of her own deportation—she came to be known by the public unlike any undocumented youth before her.[30] Her story rose above the scores of anonymous glimpses of undocumented honor students in the media.

Marie's case was used effectively to draw the DREAMer distinction in popular discourse about undocumented immigrants. "Whatever one may think of her parents' culpability on these matters," Harold Meyerson wrote on the editorial page of *The Washington Post*, "the case for deporting a young woman who's only known Missouri as her home just underscores the gap between law and justice."[31] Marie's case also left a deep impression on an emerging generation of young undocumented activists. She modeled a more hopeful, active path of public organizing for advocacy and self-protection.

CCC's public campaign, "We Are Marie," was instrumental in blocking her deportation. Next to NILC, CCC was the nonprofit most directly involved in the political organization of the DREAMers. CCC entered the field of immigrant advocacy a few years before the Marie case, at a moment of increasing insecurity for undocumented immigrants and just as the DREAMer story started to catch media attention. A well-established organization with origins in the civil rights and anti-poverty activism of the 1960s, CCC was a latecomer to the nonprofit immigration field, but it quickly became a big player.

CCC has a long history advocating for poor people. It emerged in 1968 as a coalition of national organizations absorbing, in particular, the Citizen's Crusade against Poverty (CCAP). Founded by the United Auto Workers, CCAP monitored and worked with the federal Office of Equal Opportunity formed by Lyndon B. Johnson's Great Society programs. CCC was launched as a coalition of organizations with an operating budget ensured by a multimillion and multiyear grant from the Ford Foundation. Absorbing the work of the CCAP, this new coalition took shape within the political context of Johnson's "war on poverty" and rising urban unrest. With a broad mission to empower low-income communities, CCC focused on housing, transportation, access to finance, and health care issues. Within these issue areas CCC supported organizing at the community level by providing leadership training, technical assistance, and expert mediation with policy arenas. Today, CCC follows an Alinskyite philosophy of community organizing. Its stated mission is not to organize low-income communities but to help these communities organize themselves. To this end, scores of organizations across the country receive assistance from CCC in the form of trainings, consultations, and grants.[32]

CCC prides itself on growing the organizational capacity of grassroots groups and training their leaders to unleash change. CCC's directors also envision the organization as occupying a mediating role between the grassroots organizing it facilitates with grants and trainings *and* the expert world of policy making. CCC claims to fill this space with its professional lobbying expertise and longstanding experience in the oversight of federal and state social programs. Gary Delgado, a longtime organizer and sociologist, refers to CCC as part of a nonprofit "network of technical assistance organizations" working in Washington, DC.[33]

Immigration is only one brief in CCC's broad portfolio of campaigns, and a relatively recent one, at that. The organization's website provides an illuminating timeline of its developing commitment to immigration reform efforts. It begins with this account of a convention of affiliated organizations in 2000:

> CCC convened diverse grassroots groups to create the National Campaign for Jobs and Income Support, a coalition to fight the conditions that create poverty. The coalition's Immigrant Organizing Committee asked the entire national coalition—immigrant groups and non-immigrant groups alike—to make immigration reform a priority issue. They agreed—but it was a tense moment, as Center for Community Change executive director Deepak Bhargava describes: "The immigration subcommittee was prepared to bring a proposal to the full campaign that we should embrace immigration reform. I could even feel some chills up my spine about a very consequential decision being made. Would the rest of the campaign embrace this issue? Would it be seen as a core economic issue or as a distraction?"

A quote on the timeline from Angelica Salas, the director of the CHIRLA, describes CCC's new focus on immigration reform as the result of "an agreement by many organizations that weren't immigrant-based, but who understood that if we were going to move forward an anti-poverty agenda in this country, then immigrants had to be included in that fight."[34] Whether pushed from below or pulled from above by expanding funding opportunities, CCC became a central node for advocacy organizations in the nonprofit immigration field. The organization's new focus on immigration reform did not hurt its revenue from foundation grants. By mid-decade, CCC appeared for the first time on the Foundation Center's "top 50" list of US nonprofit recipients of grants to work with immigrants, migrants, and refugees.[35]

In 2004, CCC gave its Immigrant Organizing Committee a new name: the Fair Immigration Reform Movement (FIRM). The name was aspirational. There was at the time no evidence of anything like a social movement forming under its auspices, but FIRM did pull together an impressive number of organizations from across the nation under one coalition. At its launch, CCC announced that "FIRM leaders from around the country will share stories of the broken immigration system, painting a vivid picture for the need for legislation to reform the nation's immigration policies." Stories from undocumented students eligible for the DREAM Act became central to FIRM's efforts.[36]

At roughly the same time as launching FIRM, CCC joined the work started by Josh Bernstein at NILC to connect organizations of undocumented students scattered across the nation. Most of these student groups emerged under the guidance of regional or state-level nonprofits plugged into the immigration field. Many of these organizations—like FLIC, NYIC, MIRA, ICIRR, and Angelica Salas's CHIRLA—were members of CCC's new FIRM coalition and grantees of the Ford Foundation and the Open Society Institute.[37] CCC, with the help of these FIRM membership organizations, worked to connect these undocumented student groups in a campaign it called "United We Dream."

One of the campaign's first actions was a mock graduation for undocumented students held in Washington, DC, in the spring of 2004. On the eve of the event, an op-ed appeared in *The Washington Post* from an undocumented student. The byline read: "Josue Torres, 17, is a volunteer in an immigrant nonprofit organization in Silver Spring and a member of Center for Community Change Real Voices." Following the DREAMer narrative crystalized in earlier media reports, Josue began his piece by relating his immigrant story, documenting his success as a student, and claiming his Americanness. "Everything I know—all of my friends, my roots—is American. But while other teenagers worry about which college to attend, I worry about being deported ... I long to live the American dream. Instead, I and thousands of kids like me find barriers at each step of the way because we are here illegally." He concluded with breaking some news: "On Tuesday I and hundreds of other high school students will gather for a mock graduation ceremony on Capitol Hill."[38]

The *Deseret Morning News* covered the event. "Three hundred youth in caps and gowns marched to 'Pomp and Circumstance' on the U.S. Capitol lawn. But it was not a graduation. It was a protest by illegal aliens." According to *The Washington Post*, CCC's director, Deepak Bhargava, told the "crowd of activists and students from around the country" that sixty-five thousand immigrants graduate from high school every year, but they cannot continue their education. "Those are 65,000 dreams denied," he said. "Our question to America is how can anyone sleep if immigrant students can't dream?" Marie Gonzalez also addressed the gathering, and she received with her fellow graduates a diploma from "the American Dream High School."[39]

At the end of the summer, CCC's "United We Dream Campaign" announced a "Fasting for a DREAM effort." For two weeks students, activists, and community leaders from around the nation held fasts and vigils. These days of action culminated on September 24 with one hundred "immigrant advocates and fasters" converging on Washington, DC, for a National Lobby Day. According to CCC's press release, "the events are meant to raise voices of immigrants during this election year and urge for immediate passage of pending immigration legislation, including the DREAM Act."[40]

CCC launched the "We are Marie" campaign that same year, organizing public pressure and lobbying politicians to stop Marie Gonzalez's deportation. CCC used the campaign as a rallying call to support the DREAM Act and as an organizing tool to involve undocumented student groups from across the country. "We are Marie" marked the first, national campaign that undocumented students could feel they had a hand in.[41] Although the role of undocumented youth in the campaign was limited, it marked for them an empowering moment of national activism and collective victory in self-protection.

This empowerment is captured in the letter penned by Marie Gonzalez to the editor of the *St. Louis Post-Dispatch* announcing her victory in the summer of 2005. The letter invoked all the elements of the stock DREAMer story, but it announced something new in the narrative. Marie was not a passive victim, but an agent in her fight against deportation:

> What a roller coaster of a ride my family has been on. The most bittersweet moment came on July 1. After much anticipation of being forced to leave friends, teachers, my congregation and the home, city and country I have known all of my life, the government notified me that it was allowing me to stay in the United States, at least for one year. My parents, however, could not, and they were deported to Costa Rica on July 5, just hours after we celebrated America's Independence.

Marie's letter described her family's immigration story and American dream:

> Many know that I have been living in Jefferson City since my parents, Marvin and Marina Gonzalez, brought me here legally from Costa Rica when I was 5 years old in search of a better life. We owned a Chinese restaurant and purchased a home. Our dog, Precious, chases squirrels in the back yard, and our parakeet, Lucky, keeps us up some nights. We thought things were going fine, and we did everything to be the model citizens we needed to be in order to apply for citizenship. A simple misunderstanding of this country's immigration system and the repeal of a law in 1997 put us in a battle to remain here.

She chronicled some of that battle and its outcome: "the Department of Homeland Security notified us on July 1 that I was being granted a one-year extension." She wrote about her sadness and disappointment of losing her parents to deportation and thanked a handful of politicians who took up her cause.

Marie ended the letter with an acknowledgement to those who had helped her and with her hope for the future:

> I want to thank my "family" in Washington, D.C.: Josh Bernstein of the National Immigration Law Center and the staff at the Center for Community Change. They have been my link to the nation's capital, allowing my family's voice to be heard and giving me a real-life civics lesson. Finally, to the 65,000 other undocumented immigrant students who graduate each year from high school with no chance to continue education and earn a path to citizenship, I thank them for being my inspiration. My story is just one of many, and I'm blessed to get the chance to share it. I can only hope Congress will reintroduce and pass the Development, Relief and Education for Alien Minors Act—DREAM—so that you don't have to read about another promising young person whose dreams were shattered and whose family was forced to separate. Just because of a mistake.[42]

The "We are Marie" campaign is as good a mark as any for the moment undocumented youth joined the national political fray. To extend Marie's words, they received in this campaign a "real-life civics lesson." Marie stopped her own deportation by going public. Her victory exposed a small window of political opportunity for other undocumented youth. It would take a few years before DREAMers would systematically exploit this opportunity, but they would eventually crack it wide open.

The campaign was a highlight of a relatively unremarkable year of immigrant-rights activism. In the fall, as they had done the year before, CCC organized undocumented students and community leaders to converge on Washington, DC, again to lobby for the DREAM Act. In a press release in late November supporting yet another introduction of the DREAM Act to the Senate, CCC's deputy executive director, Cristina Lopez, said the "passage of this important bill is imperative and represents a significant first step toward comprehensive immigration reform." The statement reflected CCC's strategic understanding of the relationship between the two legislative agendas. The DREAM Act was legislation that could pass now and help build momentum for the longer push for comprehensive immigration reform. CCC's position reflected a widely held position by reform advocates at the time.

In many ways little had changed since the first introduction of the DREAM Act at the start of decade. Any claim at the time about the existence of a popular movement for immigration reform, put forth by CCC or other advocates in the nonprofit immigration field, could only be described as aspirational. As the Senate debated the DREAM Act, the GOP-controlled House passed a very different immigration bill, HR 4437. Commonly referred to as the Sensenbrenner Bill, after its Republican sponsor, the Border Protection, Antiterrorism, and Illegal Immigration Control Act of 2005 passed along partisan lines in the last legislative days of the year. It defined undocumented immigrants and those who aid them as felons. It called for state and local law enforcement agents to turn over to federal authorities any undocumented immigrants they detained. For advocates of immigration reform, the Sensenbrenner Bill marked a nasty end to a legislative year of disappointments.

The Sleeping Giant Awakes

HR 4437 turned out to be a slow-burning fuse that ignited massive immigrant protests in the coming months, but at the time of its passage in the House few saw the coming explosion. The bill, after all, had no future in the Senate. As late as February 2006, CCC directors were preparing regional leadership training sessions for undocumented students in Chicago, Newark, Phoenix, Portland, and Nashville, with an eye toward advocating for the immediate passage of the DREAM Act.[43] But the political ground under their feet was about to shift, and along with it their policy calculations for immigration reform.

In March, mass demonstrations exploded across the country. The earliest rallies occurred in Washington, DC, on March 6 and in Chicago, IL, on March 10. These rallies were impressive in size but they were dwarfed by the protests later that month. On March 25, half a million marchers descended upon downtown Los Angeles, CA. Over the next two weeks mass rallies were reported in well over a hundred different cities and in every state of the nation. At the same time, more than a hundred thousand students walked out of scores of schools across the entire length of the country. The walkouts started on March 24. Almost everywhere, these student protests preceded, and in some cases prompted, the mass rallies involving whole families. In Los Angeles, students walked out the Friday before the rally on March 25. In Texas, the student lead was even more pronounced. A remarkable feature of these demonstrations is that they exploded almost simultaneously across relatively disconnected communities with little planning or support from established immigrant rights organizations. Upward of 270 demonstrations took place across the United States over a two-month period, bringing many millions into the street.[44]

This massive wave of protests altered the policy calculations of the directors of the large nonprofit organizations in the immigration field. The "mega-marchas" and student walkouts suggested that something more ambitious than incremental reform was possible, and the directors at CCC believed that they could be brokers between what appeared to be an emerging social movement and a new legislative initiative by policy elites and politicians to support comprehensive immigration reform.

CCC's website boasts of its role in the mass mobilizations of 2006. This account betrays a subtle inversion of the sequence of events and misleads with the implied causal role of FIRM:

> In response to a proposed federal law that would make it a crime to be undocumented or to help anyone who was undocumented, FIRM groups across the country worked with diverse community, labor, faith and media partners to organize rallies that brought millions of people into the streets. In March, Chicago groups held a demonstration with 100,000 people and Los Angeles with 500,000. In Washington CCC and FIRM brought 300 members of the clergy and 3,000 grassroots leaders to the Capitol as the Senate was considering a comprehensive immigration reform bill. On April 10th, immigrants and their allies in 102 cities held rallies of unprecedented size and scope, followed by still more demonstrations in May.[45]

The narrative suggests that FIRM member organizations were out ahead of the events, organizing the popular reaction to HR 4437 into protests that mobilized millions. In fact, almost all the large nonprofits and labor unions in the immigration field were caught by surprise when the "mega marchas" and student walkouts exploded in March. CCC's account also welcomes a misreading that the mass protests represented popular demands for a comprehensive immigration reform bill. Such a bill was hastily thrown together in Washington, DC, to capitalize on the momentum of the spontaneous mobilizations in March. CCC's retelling of the events put FIRM and comprehensive reform bandwagon before the horse.[46]

In reaction to the mass demonstrations of March, an array of nonprofits, including FIRM members, and labor unions *did* organize rallies. The organizers of these April marches sought to capitalize on the momentum of the mass protests and to discipline the look, feel, and slogans of the earlier actions. They worked to ensure that white t-shirts, American flags, and messages of future civic engagement and voter turnout replaced the colorful Mexican and Central American attire and Spanish language messages of the March mobilizations. In these later rallies, CCC and FIRM were not leading the mobilizations but trying to work the rudder of a bandwagon to steer "the movement."

No matter the causal role played by CCC in the wave of protests, its leadership framed the events as evidence of a massive social movement demanding comprehensive immigration reform. This altered CCC's work with undocumented students and its policy priorities. This change is captured in a May 24 press release for a youth lobbying event on the Hill:

> "After organizing in their local communities, immigrant youth and their friends are gathering to make the point that the lives and perspectives of young people matter in this immigration debate," said Deepak Bhargava, executive director, Center for Community Change. "No one can better convey the importance of Congress enacting a compassionate immigration reform bill that keeps their families together and allows them to fully participate in the promise of this country. These young people are not only leaders today, but they are part of a growing constituency that will vote and organize for years to come."

The shift in messaging from 2005 was clear. Calls for the DREAM Act were replaced by a new policy agenda of more comprehensive legislation to keep families together. The press release also quoted Marie Gonzalez:

> "I will never forget the day last summer when my parents were taken away from me and forced to deport back to Costa Rica because of our unfair and broken immigration system," said Marie Gonzalez, whose deferred deportation is expected to expire in six weeks. "This immigrant rights movement has gotten young people politically motivated in a whole new way. Those

of us, who can vote, will do so. Those of us that can't vote have friends that can."[47]

That same week, at the launch of a new CCC campaign to register one million immigrant voters before the midterm elections, Bhargava described its goal: "we want to capitalize on that movement energy and translate it into a real political voice for immigrants."[48]

Even as the popular momentum of the rallies stalled out and legislative bids for reform failed, CCC messaging articulated a mystifying history of a social movement they claimed to have "played a crucial and largely hidden role" in seeding at the grassroots. It claimed that the hundreds of FIRM member organizations "were the cornerstone of the people-led movement." It portrayed the coalition of organizations CCC helped build with funding support from Ford Foundation and OSI as transforming the nonprofit immigration "field into a full-fledged social movement."[49] Undeterred by temporary policy setbacks and a mysterious disappearance of popular mobilizations, CCC promised to guide this social movement toward its animating goal: comprehensive immigration reform. The achievement of this goal was all but inevitable. The popular momentum to legalize most undocumented immigrants was irresistible.[50]

A more critical interpretation of the events would suggest that the nonprofit organizations in the immigration field were disconnected from the grassroots of communities they claimed to organize. They had not seen the massive protests of 2006 coming. As they tried to harness the people-power of these protests for voter registration drives and comprehensive immigration reform, the protests disappeared as fast as they appeared. The professional directors of these nonprofit organizations did not know when or if this movement momentum would return. And any confidence in a near or medium-term legislative win to legalize ten or twelve million undocumented immigrants was sanguine—as suggested by the fate of immigration reform and voter drive efforts later that year.[51]

***

In the wake of 2006, where did this leave the relationship between emerging undocumented youth activists and the nonprofits in the immigration field trying to organize them? Drawing on interviews with undocumented students active in DREAM Act advocacy during these early years, the next chapter directly addresses this question. But from the archival analysis in this chapter, it is clear that this relationship was situated around two inchoate, abstract cultural projects that by 2006 appeared to fit awkwardly together: a DREAMer narrative tied to a legal distinction drawn by a failed bill distinguishing an exceptional category of undocumented youth from the larger population of unauthorized immigrants, and myth-like claims of a massive social movement awakened by the 2006 mass protests and propelled by a collective demand for the legalization of all undocumented immigrants. From the strategic perspective of the professionals leading the nonprofit immigration field, the subject of the first project was instrumental to the success of the second. The DREAMer could act as the public face of the movement.

At a Nashville, TN, training session for undocumented students in May, just as the marches had peaked and as a nativist counterattack raised its voice, Rich Stolz of CCC told the gathered youth that "together" they would be decisive in shaping the emerging movement. He said, "when the tough times come . . . youth will be important in keeping it going."[52] Tough times were coming, and undocumented youth would be called on to keep the movement going. But, with the momentous events of 2006, the policy priorities of nonprofit immigration field had shifted. The DREAM Act was no longer the first step in policy experts' plan for immigration reform. It was now a piece of legislation to be subordinated to a more comprehensive reform bill. The indispensable DREAMer would be asked to fight for their parents and families and to defer their personal dreams for a time, in the service of bigger victories for a broader movement. It was a reasonable ask, so long as undocumented youth and the professional advocates agreed on the character of this movement and the unifying goal propelling it.

2
Campus DREAMers

The first undocumented student organizations trace their origins to a time before the mega-marchas and student walkouts of 2006. It is easy to ignore these early organizational stirrings of activism because the mass mobilizations of that year constituted a real rupture in organizing efforts for immigrant rights. When the mega-marchas and walkouts hit, undocumented student organizations already existed. They were few in number and scattered across the country, but they were also active, growing, and starting to learn of each other's existence. For the undocumented students leading these early student groups, their first "real-life civic lessons," to use Marie Gonzalez's words, came from establishing and building these campus organizations.

Membership organizations of the FIRM coalition guided the local development of many of these fledgling student groups. At the national level, as discussed in the previous chapter, CCC started to draw them together in communication and through national meetings beginning a little over a year before the mass demonstrations of 2006. In December 2008, representatives from these student organizations came together in a formal national network named after the early CCC campaign, United We Dream (UWD). Drawing on interviews with leaders of student groups from Texas, Florida, and California, this chapter chronicles the early development of these student groups and their organizing work leading up to the formation of the UWD network.

Most of these early undocumented student organizations emerged in close interaction with state immigrant-rights organizations affiliated with FIRM. For example, the Student Immigrant Movement (SIM) in Massachusetts started in 2005 as a project of MIRA. The organization formed by City University of New York students, New York Student Youth Leadership Conference (NYSYLC), was housed in the offices of NYIC. The Florida group Students Working for Equal Rights (SWER) started under the guidance of FLIC. And the organizational infrastructure for the California DREAM Network was established by CHIRLA. Student organizations in Texas, where a 2001 state law provided in-state tuition for undocumented immigrants, followed a different path. Texas was the first state to pass such legislation. One effect of this policy was to create a state-sanctioned categorical distinction around which undocumented students could organize. Characteristic aspects of undocumented youth activism that developed nationwide around the DREAM Act unfolded first in Texas over in-state tuition.

Texas and the University Leadership Initiative

The first undocumented youth organization in Texas emerged in Houston in the late 1990s as educators and politicians debated providing undocumented students the same access to community colleges enjoyed by other state residents. The Houston organization was called Jóvenes Inmigrantes por un Futuro Mejor (JIFM). It provided the model for a student organization formed later at the University of Texas at Austin, the University Leadership Initiative (ULI), that would go on to play a central part in the founding of the national UWD network.

Julieta Garibay, with the help of her older sister Montserrat, formed ULI in January of 2005.[1] She was born in Mexico City in 1980. Montserrat is a little over a year older than Julieta. Their mother divorced their abusive father when they were very young. She struggled alone to provide for her two daughters a middle-class existence. She enrolled Montsy and Juli in a private Catholic school. She worked as a secretary but could not make ends meet, so she entered the grey market as a *fayucera*. She would travel to Laredo, Texas, and buy perfumes and other goods to bring back to sell in Mexico City. The Garibay sisters had another connection to Texas: an aunt in Austin who they had visited a few times. After years of struggling to make a life in Mexico, their mom decided to follow her sister and move to Austin, TX.

The Garibay family came on tourist visas, but the intention was always to stay. The family moved into a working-class neighborhood in north Austin. Their mother worked cleaning nursing homes and private houses. Following the lead of their cousins, the sisters enrolled as transfer students in a public middle school in a leafy neighborhood northwest of downtown. Juli recalled "the kids would call us wetbacks." Montsy said that, at first, they were placed in very small ESL classes with "amazing" teachers. By their second school year, they were in mainstream classes speaking, reading, and writing English.

After graduation from middle school, the sisters moved with their classmates to the public high school in the same affluent neighborhood.

When I asked Juli to describe herself during those years, she said, "I was nerdy. I was good at school." Her mom always emphasized the importance of education. She would tell her daughters, "Tu unica tarea es la escuela. I don't have anything to leave behind but your education." She did not say "I want all A's," Juli recalled, "we just gave her A's." Their mother was loving and strict. The sisters' childhood in the United States revolved almost exclusively around school and home. Discipline protected them from the risks of being undocumented. Their mom taught them to stay in school and stay out of trouble. When they were not in school, they were at home studying.

As careful as they were to stick to the safe spaces of school and home, the fear of being undocumented was never far away. In separate interviews, both sisters described how deeply disturbed they were by a jobsite immigration raid they witnessed as kids. They were sitting in a car with their mom, stopped in traffic, when suddenly they saw people running into the street weaving between the cars with "la Migra" behind them in pursuit. After this experience, Montsy remembered being dropped off at school by her mom and worrying if she would return to pick her up. Juli recalled thinking, "this is what it means to be undocumented." She recollected another time when the same harsh realization hit even closer to home:

> [M]y mom got home from work and she just looked really sad and worried, and she said, "me preguntaron por los papeles"—they asked me for my papers. And I think that was the first time that I was like being undocumented wasn't just a name or a label. It is more like this is the life we are going to have to live. And I remember my mom never returned to that job again. Soon after, we moved to another apartment, because we were afraid that they could call immigration on us or that something could happen. That's when I started thinking you know, this is our home and how could someone just come and say you have to run? I think that is when I also realized that it is not just a label, it is a status, and it means that whenever anyone asks me for my papers I need to run away. And that was when I was 16 or 17.

For most undocumented students, the end of high school meant an educational dead end. Title V of Section 505 of IIRIRA prohibited states from providing undocumented immigrants postsecondary educational benefits. It required the imposition of out-of-state or international fees, which made college prohibitively expensive for most. When Montsy graduated, her mom sent her back to Mexico to live with family in Guanajuato, where she could afford to enroll in college. Montsy taught English to schoolchildren to help pay her way. After a year of college and work, she applied for a tourist visa and returned to Austin. Once back in Austin, she found a sponsor for a student visa and enrolled in Austin Community College.

When Juli graduated from high school, she followed her sister's footsteps and returned to Mexico. When she went to the US consulate for a tourist visa, just as Montsy had before her, she was turned down. Now she was stuck. She had no way of coming back the "right way." Staying separated from her mom and sister was never an option. She crossed back into Texas by car without papers through a port of entry near the University of Texas at El Paso. "The border patrol just waved the car through," Juli recalled. "I guess they just thought [I] was another student."

Back in Austin, Montsy was now studying education at the University of Texas. Juli was not sure what to do next. She dreamed of becoming a nurse. It was Montsy who discovered a new opportunity that had just opened for undocumented students in Dallas and in Houston. Juli explained:

> [Montsy] learned about this pilot program in the Dallas and Houston community colleges where they were allowing DREAMers to go, but we weren't called DREAMers then, you were just undocumented people. My mom and I drove to Houston and then we drove to Dallas. And in Dallas I was like this is where I want to go. And I remember registering and my mom and I walked out . . . and I was literally jumping.

Dallas was the first municipality in Texas to admit undocumented students to community colleges as state residents, allowing them to pay in-state tuition rates. Houston soon followed suit. These Dallas and Houston community college programs preceded the drafting of the DREAM Act at the national level and the passage of any state laws granting undocumented students in-state tuition to public universities.

The Dallas program came first. It responded to multiple concerns, including stories of exceptional students with no path forward for higher education and concerns over rising high school dropout rates among immigrant youth. David Johnston, a high school teacher at Robert E. Lee High School in a largely immigrant neighborhood of Houston, organized undocumented students at his school into a support and advocacy group to push for a similar program in Houston. Alejandra Rincón, who worked as a director of multilingual programs in the Houston public school system, joined with David Johnston and his students to push Houston's community college system to follow the lead of Dallas' program. The Lee student group was likely the first undocumented student organization in Texas.[2]

Success at the municipal level in Houston and Dallas led to a push for a new state law. Immigrant rights advocates, educators, and politicians argued that high school dropout rates among immigrants were to be expected given the lack of opportunity many faced for higher education. Pointing to the programs in Dallas and Houston, they argued for an extension of these in-state tuition policies for undocumented students to all state colleges and universities. With the help of state representatives Rick Noriega from Houston and Domingo Garcia from Dallas, they spearheaded the 2001 push for HB 1403—a bill for in-state tuition for undocumented students.

The campaign for HB 1403 publicized the cases of promising undocumented students blocked from college. A pattern that would be repeated at the national level in support of the DREAM Act. These stories, according to Rick Noriega, provided the needed "human element" animating the political campaign. Undocumented immigrants from the student organization formed at Lee High School in Houston, along with others from across the state, testified in front of the Texas Legislator in support of the bill. HB 1403 passed almost unanimously through the Legislature and was signed into law by Rick Perry in June of 2001.[3]

With the passage of HB 1403 and the continued advocacy of David Johnston and Alejandra Rincón, the organization first started by Houston high school students grew into a small network of college organizations, JIFM. Instrumental in JIFM's growth was a partnership Alejandra Rincón established with the University of Texas at Prairie View to include undocumented youth in its pre-college summer camps. The summer program became a recruiting ground for undocumented students, plugging them into an emerging JIFM network with chapters in colleges in Houston, Dallas, and Prairie View.[4]

When Juli finished her associate degree in nursing in Dallas, the new law made it possible for her to pursue an advanced degree in nursing. She had done well in her studies in Dallas and was admitted to the prestigious University of Texas School of Nursing at Austin. It was a great opportunity but deciding to enroll was a leap of faith. She was committing to training in a profession that she could not practice in the place she called home.

It was back in Austin, enrolled as a nursing student, when she first learned about the DREAM Act. It was Montsy who brought her the news of its promise. "She was like I found . . . your solution Juli." It was also Montsy who introduced Juli to Alejandra Rincón, who had moved from Houston to Austin to fill the position of Immigration Counselor for the Austin Independent School District and to work on a graduate degree in education at the University of Texas. Montsy had read about the Prairie View summer camp in the newspaper and reached out to Alejandra:[5]

> We met and we started talking, and [Alejandra] started telling Julieta and I, "oh, well there's this other organization in Houston, Jóvenes Inmigrantes, and this is what we are doing. We are doing educational forums." And we are like "we want to do that. We want to start something like that here in Austin."

Alejandra's vision of educational advocacy for undocumented students spoke directly to Montsy, who felt called as an educator:

> She knew all the high school principals and all the counselors here in Austin, so she was really important because every time that she would do an educational forum, she would invite us. And then we would go and tell our story.

It is from the discussions and work with Alejandra that the Garibay sisters got the idea of forming a support group for undocumented students at the University of Texas, an Austin chapter of JIFM.

Juli sent a notice for the first meeting through a listserv for international students that the university used to send information to undocumented students enrolled under HB 1403, "because," as Montsy explained, "that's who HB 1403 students are, right!?" The notice was crafted around Juli relating her own experience as an undocumented student in Texas:

> We sat down on a Sunday morning, it was January [2005], it was cold . . . sitting in our dining room and I wrote out my story, like literally coming out. And we just sent it out on the server, "if you want to help me just come." I had no idea if there were other DREAMers at UT, it was just

[shrugs shoulders]. And that's how we started it. It wasn't like "oh, this is my theory of change, this is how we should do it," no it [was nothing like that.]

There were others. When Rebecca Acuña read Juli's email, she thought "that is my story too."[6]

Rebecca was born in 1983 in El Fuerte, Sinaloa, Mexico. Her parents ran a restaurant. When she was very young, her dad started doing business along the Texas border. Around 1990, her father bought a restaurant in Reynosa, Taumalipas, just across the Rio Grande from McAllen, TX, and her family decided to leave Sinaloa. In our interview, this is how Rebecca described the family decision about where to settle:

[DREAMers] always say "my parents didn't ask me where I wanted to live." My parents did ask. They asked my sister and I "where do y'all want to live? Reynosa or McAllen?" We said Reynosa. We don't want to go to the US. We want to live in Mexico. My mom didn't care and we went to McAllen . . . We weren't fleeing anything. My mom just thought we'd have better opportunities living on the US side. So, we lived in McAllen, even though my father's restaurant was on the Mexican side.

Rebecca did not think about her immigration status as a kid. Growing up in the Rio Grande Valley, where many can claim that the border crossed them and not the other way around, she never worried about being deported or separated from her family. Her father had a visa allowing him to cross the border at will. She went through elementary school and middle school in McAllen and then her family moved to Laredo. School was easy. She excelled and graduated from high school at the top of her class.

Rebecca was fortunate to graduate in 2002, the first year after the passage of HB 1403. She found out about the law from her mother: "My mom was like 'oh my gosh I saw on Univision that you are going to be able to go to college.'" She applied to the University of Texas at Austin:

Initially, when I applied, they didn't know how to treat people like me, so they sent me a foreign student application and they were asking me about my test of English as a foreign language results. They were asking me for my high-school transcripts from Mexico. They were asking me for all sorts of things that I didn't have.

The decision letter she received brought bad news:

> I actually got a rejection letter from the University of Texas saying, "we did not get your scores on time so you can't come." And I was like "oh, damn that sucks. I'll stay home and I'll try again next time." And then my mom saw it and she was livid. She takes it to my high school counselor, who was amazing, Carmen Castillo. She was so helpful. She at that moment was like "I don't understand." So, she calls the university and says "you can't deny her admission she's in the top ten percent."[7]

After pressure from her counselor, the admission office reversed its decision, and she enrolled in classes for the fall of 2002.

Sitting in my office at the University of Texas at Austin, more than a decade after the fact, Rebecca told me that she was not "mad at the university" for making her go through this emotional roller coaster. At the time, she "felt lucky" and even a little guilty:

> I didn't view it like a civil rights thing yet. It was more like I still felt I had done something wrong . . . I felt like despite that I haven't fixed this thing in my life, I am still getting to go. They are still letting me go. And not only that, but, so you know my parents, at that point, my mom was a waitress. I didn't know how I [was] going to pay for college. I couldn't work. I wasn't working. So, there was that anxiety about paying. And so, I got here still not knowing how I was going to pay my first tuition installment and then I realized [HB 1403] gives state aid to undocumented students. That was a huge blessing. . . . I just felt lucky. Not only did I get to, despite my having at some point done something—that I couldn't understand—wrong, I could still come and I could still get state aid and go to this university.

Rebecca picked government as her academic major and became active in the Latino Leadership Council and the League of United Latin American Citizens (LULAC). Her interest in politics and civic engagement followed directly from the personal impact of HB 1403. She explained its effect in our interview:

> I saw my life change because of one bill the state legislature passed, when no one was paying attention, when no one was talking. [It] completely changed

my life. I was like this is how government affects people. This is how one bill changes peoples' lives. So, I think that's kind of what made me so [interested and engaged in politics].

As she settled into campus life, Rebecca had no idea if there were other students in her situation, until she read a story published in the student newspaper:

Second semester, the *Daily Texan* does, and it's on the first page, does an analysis of, it was called "House 1403 students," of how many students are studying under it and there are 12. As small as that number seemed, I was like "oh my god it's a *thing*!" It's not just me.

Rebecca punctuated the word "thing" and then repeated it. "I didn't know it was *a thing*, outside of me." The article was coupled with an opinion piece by an editor that questioned the right of undocumented students to be enrolled as residents of Texas. Rebecca felt attacked by the article, but she was at the same time thrilled to know that she was not alone, that she was part of a larger "thing."

Rebecca's description of the power of the categorical distinction drawn by HB 1403 to turn undocumented students into "a thing"—like the power of the distinction drawn in the proposed federal legislation of the DREAM Act—nicely captures how this "reification" of a particular social condition and identity could be affirming, and even liberating. As counterintuitive as it sounds, reification in this instance was valorizing for Rebecca. It had collectivizing effects, too.[8]

At the start of the spring semester of her second year, she was following policy debates and activity in the Texas legislature when she received "the email from Julieta." It brought politics and biography together:

I'm sitting after my Italian class. I'm sitting in one of the six-pack buildings, at the computer lab, and I'm checking my email. By then I was involved in Latino Leadership Council, LULAC, Latino based organizations, and Dr. Margarita Ariana forwards an email from Julieta. I read it and it was [from] someone that could have been me. It was just sharing her story: "I came to this country at this age, going to school under this bill. We have a meeting to address what we can do next Tuesday." Or something like that. I was "it's just not me on this campus!"

Rebecca recalled that when she read the email, "I wasn't out, that's the way I describe it. I wasn't out. I wanted to go to the meeting, but I was like 'what if someone is there that I know?'" This fear of exposing her status did not stop her:

> I remember going and I was kind of walking by the classroom, is someone going to know me in there? What are they going to say? So that was the first time and it was Montserrat, and their mom and Julieta, and maybe a handful of other students.

Juli was not sure anyone would even show up for the meeting. She did not know if other undocumented students would identify with her story. Her account of Rebecca's joining of the group is revealing of the "closeted" environment for undocumented students on campus at the time. For the first few meetings, Juli remembered, "I thought how nice of Rebecca, who belongs to LULAC, to come to our meetings." She assumed Rebecca was a citizen.

The Garibay sisters saw the organization they formed primarily as a support group for undocumented students. Meetings provided a safe space for undocumented students to talk about surviving and succeeding at the university. It was precisely the kind of space Rebecca hoped to find when she cautiously scoped out the first gathering. From the beginning, the Garibay sisters' mother was active in the group. To this day, parents are welcome and active in ULI. In our interviews, Montsy and Juli repeatedly referred to ULI as "a family" and spoke of the members they have seen come through the group as they would of younger siblings. The group, for them, was first and foremost a haven for undocumented students in an often cold, judgmental, and occasionally treacherous world.

ULI's involvement in politics developed organically from its interest to protect its members and their future. The leaders of ULI first cut their activist teeth on local politics. According to Rebecca and Juli, their first public demonstration on campus was to stop a planned "illegal immigrant hunt" sponsored by the Young Conservatives of Texas (YCT). The "hunt" was a "game" that the YCT first hatched at the University of North Texas in Denton. It involved some members wearing clothing marking them as "illegals" and the rest hunting for them across campus and being rewarded with candy if they were successful in the catch. The YCT at UT-Austin planned the hunt for March 2005. ULI organized a pre-emptive protest that drew considerable support on campus and the YCT repudiated the game before it ever came off.

ULI's first involvement in wider state politics came that same year in the fall as it played a key role in the organization of a counterprotest to a Minutemen rally at the Texas Capitol. ULI was the point organization for this event coordinated by Mexican American and immigrant rights organizations from across the state. ULI, as the sponsoring organization, applied for the permits for the rally, helped coordinate the event onsite in Austin, and marched at the front of the demonstration.

With the help of Alejandra, the organization developed an outreach program to educate undocumented high school students (and their teachers and counselors) about HB 1403. The organization also acted as an advocacy group to protect HB 1403 from repeal efforts in the state legislator. As it took a leading role in local demonstrations, educational outreach, and state politics, ULI operated as a typical student club. Following the organizational model of other campus groups, it raised money through carwashes, bake sales, and selling T-shirts. It elected officers and held monthly meetings. National politics soon beckoned.

Juli went to an NCLR conference in Philadelphia the summer after forming ULI. She was grouped together on a panel with two other undocumented student leaders: Carlos Saavedra from Massachusetts and Walter Barrientos from New York. Carlos represented SIM, a brand-new student project under MIRA. Walter, a student senator from the City University of New York's (CUNY) Baruch College, was at the center of undocumented youth organizing in New York City that would lead to the formation of the NYSYLC, housed in the offices of NYIC. Felipe Vargas, representing an undocumented youth group he helped form at the University of Indiana in Bloomington, was also on the panel. This was Juli's first contact with undocumented students outside of Texas. The meeting was an important first encounter between local leaders who would be instrumental in forming the national network that would become United We Dream. Carlos, Walter, and Juli would become founding members of UWD. At that NCLR conference, Juli realized that undocumented students in Texas enjoyed privileges because of HB 1403 that others, even in much more liberal states, did not.

Rebecca and Juli's understanding of how HB 1403 came to pass and their efforts to block attempts to repeal the law in Texas influenced their subsequent activism for the DREAM Act. As Rebecca explained, the bill passed "when no one was paying attention." This is a bit of an overstatement, as she would readily admit, but it reflects what she saw as a central truth about advancing immigrant rights. Legislative actions benefiting immigrants typically passed low on the political radar screen. HB 1403 was framed as an education bill and as a solution to address high school dropout rates, not as immigration policy.

Apart from the two public actions organized against the Minutemen and the YCT, ULI kept a rather low profile on campus, focusing its work on creating a safe space for undocumented students and conducting education forums at local high schools. Its leaders knew that with HB 1403 they had something very valuable to protect, and controversial public actions might jeopardize their benefits under the state law. Every legislative year, Juli and Rebecca led ULI members to testify against proposed laws aimed at taking away in-state tuition. When ULI moved into public debates, it moved cautiously, making sure to have behind it the support of allied, mainstream Latino organizations, like LULAC, and influential Democratic politicians.

The considerable political acumen Juli and Rebecca developed running ULI owed much to the help of Ana Yanez-Correa from the Texas Criminal Justice Coalition. Formerly the interim LULAC director for Texas, Ana introduced them to the state directors of the ACLU, MALDEF, and of course LULAC, as well as potential local allies like the Austin Immigrant Rights Coalition (AIRC). Ana let ULI members use her office as their own. Montsy recalled, "she said 'you all can come here and start organizing here, and you can have all the copies that you want. Use the computers.'" Ana also helped them strategize. "Any idea that we would have she was like 'how can we do this?'"

It was through Ana's connections that ULI was invited to an ACLU training in 2006. "It was going to be a legislative year, so they were teaching us about how to talk to the legislators," Montsy explained:

> And then this issue came up of our name: Jóvenes Inmigrantes por un Futuro Mejor. And we had a big conversation about our name and they kind of told us imagine you, I mean about being strategic, imagine you go to a Republican legislator or representative. They are going to shut down as soon as they hear Jóvenes Inmigrantes por un Futuro Mejor. Well, yeah that's true. We started really talking about strategizing and you know because our name was in Spanish that was only helping the Hispanic students and the Mexican kids, and we really wanted to open[-up] to other kids, so we decided as a group to change our name. That's why we changed it to University Leadership Initiative.

The UT-Austin group brought the proposed change to the other established JIFM organizations at a Houston meeting. Montsy described the reception:

> Every semester we would get together and talk to them [about] what are we going to do. And we brought it to them, and we said look you know we need to change our name and they were like nope, it's Jóvenes, we need to take pride of who we are. And we were like yes, but at least change it to Young Immigrants for a Better Future.

The other groups rejected even the proposed change to English. This led to an unhappy split between the newly named ULI and JIFM and a chill in the relationship between the Garibay sisters and Alejandra Rincón.

Alejandra remembers the name change as symbolic of how close the UT group had been pulled into the institutional politics of Texas Democrats and away from the more community roots of JIFM in Houston.[9] The resulting rift with Alejandra still hurts Montsy to this day. She, more so than Juli, was very close to Alejandra, and identified with her as a fellow educator. Montsy said in our interview, with tears rolling down her face, that although the split with Alejandra and JIFM was emotionally difficult, the UT group, with its growing political connections, was ready to go it alone.[10]

The year 2006 was a watershed year for ULI, as it was for many organizations advocating for immigrant rights. Rebecca captured how different activism was before and after that year in the following exchange in our interview. "My first, I guess, out time"—Rebecca paused to make shadow quotes with her hands—"was at the state capitol in 2005." She continued describing the event where she first "outed" herself:

> That summer I testified at my first committee at the state level. They had a bill on driver licenses for undocumented students. And I testified as an undocumented student. And I was like, "hey, I drive every day. I'm sorry to tell you this, but I do, and even if you don't pass your law, I'm going to continue to drive. So, would you prefer that I have insurance and that you know where I am?" And that was my first time, and I was on the record . . . and these are legislators.

I asked her "did you ever regret saying it? Were you nervous afterwards?"

> I think I get nervous now, like thinking back, how's this going to hurt my boss, if they find out, stuff like that [laughing].[11] Nobody knew about

DREAMers. People here didn't know undocumented students . . . It wasn't, I guess, without trying to say something very nice about ourselves, we were kind of paving the way for future activists. People didn't have walkouts or hunger strikes. . . . It just felt like you were alone and you were doing it for the very first time, and my whole reason was because it had been so hard for me to go to college that I just wanted to tell other students, hey this is how you can do it.

The events of 2006 ended this feeling of being alone:

And then the Sensenbrenner Bill happened, and one day they had these huge manifestations in his home state, in Milwaukee, in Wisconsin . . . . When we saw it on TV the next day . . . we were like, oh my god did you see how many people were marching? Like this really isn't just a few of us. People care about this issue. Immigration is an issue. Um, a few days later they had manifestations in Chicago, which I remember again watching those on my computer. Wow, that was huge. We saw those two and that was when you feel there is a movement around this.

As they witnessed the mobilization of mass demonstrations across the country, Rebecca said ULI members figured, "hey, why not Austin?"

On April 10, 2006, ULI, working with AIRC and Workers Defense Project, led the largest immigrant rally in Austin's history.[12] After the Austin demonstration, ULI became increasingly active in the national politics of immigration reform. Juli had already attended the NCLR conference the year before where she met other undocumented youth leaders. Through Alejandra, she had contacted Josh Bernstein and was participating in regular NILC conference calls with other undocumented student leaders. She had attended an interregional meeting of undocumented students organized by CCC earlier that academic year and brought back what she learned to Austin. But ULI's national involvement really started to accelerate only after the mass mobilizations.

The winter after the mega-marchas, Rebecca and Juli drove together to a NILC and CCC organized meeting in Kansas City. Rebecca described it as the "first ever . . . DREAM Act Congresso." She remembered representatives from "CCC, NILC, NCLR and a bunch of student groups" at this meeting. She recalled vividly "little things, like Josh Bernstein with NILC. I would read his name in the paper, so I was like 'oh my gosh, it's Josh Bernstein.'" She also remembered Marie Gonzalez: "She was one of the first, big, high-profile DREAMers." But "the coolest thing I remember," Rebecca said, was the "research" circulated by NILC:

> It gave every member of Congress, every targeted member of Congress, a rating of one to seven, seven being the most anti-immigrant and one being the most pro. . . . I thought that was so cool because it was all this research and . . . it wasn't just shooting in the dark, but you knew like this is who we should focus on. I thought it was amazing.

That same year, "I think it was 2007," Juli recalled, "we were invited by a national organization to be part of their DC event and, also, we were doing our graduation." That spring, FIRM coordinated a large gathering of member organizations aimed at pushing comprehensive immigration reform, scheduling it to coincide with the annual mock graduation of undocumented students CCC had been organizing over the past three years. Juli described the reception of undocumented students at the FIRM gathering:

> They had told us "yeah, we will have space for DREAMers." Then we got there and there was no room. They basically gave us a closet, where they were keeping all the bags. And to a lot of us, we were like [laughing] "did we just get sent to the closet?" I think that's when we were like "no, this shouldn't be." We are the people who are being affected by this, and this is not how it should work. You don't, number one, you don't send anyone to the closet. Number two, we are the ones being affected. We need to have our own space where we call our own shots. And we also need to be a part of the table that's making the decisions. That's when a lot of us started saying "we need to have our own organization, our own network." And that's when we really started getting serious about becoming a formal organization as United We Dream.

Prior to that meeting, according to Juli, the national organizing of undocumented students amounted to little more than conference calls set up by Josh Bernstein and a few interregional face-to-face meetings:

> We would get on calls and try to figure out what's our action, what are we going to do, what states do we need? But it was very small. It was the usual

suspects: CA, TX, FL, NY, MA and very few states. But it was just conference calls and then every now and then we would try to get together.

That changed with this meeting in Washington, DC, in 2007. "That's when we are like, ok we are forming our own organization." It would take a little over a year of planning, but "it was in 2008, December, when we became officially UWD."

Juli resented how professional allies held all the seats "at the table" and took undocumented youth for granted, but she fundamentally trusted their political analysis. She and Rebecca were impressed with the research NILC provided to undocumented students to inform their lobbying of elected officials. A few years later, when UWD engaged directly in the politics heating-up again around comprehensive immigration reform and the DREAM Act, Juli and Rebecca approached working with the directors of the large, national nonprofits, much as they had with political allies in Austin when defending HB 1403. They steered ULI into the ranks of the moderates, trusting in the political acumen of the allies directing NILC and CCC—but the discussion of that historical juncture is still to come.

Undocumented students in Texas followed a somewhat different path than most of the other early DREAMer organizations. In Texas, there was no FIRM-affiliated organization leading and supporting undocumented students. Ana Yanez-Correa from the Texas Criminal Justice Coalition and her connections with LULAC served somewhat as a functional equivalent to FIRM organizations. Ana provided resources and training to ULI, but she and LULAC were not directly geared into the national politics of immigration reform or the DREAM Act. The policy effects of HB 1403 provided crucial institutional supports for the organizational development of ULI. HB 1403 made being an undocumented student, as Rebecca put it, a unifying *thing*: a thing to share and identify with and to organize around. The categorical distinction it drew for undocumented youth raised in Texas provided the institutional channels Juli used to organize a support group that gradually turned into an advocacy group for the DREAM Act and DREAMers.

Florida and Students Working for Equal Rights

Another early and prominent student organization, SWER, emerged in Florida under the charismatic leadership of Maria Gabriela Pacheco. Gaby was born in 1985 in Guayaquil, Ecuador.[13] Her family was well-off, traveled to Florida for vacations, and even owned an apartment in South Miami. Her parents ran a currency exchange business. When Gaby was eight years old, they left Ecuador for good and settled in Miami. She remembers the move vividly: her family suddenly selling all their belongings, including her beloved bike. But, being so young, she did not appreciate its finality. In her eight-year-old imagination, she thought Miami was just another city in Ecuador.

Her parents' reasons for leaving Ecuador were many and complicated. One of her two older sisters was receiving medical treatment in Miami for a hearing problem. Her other sister had grown to love Miami from family visits and was already going to school there. Her parents were weary of violent crime in Guayaquil. Crime felt like it was all around them and increasingly menacing. And, maybe most importantly, Miami offered a chance to interrupt a destructive cycle of personal problems that threatened their marriage. Miami appeared to present a new beginning for the family.

The family entered the United States on temporary tourist visas. The children—Gaby, her two older sisters, and younger brother—received student visas as they started school in Miami. Gaby thrived in school, her parents got the clean break they hoped for, and the Pacheco's grew to love their new home. But the family's immigration status soon turned into a problem. Through a series of mistakes by the family and their immigration lawyer, Gaby and her siblings fell out of "status" and entered, at first without knowing it, into the legally precarious world of the undocumented. Gaby, through luck or just dogged persistence in pressuring a bureaucrat at US Citizenship and Immigration Services, was able to reinstate her lapsed student visa, but it provided only temporary protection.

In our interview, Gaby described herself as "a nerd" and "the teacher's pet." Early on in elementary school, Gaby dreamed of going to college. In the eighth grade this dream appeared scuttled by a sudden realization of the precariousness of her legal status in the United States. As her older sisters discovered after graduation from high school, the limits they faced because of their immigration status were hard and narrow, but Gaby was not deterred. She pushed harder and became the "highest ranking JROTC student in her high school."[14] Rather than hiding her immigration status, she trumpeted it. She hoped that by sharing her legal predicament she might find someone who would know how to fix it. She got lots of advice, but most of it was not good. Her Advanced Placement US History teacher, playing around, would say to her: "Hey Pocohontas, how are you? Have you been able to find your John Smith yet? Have you gotten married so you can get your papers?" It was a mean joke, but, as she told me, "that was my reality."

It was also in high school that she learned about the DREAM Act. It offered a different kind of hope. She researched the proposed legislation and became a self-taught public advocate. She spoke publicly about her story and the promise the DREAM Act held for her and other students like her. A brilliant public speaker, Gaby became a student leader at Miami-Dade College. She went on to become the statewide president of Florida's junior college government. As a statewide student leader, Gaby championed undocumented students in public addresses. The controversial issue that she gave voice to, and her talent for public speaking, brought some fame and some notoriety. Gaby said in our interview that she frequently used this "favorite line: How is it that the most powerful college student in the state of Florida, representing over 1.1 million students, cannot even vote? I'm undocumented." In fact, Gaby was not undocumented: "I had a student visa, but it was just the way I described myself. How I felt." And, besides, her legal status was very tenuous, and the rest of her family was undocumented.

Her talent for public speaking is preserved in a November 2010 video of an impromptu speech immediately after the arrest of four DREAMers occupying Senator McCain's Washington, DC, offices. (The sit-in, which led to the nasty fight between Mo and Gaby, is discussed in the Preface of this book). It was a dark and cold November night. She was feeling hated and isolated from fellow undocumented activists:

> We want to call on every single DREAMer in this country, in the United States of America, to wake up.
> Let this be the last time that we put one of ours at risk.
> Let this be the last time that a DREAMer doesn't wake up and realize that their voice is powerful, that they have rights.
> Let this be the last time that Latinos in the United States of America forget where they came from, forget that they were immigrants in this country too.
> Cubans, Puerto Ricans, Mexicans, Hondurans, Ecuadorians, immigrants from Europe, immigrants from Canada, let this be the last time that they don't pick up a phone and call their senator and say pass the DREAM Act.

Her tone is sad, despairing. She speaks slowly. The somewhat awkward, but arresting, rhythmic refrain of "let this be the last time that we don't do something," all but concedes defeat:

> Let this be the last time that conscious people, people that believe in justice, don't do something for young people like ourselves, for those four young people who are risking it all.

The crowd around her is silent. Gaby suddenly flashes anger. Punching the air with an accusatory finger, she raises her voice to a near yell. And the words race out:

> McCain, shame on you.
> Shame on you Senator McCain and every other senator who once stood with us, and are turning their backs on us.
> Shame on you.

The quiet crowd suddenly erupts with shouts of "shame on you." Gaby appears to struggle to control her anger. Another DREAMer involved in the action, steps in to address the gathered. When he stops, Gaby, now composed, says resolutely but more softly than before:

> We're doing this for Guillermo,
> for Alma,
> for Jorge,
> for Noemi.

The names of the arrested DREAMers sing out, smoothly and rhythmically. She ends returning to her opening theme:

> I'm doing this to wake up other DREAMers.
> So that other DREAMers wake up
> And start [pauses and tailing off]
> realizing their lives.[15]

Gaby quickly gained a reputation as a powerful speaker with a good story. "I was asked to go to the national press club and tell my story. I would get flown all over." And then, in 2005, Maria Rodriguez, the director of FLIC, approached Gaby and asked her: "Why are you doing this by yourself? There are other students like you." Maria challenged her to start organizing undocumented students. That same year, Gaby, along with a couple of other students introduced to her by Maria, formed SWER.

Gaby describes SWER's early work very much in the same way as the Garibay sisters understood the founding mission of ULI, as a support group and educational resource for undocumented students:

> It became a very powerful organization in a small amount of time. And this is when SWER started meeting up with all the other organizations and pockets of communities that started the same kind, maybe not the same story, but they started organizing and building community and saying: "Oh, I don't have papers. Oh, you don't have papers. You went to college. How did you go to college?"

Unlike ULI, Gaby's organization, with its founding relationship to FLIC, was from the get-go plugged into CCC and the national nonprofit immigration field.

Gaby described the early landscape of undocumented student organizations as being under the care of "parental" nonprofits in the immigration field:

> Not all of us, but the majority of organizations are children of a parent organization or had support from a national or statewide coalition or organization that are part of CCC, FIRM, and all these other bigger kinds of groups.

It was at CCC's national gatherings that she first met undocumented students from other states. There were some nuanced differences to the organizational histories of their groups, but most seemed to her to have developed in the orbit of FIRM affiliates, as SWER had formed under FLIC. Her view, of course, was shaped by her experiences, but she was not wrong.

CCC mediated the early collective action between Gaby's Florida organization and undocumented student groups from other states:

> The first time that something really major just brought some of us together was in 2005 ... [T]here was a whole campaign that happened in Washington, DC, called the "We are Marie" campaign. The "We are Marie" campaign was

the first time that people got a glimpse of organizing power, and that when people came together, that things could happen. And [Marie's] deportation was stopped. And people were like, "wow, this happened!" Her parents weren't able to stay, but the fact that this student—she got the criteria that all of us had, right—was able to stay in the country was just monumental!

What was the criterion that they all shared with Marie? The categorical distinction that united them and might save them from deportation, like it did Marie: Eligibility for the DREAM Act. The campaign showed that this categorical distinction could prove material in saving an undocumented student from deportation. It was empowering and it propelled further student organizing.

Working with CCC was not always empowering. Gaby described in our interview the resentment undocumented youth felt at how "the DC people" treated them as pawns:

> I feel that more than anything they were trying to organize us and take us, because they started to see how powerful we were. In 2005 or 6 was the first training that we did that they brought together all these young people. And it was funny because we were so young, and we didn't really think we [knew much]. We'd share and talk... [And] there was a resistance, from having the adults tell us what to do. But it wasn't, we didn't resist it as much. Right? And so, I do remember once, we were, you see, I wish I would have been writing all this stuff [down]. To me it was just like ahh, we are going to another meeting, right? So CCC hired Corina. And Corina became the first national organizer. And this is before Carlos Saavedra [became the national organizer of UWD in 2009]. And so, Corina was supposed to be organizing us. And it would be really interesting to talk to Corina. Corina has not wanted to talk to anybody about this, right, and how they used to tell her to kind of brainwash us. And how she would get this perspective from us because we felt how she would try to brainwash us and tell us what to do, and how her bosses and everything would mistreat her because she wasn't getting the results of what she was [supposed] to get us to [do] ... That was the first glimpse of a national organization that would bring us together ... That's what nobody talks about.[16]

Gaby had already developed a statewide reputation as an immigrant-rights advocate in Florida when the 2006 demonstrations hit. That spring and into the summer, she became even more visible in state politics as she spoke at rallies. On July 26, after a weekend rally for immigrant rights where Gaby and her father spoke, immigration authorities executed a dawn raid on the Pacheco home. They were looking for Gaby, but they bungled the raid, sweeping up her sister instead and leaving Gaby at home. The agents acted like Keystone Kops and Gaby laughed hard when she retold the story and her understanding of what happened:

> Somebody within politics in power made a call and said: "Here's this woman who's undocumented. She's bothering me. You need to go after her," right. Because I used to go after politicians really, really hard. So, Immigration came and was looking for me, but the problem is I live with my family. When they came in they actually rounded us all up. They put us in the living room and they started saying who's Maria Pacheco. The problem too is [laughing hard] that, if you know a lot of the communities, we are all Maria. We are, like all of us! The agents are like, ok, so they start getting all the IDs, and they're looking at it and then the bad thing for them and good thing for us was that my sister Erika and I look alike, a lot. We even used to pass as twins everywhere we would go. So he's looking at her ID, at my ID, at my other sister's ID, at my mom's ID, and he picks up my sister's, Erika's, and says "who's Erika Maria Pacheco?" And she's like "that's me." "You're coming with us." They thought I was her.

After taking Erika into custody and interrogating her, the immigration police realized their mistake.

Gaby laughed at the story as she retold it, but at the time she felt terribly guilty. Her actions had placed her whole family in the crosshairs of the authorities. "Now the fight wasn't so much about other people and just immigration as a whole," she said. "Now the fight became personal, now the fight was like I need to fix this 'cuz I broke this." Gaby's family was eventually put into removal procedures, and she fell into a deep emotional funk and took a step back from organizing. Gaby's withdrawal was actually a good thing for SWER, she said, as new leaders came to the fore. With the support and guidance of FLIC, who had hired José Luis Marantes as a youth organizer to recruit and train undocumented youth leaders, SWER continued to grow. At national meetings in 2007 and 2008, new leaders like Juan Rodriguez took Gaby's place as SWER's representative.

Undocumented youth across the nation looking for models and guides looked to SWER. As Mo recalled in our first interview, "before I had met too many undocumented activists in person . . . I had been following the folks from Florida online, the SWER folks. I thought they were really amazing people and awesome."

Another early hub of undocumented student activists, and by far the largest in the country, was in California, where CHIRLA coordinated a network of undocumented student organizations that spanned the University of California and California State University systems.

Lizbeth Mateo and the California DREAM Network

Lizbeth Mateo, a statewide representative for the California DREAM Network, was in Washington, DC, in the summer of 2007, the same summer Julieta attended the FIRM meeting where they confined the DREAMers "to the closet." In our interview, Lizbeth echoed Julieta's characterization of that summer as a pivotal time when undocumented youth started making concrete plans for a national network of DREAMers. Lizbeth had been sent by CHIRLA to lobby for the DREAM Act. The following year, Lizbeth and Julieta, representing their respective states, would attend the official convening of the UWD network. Up to that point, Lizbeth and Julieta had followed similar trajectories of engagement. From a distance, the two appeared to have much in common. Both were Mexican-born, talented students with professional ambitions, organizers of undocumented student groups from the two states with the largest populations of undocumented youth and singled out by elites as effective political leaders. But Lizbeth left these experiences in Washington, DC, on a very different trajectory than Julieta.

Lizbeth was born in 1984 in a small town in Oaxaca, "not too far from the capital of the state."[17] Her dad made money driving a taxi, and her mom worked at home raising a family and running a small store adjacent to their house. Lizbeth is the oldest of three children. In 1990, her father started to work in the United States for stretches at a time to send money back home. Lizbeth recalled that the periods of separation were hard on him and the family, so they started to think about moving the whole family to the United States.

Lizbeth was fourteen and her two younger brothers were twelve and two when the family decided to move. "We were kids and we were like 'sure let's go,' not thinking if we were going to stay here forever." Lizbeth had finished the equivalent of middle school, or eighth grade, in Mexico. She loved school and excelled at it. She had plans to go to college. She dreamed of being a lawyer:

> But my parents knew how difficult it was going to be for them to pay for that, and for me to pay [for] that as well. It was just going to be impossible. I was too young to understand the stress that my parents were under. I had good grades, so they knew I was going to go to college. They just didn't know how they were going to pay for it. I think that's what drove my dad to make the decision of immigration.

In 1998, the family packed its belongings and made the difficult and dangerous decision to leave Mexico.

They were not leaving everything behind. They had family who had gone before them. "Most of my dad's siblings are here, in the US. Half of my mom's siblings are here." The family decided on Los Angeles, CA, as their destination—the city where Lizbeth's aunt and uncle lived and where her father had worked. The family crossed the border in two stages:

> We took a place in Tijuana, and from there my two younger siblings crossed the border before us, before my parents and I. And so, they went ahead. When we knew that they were safe and were with my uncle and his family, then my parents and I crossed the border. I don't remember the exact location, but it was close to TJ. It was during the day; it wasn't at night. And it wasn't necessarily in the desert, but it was like running, hiding from border patrol, and it was intense. It was pretty intense.

Unlike some DREAMers I interviewed, Lizbeth knew she was undocumented the moment she set foot in California. She came running and hiding from the authorities. Where she settled in Los Angeles, she was not alone. She lived with and went to school with many people who shared her immigration status and similar experiences of crossing over.

Lizbeth enrolled in the ninth grade at Venice High School. She was coming from a rural Oaxacan school with maybe a few hundred students across all grades and was thrown into a massive, urban American high school with thousands of students. "I had an awful time," Lizbeth recalled:

I remember crying a lot when I got home after school and just telling my mom "I don't want to be here." And I mean I thought about leaving right away. My mom was like "OK, well, let us just save up some money, and then we'll send you back to live with your grandma." But I kind of decided to stay. It was mostly a teacher of mine. She was like "you can't leave. After all the sacrifices your parents made to bring you here, you can't just leave like that, suck it up, and try to do your best." And so, I did.

Life at school gradually got better. She made friends. "There were a lot of kids who had just come across the border from Mexico . . . so that helped." In time she built a strong and lasting network of friends.

Her parents found jobs at a factory close to home. Her dad worked cutting and machining acrylic. Her mom worked in the printing division of the same factory. After graduating from high school, Lizbeth hit that impasse that snuffs out the ambition of so many undocumented youths when they finish secondary education, but she was luckier than those who came of age just a few years earlier. In June 2002, California followed Texas's lead and passed its own in-state tuition law for undocumented students, AB 540. Money remained an impediment, however, so she started working as a salesclerk and taking classes part-time at a local community college. At that time, her dream of becoming lawyer was frankly impossible.

It was during her first year out of high school, sometime in 2003, when she learned about the DREAM Act. It was an accidental education:

> It was, I think, I want to say it was my freshman year, at some point in my freshman year. I met a student who was also undocumented and she had this application, not application, this petition. It was a letter to President Bush asking him to support the DREAM Act. And so, I was on my way to work, and she was on the bus, and she was asking people on the bus to sign it.

Lizbeth asked her for a copy of the petition:

> I read it and I was "oh, this would benefit me." I didn't say anything at that moment. I said "hey, give me a few more." You know, "I'll sign this petition but give me a few more." It was, I don't know, I put all my hope into that little piece of paper.

She did not understand how the proposed law would work, but she threw herself into the work of supporting it:

> I went to Staples or Kinkos, I can't remember. I made like 100 copies of it. And I worked in Venice Beach at the time, so I just stood in front of the boardwalk or on the boardwalk, and I was passing out petitions and asking people to sign it, and explaining what little I understood about what the proposal was. And I got pretty much all of them signed in a weekend. And the next week, I went to a meeting of a club that this student was a part of, and I joined the club, and I said "here are 300 or 100 petitions," I can't remember, "let me know what else I can do." And so that's how I became involved with it.

This accidental encounter not only marked the beginning of a lifelong political struggle, but also the beginning of a close friendship. Alma, the woman who gave her the petition on the bus, "she became my best friend."

Lizbeth enrolled in California State University, Northridge (CSUN) after finishing community college. She wanted to go to the University of California, Santa Barbara, but could not afford it. CSUN was more affordable, and it was also close enough to home for her to commute by public transport:

> At first, I would take the bus. It was like 2 hours to get to school. I would leave 6:20AM and get to school around 8AM or so, and then come back pretty late. And that would take longer because of traffic.

Alma had made the same move to CSUN. They both were eager to organize for the DREAM Act at their new school, but it took some time before they got started. For her first semester, Lizbeth focused on schoolwork and adjusting to the long school days. Then her younger brother fell ill, and she needed to spend her free time with the family, helping out at home. "So it took me awhile," Lizbeth recalled, "to actually start 'Dreams To Be Heard' with Alma and other students."

At their community college, Alma and Lizbeth organized for the DREAM Act under the Association of Latin American Students. Lizbeth described the association "as our safe haven" but "at CSUN we had nothing."

> I mean there was MEChA,[18] but MEChA was also really broad and we wanted to be more ... We started talking about forming a group, forming a

support group at first. The main thing just being *that*, a support group, and it quickly became an advocacy group. And we became very open about our status with everyone.

The openness and visibility of their new official campus organization for undocumented students, Dreams To Be Heard, made faculty advisors and administrators very nervous:

> The administration was against it at first. They were just concerned. Well, they said they were concerned about our safety, but the other concern they had was that if we were so open about our status, then people would challenge AB 540 as a law. Because some of the administrators were part of the original network who actually pushed for the law, they had all these concerns. And they made it known, and we had a lot of disagreements with them at first.

The excessive cautiousness of academic leaders from whom Lizbeth had expected political inspiration was disheartening. She was stung by their timidity:

> I think the first day I met with the Chair of the [Chicano Studies] department, who was my advisor at the time, she told me, "Whatever you do you don't tell anyone because even though they are supportive here, you know, you don't know what their views are on immigration always." And that felt wrong. Part of the reason I wanted to go to CSUN was because I wanted to study Chicano Studies, and a lot of the people I had read about were professors at CSUN. I had this idea that they were pretty, you know, liberal, not just liberal, but understanding, and that they were going to be supportive, and I was going to have this amazing experience. And my first impression wasn't that.

Against the counsel of faculty and administration, Lizbeth refused to hide her status and blazed a very public path of activism at CSUN.

Lizbeth and Alma organized Dreams To Be Heard in the immediate wake of the mega-marchas and walkouts of 2006:

> I think that's what sort of drove me to be more open and say "ok, we are not going to stay quiet." You know, whatever the administration feels like we

should do, we are not going to do that. We are going to start a group. We are going to be more vocal. We are going to be more open. I mean we have kind of shown that we do have power and when we come together and organize we can make things happen. So those marches, not just in LA, I mean the LA one was huge, it was amazing, but then seeing all the images on TV and the coverage in the media was amazing.

With public attention transfixed by the marches, Dreams To Be Heard set to work:

We're setting up tables outside the library, getting students to sign petitions, doing different events on campus, presentations in classrooms, presentations with high school students, with the staff and the administration. And then we did something along the lines of the mock graduation, like a smaller-scale graduation, where basically we shared our stories in front of the library. And I remember at that time we didn't have a permit, so we almost got kicked out, someone at the library got pissed off.

Not too longer after launching the CSUN organization, they became involved in the statewide network of campus organizations of undocumented youth brought together by CHIRLA:

I don't remember how we got involved with CHIRLA, but we at some point started going to their meetings. We were invited ... They have these retreats, I think twice a year, in different areas in California, and all the campus groups come together. And I mean the idea, at least then, I truly believe that the idea behind those retreats was to actually, as a youth-based network, to come up with one or two goals to organize work together.

Lizbeth quickly emerged as a leader in this statewide network and caught the attention of CHIRLA's directors.

At these statewide meetings and retreats, CHIRLA staffers set agendas, framed messaging, and identified and trained the undocumented leaders of the mostly campus-based organizations. This is how Lizbeth described her interaction as a young, inexperienced organizer with CHIRLA:

I didn't know how to get access to some things, the media, how to get access to an elected official, and all of that stuff ... I thought at first it was a very difficult thing to do. And so, I just kind of let, and I think a lot of us just let, CHIRLA lead everything and tell us, "okay, this is what's happening in Congress, and this is what's happening in other locations across the country, and this is what we are going to be doing. This is the messaging."

Lizbeth was good at the work CHIRLA taught her to do. She was good at speaking with the media, and she liked coordinating communication among the many different student groups within the state. Within months of working with the network, she became the representative of the central region in California, one of the three regions in the larger DREAM network:

I was in charge of being, along with another student, being in contact with all the schools, making sure that whatever plan we had as a network, whatever action we planned to do as a network, following up with the students and making sure they were doing what they were supposed to be doing. That was, I think, when I really understood, or started understanding, what organizing meant at a larger level—not just with my friends at school, but you know fielding conference calls, and being glued to my laptop, and sending emails, and all this kind of stuff.

Toward the end of the summer of 2007, the summer Julieta described as pivotal for the national organizing of undocumented students, as hopes in Washington, DC, for passing comprehensive immigration reform faded and entered a waiting period for the outcome of next presidential election, NILC pressed to make a late legislative push for the DREAM Act. CHIRLA tapped Lizbeth to participate in lobbying efforts:

I was asked to go to DC in September to speak at a conference, at a press conference, and go lobby for the DREAM Act. Surprisingly enough, CHIRLA was in support of moving the DREAM Act as a stand-alone bill, if [comprehensive] immigration reform was [not] going to happen. There were several students that went, and I was one of them. We lobbied for a couple of days.

Josh Bernstein from NILC and Rich Stolz from CCC guided her through the lobbying visits and the media events:

I got prepped to do the press conference, my first sort of major press conference. And you know presented my story, but in a very, I don't know how to put it, but in a very homogenized way, very apologetic. And that was the message and that was the way that my story was framed, or as I was told to frame my story.[19]

As with all the DREAMers brought to Washington, DC, by NILC and CCC that year (and later), Lizbeth was there to tell "her story."

Lizbeth says she did not have serious misgivings about the way she was told to tell her story in front of the press or to present herself to politicians. Although she described it retrospectively as homogenized and apologetic, at the time, she "was pretty convinced that that's the way that I had to say it. You know, because I had to gain the sympathy of people. And it wasn't so bad. I wasn't throwing anyone under the bus." That is not to say that she felt in control of the story and the stage. She was there at the bidding of professional allies to play the role of a scripted character in a crafted political strategy:

> I think it was very clear for all of them, and to some extent for us, that we weren't in power. We were not at a point where we could just say "I'm undocumented and I'm not afraid of what you can do to me," or whatever.

Lizbeth and her fellow undocumented youth leaders were just starting to grasp the complexity of the politics of immigration, and to discover their voice in this fight. At the time, they depended on professional allies to assess the risks of public action, and these allies reminded them of their existential vulnerability in the contentious politics of immigration.

This vulnerability hit home for Lizbeth immediately after her return from the lobbying trip:

> We came back from DC, about maybe three days, I can still remember this, maybe three or four days after, there was a raid at a company three blocks away from our school. It was the first time we ever heard about an ICE raid so close to us. That was huge. I was scared. I was scared for my family. We talked about it. We just didn't know how to react to it.

Almost immediately after hearing about this workplace raid, ICE raided the home of the family of Tam Tran, a leader of the UCLA undocumented student group, IDEAS. Tam had testified in front of Congress earlier that year. Many, including California Congresswoman Zoe Lofgren, who had invited Tam to testify, saw the raid as a reprisal for her public testimony. In these early days of activism, for obvious and sound reasons, undocumented youth felt dependent on their citizen allies and powerful patrons for protection. They really had no option but to rely on them. Lizbeth would grow to hate this dependency and would commit all her energies to breaking it, but that definitive break would not come for a few years.

After the failure of DREAM Act in the fall of 2007, the national advocates for immigration reform entered a holding pattern as the nation geared up for the presidential election cycle. Lizbeth turned to efforts to pass the California DREAM Act—a bill that promised to extend financial aid to students covered under AB 540. The state legislature passed the act in the fall of 2007, and again in 2008, but Governor Schwarzenegger vetoed the bill both times. At CSUN, Dreams To Be Heard pushed the student senate to back the California DREAM Act. When it failed to pass a resolution of support, Lizbeth ran with a slate of seven undocumented students for seats on the senate. Their unprecedented victory triggered a controversy over whether undocumented students without social security numbers could be paid student government stipends. And then, at the start of the summer of 2008, Lizbeth graduated from CSUN, and everything for her just came to a stop.

With graduation came an abrupt end to years of academic work and mounting school-based activism. Lizbeth scrambled to find a new field for organizing:

> Right after I graduated, the day after, I went to CHIRLA and I said: "hey, a lot of us graduated this year, and so why don't we start an alumni network [of the] California DREAM Network." And they were like, "oh sure, that's a great idea, but we just don't have money to do that. We don't have anyone to staff it." I think that was the first time I sort of realized, ok, these people move when there is money. And if there is no money, they don't.

Opportunities suddenly appeared limited. She received job offers "through my professors who kept forgetting that I couldn't work." In our interview, at first laughing as she recalled the irony of offers that could never be delivered, Lizbeth's attitude then turned steely as she described how she felt:

> That was pretty upsetting. I went through a period where I was really angry at everything. I wanted to study for the LSATs and go to law school, but I'm like I'm never going to be able to make it, and so I was in a state of anger. Not so much depression, but I was just in a state of anger.

She seriously considered returning to Mexico. "And then CHIRLA calls me."

It was late 2008. CHIRLA directors asked her if she would go to a national meeting of DREAMers in Washington, DC, organized by NILC. This was just after the November elections and the Democrats' victories in gaining control of the White House, the House, and the Senate. CHIRLA was backing away from its earlier support of the DREAM Act and firmly positioning itself in a growing camp of advocates prioritizing comprehensive immigration reform (CIR). Lizbeth described how they pitched her the assignment, if she chose to accept it:

> We have the California DREAM Network retreat and we can't go [to DC], at least the two organizers, the youth organizers, couldn't make it, and people were like but I think you should go and then you'll come to the retreat when you come back and tell us what happened. And from whatever happens from this meeting, we'll decide what our goals are going to be for the year. And I was like sure I'll do that. And I went. First time traveling to DC by myself. I told my mom I'm going to Sacramento [laughing]. I'll be back and I'm not going to be by myself. I go off to DC. I was gone for just a day and a half. It was so quick. And that's where I met Mohammad, Felipe, and a bunch of other students. I think that's when I met Julieta too.

The goal of the meeting was to begin organizing a national network of DREAMers:

> And so, they talk about starting this network of undocumented youth. The idea of United We Dream already existed, but it was very small at the time, it was a small group, and I think it had a different name, but they had started using United We Dream. And it was started by CCC. And so, I think Josh was in the room, I want to say Josh [Bernstein] was in the room, yeah. Um, Rich [Stolz] was also there, but he was against it.

CHIRLA was against it too. That is why they only sent Lizbeth, and they sent her really only to keep tabs on what was unfolding and to state CHIRLA's opposition.

CHILRA staffers had coached Lizbeth to argue for comprehensive reform over the DREAM Act, and they expected her to represent the organization's interests. Lizbeth was told to keep her phone on so the home office could hear what was going on during the Washington, DC, meeting. As discussion turned to CIR versus DREAM Act, she was having serious misgivings about her role at the meeting and working for CHIRLA's interests. At a certain point, she turned off her phone. Lizbeth explained what happened next:

> Because I wasn't answering my phone, CHIRLA sent the husband of the ED who was actually in DC. He works for CCC, he was there. And so, they sent him to the meeting. And he sits next to me. And there's this guy, real creepy guy, and he tells me: "so you're Lizbeth, right?" And I was like "yes." "Well, don't you think they are being selfish? They're forgetting about their parents." Blah-blah-blah. It was like there, during lunch break or something. And I was just like who is this person? And later I realized who he was. And I was like, ok, that was really shady, that was awful.

He hit a nerve. Lizbeth was already feeling guilty about her parents. She had never been completely open about the extent of her activism and was plagued by feelings of guilt and selfishness:

> I had not been very honest and open with my parents about what I was doing. I mean I had told them that I was going to Sacramento. I didn't tell them I was in DC. I didn't tell them I had participated in a bunch of other events and I was very open about my status and you know all this other stuff. [I didn't tell them] because in my mind I was in a way protecting them so that they wouldn't worry. I think once I sort of woke up to my parents and told them, ok, this is what's going on. This is what I'm doing. This is what I want to do, blah-blah-blah, which was much later, I realized my parents want immigration reform, but if they can't get immigration reform, they don't want their children to just wait. They don't want their children to struggle. If there's a chance to get something done, get it done.

When the professional advocates for comprehensive immigration reform, embodied in "the creepy guy" from CCC, pressed Lizbeth to think of her parents and to not be selfish, they hit a chord that unsettled her, but it was not the chord they intended to play. For Lizbeth, it sounded an alarm and a defiant reaction in her.

Lizbeth described the meeting as "pretty awful for me" and not just because of the emotional manipulation of the allies. There was also tension with fellow undocumented students. When she introduced herself to the other youth as representing CHIRLA, the reception was cold. "I told them that I was there representing CHIRLA [and] everyone was just like really quiet and didn't really know how to deal with me." "There were some people from California," including the blogger, Prerna Lal, and Tam Tran, "who did not agree with CHIRLA. Lizbeth adjusted to the situation at the meeting by making a clear distinction between her position and CHIRLA's:

> [W]hen I participated in the conversations I was like very clear look this is me as an individual. I don't know what CHIRLA is going to do. I don't know what the network is going to do. I have to take it back to them. But me as an individual, yes I'm committing to this. And then I went back.

Lizbeth returned to California, unsettled and agitated.

She had been on the verge of returning to Mexico before the trip. CHIRLA had rebuffed her idea of establishing an alumni network. The invitation to go to Washington, DC, had come out of the blue, and there in the midst of an emerging national network she witnessed an ugly dynamic of "allies" pushing undocumented youth away from the DREAM Act with the charge of "don't be selfish," and some of them pushing back. She was drawn to pushing back:

> I was crying when the meeting was over. I went to the airport. I got lost. I was crying on the streets of DC because I knew what CHIRLA was trying to do, and I knew that they were already, they were set on what they were going to do. I started to realize they have a plan, and they are not going to let the [California] network decide what they want to do. That was a pretty awful realization for me. Even though I kind of suspected it before, it just became so clear.

Lizbeth felt played. They were toying with her emotions to prod her into a particular line of action in service of their plan. Lizbeth did not resent the allies for their detached, game-like approach to this struggle. It was not even so much that they were manipulating her. What unsettled her most was the realization that what these professionals saw as being at stake was essentially different than what she and other undocumented youth felt was at stake.

3
DreamACTivist.org

A few months prior to the 2008 convening of United We Dream in Washington, DC, Marisol Ramos, a founding member of NYSYLC, conducted a national "landscape analysis" of undocumented youth groups and their parent organizations. She pulled together her findings in a report that UWD submitted as a grant proposal to private foundations. Her analysis also informed the invitation list for the Washington, DC, convening. The report highlights the undocumented student groups that developed in close contact with FIRM-membership organizations. It lists SWER in Florida as a "project" of FLIC, the DREAM Network in California "anchored" by CHIRLA, SIM in Massachusetts "hosted" by its "parent" organization MIRA, and NYSYLC in New York with its "fiscal partner" NYIC. The report also included a map of all organizations Marisol could find organized by or working with or on behalf of undocumented youth. The map included student organizations without clear parent sponsors, such as ULI and JIFM in Texas. It also included a handful of online forums for undocumented youth and blogs by and about undocumented immigrants. These online forums represented a fast-growing arena of undocumented youth activism developing off campuses and outside the influence of the nonprofit immigration field.

Marisol knew better than anyone the landscape of undocumented youth activism and its ties to established nonprofits. She worked at the time as a program associate for the New World Foundation's Phoenix Fund. For the fund she would do site visits to immigrant rights organizations across the country. Her work brought her into contact with many of the parent organizations of the first undocumented youth groups. In this capacity, she was also tasked by her boss to carry out regional landscape analyses of these types of organizations to help guide the Phoenix Fund's grant-making decisions. In her 2008 report, "Youth Organizing for the DREAM Act," she applied this skill toward what had developed for her as an urgent calling: finding the resources to build an autonomous, national network of DREAMers.[1]

Before working at New World, Marisol attended Hunter College where she founded the college's first Mexican student group.[2] When I interviewed

Marisol, she joked that the main challenge she faced in forming the group was that there were practically no other Mexican students on campus. Organizing at Hunter brought Marisol into interaction with student government at CUNY. It was through CUNY Senate that she first met Walter Barrientos and Cristina Jiménez. Walter went to Baruch College and Cristina to Queens College. Both were undocumented, Marisol was not. "Born in the Bronx. Not a DREAMer. Never was. But my parents were undocumented." While enrolled at Hunter, Marisol also worked as a summer intern for a Harlem nonprofit, Esparanza del Barrio, where she worked to organize the children of unlicensed Mexican street vendors. She organized them into a group that they called Sueños del Barrio. Many of the kids were undocumented.

After graduating from Hunter, she turned the internship into a full-time job. It was late 2005 and NYIC was convening various immigrant youth groups from across the city into a project funded with CCC money. The project pulled together Marisol's group, Sueños del Barrio, with other youth and student groups into citywide meetings and a loose coalition. Walter was working with NYIC as an intern on this youth project. Cristina was interning for a nonprofit in Queens also involved in building the coalition. One of the urgent issues raised by the youth coalition was advocacy for the DREAM Act.

After the mass mobilizations in the spring of 2006, Marisol said NYIC appeared to lose interest in DREAM Act advocacy. Drawing on what she was learning about foundations from her new job at the Pheonix Fund, Marisol started to investigate who might want to fund a New York youth organization focused specifically on the DREAM Act. With Cristina and Walter, she drew up a proposal for funding. Together they formed a board, secured a fiscal sponsor in an aloof NYIC, approached funders, and planned for site visits from prospective suitors. Their efforts were quickly rewarded. They won a small multi-year grant, hired a part-time director, Kiran Savage-Sangwan, and launched NYSYLC in 2007. The following year Marisol's ambition turned national.

She used her landscape analysis as a grant proposal to pitch to foundations the opportunity of funding what she called a national "peer-to-peer network" of undocumented youth. With Democrats poised for victory in November 2008, CCC and FIRM membership organizations were increasingly focused on comprehensive reform and, according to Marisol, no longer prioritizing work with undocumented student organizations focused on the DREAM Act. She witnessed this directly with NYIC's fading interest in working with undocumented youth in New York and CCC's neglect of its own United We

Dream campaign. Only NILC still appeared eager to organize DREAMers. It stepped-up as a fiscal sponsor and an initial donor of seed money to help establish this new, national network of undocumented students.

NILC had no experience in this kind of work. Essentially an organization of lawyers, it had no track record of winning grants to help organize immigrants. Marisol understood that to find funders, the network needed to demonstrate their organizing potential. A national convening of leaders from the groups mapped in her landscape analysis would do just this. With NILC's support, members of NYSYLC, SWER, and MIRA took the lead in organizing the convening.

It was Marisol's idea to invite some of the online activists included in her report. It was a bold move. Little was known about these undocumented youth except for their online presence. In contrast to the student organizers who knew of each other from occasional meetings organized by CCC and through the communication facilitated by NILC, the online activists were outsiders and wild cards. Would they even show up?

The Adventures of "Quaker" and "QueerDesi"

One of the online groups invited to the convening was a new Web 2.0 site with a lot of buzz: DreamACTivist.org founded by Prerna Lal and Mohammad Abdollahi. In good new-media fashion, Marisol tweeted their invitation. Josh Bernstein said that there was "a lot of excitement" around the convening because it was bringing together "campus organizers with bloggers and online activists."[3] It would prove to bring more excitement than Josh could have predicted or likely wanted. If Marisol was looking for a disruptor of the nonprofit professional management of undocumented youth organizing, a form of management she was growing to mistrust, she found it in Prerna and Mo.

Prerna started blogging in 2007 about her "adventures as a Queer Indo-Fijian" in America. Her blog gave voice to an attitude that stirred many of the "1.5 generation" of undocumented immigrants who felt increasingly unapologetic, ungrateful, and unafraid about their existence in America. She was fourteen years old when she arrived in the Bay Area in 1999. She hated her father for taking her away from her life in Fiji. Later in life she came to terms with his actions but, when she started blogging, she was still smarting from being ripped from the world she knew and transplanted to a strange country. Angry about being in the United States, not identifying as American, and not wanting to become one, Prerna's blog inspired an inchoate online network of radical undocumented youth who did not recognize themselves in the DREAMer narrative.

The Lal family enjoyed considerable social and economic capital in Fiji. They were also politically active. The spiraling social conflict of the 1990s made them increasingly fearful of their situation at home. America was not the family's first choice of refuge. Before emigrating to California, Prerna's family tried to gain access to Australia and New Zealand, but without luck. Her mom had family in the Bay Area, so America became the obvious backup plan. Shortly after Prerna arrived in the United States, a political coup by Fijian nationalists ousted the Indo-Fijian prime minister and foreclosed any chance of return for her family. In our interview, Prerna said the coup "confirmed" the family's "fears for a long time of where the country was headed."[4]

The family first moved in with her aunt in Hayward, CA. From there, they moved to an apartment in a nearby low-income housing complex. The next stop was a mobile home in a trailer park, and finally, in 2005, to a home they bought in Antioch. When I interviewed Prerna in the fall of 2015, she had recently returned to the Bay Area after years of law school and work in Washington, DC. She was working as a lawyer at the East Bay Community Law Center and as a clinical professor at Berkeley Law and living, once again, in the family's Antioch home.

As a young teenager adjusting to culture shock, Prerna threw herself into her studies. "There was little else to do," she explained. She did not at first connect with her peers. In high school and college, she spent more time hanging out with her teachers than with fellow students. Online gaming, web development, and social media became a portal to escape isolation in a strange country that she struggled to understand. She describes herself as an introvert. If you have read her blog or tweets, @AQueerDesi, this claim may strike you as incredible, but when you spend some time with her in person it makes sense. She is warm, magnetic, and sharp-witted, but slightly awkward, fidgety, and even a little nervous. Her fiery, self-assured online persona is something of an alter ego.

She did not know any undocumented youth during her first handful of years in the United States. She told no one about her immigration status, except for a college counselor and a high school teacher for whom she worked as an assistant. She raced through secondary and tertiary education, graduating high school early and finishing a Bachelor of Arts degree in roughly two years. For college, she enrolled first in Chabot Community College and then transferred to California State University, East Bay. Apart from helping with her mother's janitorial business, school consumed all her time. She participated in student government serving as student-body president at Chabot, joined the debate team, and became active in several political causes on campus, including racial justice, LGBTQ rights, and anti-Iraq war protests.

Prerna did not identify as a DREAMer in high school or college. "I didn't really relate to it a lot because I was like: 'I have papers, somewhere, that are processing, some day they will be done,' whatever." This changed in 2006:

> I go to a lawyer. I go to a stupid lawyer in the Bay Area, you know, one of *those* lawyers. My mom wanted to see where the [family] petition was and what was happening with it. And then the lawyer told me "you're twenty-one, you can't benefit from your grandmother's petition anymore." What else was it? Oh yeah, but you know "you're young, you can just get married." You know, like a bunch of bad advice.

Prerna is gay, so the lawyer's advice to not to worry and just get married—offensive in its own right as legal advice to anyone—was particularly useless and did nothing to allay her fear. As it turned out, marriage *would be* the route to legal status for Prerna, but that was still years off in the future and would depend on, among other things, a remarkable political and legal revolution for marriage equality.

In our interview, Prerna reflected on all the bad advice her family received from immigration lawyers over the years. One lawyer recommended against her family applying for political asylum. Prerna thinks "they probably would have gotten it if they had." (Prerna has won asylum cases as a lawyer, so she would know.) Lawyers hold a special place in hell in the imagination of radical DREAMers. A common refrain I heard in my interviews was that the immigration system is not broken. It works perfectly to enrich feckless and fraudulent lawyers who dole out bad advice and destroy the lives of their clients.[5] Prerna captured this shared disdain for immigration lawyers in a June 2009 blog post about the deportation case of Ewelina Bledniak—an eleven-year-old facing removal proceedings even though her father was a naturalized US citizen and her mom a legal resident. Prerna blasted the family's immigration lawyer for the girl's precarious legal situation: "It's too bad these immigration lawyers aren't deported each time they toy with our lives."[6]

The year 2006 was a big year for Prerna, as it was for many undocumented immigrants. She turned twenty-one years old. She was finishing up a master's degree in international affairs at San Francisco State University. She was without papers, unable to work, and, having aged-out of her grandmother's petition, with no clear way to adjust her immigration status. The megamarchas of that year left an impression on Prerna. "They were big, not for me personally and not in my community," but they were part of a collective immigrant awakening that seized her attention. The following year, finished with school, with a practically useless master's degree framed on the wall and nothing but time on her hands, she started to look earnestly into immigration politics and the DREAM Act:

> I'm sitting at home. We don't think I can work legally. I'm helping my mom with the cleaning business. And I just feel I don't know what to do. I sort of knew what the DREAM Act was. I didn't really relate to it.

After all, "the DREAMers" are "American children," and since arriving in the Bay Area, she resisted the idea of becoming American. Although she never felt "very connected to this idea of the DREAMer," she said, "as it was written, the DREAM Act still applied to me and would benefit me." At a personal legal impasse with protests erupting all around, "I started Googling about it."

These searches led her to the DREAM Act Portal (DAP)—an online forum created by and for undocumented students.[7] It was through DAP that she first met other undocumented youth and started to appreciate the sheer number of young people stuck, as she was, in what she described in her blog as a juridico-political "waiting room." With a handful of peers that she met through this forum, she started to devise ways of turning all these young, undocumented denizens of the state's waiting room into an online activist community.

Steeped in critical social theory, Prerna seized on the "interpellation" of undocumented youth by the DREAM Act and their intense frustration over the drawn-out institutional politics around this piece of legislation, as an opportunity to forge a shared identity that could unleash collective action.[8] Prerna grasped that the collective frustration of these undocumented youth, brought together by their shared experience of being made to wait for the ever-deferred DREAM Act, could trigger movement:

> The critical geographers liken the "politics of waiting" with a "politics of control" over migrant bodies. Since we think and speak in terms of spatiality (while the historians are better with temporality), we have only

recently come to address timelessness and temporal status when it comes to migrants. Think about DREAM Act beneficiaries. We are constricted to both SPACE and TIME; in effect, a temporal status. This is the institution of massive control over our bodies, both in space and through time. Do these "waiting rooms of history" (Dipesh Chakraborty), contribute to the creation of a "community?" Guess what, I can point over to the DREAMers and say we have come together, from completely diverse backgrounds, and only created community because of our PLACEMENT in these waiting rooms.[9]

Prerna saw in this waiting room a gathering of potential DREAM activists. And online forums like DAP could be used to mobilize these undocumented youth—not yet citizens of the state but turned into "patients of the state" by the ever-promising but always-deferred DREAM Act—into a political force.[10] Quoting Garth Henrich, she counseled: "The person who is waiting for something to turn up might start with their shirt sleeves." As she saw it, "'Waiting it out' is not an option. Expecting politicians to do the right thing on immigration without nudging them is never an option." Nudging would soon become too weak a word for Prerna's increasingly radical vocabulary of action.

Campus DREAMers first joined fellow undocumented students in political action through college organizations supported by institutional allies and nonprofit organizations. A very different and more dispersed network of undocumented youth first met online. Their early lessons in activism were mostly self-taught and developed at a distance from the political mediation of the advocates directing nonprofits and private foundations. This original independence from the professionally managed DREAMer organizations was instrumental in shaping the radical impulse they would bring to undocumented youth activism.

It was through DAP that Prerna made a fateful connection with "Quaker," the name Mohammad Abdollahi used on the forum. Reflecting on her early interactions on DAP, Prerna told me, Quaker "seemed like the most active person who wanted to do something." Mo shared Prerna's impatience with the promises of the DREAM Act. He was restless, looking to do something. Prerna's political confidence, smarts, and vision gave him courage and purpose.

Mo was born in Tehran in 1985. He was not yet four years old when he came to America, as he likes to say, "the privileged way."[11] With his parents and older brother, he passed through a US port of entry with a passport and a visa. Years later, when his family's visa expired, he became undocumented, but not before receiving a social security number and a driver's license—more privilege. The family moved from Iran so his father could study engineering at the University of Michigan. His sister was born the same year the family arrived. In our first interview, Mo referred to her as an "anchor baby." A few years later, his second brother was born. When his sister turned twenty-one, she adjusted the immigration status of their parents, but Mo and his older brother remained undocumented.

Mo described himself as "the black sheep in the family." His parents are religious and prize education. Mo is neither religious nor drawn to school. After graduating from high school, he worked in a "nice office job" for a few years. Boredom led him to take a few courses in social work at a local community college. He would work from nine to five and then take night classes. After racking up some credits, he planned to enroll in Eastern Michigan University to pursue a degree in social work. He was accepted, but a final check of his application by an admissions officer caught that he was not a citizen. With an admission letter in hand, he was told, in Mo's words, "to go get in a line."

In our first interview, Mo credited this event as his politicizing moment. He has told the same story many times: the first time in an interview Prerna posted on her blog in early 2008, again in the companion book to the movie *Papers*, and to scores of reporters over many years. This "official" story fits the stock DREAMer narrative of a balked educational and occupational dream, yet Mo readily admitted in our first interview that the story is somewhat disingenuous. He never actually identified with being a college student. He said he always hated school. He bristled at the idea of ever having *dreamed* of going to college or becoming a social worker, much as Prerna rejected the idea of ever wanting to be an American or dreaming the American dream. When asked if training to be a social worker informed his work as an activist, he quickly retorted, "fuck that shit." Mo was a bad DREAMer from the start.

Mo's college-rejection story is also misleading because it did not motivate his initial engagement with DREAM Act politics. Even before his rejection, Prerna says Mo was expressing impatience with the lack of meaningful political action on DAP. In his own description of his frustration with the online forum, he made clear that interest in the DREAM Act and connecting with other DREAMers came before this college rejection:

> Three or four months before that, my mom told me about there's this thing called the DREAM Act. It could help fix your status. And then she told me,

but don't ever search for it or anything because the government is going find us and know who we are. So, the first thing I did was I Googled it. And I found other undocumented folks, so that's when I started initially connecting with other undocumented kids, other undocumented students. I met three or four other ones and then we became friends online. We would chat all the time and that kind of stuff. But it wasn't really politically active. It was just talking to other folks. And then when that school thing happened, I was in touch with a couple of folks and then from there it kind of spurred to become more active.

Regardless of whether these early talks constituted political action or not, the handful of individuals Mo initially connected with on DAP became his activist companions going forward.

Launching DreamACTivist.org

This small group of online companions quickly realized that DAP was not going to be a forum for political action. Mo explained:

We were getting very pissed-off about the people on the online forum. In the sense that everyone was talking about being undocumented and you know about our feelings and issues and stuff like that, but there was no action behind it. So, we tried to get them to change, like the people who ran that network, and it didn't really happen, so we got kicked out.

Exiled from DAP, this group of five undocumented youth, scattered geographically—Prerna in California, Mo in Michigan, Kemi in Texas, Maria in Pennsylvania, and Juan in Florida—launched DreamACTivist.org. With no connections to DREAMer campus organizations, FIRM membership organizations, or any other nonprofit organization, they held their first organizational meeting over the phone in November 2007.

Prerna said the original idea behind DreamACTivist.org was simply to "find some way to bring the stories of undocumented youth to the limelight," and through sharing these stories "to organize and mobilize" online. That was it: "Start small, nothing ambitious. No master plan. And I knew how to design websites." Back in Fiji, she was one of the first kids she knew who had a home computer with dial-up internet service. As a child, she expected to become a computer scientist. This career ambition was now gone, but she put her computer skills to work to build the website.

Prerna posted a few of these stories of undocumented youth on her blog before the official launch of DreamACTivist.org. She described them as "part of an experiment" to "get more DREAMers featured on this blog." One story featured a short interview with Quaker (Mo) about being queer, undocumented, and working for the DREAM Act. This was followed with an open solicitation for more stories from "DREAM Act students." In April, Prerna announced on her blog a "slow release" of these stories on DreamACTivist. org and implored her readers to "come out, come out, come out."[12] The first story came from K. B. It was Kemi's story, one of the co-founders of the new website. Over the next few years, the posting of coming-out stories constituted a defining feature of DreamACTivist.org.

In our interview, I asked Prerna about the stories that appeared in the early days of website. Did they deploy the story of the good DREAMer, following the frames crafted by the directors of nonprofit organizations that Lizbeth described as homogenized and apologetic? She did not hesitate in response: "No, because we didn't have allies, right, to start with." And she added, "I don't think we had those templates." But she admitted that the good DREAMer characterization nonetheless shaped the stories they posted:

> I don't think it was conscious. I think there were some subconscious elements that we had to present ourselves as ideal, in order to look deserving. But I don't think it was strategic in that sense. I think a lot of our stories did lend themselves to the picture-perfect stories, right, with happy endings. I think there was a lack, I mean none of the people who first started DreamACTivist, you know, had criminal records ... There was some subconscious, obviously, bias towards trying to make ourselves appear good or positive. Right? We are crafting our stories, you know, the migration history, where it begins, how we end up here, discover we are undocumented. All the stories are similar: Do well, despite the odds, blah-blah-blah. [But] I think it was not intentional, at all.

As with the DREAMer narratives in the mainstream press, the categorical distinctions of the DREAM Act shaped the stories posted on the website. But there was an important difference. Most of the stories on the DreamACTivist. org were tales of "doing well, despite the odds," but they were not the thin, biographical accounts that they tended to be in the media. The DREAMer stories posted on the website told of complicated migration histories, difficult family and social histories, and emotional disclosures of personal secrets.

These stories, and Prerna's growing online persona as an unapologetic voice of undocumented youth, drew traffic to DreamACTivist.org. She recalled how the site's success surprised the five founders:

> It was kind of bizarre how quickly [it took off]. I mean, right, a lot of students are sending us stories to put up, from all over the country. We start getting a lot of emails from queer people, queer undocumented people, quite early on, who wanted to organize in this space.

From the outset, they intentionally created a welcoming space for LGBTQ undocumented youth by featuring stories of queer DREAMers. DreamACTivist.org provided a meeting space for a dynamic intersection of undocumented and queer experiences. Prerna described the boost the new website received from this powerful intersection:

> Mohammad was very out as gay. I was very out as gay . . . A lot of the stories we were putting up initially were about people who were queer and undocumented. There was a lot of buzz about that stuff. We had a whole LGBT section as well. And then because we had an LGBT section, people contributed more LGBT stuff. It becomes its own thing, at some point.

Starting with Prerna's Quaker interview, these stories highlighted how being queer and undocumented meshed in illuminating ways. In that interview, Mo talked about strategic dilemmas of how to handle disclosures of the self when lobbying for the DREAM Act:

> I'd think to myself, "now would they even give me the time of day if they knew I was also gay?" I always find myself having to think a bit on how to answer certain questions and whether it is worth the risk of exposing myself to them. . . It's frustrating, because even though you are out, you cannot share who you are. I also find it amusing how similar the "should I tell bf/gf/friend that I am illegal" is to what we have to go through when coming out.

DreamACTivism.org was the first public space where DREAMers really started to come out; and in this virtual space, queer DREAMers took the lead.[13]

The influence of the LGBTQ movement on the immigrant rights movement has attracted attention in a growing sociological literature on inter-movement linkages. Much of this research points to collective acts of "coming out" as a powerful link between the two movements. Sociologists speak of this connection as an instance of the transposition of a highly resonant cultural schema or repertoire of contention from one movement to another.[14]

Following a similar logic, professional advocates of immigration reform claimed their movement was drawing on models from LGBTQ activism when it harnessed the power of coming out. In a retrospective account published in 2013, Frank Sharry asked, on the op-ed page of *The Washington Post*, "How did we build an immigrant movement?" His answer: "We learned from gay rights advocates":

> Gays and lesbians have created a monumental shift in American culture. They did it, first and foremost, by coming out to family and friends. They did it by infusing popular culture with popular characters, from Ellen to Will to Mitch and Cam. They did it by being brave and loud, out and proud. We had nothing of the sort. To most Americans, undocumented immigrants were unknown and invisible. To some, they represented a menace. But then, just a few years ago, Dreamers—who take their name from the Dream Act, which would create a path to citizenship for young people who go to college or serve in the military—started to come out as "undocumented and unafraid."[15]

By coming out, Sharry claimed, DREAMers "became the heart of the movement, and their courage opened millions of minds... Suddenly, the human faces and personal stories so sorely missing in our debate broke through as never before." Set aside for a moment his breathtaking phrasing that simultaneously identifies with and reifies the movement and the agency of undocumented youth—*we* had no*thing* of the sort but then DREAMers started to come out. Sharry's movement analysis of "we learned from gay rights advocates" misses a simpler more direct explanation: the protean resistance of queer undocumented youth.

Prerna, in a *Huffington Post* article, co-authored with Tañia Unzueta, charged that Sharry's piece erased "the work and existence of queer immigrants." Their answer to the question Sharry used as a conceit to frame his piece was devastatingly straightforward: "Next time someone asks how the contemporary immigrant rights movement came about, tell them that queer undocumented youth built it."[16] The explanatory framework of one movement learning from, inspired by, or transposing schemas from another movement analytically distinguishes what the intersectional undocu-queer experience fused. Explaining the connection between the two movements as the transposition of schemas across two cases or sociohistorical contexts is to take a logical leap passing over the agency of queer undocumented youth who shaped the migrant rights movement and whose experiences blurred the lines between the two movements.

When I interviewed Mo for the first time, I asked him, in the context of discussing the coming out actions organized by undocumented youth, how he thought LGBTQ activism had influenced DREAM activism. My question implicitly betrayed my hunch that the answer had something to do with how the schema of coming out was transposed from one movement to the other. His response is cheeky:

> I'm really bad because I've never done any gay organizing and stuff. I'm a let down to my people there [is that a smirk on his face?], but I think there were a lot of connections for us from the get-go. I think Prerna did a series or a blog post way back when, it was like way before all the undocuqueer people came out, it was like March of 2008, way back when.

Still responding to my question of cross-movement influence, Mo described how Chicago DREAMers from the Immigrant Youth Justice League (IYJL), led by Tañia Unzueta, did the first coming-out collective action and how they used quotes from Harvey Milk drawn from a recent documentary film about his life to publicize the event. But he then quickly qualified this observation with the claim that the influence from LGBTQ activism was largely "a happy accident":

> I don't think, personally, ... we've ever been like let's study the past and let's replicate, but rather when it's convenient, things kind of mesh-up and then we connect the dots: "Oh shit, okay now it makes sense why this is working, it's the same thing that happened [back then]." At least, that's for me, that's how it's been. It's been analysis after the fact in making those connections.

Mo's account does not describe an intentional process of activists learning from or building off past movements. He highlights the influence of queer youth following a kind of pre-reflective common sense. Their decisions about public disclosures of self were guided by a pragmatic know-how of the strategic uses of identity in a politics of visibility. In our interviews, Mo consistently expressed impatience with abstract theorizing about social movements. Academic talk about the transposition of schemas seemed irrelevant to him. Mo summed up his thoughts on my questions about cross-movement influences with this simple observation: "The majority of the leaders in this movement are also queer. It has always been that [way]." From his pragmatic view, what more did you need to know?[17]

A few months after they launched DreamACTivist.org, Mo emailed Prerna about a Change.org competition: "Ideas for Changing America." He suggested that she submit the DREAM Act as an idea. "We'll get about a hundred votes for this if we submit something," Prerna remembered Mo telling her. "I'm like this is one of your stupid ideas, but I'll write something up. And then he starts promoting it everywhere. It spirals into something huge." Mo mobilized the website's burgeoning network of followers to cast thousands of votes in support of Prerna's submission. The DREAM Act placed as one of the top ten ideas, just behind legalizing marijuana. This startling finish put DreamACTivist.org on the radar screen of national advocates for immigration reform. Prerna recalled, "We start getting calls from everywhere. How do these five people start something as big as this and get 15,000 votes for a dead bill?" Marisol Ramos's Twitter invitation to DreamACTivist.org to attend the UWD convening came shortly after this surprising showing in the Change.org competition. It was at the December 2008 convening of UWD, in the Washington, DC, offices of NILC, that Mo and Prerna first met face-to-face.

"There was a lot of buzz and excitement in the room," Prerna remembered, echoing Josh Bernstein's recollection of the event. Prerna and Mo were introduced to many of the leading campus organizers. Julieta Garibay from ULI was there. Tam Tran from UCLA was there too—"We got really close," Prerna said in our interview. Matias Ramos, also from UCLA, was there. Felipe Vargas from Indiana was there. They also met Cristina Jiménez and Marisol Ramos from NYSYLC. They met fellow blogger and online activist Kyle de Beausset, from Citizen Orange, and powerful DC "allies" including NILC's Josh Bernstein and Joe Zogby, the chief counsel of Senator Dick Durbin of Illinois. "That's also when I met Lizbeth Mateo for the first time," Prerna recalled. "She was a CHIRLA representative. That's hilarious. I was like get away from me, you are from CHIRLA." Lizbeth remembered the same interaction and how the thrill of meeting the person behind DreamACTivist.

org was quickly dashed by Prerna's cold response. She was left wondering "why are you being so mean to me."

Organizing with United We Dream

I asked Prerna what NILC was thinking of when it backed this convening. After all, wasn't comprehensive immigration reform (CIR) already emerging as a unifying agenda for the immigrant-rights advocates in Washington, DC:

> It was weird, right. I think NILC was smarting from pushing for the DREAM Act in 2007 and losing and didn't have a lot credibility in the immigration reform community in DC. I didn't realize this at the time, by the way. So, there was some of that. And they're convening a bunch of DREAMers, again, and I'm not quite sure why.

She continued, thinking through the puzzle, out loud and as if for the first time, but arriving at answers she discovered long ago:

> I think it was a pet project. I think it was like "yeah, we still have a lot of DREAMers and they are here and they want to organize and mobilize and let's just connect them to each other," and, I'm not sure. Yeah, I think NILC felt this was their project because this was the one thing they pushed for, lost, and then got a lot of flak for. I think a lot of us in the room must have felt like NILC was the only one who had our back. I don't know, at the time at least, but obviously they were using us as a way to keep afloat, to get funding, and all that stuff.

Prerna emphasized that her analysis of NILC exploiting DREAMers for funding purposes was something she formulated only later. At the time, "I was very naïve."

Mo used the same self-descriptor when he talked about his understanding of the motives of the professional advocates participating in the convening:

> There was this guy from CCC there, Rich Stolz? Rick Schwartz? Or something, looks like a cat, and he was there at the meeting. And I always thought it was really weird, and then towards the end of the meeting I heard chisme from somebody that he had essentially approached the people at lunch

and told them that you guys need to stop working for the DREAM Act and every time you work for the DREAM Act it hurts CIR more. So that was sort of my first introduction to that. But I was just starting [to understand], I was very naïve, very innocent, I was like wait what could us, you know, trying to fight for the DREAM Act, why would that hurt anybody?[18]

Mo and Prerna may have been naïve, but they both sensed, as Lizbeth did, that something was off in the intentions of the professional allies who attended the convening. All three recalled interactions that conveyed that "weirdness."

According to Prerna, "everyone was pitching their organization to us. They wanted to know where we were getting funding from, a lot of questions like that, for us, and for me." One interaction and question from a staffer from NILC stood out to Prerna:

> I didn't know her at the time. I had no idea who she is, what's her background, why was she asking me this question, asks me in a scribbled note, if she, whether NILC, could take over the campaign on Change.org that we were running?

The "Ideas for Changing America" competition had a second stage, a run-off election for the top-ten ideas from the first stage. The staffer was suggesting that DreamACTivist.org turn the sponsorship of the DREAM ACT idea over to NILC for this run-off stage:

> And I was like I don't really know how to do that. I put it up as an idea. People are voting for it. I'm not quite sure what you mean by take it over... It didn't make sense technically, in my head, and also it didn't make sense to me politically. Why would you care? I had no idea why you would care? I was that naïve at the point.

But this was the first of a pattern of bids by directors of nonprofits to take over work that DreamACTivist.org initiated and brought to success. Prerna was just beginning to learn the lay of the land of the nonprofit immigration field and to get to know the people in it who were fighting for turf and resources. "I have no idea who these people are and why they care. And why they are there? Why are they in the room? Right? Are they interested? Whatever. I didn't question people's motives at this point. I'm also, I'm only twenty-four."

At the convening, Mo and Prerna, on behalf of DreamACTivist.org, agreed to do website hosting for the new United We Dream organization.[19] They were promised funding for this. Prerna joined the steering committee and became chair of the communications. Mo joined the organizing committee as well as the steering committee. These three committees constituted a provisional organizational infrastructure for the new UWD national network. To facilitate the work of the committees, the members formed "Google groups." Across these three committees, roughly two dozen active members built the organizational foundation for United We Dream. These active members included paid allies working for NILC, National Korean American Service & Education Consortium (NAKASEC), SEIU, and FIRM membership organizations such as FLIC; a few undocumented interns working at these nonprofits; and a larger number of volunteer undocumented youth and allies from student organizations (e.g., SWER, NYSYLC, ULI) and DreamACTivist.org.[20]

The excitement of the UWD convening sustained vigorous work well into 2009. Obama's inauguration buoyed optimism. UWD held its first national conference call on February 18. Juan Rodriguez, who had replaced Gaby as the leader of SWER, facilitated the call. José Luis Marantes, a paid youth organizer for FLIC, welcomed the callers with an introduction to "Who United We Dream Is." Also speaking on the call were Joe Zogby and Adey Fisseha, the Interim Federal Policy Director at NILC. By March, the Google groups for the committees were up and running with discussions of how to organize their work going forward. The DREAM Act's re-introduction on the Hill that same month thrilled the members of the new UWD committees. They hastily organized a week of actions to call attention to the bill. NYSYLC called for a rally in front of Senator Schumer's office and hand-delivered a petition asking him to co-sponsor the DREAM Act. Matias Ramos, a DREAMer from UCLA interning for NILC and an active member of the UWD steering committee, appeared on CNN telling his story and advocating for the act. By May, twenty-two senators and sixty-two congresspersons had signed on as co-sponsors. It was salad days for the "Dreamies"—as they would sometimes affectionately refer to each other. But, unbeknownst to them, the legislative agenda had already shifted in ways that would doom the prospects for the DREAM Act in 2009 and weaken its chances for passage in the following year.

First, Democrats were settling on health care reform as their legislative priority, and this would leave little space for other major business on the

111th Congress's calendar. Second, leading national advocates for immigration reform started to organize a campaign to rally all pro-immigrant organizations behind the all-or-nothing goal of CIR. With the financial backing of the Four Freedoms Fund, CCC, NIF, America's Voice, SEIU, and a half-dozen other organizations in the immigration field planned a June roll out for a "new campaign" they called Reform Immigration for America (RI4A). They sent out invitations to organizations across the nation to join them as they launched what was described as an "exciting grassroots movement to reform immigration."[21]

The leaders of the new UWD worked through the spring as if there were no essential contradictions between their advocacy for the DREAM Act and the emerging RI4A campaign for CIR. Prerna drafted a talking-points memo on CIR and the DREAM Act for committee members. The memo described the DREAM Act as "the most politically palatable piece" of immigration reform. The memo promoted it as a "building block" for wider reform, "a litmus test" for what is possible. "If we cannot pass the DREAM Act, we know that we do not have necessary support for comprehensive reform." Prerna argued that supporting the DREAM Act does not take away from advocacy for CIR. Its passage would energize and empower the immigrant youth who are "critically needed in the larger movement" and "hard to demonize" by the anti-immigrant opposition. In emails to UWD committee members, Prerna described her talking-points memo as a guide for discussions with allies "who are tentative about the way we are pushing DREAM."[22]

Prerna may have been naïve to believe that undocumented youth could influence the policy strategies of professional advocates. She was, after all, an outsider to the nonprofit immigration field. But she was now working with others at UWD who had considerable experience interacting with organizations in the field. José Luis Marantes, the nominal national director of UWD, was a FLIC employee. Tolumo, the media spokesperson for UWD, was an intern at NILC. Juan Rodriguez, another important member of the steering committee, was a SWER member with a longstanding work relationship with FLIC. Matias Ramos, from UCLA, worked closely with NILC. Walter Barrientos and Cristina Jiménez from NYSYLC had long histories of working with NYIC. These campus DREAMers believed that the nonprofits pushing CIR were at the center of a larger movement in which they, as DREAMers, played an important role. And they, too, saw no contradiction between undocumented youth advocating for the DREAM Act as this wider movement pushed for CIR.

Marisol, who possibly understood better than anyone else at UWD the interests of the professional directors of the nonprofits, was from the outset very wary of their intentions when it came to working with DREAMers. Mo and Prerna found an ally in Marisol. They learned much from her about how agenda setting and decision making worked in the nonprofit immigration field. Mo called her the "puppet master" because she knew all the strings the directors of the nonprofits and foundations could pull.[23] She helped Mo and Prerna see behind the nonprofit curtain of expertise and pierce the myth of the so-called movement to reform immigration.

Marisol believed that the nonprofits acted only when there was grant money earmarked to do so. Her view squared with what Lizbeth had discovered working with CHIRLA. Marisol's experience came from both the foundation side, working for New World to screen nonprofits applying for grants, *and* from the nonprofit side, trying to secure grant money for NYSYLC and UWD. Having navigated both sides, she saw little chance of a genuine social movement arising from these organizational interactions and relationships. In our interview, when I described how CCC publicly claimed to have help build a "movement for immigration reform," she answered back, "They talk a lot of shit." From her admittedly jaundiced view, CCC directors pitched "the movement" to funders to win grants. They claimed their expenditures of grant money went to seed and advance the movement. But after a lot of money was spent, she said CCC was astonishingly disconnected from the immigrant communities they claimed to move. In conversations with Mo, she contrasted CCC and FIRM's community outreach to what DreamACTivist.org had accomplished in one short year with no grant money. Mo and Prerna's website had built strong, meaningful connections with tens of thousands of undocumented kids from across the nation, whereas CCC had no comparable connections to undocumented immigrants.

Marisol nonetheless believed UWD needed foundation money to establish independence from CCC and the new RI4A campaign. Undocumented youth were on the horns of a dilemma. Without direct funding from foundations, they could not build the organizational capacity needed for autonomy, but this funding would bring its own incapacitating risks. Marisol was instrumental in winning the first big grant that provided UWD with financial resources to build an organizational infrastructure. She turned her landscape analysis into a grant proposal, and then pitched it to potential funders. In April, Unbound Philanthropy contacted Marisol expressing interest in a funding relationship. As UWD worked to secure this funding, directors at CCC/FIRM approached the same set of foundations for grant money to mobilize immigrant youth leaders for their CIR campaign. Marisol saw bad intentions behind their renewed interest to fund work with undocumented youth. She suspected they were trying to suck the oxygen out of the room to stop UWD's growth.[24]

In late April, José Luis Marantes announced to the committees "an opportunity to set up a UWD Strategy meeting" to coincide with the RI4A rollout. Marissa Graciosa, the campaign coordinator for FIRM, promised space for DREAMers at the event scheduled for the first week of June. In a follow up email to the steering committee, José Luis suggested that during the visit to Washington, DC, "we all take advantage" of the day of lobbying set up by RI4A and "show some solidarity for our movement." He also reported "good news" from conversations "with our friends at FIRM" of an opportunity to "set up our very own DREAM at 69865 Mobile Action Network." This text messaging network would be set up as a subset to FIRM's wider Mobile Action Network and allow UWD "to send out special messages moving DREAM . . . while larger messages moving CIR will be sent to our DREAM list." Prerna reacted quickly and angrily to this "good news." She asked, "Is FIRM building its phone spamming list on the backs of DREAM advocates now?" She saw FIRM's offer as a cloaked attempt to gain access to the rapidly growing DreamACTivist.org list. Her forceful pushback placed the Mobile Action Network agreement on hold.

Heading into the June strategy meeting, the first face-to-face gathering of UWD organizers since the December convening, two big issues stirred controversy within and across the committees. The first was over establishing rules that should govern the agenda-setting and decision-making of the steering committee, especially the role of allied organizations in shaping UWD's agenda and control of organizational funds. The second was over whether to allow allied organizations access to the growing DreamACTivist. org email list. The June meeting in Washington, DC, did not put these controversies to rest. It exacerbated them.

For some within UWD, the meeting in Washington, DC, forged closer relationships with allies at the big nonprofits. Julieta Garibay was invited to speak at the RI4A meeting. She told her story in front of hundreds of delegates from across the nation. She showed solidarity with the "larger movement," as José Luis had suggested they do; and, in return, she felt seen and listened to by the allies.[25] Two days after the meeting, Prerna blogged about a completely different experience at the RI4A roll out:

This is my biggest peeve with the so-called pro-immigration movement or what we are calling the "Reform Immigration for America." Don't shout down at migrant youth. Don't tell us what to do and what stories to tell, and what to marginalize.

Her disdain for the "so-called movement" fueled an alternative, subversive DREAMer strategy:

We need to flip this picture upside down. And that requires 4 M's—We need a clear **manifesto** outlining what we stand for and no compromises on that. End raids, end deportations, roll back migrant-military complex, include LGBT partners in any comprehensive bill. Pro-enforcement policies are not going to cut it. We need **money**. Incorporate away, charge for consultations. We need a loose structure in place, not hierarchical but certainly some mechanism to **manage** money, press relations. And finally, we need to whore ourselves out to the **media** with a counter-narrative derived from the manifesto.[26]

Prerna's post sketched a way forward for those DREAMers starting to grow wary of UWD's relationship to the nonprofits behind the RI4A campaign.

Two radical insights jump out of this pivotal post, and they both hinge on DREAMer objectification. First, Prerna called on undocumented youth to resist the exploitation of their unpaid labor by nonprofits flush with grant money to organize the DREAMer. In an article co-authored with Tam Tran and published a couple of months later in *Nonprofit Quarterly*, Prerna described in greater detail the many ways nonprofits not only exploited the unpaid labor of undocumented youth but also profited from their very existence as DREAMers.[27] For self-protection, undocumented youth needed to charge nonprofits for their work as consultants and incorporate their own autonomous organizations. Second, while sounding the alarm of their exploitation by nonprofits, she announced with urgency that DREAMers engage in self-instrumentalization: "we need to *whore* ourselves out to the media," as a weapon of self-defense and strategic empowerment. This mind-bending dual insight linking DREAMer objectification to both to the ugly reality of their exploitation by nonprofits and the emancipatory potential strategic self-instrumentalization was, at that time, beyond the grasp of most committee members at UWD. But it would soon guide the radical leading-edge of undocu-activism.

Prerna's ability to speak matter-of-factly about strategically using the DREAMer narrative to subvert it may have stemmed from her not having ever strongly identified as a DREAMer or from her appreciation of queer theory's rebellious deconstruction of identities and essentialisms. Be that as it may, her anger over the exploitation of her work by nonprofits came from interactions she was having with the directors of these organizations.[28] While attending a RI4A Web 2.0 conference in June, Prerna was approached by Shuya Ohno from NIF. He started "pitching to me about 'oh, you should just give us your list of people that you have,'" Prerna said in our interview:

> I can quote this from memory. Kyle was there, he can verify this. [Shuya's] like "we paid for you to come out here for this convening. You should work with the RI4A campaign and give us your email list." Like straight up. And I'm just shocked that this is something that he would actually say to me. And also, still at the same time, didn't quite understand. You guys have a lot of money and you have no fucking infrastructure. No like nothing. And why do I have this? You know? And why am I seen as somebody who has a lot of power because all I have is an email list? People were really after the DreamACTivist email list, from day one. And it was something that Mo, organically, really did on his own. It grew organically. Not something that we did for [money] or put money in to. It just was very organic.[29]

Immediately after Shuya's request, SEIU asked for access to the DreamACTivist.org email list as part of a joint blast to its members and UWD supporters to promote the upcoming annual DREAM graduation in Washington, DC. Their idea was to send out "asks" for people to sign "diplomas" to be presented at the mock graduation. They would of course collect information on those who responded.

José Luis backed the SEIU idea to boost publicity and participation for the graduation. He wrote to the UWD committees, "the more info thru the most channels is ideal to make our mark on history next week." Initiating a long thread of emails, Prerna pushed back, again: "This is going to happen a lot more in the near future—people wanting to use our list and groups because we have real power online (and they don't)." Marisol backed Prerna, but the issue did not die. Prerna dug in, shooting back with her angriest email to date on the Google groups:

I am a new media person and not about to fall for the BS. If the logic of this "diploma" is to ONLY be a diploma, then don't collect emails and zipcodes. Otherwise, let's not try to be dishonest, especially not with DreamActivist. This is going to happen A LOT. It's precisely why my ticket to D.C. has been free with RIFA/FFF footing the costs. They want IN; they want to exploit our online media networks. Period. I don't want to see this exploitation anywhere near our FB. If I do, I'll take admin powers away from people TRUSTED with the messaging. End of discussion.

Kyle de Beaussett, the blogger from Citizen Orange, intervened forcefully on the issue to side with Prerna. He understood the value of what DreamACTivist.org had built and the need to protect it:

I've been at the RI4A Web 2.0 convening with Prerna all day, today, and I've been watching her get pitched endlessly in all manners to use the DREAM Act lists. The power Dreamactivist.org has built online without funding of any kind is incredible, and there's no question that everyone wants a piece. I hope people realize that the online power Dreamactivist.org has built rivals that of even the largest pro-migrant organizations in the U.S. Asks like the one made by SEIU here are extremely sensitive.... [T]his ask only builds SEIU's lists, and it does nothing to build Dreamactivist's lists. From an online organizing perspective, that just doesn't make any sense.

As with the FIRM Mobile Action Network issue, no agreement was arrived at by the UWD committees, and the SEIU "offer" was turned down.[30]

The DREAM graduation that summer was, by all accounts, a smashing success. Mo, leading the UWD organizing committee, steered UWD away from initial plans for allies to play prominent roles in the ceremonies and organized an event led by undocumented youth. Unlike past graduations, undocumented youth organized the whole event, coordinating simultaneous graduations on the west coast and in the Midwest with the Washington, DC, event. In Washington, DC, Mo and Lizbeth emceed the event. Kemi, one of the founders of DreamActivist.org, gave the keynote address. Two DREAMers who had just managed to stop their own deportations, Walter Lara from Florida and Benita Veliz from Texas, told their stories at the graduation. Walter and Benita's participation highlighted an emerging priority for UWD: ending deportations. José Luis, writing to all UWD committee members, declared the graduation "amazing, inspiring, historic."[31]

"It All Started With and Goes Back to Deportation Cases"

Even as they became deeply involved in committee work at UWD and webhosting for the organization, the leaders of DreamACTivist.org continued the independent work they had started the year before—principally, sharing DREAMer stories online as a vehicle to connect undocumented youth with each other, and tapping this growing network with calls for action. Prerna described her full vision for the website in a blogpost entitled "Facebook Meets Daily Kos for Color of Change":

> **Think about it.** You are the only immigrant student at your high school in Georgia. But you go to DreamActivist 2.0, register and find out that you can click on your "Region" and find local groups and students in your area. You can even PM the other members directly and get to know them! And best of all, you will be able to access your own group and state blog, see upcoming events via an events calendar, pressing actions you can take for your state and even suggest your own. As you grow more comfortable, you can also start contributing blog posts that will be under yourname.dreamactivist. org. There is a WIKI for all your pressing questions, a forum for additional support and socializing, and more exciting features such as weekly chats.[32]

In my second interview with Mo, I asked him how close DreamACTivist.org came to Prerna's vision. Mo said they came close and might have realized it if the exigencies of organizing had not pulled them in another direction. The strongest of these organizing pulls came from campaigns to stop DREAMer deportations. The year 2009 was record-breaking for "removals" with almost 400,000—as the Obama administration moved to enhance the Bush administration's aggressive enforcement policy. And DreamACTivst.org started to commit much of its limited resources to organize online campaigns to defend fellow undocumented youth placed in removal procedures.[33]

Prerna recalled that it was Mo's initiative to organize the first campaigns to stop deportations. These campaigns then grew organically as DreamACTivist. org's expanding network of undocumented youth brought more and more cases to Mo's attention. This is how she explained this development:

> As people were brought to our attention, people who are like . . . say Noe in 2008, who was in [removal] proceedings and there's an article in Missouri that Mo read about, and he like contacted the person through Facebook,

because he has so much time on his hands. I don't know what he is doing at work. I guess this is what he is doing. He is contacting random people, and helped to put an end to his deportation case. One of the first known cases of people given deferred action. So, once we start understanding what deferred action is, we start trying to get more cases.... Every single week we were working a different case. And it was very organic. People reached out to us because they heard about us from somebody else's case.[34]

Prerna said Mo made these "Education Not Deportation" or END campaigns the centerpiece of DreamACTivist.org's mission.

The empowerment that flowed from successful END campaigns contrasted starkly with the frustrating spinning-of-wheels at UWD as committee work became paralyzed by disputes over the network's organizational structure and its associations with the nonprofits prioritizing CIR. These disputes extended through the summer. Prerna framed the contrast in our interview:

> The one thing I remember clearly is Mo pulling me aside in New York, during one of the UWD, the actual UWD let's put a structure together, boring-ass meeting, and I was like I can't deal with this right now, you know, and pulling me aside and being like "let's go work on Taha's campaign," and "if we can stop his deportation, we can stop any deportation." I remember this very well, him saying that. I was like this is one of your crazy ideas. He's like out there completely, I thought, but you know, we did it. He went to Taha's family. He sat with them. He talked to them. He got his mother deferred action for a long time... And a little after that I think it was that Lara got his deferred action done. So, he had like three campaigns that summer at the same time.[35]

This New York meeting, the one Mo skipped out of to work on Taha's case, took place in July. It was called by UWD leaders to address issues that continued to vex the work of the committees: chief among them was how to respond to allies who wanted to access their email lists and to establish an agreement on UWD's organizational structure before the first major grant installment from Unbound Philanthropy.

A key agenda item for the meeting was to get DreamACTivist.org to sign a "Memorandum of Understanding" about the use of this list and sharing it with allies. Up until that point, Mo and Prerna, with the support of Marisol and Kyle, had managed to protect the DreamACTivist.org email list from falling into the hands of other organizations. The list now stood at over thirty thousand contacts, and in contrast to comparable lists, a very high share of these contacts actively engaged with calls for action. The other major item was how to hire UWD's first full-time, paid, national coordinator.

Prerna started to lose faith in UWD at this meeting. Although she remained an important online advocate for DREAMers for years to come, as a blogger and through social media, this is when she started to disengage with direct participation in UWD committee work:

> I was promised, like you know, you will get funding from UWD to do this and then we will all work together in partnership and move forward together. Six, seven months in, I'm like, there is no funding. Nobody is doing anything. Like there is no traction, no movement in the Obama administration. It's all about health. 2009 is like a disaster. It's all about health care. And like there's nothing on immigration moving. Nothing's happening. There's no funding coming through. So then I started getting frustrated. And I'm also, at this point in my life, I have my own immigration shit to deal with. My mom's petition becomes current. She gets her papers. I don't. I want to go to law school. Studying for the LSATs. I'm doing a lot of things in 2009 that are personal to me and . . . I just decide to not work on UWD shit anymore. I'm like, Mo, you go to the meetings. You fucking deal with these people. I have to deal with my own life. I sort of take a step back.

Mo remained involved in UWD committee work well into the following year, but he refused to relinquish control of DreamACTivist.org's growing email list.

Mo mined this list to find more removal cases in his expanding work on END campaigns. He would search for people who had left comments about themselves, friends, or family members being in deportation proceedings, and reach out to them to help with their cases. His strategy for END campaigns was simple. Mo would feature the DREAMer's story online and then mobilize DreamACTivist.org's growing list of followers to pressure allies, politicians, and ICE to stop the deportation proceedings. With every successful campaign, the website grew still larger as a forum where DREAMers would come out with their stories, and so did its email list and its power to stop deportations.

Somewhere along this iterative process, Mo realized that any DREAMer with public visibility and organized support was, in effect, *un*-deportable.

The case of a leader of Chicago's IYJL, more than any other deportation case, crystallized this revelation. Rigo was pulled over for a traffic violation and failed a sobriety test. With a DUI, his deportation was all but certain. A strong immigrant community of supporters in Chicago nonetheless came to his defense. Mo coordinated the online support for the defense through DreamACTivist.org. Against great odds, the campaign pressured ICE to grant prosecutorial discretion and the deportation was suspended. It was a triumph that Mo would not forget.[36]

I directly asked all the undocumented youth activists I interviewed about the source of the initiative to involve DREAMers in direct actions that risked arrest. Many were not sure where the initiative came from, but of those who did proffer an answer, all agreed it came from Mo. He was the author of this radical shift in the repertoire of protest of undocumented youth. The first signature movement in this new choreography of protest occurred in 2010, and then lead to escalating variations on it over the next three years. This escalation and the creative variations are the subject of chapters to follow, but the origins of this creative line of collective action reach back to 2009.

I asked Mo several different times in our interview to return to the point where he started to think about using civil disobedience to fight for the DREAM Act. Each time he responded by saying that "it all started with the deportation cases." Once it became clear to him that public campaigns initiated by undocumented youth could stop the deportation of any DREAMer, and that these successful END campaigns drew more undocumented youth into engagement the cause, Mo linked this realization that DREAMers were un-deportable to Prerna's audacious call that DREAMers engage in self-instrumentalization to power an insurgency within and against the nonprofit immigration field. Mo started to imagine what undocumented youth might achieve if they dared to engage in protests that risked or, better yet, forced authorities to arrest DREAMers.

Nonprofits, UWD, and DREAMer Autonomy

UWD received its grant from Unbound Philanthropy in the fall of 2009. It finally had real money to spend for its own purposes. With the new funding, UWD hired Carlos Saavedra as its national director. Carlos, a veteran leader of SIM and youth organizer for MIRA, had recently adjusted his immigration status, so paying him for his work was legally straightforward. But, strictly speaking, he was now an "ally" and not a DREAMer. The distinction was of material and symbolic significance. Gaby Pacheco, when describing the early work Corina Garcia did for CCC to organize undocumented students, commented on a challenge Corina faced as an ally paid to organize them:

> She was a citizen. She was Mexicana, but that's the other thing, we were like "oh, you're not undocumented. You can't know how we feel. You can't, you just can't." That's [a] big, big one. People resent that.[37]

Well-known and respected by many within UWD, Carlos still ran up against a similar resentment. He consulted with DREAMers before taking the job. He told Prerna that he would work inside the nonprofits for the interests of DREAMers. Prerna told me that she initially trusted Carlos, but that trust did not last long. She also made a point to emphasize in our interview that Carlos had an impossible job balancing the pressures from his former bosses at FIRM and MIRA, current directors at NILC, and the growing expectations of increasingly restless DREAMers led by Mo and Lizbeth, who wanted an autonomous UWD run for and by undocumented youth.

If at the height of the summer, with the DREAM graduation, UWD seemed to be evolving into an organization for and by undocumented youth, by the end of the fall season, it appeared to some to be reverting to its roots in CCC and dependency on the nonprofit immigration field. UWD still did not have clear by-laws for governance. There were no recognized rules governing representation and decision-making. The New York meeting in July failed to develop clear organizational procedures and a shared understanding of the proper relationship between UWD and CCC/FIRM and the RI4A campaign. To Mo and Lizbeth, and to the undocumented youth drawn to their orbit of influence, it was clear by the end of the year that UWD, as structured, could not actualize the political autonomy necessary to unleash the agency of DREAMers. UWD failed in its first full year of operation to build an organization with even the semblance of rules and practices designed to ensure some measure of accountability to its undocumented youth constituency. It is hard to find an explanation for this circumstance that reflects well on CCC, FIRM membership organizations, and NILC. CCC's stated mission is "to build the power and capacity" of "the people most affected by injustice . . . to change their communities and to improve the policies that affect their lives." And yet this resource-rich nonprofit organization left DREAMers with next to no organizational capacity when it brought to an end its direct involvement in the original United We Dream campaign.

Negligence might explain why UWD failed in its early organizational mission, but Mo, Prerna, Lizbeth, and Marisol saw darker motives. Mo recalled asking at the 2008 UWD convening "why don't you guys already have a website?" José Luis Marantes responded with an explanation along the lines of "whenever we said we needed something like a website, CCC said we will do that and then nothing would get done." Prerna saw something very similar happening in California that she described in a message to the UWD Google group as "CHIRLA's incapacitation of the California Dream Network." From Marisol, Mo learned about the fraught relationship between DREAMers and their former sponsors at CCC. Marisol's detailed knowledge of the financial and personnel networks shaping the nonprofit immigration field helped make sense of Lizbeth's description of how CHIRLA controlled California DREAMers by turning on and off the flow of resources. Together, they concluded that the nonprofit allies of UWD never intended the organization to build the independent capacity of undocumented youth to act, but instead saw the organization as a project to draw foundation money. "The big orgs" of the nonprofit field considered the UWD network and the undocumented youth connected to it as a resource to be exploited.

From the perspective of even the most disaffected DREAMers, not all UWD's work that year was co-opted by the nonprofits or for naught. Undocumented youth made valuable contacts with congressional offices through lobbying visits. Early that year, when initial hopes of passing the DREAM Act were high, they forged relationships with key congressional staffers that fed them crucial information about behind the scenes negotiations. Marisol described how, before these contacts were forged, they would go to CCC and NILC gatherings to hear "the latest word" from "Papa Durbin" about the chances of passing DREAM on the Hill. In 2009, they cultivated their own contacts with congressional staffers and opened independent lines of intelligence.[38] Mo and Marisol credited Kiran Savage-Sangwan in New York with NYSYLC, Lizbeth and Neidi Dominguez in southern California with DREAM Team LA, and Tañia and Rigo in Chicago with IYJL, for building many of these valuable relationships.

**

Early in 2010, Prerna was invited to a RI4A event for LGBTQ bloggers sponsored by the Four Freedoms Fund. The event featured a pitch about why LGBTQ activists should support CIR, even though the proposed legislation excluded key issues for queer undocumented people, such as those included in the Uniting American Families Act (UAFA). UAFA shared a similar legislative history as the DREAM Act, first drafted in 2000 as the Permanent Partners Immigration Act and reintroduced in 2003 and 2005, and then again in 2007 and 2009. The act, which died in committee each time, would have amended immigration law to provide same-sex, bi-national couples equal treatment as straight bi-national couples. Prerna chronicled on her blog what she saw as RI4A's "epic fail" in its approach to LGBTQ activists.

Prerna feared that RI4A's clumsy handling of the summit undermined the bridgework that queer DREAMers had accomplished over the past year. "The high point of the blogger summit," Prerna wrote, was when Felipe Matos and Juan Rodriguez "called in from the Trail of Dreams." Juan and Felipe, along with Gaby Pacheco, were on a trek from Miami, FL, to Washington, DC, drawing national attention to the plight of undocumented immigrants. "Juan is documented while Felipe is undocumented," Prenra explained to her blog readers:

> Their only legal recourse to stay together is either passage of the DREAM Act or the Uniting American Families Act, since immigration law will not recognize their partnership. Their bravery and willingness to not only speak out, but risk detention and their lives, by walking hundreds of miles through Klan-country was awe-inspiring. But the solidarity lasted only a few minutes.

Frank Sharry then made a "dismal and uninspiring showing," followed by a short talk from Ali Noorani of NIF, which was "enough to obliterate any bridges under construction" with LGBTQ advocates:

> He admitted that there were no LGBT organizations on the Reform Immigration for America management team, allegedly to appease conservative religious organizations—the same community that queer advocates have been fighting against to gain equal rights for so long. Noorani also went out on a limb to say that the Uniting American Families Act (UAFA) was not a winning strategy for the campaign to adopt, which made little sense given that UAFA has more cosponsors than even the popular DREAM Act and the tanked Gutiérrez [CIR] bill.

Then Noorani dared to "rank oppressions" as he talked about the courage of Felipe and Juan. "They won't be detained for being gay, they would be detained for being undocumented":

> This blatantly ignorant statement demonstrates a complete and utter failure at understanding intersectional oppression: Felipe is still undocumented because Juan is a queer male and they are in a same-sex relationship—these multi-dimensional identities are so intrinsically linked that it is hard to elevate one over the other, let alone rank them.[39]

When I interviewed Prerna, she returned, unprompted, to the personal impact of this event. The RI4A leaders asked for support but "told the room we won't include your issues, because your issues will derail CIR":

> And the room was like what the fuck is wrong with you? What are you smoking? . . . It was a really terrible way to use Felipe and Juan, I think, because I knew them personally, and they wouldn't be asking for this either, so why are you using their story to ask for this? The room was not very happy with them. It was like a failed effort, I think, to reach out to the LGBT community by telling them "oh, sorry, you don't belong."

Prerna said she knew then that she was done with what she called "immigration reform-ville" and its so-called allies.

The reform-ville allies wanted only one aspect of her—the DREAMer aspect. Their objectification of her had been unmasked, not just then, but also gradually over the year she worked with UWD:

> When I'm told in that room, your issues don't matter to me, but this other piece of you does matter to me a lot, the gay part of you doesn't fucking matter, it was really personal. It was a personal attack. I took it very personally. I started hating people who worked on CIR . . . . I was still very young and impressionable, and being told by people who were supposedly progressive or liberal or whatever on issues of immigration that, like you know, we like a part of you, we don't like another part of you, that seemed very hurtful. And I think a lot of young people who are undocumented and queer felt the same way as I did. Just hurt and excluded and told that, "oh, you know, we want you to be like the voice, but we don't want this other part of you."[40]

Prerna now felt the reification of the DREAMer and its instrumental use by the allies as violence, cleaving her into pieces, separating the "good" from the "bad."

Prerna attended another conference that same winter, a Netroots Nation event in San Francisco, CA, where DREAMers were criticized for their "piecemeal approach" to immigration reform by a speaker from Nancy Pelosi's office. In her blog, she expressed exasperation that undocumented youth "are so derided" for taking the "reins of their own cause." "It's like accusing queers of only wanting marriage for themselves. Now regardless of what we think about marriage, WHO goes around saying that?" And yet allies insisted on charging DREAMers with a similar absurd particularism:

> I have no interest in listening to citizens talk about immigrants and "their rights." That's like being gay and sitting in a room where straight people are lecturing about tenets of the LGBT movement. My mind is not colonized enough to accept that. For the "white liberal racist" we are mere tokens, only for interest when it comes to collecting stories and posing for documentaries. And when their million-dollar strategies fail to bear fruit, we are blamed for "ineffective advocacy." We, the immigrant youth, fighting to keep our homes, find and hold down jobs, somehow get 3 meals per day and struggling to grapple with refugee status in our own homes just did not try hard enough to lobby for ourselves. We failed even though we are mere caricatures in a simulated game.[41]

The post is prescient and uncanny. If it had been written a year later, after the failed push for the DREAM Act in 2010, it would have read as the sharp retrospective analysis from a DREAMer who fought the immigration-ville allies and was now calling them out for their hypocrisy as they dared to point their fingers at the petulant DREAMers for the failure. But all of that was still to come, and Prerna saw it coming.

4
2010, Act I
"The Dream Is Coming"

In 2010, against long odds, undocumented youth succeeded in making the DREAM Act a legislative priority in Congress. It was a year of almost continuous collective actions. A year of political triumphs, punctuated by the passage of the DREAM Act in the House on December 8, only to be followed eleven days later with crushing defeat in the Senate. Powerful obstacles stood against Congress voting on the DREAM Act. The first came not from politicians but from the erstwhile patrons of the DREAMers in the nonprofit immigration field. This chapter covers the first half of the year and the actions of undocumented youth that succeeded in placing the DREAM Act on the national political agenda. The following chapter tracks the second half of the year, culminating in the congressional votes and the splintering of undocumented youth activists into opposing camps.

The nonprofit and labor leaders aligned behind the RI4A campaign expected Congress to turn to CIR after the passage of the Affordable Health Care Act. They planned accordingly, spending millions of dollars in the first quarter of 2010 on a national media campaign to culminate in a massive march on Washington in the early spring. They spoke confidently about the chances of passing CIR, but even before they could demonstrate popular support for the cause, they faced serious challenges that threatened to derail their plans.

In January, Arizona Republicans introduced a sweeping anti-immigrant bill to the state legislature. Drafted by political leaders of the nativist Right and corporate interests invested in the private prison industry, SB 1070 moved quickly through the Arizona House and Senate. Immigrant advocates in the state sounded the alarm and called for resources to try to block the passage of SB 1070. Across the nation, immigrant rights groups struggled to mobilize resources both for RI4A's CIR campaign and actions countering SB 1070 and similar state and local initiatives enhancing the policing of immigrants. Local imperatives of self-defense inevitably competed with the RI4A campaign for the time and resources of activist groups.[1]

At roughly the same time, two independent actions organized by DREAMers caught national attention, raising doubts about the legislative priority of CIR. In the first of these actions, the Trail of Dreams, the challenge to the RI4A campaign was mostly implicit. As the DREAMers on the Trail wended their way on foot from their homes in Miami, FL, to Washington, DC, the directors of RI4A succeeded in integrating the message of the undocumented trekkers with the goals of their CIR campaign. The second action, a sit-in by four DREAMers in the Tucson offices of Senator McCain, could not be absorbed. This second action exploded directly in the unsuspecting faces of the professional advocates for immigration reform and threatened to wreck their legislative designs.

The Trail of Dreams

After a long hiatus spent tending to her family's deportation case and her own health, Gaby Pacheco literally stepped back into the politics of the DREAM Act on January 1 when she joined fellow SWER members Juan Rodriguez, Felipe Matos, and Carlos Roas on the Trail of Dreams. According to Gaby, Juan came up with the idea for the Trail. His idea, loosely inspired by the Underground Railroad, was for undocumented immigrants to walk to Washington, DC, for their freedom. The initial reaction Juan got from fellow DREAMers and allies was discouraging. He was told that it would cost too much in time and money to pull off, and that UWD's scarce resources were better spent on actions designed to pressure targeted politicians needed to win a vote on the DREAM Act. When Juan first raised the idea with Gaby, she said it immediately resonated with her.

There was, for Juan, an added personal reason for undertaking the trek. Felipe Matos, his partner, was at the time in acute despair. He had gained acceptance to a prestigious Bachelor of Arts and law program, but Felipe could not attend because of his lack of papers. He was on the verge of giving up. Juan started the walk, alone, in late 2009 as an intervention of sorts to shake Felipe out of this despair. According to Gaby, Felipe told Juan to return home, and he promised "we will walk together, we'll call some friends, and do it on January 1st, the start of a new decade." They called Gaby first and she immediately said yes. She said the idea uncoiled an inner emotional need like a spring: "After what happened to my parents, I had that urge: I'm so angry. I'm gonna take it to the streets and I'm gonna go walk and just go to DC, right to the president." Gaby explained their joint commitment to walk to Washington, DC, as forged by a shared anxiety, anger, and restlessness. "We were so frustrated with the marches, with the rallies, with all the stuff that wasn't working. We were like our lives are at risk every single day. We need to put ourselves out there."[2]

The four trekkers were all members of SWER and active in the national DREAMer network, but the Trail of Dreams was not an official UWD action. The action received initial modest support from FLIC, SWER's longtime sponsor; but it was Presente—a new online advocacy group with a mission to amplify the Latin@ vote in politics—that provided most of its funding. With Presente's help, the Trail garnered considerable media attention, much of it glowing, "with over 300 articles written about the walk and interviews with trekkers on several major networks."[3]

The DREAMers braved cold weather, fatigue, physical ailments, and even intimidation from the Ku Klux Klan (KKK) in rural Georgia as they walked more than a thousand miles. Extensive media coverage made the trekkers de facto spokespersons for the national network of DREAMers, even though the action developed outside of the formal auspices of UWD. Gaby already had a high profile in immigrant rights circles, but it was on the Trail that she became the most prominent DREAMer in the nation. Presente, recognizing her popular appeal, hired Gaby as an official spokesperson after the completion of the trek.

Despite its name, the Trail of Dream's messaging did not focus on the DREAM Act. Over four long months of walking and scores of public events staged along the way, the trekkers were careful not to challenge the political wisdom of RI4A's singular focus on CIR. They faced considerable pressure from some of their peers to do just that. Mo was in regular contact with Felipe Matos. He pushed Felipe for a more forceful message of supporting the DREAM Act and suggested lines of action that would break with the expectations of the nonprofits prioritizing CIR. Felipe Vargas, who drove a supply van for the trekkers, regularly voiced suspicion to the group about the motives behind Presente's support and echoed Mo's critique of RI4A.[4]

On May Day, the four DREAMers walked from Alexandria, VA, into Washington, DC—the final four miles of their journey. There they joined a demonstration in front of the White House. Organizers of the event planned for dozens of protesters to be arrested to call attention to the urgent need for immigration reform. A *Washington Post* article reported that participation in the planned civil disobedience was "a step too far for the undocumented trekkers from Miami." It quoted Gaby on this point: "We don't want to do anything to make us seem radical. We want to show our love and all our passion and our desire to stay in the country."[5] The demonstration included prominent politicians and directors of the nonprofit immigration field. Representative Luis Gutiérrez from Chicago, speaking directly to the crowd, gestured symbolically to President Obama: "We shall not move unless we are arrested or until you sign comprehensive immigration reform." Before the police started with the arrests, the Trail of Dream trekkers departed, leaving behind their shoes. Gutiérrez, Ali Noorani, Deepak Bhargava and thirty-one other allies were arrested in their place. As he was gently led away in handcuffs, Gutiérrez was sporting a white t-shirt emblazoned on it in with red capital letters "arrest me and not my friends."

An emerging faction of DREAMers within the UWD network believed the agency of undocumented youth was left behind with those shoes. These DREAMers did not share Gaby's reluctance to appear radical. They had come to believe that CIR was already dead and that if undocumented youth did not turn to radical actions, an opportunity to pass the DREAM Act would be squandered. As the May Day action unfolded and the Trail of Dreams came to an end, these more radical members of UWD were putting the finishing touches on plans for a sit-in that would lead to the arrest of DREAMers in Arizona.

Noodles

Earlier that year, at the January UWD convening in Minneapolis, MN, leaders of IYJL initiated a discussion about "escalating" actions to push allies and politicians to advance the DREAM Act on the Hill. From this discussion, members of an emerging radical network arrived at a rough consensus that if, or more likely in their opinion, *when* the RI4A push for CIR faltered, they had to be ready to forcefully push allies and politicians to support the DREAM Act as a standalone bill. By February, leaders of this inchoate radical network were hearing from congressional staffers that Washington insiders believed CIR faced zero chance of passing in the current legislative session, but pro-immigrant politicians were not yet ready to admit this. Convinced that RI4A's legislative agenda was already effectively dead, DREAMers in this radical network started to watch anxiously as the time left on legislative calendar began to dwindle. They believed that the likelihood of passing the DREAM Act in 2010 was tied to how long it would take Democratic leaders in the Senate and House to acknowledge the death of CIR.[6]

Meanwhile the RI4A campaign was spending millions of dollars on organizing a massive "March for America" scheduled for March 21. The professional advocates and liberal politicians who recognized that CIR faced very long odds shared, nonetheless, a concern not to embarrass RI4A and the powerful organizations behind it. Mo was still on the steering committee of UWD at the time. On weekly conference calls, he would relay to committee members what Kiran Savage-Sangwan and Lizbeth Mateo were hearing from congressional staffers during their lobbying visits. Mo argued that CIR was already dead and that UWD could not afford to waste any more time. They should be pushing congressional leaders to advance a standalone DREAM Act in its place. Members on the UWD steering committee with closer ties to the leadership at CCC/FIRM and RI4A argued for patience and a greater trust in the legislative strategy of their allies. Carlos Saavedra, the new director of UWD, backed by a majority of the members sitting on the steering committee—including José Luis Marantes, the four Florida DREAMers from the Trail, and representatives from SEIU and NILC—argued that there should be no advocacy for a standalone DREAM Act ahead of RI4A's planned March for America. Waiting for the RI4A march to come and go was excruciating for DREAMers, who did not see a path forward for CIR. Witnessing the colossal expenditure of resources for a massive march to support an already dead bill was maddening.

In an apparent break with RI4A, the American Federation of Labor and Congress of Industrial Organizations (AFL-CIO)—joined by the National Education Association, the American Federation of Teachers, and MALDEF—started planning a joint public announcement of support for the DREAM Act ahead of the march. These organizations called for a press conference scheduled for the day after the march. With this public endorsement of piecemeal alternatives to comprehensive legislation, an influential bloc of labor, education, and civil rights advocates appeared poised to break with the CIR orthodoxy of the RI4A campaign. For Mo, the planned press conference presented UWD with an opportunity. He wanted UWD to time the launch of a national campaign for a standalone DREAM Act with this AFL-CIO event. A steering committee conference call in mid-March discussed the press conference. Mo recalled Josh Bernstein of SEIU and José Luis Marantes saying, in effect, "we got to find a way to shut this down. This is going to make them look bad. This can't be the day after the March for America. You know they are going to think we planned this."[7] According to Mo, Josh and José Luis argued that taking advantage of the AFL-CIO event, the morning after RI4A's big march, would embarrass their allies and be a political blunder.

After the conference call, Carlos Saavedra sent an email to the members of UWD's working committees. "Comprehensive Immigration Reform seems like it's having a slow death," he wrote to them. "The possibilities of passing reform are very small now and the conversations that everyone is having is about 'Where do we go from here?' and 'When do we start pushing for DREAM?'" Carlos' understanding of the legislative fate of CIR appeared to be approaching that of the radicals, but he did not share their sense of urgency about the diminishing time left on the legislative calendar. He still cautioned patience:

> There are a couple of pieces that we need to move forward in order to advance DREAM but first of all we need to let CIR have its final chance. Now what I mean by this is that this Sunday (3/21) we have a 100,000 people march, more than a million dollars have been invested in making this action happen and it will definitely get a reaction by Wednesday, March 24th. That is why it is important that any public message about CIR is dead happens after we get a re-action from the March for America Action, if we blow the whistle too soon we will just get the immigrant coalitions, advocates and other possible supporters alienated because of our message. We will also participate on the press conference with the AFL-CIO on their support to the Dream Act this upcoming Monday, to show the viability of dream but without getting burned from any internal DC politics.[8]

Carlos's message was weighed down by the tension of being pulled in opposite directions. From CCC, SEIU, and NILC, the pressure was to remain supportive of the CIR campaign through the wake of RI4A's "March on Washington." From radicals came the urgent call to start mobilizing around a clear message of DREAM Act now, before it was too late.

Mo said he sent an email saying "adios" to the UWD steering committee after its slow and trepid response to the AFL-CIO opportunity. He thought time was too precious to waste energy talking about how to protect the reputation and feelings of the leaders RI4A and the March on America boondoggle.[9] The failure of UWD's leadership to seize the opportunity presented by the AFL-CIO announcement confirmed Mo's suspicions that the steering committee would never defy "the big orgs" behind the RI4A campaign. It also signaled to him "that our leadership doesn't do what we say":

> Just because they say they are on our side, doesn't mean that they are on our side. And they could actually be hurting us more than they are helping us. I think February 2010 is when the division in UWD started and when we found out who was on our side.[10]

This is also when concrete planning for the Arizona action started. As winter turned to spring, as the March on America came and went with no sign of change from above, a network of radical DREAMers started to coalesce around a forceful response to the inaction of UWD leadership.

A common refrain radical DREAMers heard from the staffers and aids to key Democratic party leaders was, "We can't be the first person to push for DREAM as a stand-alone." Politicians did not want to get out ahead of RI4A and declare CIR dead by backing the DREAM Act as an alternative. RI4A still held the confidences of the principal politicians heading the Democratic initiative on immigration reform. And when it came to media coverage of the national debate over immigration policy, RI4A and these politicians held a monopoly over setting the pro-reform legislative agenda. With UWD leadership unwilling to announce a public break with this agenda, the radical network designed an action to break RI4A's stranglehold.

Mo warned Carlos of their plan to break with UWD leadership in an email at the end of April. He emphasized that "May is the month to get DREAM out there" and asked about "discussions happening inside to get this moving":

> I am asking because we are ready to give up on you all inside as you have had too long to make these things happen and you have not done it. We are getting ready to do a push ourselves, one of the things floating around is a national campaign/sign on letter targeting Stolz, Deepak and Josh: "Why are you holding our dreams hostage?" It's looking more and more like DREAM ain't happening at all this year but before we are going to accept it we are going to make one final push, a real push, and we aren't going to look back, so if you have any info now is the time to share.[11]

Carlos' response was terse. It acknowledged Mo's threat but suggested no real change of course for UWD. "We have the same information. The strategy is clear... You go ahead and do what you need to do."

The radicals' reaction to UWD inaction turned out to be more forceful than a sign-on letter calling out Rich Stolz, Deepak Bhargava, and Josh Bernstein. Mo had considerable help in planning the action, but everyone I interviewed agreed that the original idea behind the action was his. This is how Lizbeth described the genesis of the plan:

> I remember getting a call from Mohammad, "Hey, would you get arrested?" It was just a big joke at first. And then we talked about it for hours and hours at night about it, thinking about it very strategically.[12]

José Torres-Don, a member of ULI, remembered a similar call. "Mo calls me and says, hey you want to get arrested." Like Lizbeth, he didn't at first think Mo was serious. "I thought it was a big joke." But José quickly realized otherwise.[13] Building on these informal phone discussions, Mo drafted a proposal for the action. Written in mid-March, the proposal listed Mo, Lizbeth, José, Tañia Unzueta from IYJL, and an unnamed "Trail of Dream walker" as potential participants for the action.[14]

The proposal provided a backstory for the action. UWD members at the Minneapolis, MN, meeting discussed the "very small legislative window of opportunity to pass" the DREAM Act—a window closing as early as the end of June. Given this timeline, "a meeting of the minds" agreed on "the need for escalation." One line of escalation raised by the IYJL members was a "Coming out Day" in March. There was no consensus within UWD on this, but IYJL went ahead with the action and many organizations in the national network followed their lead. IYJL members also suggested "confronting ICE and Senator Durbin" to build a sense of urgency. "We left the MN meeting without a clear point of escalation," and then, according to the proposal, something unexpected happen:

> The Monday after our meeting Matias [Ramos] was detained leaving the MN airport. As word spread about his detention leaders became angrier and more fed up. We contacted all of the leaders and each would ask what they can do to get him out, how they can step it up? During the 12 or so hours we had no news about Matias, several of us were ready to be in MN in the next few hours to get things set up for his campaign. Really Matias

getting detained shook a lot of us to the core and, was potentially, the type of action that would lead us to create chaos within the movement. Matias was released due to inside connections and maneuvering by NILC with players in DHS and ICE. There was no time to alert the base as to what had happened and to mobilize them. An opportunity was lost, but it led us to think, what would happen if leaders of the movement were detained?[15]

If it was a lost opportunity, as the proposal stated, Mo and those close to him quickly realized that they could contrive a similar opportunity. They could design an action to get leading DREAMers arrested to mobilize the UWD network and its base of undocumented youth.

The proposal stated that this kind of action could trigger "chaos within our movement to create a sense of urgency to push the dream act forward." To the public, the action would appear as a high-risk gambit, an act of courageous self-sacrifice, almost martyrdom: undocumented youth risking deportation, sacrificing their future in the United States, to push the DREAM Act. But Mo knew the risk of deportation for such an action was slim. DREAMers, especially prominent DREAMers with community support, were in effect un-deportable. Matias, after all, remained detained in Minneapolis for only hours. Yes, he had connections with political elites, but the END campaigns of 2009 taught Mo that DREAMers with no inside connections could also be saved from deportation by a well-organized campaign of public support.

The principal participants of the proposed action met in Boston in early April. After this meeting, Marisol Ramos established a closed "Google group" called "Noodlesforo" to facilitate communication and planning. She sent out the first group message on April 8. "Noodles" was the name given to the DREAMers selected to carry out the action. In a message responding to Prerna's query of how they arrived at such "a stupid name," Flavia, a member of DreamACTivist.org from Texas, explained: "It alllll started in a food court in D.C.. Cris said Mo was long and skinny like a noodle. I nicknamed him Noodle. Then it became Team Noodle. Now each future detainee is regarded as a Noodle." The Noodles Google group connected a loose network of un-documented youth and co-conspirator allies from across the country. It purposefully excluded UWD leaders, who the founders of the Noodles Team believed to be disinclined toward escalation and too inclined toward complying with the wishes of the directors of the big nonprofits. Team Noodle worked hard to keep the planning within the closed group a secret.[16]

Noodlesforo included organized clusters of DREAMers and allied youth from New York's NYSYLC, Chicago's IYJL, California groups alienated from CHIRLA, and organizations from Kansas City, MO, and Ann Arbor, MI. A sprinkling of more isolated individuals joined the Google group from places as far and wide as Miami, FL, Austin, TX, and Bloomington, IN. Most in the group had not known each other before the 2008 UWD convening, and many had never met face-to-face. All told, there were around fifty people directly involved in the online planning of the Arizona action though Noodlesforo.[17] The members of this Noodles Team were a diverse lot joined by a shared sense of urgency that time was running out on the legislative calendar and by frustration with UWD's failure to initiate purposeful and independent action designed at advancing the DREAM Act.

The Noodles—those who were to be arrested in the action—first included six undocumented youth: Mo from Michigan, Lizbeth for California, Yahaira from Kansas City, Tañia from Illinois, Renata from Massachusetts, and José from Texas.[18] Weeks before the action, it was decided only four Noodles would go forward with the civil disobedience. José and Renata dropped out. The Noodles Team concluded that José did not have enough support in Texas from ULI. The reasons for Renata dropping out were unclear. José remained active on Noodlesforo working as a liaison to DREAMer organizations not directly involved in the planning of the action.

Rather late in the planning process, the group settled on staging the action in Arizona. Their public rationale was to target Senator McCain, former presidential candidate and early supporter of the DREAM Act, who was now conspicuously silent on the matter as he faced a tough primary challenge.[19] More importantly, because of the passage of SB 1070, Arizona had become the focal point of media attention on immigration enforcement, providing a bright stage for their planned "escalation."

Most of the preparation for the action unfolded online through Noodlesforo and over regularly scheduled conference calls. By mid-April a website, TheDreamIsComing.com, was up and running to tease the escalation. The site featured nothing more than a banner with the words "The Dream is Coming" and a ticker counting down the days and hours to the action. Mo got the idea from a KFC promotion campaign for a new fast-food item.[20] The webpage offered no details about the event, creating a sense of mystery and suspense as the ticker counted down. DREAMers not connected to the Noodles Team started referring to them as "The Dream Is

Coming" group. The two names— Noodles and The Dream Is Coming— would stick for the rest of the year as referents used by DREAMers for the radicals within UWD.

The Noodles Team designated four national managers: two project managers, Cris (Illinois) and Marisol (New York), and two media managers, Flavia (Texas) and Juan (Florida).[21] Behind each of the four Noodles, they created local support groups. These local groups created a database of their Noodle's most important contacts (e.g., work and professional contacts, and supporting professors) and a phone tree to activate on the day of the action. The national managers then merged these lists in preparation for a coordinated email and text "blast" on the day of the action.

The local groups crafted biographies and videos of their Noodle to be released on the day of the action. Local media managers also collected passwords for the Facebook and Twitter accounts of the Noodles, so they could take over their social media accounts on the day of action and for as long as the Noodles remained detained.[22] Across all the local Noodle groups, media managers worked to assemble one media database with information on all "local and national, print and media" contacts who might cover the action. A month before the action, Flavia wrote on Noodlesforo that the database "will be a monster. It is already quite monstrous."[23]

The four Noodles sought legal advice to assess the risk of deportation they faced if arrested for civil disobedience in Arizona. They enlisted David Bennion as their team lawyer and secured the help of an Arizona lawyer, Margo Cowan, to represent them at their court arraignment after the action.[24] Mark Silverman from the Immigrant Legal Resource Center and Chris Newman from National Day Laborer Organizing Network (NDLON) provided additional advice. No one could say for sure that the arrests of the Noodles would not lead to deportations. Their lawyers, trained to anticipate all possible consequences and risks, did not dispel fears of removal. The Noodles were in uncharted legal waters.

Mo thrives in these situations. He can be cold and calculating in situations of uncertainty and threat. When I asked Mo if he worried that the Noodles might get deported, he replied, without hesitation, "not for a minute." The action was building upon what Mo had learned from the END campaigns. Following the model of these successful campaigns, the Noodles Team was ready to activate campaigns on behalf of the arrested DREAMers to trigger public support, draw media attention, and pressure local and national politicians. Mo was certain that these ready-to-go public campaigns and all the media attention the arrests would attract foreclosed any chance of deportation for the Noodles.[25]

Lizbeth felt at the time a little less sanguine than Mo. She recalled that the lawyers tried to dissuade her from participating. They considered Lizbeth's risk of deportation to be greater than some of the others because she was straight. Mo, gay and from Iran, could slow any removal process by claiming fear of political persecution if he was forced to return to his country of birth. Yahaira, from Mexico, had come out in 2007 and the lawyers thought her sexual orientation could also be used to stop her deportation. Tañia's case was altogether different from the others. She had returned to Mexico after graduating from high school in the United States. She was re-admitted into the United States on the grounds of humanitarian parole. Tañia's case raised the most concerns for the lawyers.[26]

The Noodles held only three face-to-face meetings before the action. At these gatherings, they hammered out sensitive details of the action they wanted to keep under wraps. But even more importantly, it was in each other's presence that they gauged their collective resolve to see these plans through. In Boston for the first meeting, the group was still undecided about the number of Noodles that would participate, what form the action would take, and where it would take place. They knew it had to lead to arrests, but little else was clear. In Chicago, two weeks before the action, they settled on the four Noodles to be arrested and chose Arizona as the general location, but the exact date and place remained uncertain. They considered changing their initial date of May 15 to May 22.[27]

A few days after the Chicago meeting the Noodles came together again in Washington, DC, to make "lobbying" visits on the Hill. Without revealing details, they informed the offices of Senators Feinstein, Lugar, Brownback, LeMieux, Menendez, Reid, and Durbin that they were planning an action of civil disobedience.[28] Joe Zogby from Durbin's office and Lugar's legislative director warned them of a possible blowback. They raised a cautionary tale of the confrontational action targeting Karl Rove's Washington, DC, home in 2003. These legislative aids argued that the Rove action prompted moderate Republicans to withdraw their support for immigration reform. Mo described the meeting with Zogby as the most productive. He reported to Noodlesforo that they explained to Zogby that the action was not aimed at calling out Republicans but at "moving [the] base and creating moral crisis within faux CIR campaign and also congressional leadership."[29] With these visits, the Noodles intended, more than anything else, to impress on politicians that going forward they should take DREAMers at their word when they announce they are going to do something. They also hoped this might undercut the mediating role of the big nonprofits in future communication between DREAMers and elected officials.

News in Washington, DC, confirmed that there was no sign of RI4A pivoting from CIR to DREAM. An email from Ali Noorani, circulated on the morning of May 10, with updates from RI4A's "Thursday's Management Team conversation," left the Noodles Team with no doubt about their Arizona action. Noorani's message read, in part: "There continues to be broad agreement on the 12 million understanding, that the AZ law creates an opportunity and a challenge, and that we need to press Congress and the White House to act in as significant manner possible." The opportunity, as the Management Team saw it, was to force "Republicans into a wedge on Arizona and CIR." On a longer time-horizon, Noorani said RI4A's "legislative team will begin doing serious homework on specific items such as DREAM and AgJOBS (keeping in mind how we can get a victory that won't have a cost that will split our movement)."[30] For the Noodles, the time to "begin doing serious homework" on DREAM had long passed. As the number of deportations skyrocketed, the message from RI4A that they would not risk splitting *"our movement"* with a near-term policy win to protect undocumented youth was offensive, and, they believed, more than a little disingenuous. In a Washington, DC, airport, as they waited to board their flight to Phoenix, Mo and Lizbeth read Noorani's letter to the other Noodles and savored the idea of how their action would create "chaos" in RI4A's "faux" movement.

To maximize this chaos, the action was kept a secret from UWD and NILC leaders almost to the day of its execution. As the Noodles Team sought to scale-up organizing support in the days before the action, they expanded the network of people in-the-know, but discussions on Noodlesforo continued to emphasize that UWD leaders—especially Carlos—be kept in the dark.[31] After the sit-in, leading DREAMers kept out of the loop, such as Julieta Garibay, found it hard to forgive and forget the Noodles for this secretiveness and lack of trust.

Late on Monday, May 10, the Noodles were on an airplane headed for Phoenix, Maricopa County, AZ. Their Arizona lawyer, Margo Cowan, had warned that "a war zone" awaited them. The county's notorious Sheriff Arpaio and his officers, empowered by the newly enacted SB1070, were squared off against what one local advisor described as "shaky coalition of organizations—now working together. There is definitely a mood of escalation, but everyone is doing it their own way. There is no super tight, strict set up."[32] The Noodles Team had no clear plan of how to navigate this local scene of activism, and they were still working out how to message their action in this local context.

They arrived in Phoenix to good news. Kyle de Beausset, under the subject line, "Mo just struck media gold," informed Noodlesforo that Julia Preston of *The New York Times* had agreed to cover the action. Her condition for participation was that her report be an exclusive. "This represents a break in the RI4A stranglehold of the mainstream media narrative on immigration," Kyle wrote.[33] What the exact action was that Preston had agreed to cover remained murky. The Noodles knew they were getting arrested—that much was for certain, but not where or how. The day after arriving in Phoenix, Mo wrote on Noodlesforo: "I know we have been a bit sketchy about the final action but we reached consensus as noodles just now. We are going with an action on McCain's [Tucson] office. It will be a sit in taken to the extreme, as in more than just walking in. Maybe having grad caps, citizen supporters outside etc. We are on [our] way to Tucson now, but will give details asap."[34] In a gesture of solidarity with local organizers, the Noodles agreed to include a Tucson activist, Raul, in the sit-in.

A finalized national press release for the action was ready on May 15. It was sent out to all local Noodles groups with clear instructions to only release once *The New York Times* story broke.[35] The local groups tweaked the national press release highlighting the participation of their Noodle and his or her ties to local communities.[36] The California team organized behind Lizbeth, which had dubbed itself Spicy Noodles, reported that NDLON was giving them access to their database to send an email blast out on the day of the action.[37] DREAMer organizations in twelve different states scheduled emergency solidarity meetings to generate support across the nation on the day and day after of the action. Civil disobedience actions to be carried out by citizen allies in solidarity with the sit-in were scheduled for May 20.[38] Everything was in place.

The group received a scare the day before the action. Details of the sit-in were circulating among some local activist groups and starting to spread. Mo sounded the alarm on Noodlesforo trying to contain the leak:

> Hey all sorry to yell, but there is a message that is going around that is TOO detailed that is revealing the action we are doing. We want to make sure that it is clear that nothing is to be revealed about the actual

CD. No one should be saying there is going to be a sit in. The only thing that can be revealed is that there is going to be a rally outside of McCain's office!!!!!!!!!!!!!!!!!!!!!

Kyle attached an email from an Arizona organization to the thread started by Mo's message. Its subject line read: "Students Risk Deportation Tomorrow at Noon in Tucson!!!" Kyle said it "went out to a list of a bunch of big whigs in D.C. This isn't good for a lot of reasons, media wise being the *New York Times* exclusive."[39] The Noodles scrambled to plug the leak, but it was too late. Word of the sit-in was out on Twitter and spreading.

Felipe Vargas was working as the "on the ground organizer" in Tucson and tasked with mobilizing local support. The leaks had come from local activists he was working with to organize a crowd of protestors outside of McCain's offices to coincide with the sit-in. Felipe took responsibility:

Breathe easy! Much luv . . . we are good! Just as all my homies on the day of the wedding freak out . . . the groom n bride should not be worried we have done what we can! I'm glad that now the noodles are sending a corrected action alert for the local community-that should help . . . although another would b kind of a risk?

;-(I dropped the ball and I take complete responsibility for Derechos Humanos mobilizing their gente early! please send that local call out n they can resend . . . other than that . . . let's ride the momentum n be ready to mobilize our bases towards our targets![40]

As the Noodles Teams fretted over losing the Julia Preston story, contact from a member of *The New York Times* editorial board raised hopes for an editorial on the action.[41]

On Monday, May 17 at 10:45 am, Rigo sent the following message out on Noodlesforo: "The noodles are inside McCain's office already. Please take command of their Twitter accounts and begin to update folks that they are inside."[42] Marisol followed-up with pictures from inside and an update:

The noodles . . . will remain in the office until 5pm Arizona time. Cops/UsMarshalls/and Border Patrol are outside waiting for the noodles to be taken out. Most likely they will be taken to the local jail and remain there for 48 hours. Outside of McCains office there are around 150 people and the crowd is growing bigger as students come out of their classrooms . . . The

Noodles want to send their love to everyone as they feel your support and love from inside.[43]

The Noodles then sent a message directly to the group: "We just got our phones for a bit, attorneys will take em br dday. Mo has a mic on him so it is all recorded. Camera got kicked out early. Cops say mccain welcomed us to stay till 5, so action will go down then. We are all still a go."[44]

Almost no one involved in the Noodles Team had any experience in organizing an act of civil disobedience, let alone one that was unfolding on a national stage. As information from the inside passed to Noodlesforo, the regional teams passed it on through their local networks, but not without distortion. They were all nervous and excited. Rigo cautioned them to be disciplined:

Can we please calm down, take a deep breath and really stick to our national and local plans. There's been a ton of misinformation that has been disseminated and also been taken down. We are looking sloppy and unorganized. Let's all be on the same page and if someone does not know about something or is unsure about something, please do not publish anything and speak to Marisol or Juan or Flavia beforehand. We cannot continue publishing more mistakes because it will hurt us in our press coverage and at the end of the day hurt the ability to have a huge impact in this.[45]

Inside McCain's Tucson office, the Noodles faced their own difficulties. Lingering fears that Tañia faced a higher risk of deportation upon arrest led to a last-minute change in plans. With the sit-in already underway, the group decided that Tañia would leave just before the arrests and serve as spokesperson for the DREAM 5. With all the messaging already queued to go, it was way too late to change the name of the action to the DREAM 4.

Tucson police entered the office promptly at 5 pm and arrested the three DREAMers and the local activist, Raul. Immediately a press release attached to the message "BLAST THIS NOW" went out on Noodlesforo. The opening lines read:

FOR IMMEDIATE RELEASE
DETAINED in Arizona: Four Student Immigrant Leaders
Peacefully Resist Current Immigration Law, Urge Passage of DREAM Act

As of 6:00 PM PST today, Mohammad, Yahaira, Lizbeth and Raul, an Arizona Resident, have been arrested and detained after their day long sit-in at Senator John McCain's Office in Tucson, AZ. Tania, who was not detained, has been designated as spokesperson and will be relating the experiences/ thoughts of the group during the action. Senator John McCain offered the students a meeting in order to discuss the Dream Act, however, the students recognize that this is insufficient and that immediate action is needed to pass the DREAM Act!

The press release described the action as a challenge "to local and federal law" aimed to "highlight the urgency of legislative action in Congress, and catalyze mass grassroots mobilization to pass the DREAM Act before June 15th." The release ended with a quotation from Yahaira: "Dr. King spoke of a dream of equality overcoming fear. Well, the fierce urgency of our dreams has overcome any kind of fear we may have had before. We can't wait."[46] Shortly after the blast, the DreamACTivist.org server went down as it struggled to handle the traffic. It was back up and running within minutes.[47] And then the media requests started to roll in.

The Julia Preston piece appeared on *The New York Times* website that very evening, followed by a wave of news reports: a *Huffington Post* piece, a radio segment on *Democracy Now*, a story in both *El Diario* and *La Opinion*, and scores of local reports. Over the next few days, the Noodlesforo group tracked ninety-six different media hits ranging from print media giants like *The New York Times* and *The Washington Post* to local newspapers like the *Contra Costa Times* and the *Kansas City Star*, from national television reports on ABC Nightly News to nightly news coverage on local Arizona and California TV stations, and from radio coverage on PRI to scores of posts on a wide range online media and blogs.[48]

The next morning, Marisol posted that the Noodles were "released and then ICE came under cover to detain dreamers. More updates to come but please keep quiet."[49] Juan replied, "It's on Twitter, somebody tweeted it and it's being spread like PB&J."[50] Flavia added detail: "The criminal court proceeding stated that no ICE hold was placed on the arrestees. However, ICE came on their own initiative and took Mo, Lizbeth, and Yahaira." Raul, the Arizona ally, was free. Flavia told everyone to stay on message: "REMEMBER: Noodles want us to push for the DREAM Act, NOT just get them out of detention. So when people ask you, 'so what are the next steps', the answer is, pass the muthafuckin dream act!!! (but no cussing)."[51] Adam, following up on Flavia's message, provided a legal update:

> At this morning's "initial appearance" hearing, Mo, Yahaira, Lizbeth, and Raul gave a not-guilty plea to trespassing charges. The court assigned a court date on June 16th, 9:00 AM with regard to the misdemeanor charges. The three undocumented noodles were given the permission to leave the state, however, they are required to appear at the June court date . . . . Between 10:30 AM and 11:00 AM, Mo, Yahaira, and Lizbeth were released on the State Court charge and subsequently taken into ICE custody. Although the court hearing did not indicate ICE intervention, within hours, noodles were transferred to Immigration custody. They were transported from the County Jail to an ICE processing facility. Margo Cowan, our immigration attorney entered Notices of Appearances (designating herself as their lawyer).[52]

That evening, a little more than 24 hours after the arrests, the following message from Azadeh appeared on Noodlesforo: "Just talked to Flavia, they've been released . . . DO NOT TWEET, DO NOT POST, DO NOT SPEAK TO ANY REPORTERS until we release a statement. sorry for the caps. she insisted;)."[53] Flavia followed with her own warning in bold font:

> **We need people to keep mobilizing. Stress the fact that there are misdemeanor charges, the homeland security watch list, everything . . . . make it sound dire. Which it is. I need to reiterate. This is NOT a victory. The DREAM Act has NOT passed yet. We are happy the Noodles are out—but remember, this isn't just about the three of them, this is about thousands of people across the country, still waiting.**[54]

The press release from the Noodle Team quoted Yahaira to frame this message:

> While we are glad to be out, remember that this action was not and is not about us as individuals. It is imperative for all to continue to push the DREAM Act, to work like we've never worked before and make this a reality this summer. We've surpassed the days of sitting idly by while others make decisions for us, while others tell us to wait. We cannot wait. Waiting is no longer an option. The DREAM Act must pass and it must pass now.

And it concluded with a public challenge from Tañia: "If our three friends can face the ultimate fear of deportation to show their commitment to passing DREAM, our community and leaders must ask themselves what they are willing to do?"[55]

Protests in support of the DREAM 5 followed. On May 20, in an action coordinated with the Spicy Noodles Team, nine students—citizen allies, not DREAMers—sat down in the middle of the intersection of Wilshire Boulevard and Veteran Avenue in Los Angeles. They demanded politicians "push for passage of the DREAM Act as a stand-alone bill." A larger gathering of "several hundred" supported the "Wilshire 9" as they were arrested.[56]

Under the title "Courage in Arizona," editors of *The New York Times* praised the "young immigrant students" who "risked everything on Monday when they sat down in Senator John McCain's office in Tucson and refused to leave."[57] Of the DREAMers, the editors wrote they "want the opportunity that others take for granted: the chance to earn college degrees, to forge better lives, to fulfill their potential in their home country. These are dreams that to them are well worth the risk." They contrasted the courage of the arrested DREAMers with the timidity of prominent politicians who professed advocacy for immigration reform but did nothing. Journalists understood the action to be unprecedented and covered it as such. In her article, Julia Preston described the action as "the first time students have directly risked deportation in an effort to prompt Congress to take up a bill that would benefit illegal immigrant youths."[58] Media coverage of the sit-in conveyed the message the Noodles Team had hoped for. The action was framed as an urgent call to congressional leaders to pass the DREAM Act and a warning of the lengths to which DREAMers would go to push for its passage. But there was another important target and message that largely escaped the news media's grasp.

The sit-in of course had multiple targets: energizing undocumented youth activism, pressuring senators and congresspersons, *and* pushing the recalcitrant allies behind the RI4A campaign out of the way. Arizona was selected as the site of the action mainly because of SB 1070. The law had triggered vibrant pro-migrant protests that departed from RI4A's mono strategy of CIR. Arizona had become the center of focus of both local and national media attention on immigration. It provided a stage to broadcast loud and clear to "movement" leaders that undocumented youth were directly challenging the political strategy of the RI4A campaign. The arrest of DREAMers in Tucson aimed to highlight the dangerous consequences of the campaign blocking or delaying piecemeal legislation that could save undocumented youth from deportation.

In weighing the balance of the importance of these different targets of the DREAM 5, Mo considered the RI4 campaign as primary:

> When we started planning it, the idea behind it was we are doing this to ask for the Dream Act as a standalone bill, but the real reason behind it was not to get McCain or anybody else onboard, it was really just to shut up, to shut up RIFA, and to push DREAM Act as a standalone bill. We knew that if we put ourselves on the line that these advocates couldn't then say "no what they really want is CIR," because we are the ones sitting in jail. You can't speak for me when I am in jail. So that was really the motive behind the McCain action, and what it really accomplished was to shut up all these folks.

The "real" target was the directors of RI4A and the nonprofit handlers of UWD allied with this campaign. The aim was to make clear and public that they were misrepresenting the interests of undocumented youth and thwarting their agency. The media accounts of the DREAM 5 may have missed this message, but it was not lost on most advocates organizing for immigration reform.

Shortly after their release from a Tucson jail, the three DREAMers received a call from Shuya Ohno, the National Field Director for NIF and a former employee of CCC. Mo told me, "It's my favorite call ever." Before describing what was said on the call, Mo paused to describe Shuya. "He looks like a turtle. They all look like animals." Then he laughed, and flashed a big, mischievous smile. A little earlier in the interview he had described Rich Stolz as a cat. These visual jokes turning the professional leaders of CIR into animal caricatures worked to rob them of their power to overawe. Mo continued:

> Shuya called one of our counterparts that was there working with us, and he then was passed to speak to me and tells me, this is two days after we get released from jail, he's like "well, why you guys doing this," whatever. And we told him like "we need you guys to support DREAM Act as a standalone." And he said, word for word, he said, "who says our communities need a win this year?" And I was just like "what do you mean who says our communities need a win this year, we want a win this year." That was really sort of the moment for me, the realization of like these guys really have an

alternative agenda and their definition of a win is completely different than what people on the ground who are getting deported consider a win.

The dispute with the professionals of immigration reform was not simply about a difference in political strategy. It was over a more fundamental difference: what and for whom was "the movement" about? Mo added that the Noodles heard through their networks that RI4A directors held "conference calls to discuss what do we do, what do we do?" Mo was thrilled that the action seemed to be stirring the chaos he intended. "That's sort of how we knew the action was a success, in that they were feeling the heat."[59]

UWD leadership was also a target of the sit-in action. It threatened to make the leadership of the national DREAMer organization irrelevant. The Noodle's official press release credited the action as "an independent undocumented youth-led project supported by DreamACTivist.org, DREAM Team LA, the Kansas/Missouri Dream Alliance, the Immigrant Youth Justice League, One Michigan, the Indiana Latino Youth Collective, and New York State Youth Leadership Council": a clear message to UWD that if it did not lead the push for DREAM now, it would be left behind by an independent network of DREAMer organizations ready for action.[60]

With the success of the Arizona action, radical DREAMers started to imagine an independent immigrant movement led by undocumented youth. The Tucson sit-in added civil disobedience to their repertoire of contention. Its law-breaking defiance put into action a crystallizing DREAMer mantra, "undocumented and unafraid." In an after-action report, Marisol informed Noodlesforo that "there is a lot of initiative to escalate . . . and a growing sense of urgency" across the UWD network. Planning for an upcoming weekly UWD field conference call, Marisol told the members of the Noodles group to make a "three prong ask" of UWD: "1. Groups need to pressure their senate targets. 2. Groups need to escalate actions whether through civil disobedience, hunger strikes, sit in . . . whatever it takes to move targets. 3. Ask needs to be the same: we need dream first, we need as stand alone before June 15th." Kiran followed Marisol's message with this short missive: "It is also important to be clear about the fact that they can collaborate with us but have no part in the decision-making process."[61]

The DREAM 5 widened the divide within UWD between the radical The Dream Is Coming group and the moderate leadership of the organization. Left out of the loop on the action, these moderates responded suspiciously to what they saw as a secretive network led by Mo, Lizbeth, and Marisol.[62]

The radicals wanted UWD leadership to immediately align with their demand for a standalone DREAM Act. Undocumented youth unfamiliar with the organization's inner workings viewed the DREAM 5 as an official UWD action. UWD leadership could not afford to disown it. They appreciated how the action had energized DREAMers across the nation, but they also resisted pressures to demand that RI4A abandon CIR and push for a standalone DREAM Act. Over the next few months, the Noodles would dance around whether they were operating within or outside of UWD. Similarly, UWD leadership would waffle on whether the escalating actions of the Noodles were sanctioned by UWD or not. Both sides vied for the growing constituency of UWD and refused to bright line the yawning breach separating them.

Back on the Hill

The professional advocates of CIR sought to spin the Arizona action as in-step with their campaign. RI4A praised the DREAM 5 for their courage and synced its public message with the act of resistance, sending out an email blast calling on organizations across the country to "Begin Sustained Campaign of Civil Disobedience." The blast described the new campaign as inspired by four "gutsy student activists at McCain's office," but it did not signal a change in RI4A's policy agenda. The message said nothing about advancing a standalone DREAM Act.[63]

A statement circulated by FIRM ten days after the action all but ignored the demands of the Dream Is Coming group. Marissa Graciosa, the Immigration Campaign Coordinator for CCC, shared it with the UWD steering committee in an email. "UWD friends—Please see below for FIRM statement about our plan moving forward. Thanks!" The statement began as an organizational brag sheet:

> The Fair Immigration Reform Movement (FIRM) is the largest national grassroots network of immigrant rights organizations in the country. We began fighting for legalization of undocumented people and family unification in the late 1990's, at a time when such proposals were not taken seriously by most in Washington and even by some activists. Over the last decade, we have helped to lead mobilizations that have brought millions to the streets, naturalized, registered and turned out millions of new voters, and won important victories at the local and state level. Over the

past 18 months we have worked with allies to mount an unprecedented organizing and advocacy campaign to achieve federal reform legislation. This work has moved the question of immigration reform from the margins to the center of the national debate and the country's politics.

It then presented five points to meet the historical moment. The first tied the movement directly to the goal of CIR:

Today, we are facing a moral crisis in our nation that has helped to inspire a social movement. The crisis has been brought about by the failure of Washington. **There can be no resolution of this moral crisis without legalization for 12 million people and policies that reunites families.**

The second point demanded that "**President Obama use his executive authority to <u>immediately</u> declare a moratorium on deportations.**" The third raised, somewhat confusingly, an openness to piecemeal reforms, yet doubled down on the position of nothing less than comprehensive reform. "We support Senate efforts to move targeted legalization for farm workers and students, but cannot support such legislation if it is paired with even more enforcement measures. **Senators should know that passage of these measures will not lessen their obligation to pass legalization for all immigrants.**" The fourth expressed solidarity with the mobilization of resistance against SB 1070 in Arizona. The last point added nothing new but simply returned to opening theme of the statement:

Today, the gravity of the moral crisis in our country together with **the failure of leadership in Washington compel us to undertake a campaign of direct action and non-violent civil disobedience to stop the destruction of our families.** Throughout American history, when confronted with unjust laws and resistance to changing them by people in power, movements have taken history into their own hands. We are doing the same to address one of the great moral crises of our day.

And lest there be any confusion of what FIRM meant by "doing of the same," this last "point" reiterated the first: "**We will not stop until we achieve full citizenship for 12 million undocumented immigrants in our country.**"[64]

Judging from angry responses on Noodlesforo, FIRM's statement marked an apogee in CCC's multi-year effort to reify the immigrant rights movement: a point where the orbit of the nonprofit's mystification of the movement appeared to travel so far away from the interests and actions of activists on the ground that it unmasked itself. The statement painted FIRM as a prime mover of a movement that was taking "history into its own hands" and framed its organizational goal of CIR as the only true solution to the moral crisis that the movement confronts. But on the ground, local activists were increasingly much more concerned with mobilizing against SB 1070 in Arizona and copycat laws being proposed in other states than with the RI4A campaign. And at the national level, the civil disobedience of radical DREAMers was directly challenging FIRM's legislative agenda.

FIRM and RI4A nonetheless retained key supporters at the helm of UWD. Gaby Pacheco was at the time still working for Presente, but she held great influence in UWD and was soon to become its de facto policy director. She said in our interview that for weeks after the McCain action she still saw the broader agenda of comprehensive reform as her mission. She described a meeting with the DREAM 5 and Carlos Saavedra in Arizona immediately after the action, where she held to this broader agenda against strong pressure from Mo and Lizbeth. She was miffed that Carlos mostly listened and did not step into support her against angry attacks. Despite Carlos' silence, he shared Gaby's resistance to the idea of UWD breaking with the legislative strategy of their nonprofit allies.

Carlos nonetheless embraced the momentum sparked by the Arizona action. "At this point, the leadership is coming from us (the youth)," he wrote in a May 24 email to the UWD committees. Using the movement-mystifying language of his nonprofit bosses, he asserted that "we are writing a new chapter in the immigrant rights movement as we speak," but departing somewhat from the image of one united movement, he concluded in bold, "**We are an Immigrant Student Movement.**"[65] Nonetheless, the official UWD press release after the McCain action did not make an explicit call for a standalone DREAM Act. Joined by other moderates on the steering committee, Carlos effectively resisted The Dream Is Coming demand that the UWD officially break with RI4A and push for a standalone DREAM Act.

The loyalty of UWD's leadership to RI4A led to a vibrant debate on Noodlesforo: Why were they continuing to support the CIR campaign? Some argued that their fellow DREAMers were being manipulated by the campaign to act against their own interests. Others offered a more sympathetic explanation. They explained the yawning difference between themselves and the UWD moderates as a disagreement over executing a public strategy versus a "private/secret strategy" to pass the DREAM Act. The moderate DREAMers, following the advice of allies at NILC, CCC, and FIRM membership organizations, were sticking with the CIR campaign to keep the DREAM Act off the radar of a nativist Right poised to counterattack, and thereby increasing the chances of passing DREAM quickly at a late hour in the legislative calendar.[66]

Mo raised two major problems with the private/secret strategy. First, the strategy provided no accountability for the actions and motives of the elites running the RI4A campaign. How were DREAMers to know if RI4A was holding to the secret strategy and not blocking DREAM in their private meetings with politicians? Second, even if the allies were faithfully executing a private/secret strategy, there was no longer any time for this strategy to unfold. The legislative clock was running out. The DREAM Act had to be pushed now through all possible channels. Mo believed the private/secret strategy was a cover for professional advocates who had no intention of backing DREAM. The UWD steering committee was being manipulated. Lizbeth made it clear on Noodlesforo that she agreed with Mo. With CIR dead, RI4A now saw long-term advantage in a legislative failure that could be pinned on the Republicans. A victory on the DREAM Act would only reduce political pressure for immigration reform in the future and remove from the struggle a valuable asset, the DREAMer. The allies at RI4A and CCC/FIRM might have sold the UWD leadership on the private strategy, but Lizbeth and Mo were convinced they did not want DREAM to pass as a standalone bill. Ohno had said as much to Mo after Arizona: "Who says our communities need a win this year?" But not everyone on Noodlesforo agreed with this cynical view. The very debate revealed that the radical DREAMers did not all agree on the intentions of nonprofit "allies."

'The Day We Broke the Campaign'

Mo saw the month of June as critical. He feared that no legislative movement on DREAM before the July 4th recess spelled doom for the bill. Kiran and Lizbeth's lobbying identified the Congressional Hispanic Caucus (CHC), along with R4IA, as the major impediments. They heard from staffers in Senate offices eager to champion DREAM that no one on the Hill was willing to take the lead. They were waiting for Senate leadership to signal that comprehensive reform was dead and greenlight alternative piecemeal approaches, but leadership was still listening to the champions of CIR at RI4A and the CHC.

At the start of the month, Mo and Lizbeth called for further escalation to "1. Get [RIFA] campaign on board with dream as stand-alone. 2. Get CHC out of way or in support of dream as stand-alone. 3. Get a senator to champion DREAM":

> This is going to take a lot of risky and bold moves to make this happen. There is a good chance DREAM has zero chance of passing this year, I think we need to all have that reality check. Essentially what we are doing is making one last effort, against ALL odds, to revive it, to get it back on the agenda.[67]

With the help of the regional Noodle teams, Mo pulled together a civil disobedience toolkit to distribute to undocumented youth nationwide. They set up an online civil disobedience intake form to identify DREAMers willing to risk arrest.

Drawing from the information gathered from lobbying work, the Noodles Team discussed actions to "call out" key politicians and drive a wedge between them and the official position of RI4A and the CHC. This brought Representative Luis Gutiérrez of Chicago into their crosshairs. Within the CHC and Congress, Gutiérrez was viewed as the national voice for immigrant communities and immigration reform. With IYJL, the Noodles Team had a powerful local organization on the ground in Chicago that could challenge Gutiérrez. Led by Tañia and Rigo, IYJL had already succeeded in pressuring ICIRR, its "parent" organization and a member of FIRM, to publicly support a standalone DREAM Act. Mo and Lizbeth pushed the Chicago group to move fast and pressure Gutiérrez with civil disobedience.

The Chicago DREAMers debated, internally, the wisdom of an immediate action on Gutiérrez's office. The group demurred and decided on a more cautious approach. Their stated reason hinged on the group's reading of the local situation in Chicago. They thought a sit-in without warning would alienate local supporters in the immigrant rights movement. IYJL settled instead on a two-step plan, first pressure Gutiérrez with an aggressive ask, give him a deadline to respond, and if he did not deliver, only then stage a sit-in.[68] IYJL's decision opened the first significant split in the Noodles Team. Unwilling to wait for Gutiérrez's response to IYJL, the group in New York, NYSYLC, launched a more confrontational approach with Senator Schumer, the lead advocate for CIR in the Senate.

On June 10, NYSYLC members carried out three simultaneous actions on different Schumer offices. The New York group was already ten days into an "indefinite hunger strike urging Senator Schumer to move the DREAM Act as a standalone bill."[69] A few days into the strike, Schumer's immigration counsel and lead author of the CIR framework, Leon Fresco, promised the hunger strikers a meeting with the senator, but nothing had come of the promise. Feeling rebuffed, the angry and starving members of NYSYLC planned a sit-in at Schumer's New York City office, but word got out about the action. Having lost the element of surprise and fearing that they would be preemptively locked out in NYC, they quickly changed to a plan of multiple, simultaneous direct actions: a die-in outside his NYC office and sit-ins at his Long Island, NY, and Washington, DC, offices. The NYC die-in yielded local publicity. The Long Island action led to arrests. But the Washington, DC, action struck gold: an impromptu and heated encounter with Schumer in which he exposed what many on Noodlesforo had long suspected about RI4A's behind-the-scenes lobbying position.

Thirty minutes into the Washington, DC, sit-in, Leon Fresco spoke with the activists and told them that there was no chance for a meeting with the senator. Leon offered to arrange a future meeting with himself and Joe Zogby to discuss the DREAM Act. The students rejected the offer. Having not made good on his earlier promise of a meeting, it rang hollow. In explaining this broken promise, Leon told the NYSYLC contingent that Schumer had met the day before with Ali Noorani, Frank Sherry, Deepak Bhargava, and "the Catholic Church." Fresco had wanted to include the New York DREAMers in the meeting, as promised, but he said that on the direct request of RI4A they were not invited. The student activists told Fresco they would not leave until Schumer talked to them.

An hour later Schumer entered the office. In real-time, a NYSYLC member posted on Noodlesforo an account of the encounter:

> He was irate and did far more yelling than talking, but it was the first time we had ever met him directly, despite several years of attempting to secure meetings. His main point was that RI4A had told him as recently as yesterday not to push Dream on its own and to continue pushing only a comprehensive bill. He said they said they want this because they represent all immigrant communities and we only represent a small segment.[70]

Mo took the news and ran with it. He quickly posted on DreamACTivist.org a public charge against the biggest names associated with the RI4A campaign.

He titled it "Schumer Says: 'Ali Noorani, Frank Sharry, Deepak Bhargava, Catholic Church (RIFA) .... Don't Want DREAM Act.'" The post read:

> The New York squad holed up in Senator Schumer's DC office just had a quick meeting with the senator. They going to continue with the sit-in because they are nowhere near happy with the results. The senator continues to stick with this line of not pushing DREAM Act this year. One of his failed promises from last week was a meeting with senate leadership and campaign leadership to talk about the future of the DREAM Act. The meeting was supposed to include Dream Act youth leaders. Schumer's office had promised this and again lied on that promise.
>
> It turns out however the meeting did happen, but instead of having youth there to defend our position we have advocates from the campaign do it for us. About an hour ago Schumer told the youth in his DC office that Reform Immigration for America, namely Ali Noorani (executive director of National Immigration Forum), Frank Sharry (America's Voice), Deepak Bhargava (Executive Director for Center for Community Change), and members of the Catholic Church and others, were at a meeting yesterday **where they stated they did not want the senator to move forward with the DREAM Act.** An aide to Schumer stated that Dream Act youth were not wanted at that meeting by the campaign. A complete list of who was at this meeting will be coming shortly. It is time to hold our 'leaders' accountable. The BIG question is why? Why are our so called leaders holding out on our communities? Why are they advocating against DREAM Act? We are supposed to be a unified movement, yet at every turn we have to fight our own advocates to even have any space in the discussion! Why? **Why would you rather have youth STARVE than to support us? Prove us wrong, and release a statement calling for stand-alone DREAM Act immediately. Prove us wrong, and include immigrant youth, who can speak for themselves, at a meeting with congressional leadership.**[71]

The post triggered a storm of angry calls from undocumented youth to politicians and leaders of RI4A.[72] It also stirred controversy on Noodlesforo.

Tañia, who had led IYJL into a less confrontational approach with Gutiérrez, responded immediately to Mo's blast:

> I know that rifa has treated us worst than bad, but my experience as a journalist tells me we should check our sources. if we really want to burn rifa we

need the exact quote, hearsay is not enough. Also a message from deepac was forwarded to me where he says that schumer's statements are false, and that at the meeting he said they did support dream. He says "I specifically said that we do strongly support moving the dream act, provided that it can be done without punitive enforcement." Not saying we have to believe him, but what makes us believe schumer? Just saying this may not be helpful for our conversation with rifa especially if schumer's statements are not accurate. He could very well be lying to us. We should decide if we want them as our allies or not, and if we do this is not helpful. If we don't, we are on the right track. But regardless of what deepac says he said, we should check our sources (schumer) and our source's reliability.[73]

Mo defended publicizing the information from Schumer to question the integrity of RI4A's leaders:

eh i think we are fine. the post was made from dreamactivist not from the dreamiscoming. ri4a needs to publicly and finally state its position. they aren't going to do it quietly, we have waited a year plus for it. this post doesn't hurt us at all. . . . so all ri4a has to do and partner orgs have to do is release their public statements of support for the dream act as a stand alone. still, even in response to this, none of them have chosen to do so. they are still play games with us. we've told em we'll retract it as soon as they prove us otherwise, they have yet to do that.[74]

Because it came from DreamACTivist.org and not The Dream Is Coming, Mo felt justified in going public with the charge without discussion and deliberation on Noodlesforo. He also thought this provided the wider group with cover. The post was not a statement from The Dream Is Coming but the charge of a blogger. Mo's use of DreamACTivist.org in this way gave him tremendous power to act independently. This had been a contentious issue within UWD, and now, with the Schumer post, some on Noodlesforo started to question this unchecked power.

Boosted by the DREAM 5 action, DreamACTivist.org's email list, donors, and active users continued to grow. In the loose coalition of organizations behind the Noodles Team, not one had a comparable megaphone. In 2010, the website raised $40,000 on almost twelve hundred contributions averaging $33.00 per contribution. That summer there was $1,700 in The Dream Is Coming's account with NDLON.[75] IYJL and NYSYLC had their own organizational resources which were also likely greater than the resources formally under the control of The Dream Is Coming. In short, this network of radical DREAMers did not have its own center of gravity to counterbalance the composite parts that came together to form it. And among these parts, DreamACTivist.org, under the considerable discretionary power of Mo, reached more people than any of the others.

Neidi, from Dream Team LA, backed Tañia's concern about the post, adding to the criticism of Mo's tactic for turning the heat up on RI4A:

> Mo ... they wont ever say Dream Act as a stand alone just like we will never say Comprehensive Reform is the way to go ... To be honest we have all kinds of court hearings coming up in the next few weeks to also deal with and SO MUCH more that I don't intend on spending my time on pitiful language games or calling out strategies. I am fully committed to our campaign and I am deeply humbled by all the tears and sweat and time we all are devoting to this and I will always speak my mind, I will not just follow orders and I will constantly challenge our strategies in a productive way. I am sorry I had to be this harsh but I think that we need to lead by example and if we believe that some of the behind the scenes politics of RI4A has been shady and messed up than why repeat the same pattern?[76]

Neidi and Tañia's messages raised several different concerns: the questionable veracity of Schumer's claims, the needless burning of bridges with allies, and that with this Schumer action and the DreamACTivist.org post, a faction within the Noodles Team was following the same guilty path they charged RI4A of paving—deceit, misrepresentation of the voice of others, and undemocratic decision-making.

The divide opened by the Schumer action roughly mirrored the lines of the debate over the motives behind the private/secret strategy. It also reflected a split between those on Noodlesforo who believed that the support and resources of some of the allied nonprofits remained indispensable for success, and those who increasingly distrusted all the established nonprofits and believed that an independent strategy of bold and risky actions by undocumented youth could carry the day. For Tañia and others in IYJL, their close working relationship with ICIRR vindicated an approach that protected ties to some nonprofit organizations. For DreamACTivist.org radicals, who never cultivated ties with the "partner orgs," and for campus DREAMers burned by their connections to nonprofits, like the radicals at NYSYLC, no relationship with so-called allies was beyond the test of direct confrontation.

Lizbeth backed Mo in the dispute over the Schumer action. She rejected Tañia's suggestion that more care needed to be taken in the relationship with RI4A and its partner organizations:

> I don't think the goal is to necessarily get the campaign on our side but rather to get them to move out of the way. Asking nicely will not get us that. The only reason they are responding and giving us meetings and conference calls is because we have put them on the spot. RI4A will never come out in support of DREAM as a stand-alone bill.

Lizbeth, with fellow members of the Spicy Noodles, had just met with CHIRLA directors who made it "very clear that RI4A is shooting to pass CIR in the lame duck session. So no way will RI4A work for us." She shared minutes from the meeting. "Angelica [Salas] started by stating that CHIRLA does support the DREAM Act and that they were the first organization to recognize the importance of organizing youth even before the DREAM Act was called DREAM Act." She made it clear, however, that "RI4A's goal is to pass CIR during the lame duck session, but said that if DREAM hits the Senate floor first they will support it." The Spicy Noodles voiced their suspicion that CHIRLA and RI4A were actively working behind the scenes to block the advance the DREAM Act:

> When we expressed our concerns . . . they got a little angry and said that was not true and questioned us on who was saying this. We told them about our meetings in DC with key congressional leaders and [they] wrote down every single name we gave them. Angelica said that as youth we can't trust politicians, that they tell us one thing and tell others a completely different one.

Lizbeth described the CHIRLA directors as patronizing and incredulous:

> Angelica and Cynthia kept asking who was doing our legislative analysis for us. They asked whether NILC was doing it, asked about the Trail of Dreams and UWD. I don't think they believed us when we said that we are the ones doing the work, that we have access to these people and that we do it with

no funding. Several times during the meeting they asked who was behind us, not in a very direct way but they did.

Then the meeting got "personal." According to Lizbeth, "Angelica said that she was very hurt when the youth that CHIRLA had organized and 'trained' abandoned (yes, abandoned) the adults and the movement in a way":

> At that point both Neidi and I reacted. I said that I also feel hurt when I hear that we are being selfish and that we are not fighting for our parents. Neidi said that the conversation was going somewhere up until that point because the tone of it had become very paternalistic and it sounded very much like they were trying to lecture us.

It ended with Angelica reiterating that CHIRLA would continue its advocacy for CIR and with the Spicy Noodles responding that they will "hold accountable those who stand in the way" of a standalone DREAM Act. Lizbeth concluded her message with this observation: "I think they were expecting us to not know much about how the legislative process works and that's why they kept asking who has doing the analysis for us and who was behind us."[77]

Three days after the Schumer action, NYSYLC released an "open letter" on the event. It was a blistering attack on pro-immigrant politicians and nonprofits "playing with our futures":

> This past Thursday, the New York State Youth Leadership Council (NYSYLC) held a series of coordinated actions, which targeted Senator Charles Schumer (D-NY) for his inaction on the passage of the DREAM Act. The request of the group was simple: respond to the voices of immigrant youth who would highlight the benefits of the DREAM Act and most importantly, move forward immediately with the DREAM Act as a standalone bill.

Responding to the offensive claim from RI4A, as relayed by Schumer, that "they represent all immigrant communities and we only represent a small segment," the letter reminded the public who the undocumented youth supporting the DREAM Act are and where they come from:

> We understand that the trauma and struggles endured by our immigrant communities goes far beyond what the DREAM Act would fix. We

understand this because we live it. We live separated from loved ones, watch our parents work hard in poor, unsafe conditions for low wages, and fear the apprehension and deportation of our families daily. So if and when there is a proposal for reform of the immigration system that would address all of the issues that we, our families and our communities face, the New York State Youth Leadership Council would fully be in support and let it be known that we would be present then as we are now. Yet absent this real possibility, immigrant communities are united on this point: We all want the DREAM Act and we want it now!

The letter described in detail the action of June 10, concluding with the pivotal encounter with Schumer:

In perhaps the most controversial part of the conversation, the students were personally told by Senator Schumer, that he would not work to gain support for the DREAM Act as a stand-alone bill because the leaders of RI4A had asked him not to, and that the students were not included in the meeting that had taken place the previous day because RI4A refused to have them at the table.

Perhaps in response to the concerns raised by Tañia and Neidi, the letter stated that they could not "be certain whether Senator Schumer is accurately portraying the sentiment of the leaders of RI4A." It nonetheless defended going public with what he said:

We are also aware of statements that have been made after the fact by all the parties involved [in the meeting with RI4A]. However, we find it unacceptable that anger has been directed at us simply for disclosing the information we received, and we encourage those organizations who have made statements in this vein to reconsider their position and speak strongly in support of the Dream Act as a standalone bill, as well as ask Senator Schumer to be honest and forthright with immigrant communities.[78]

The letter's ultimate charge was irresistibly simple: "No more youth should suffer while politicians and special interest groups play with our futures."

The Noodles Team did not agree on the wisdom of disclosing the information gained from the Schumer action, but the effect of the public exposure quickly became undisputable. Mo described the exposure of the Schumer exchange as "the day we broke the campaign."⁷⁹ In reaction to the action and the DreamACTivist.org post, first Frank Sharry of America's Voice, and then Deepak Bhargava of CCC, felt compelled to make public that they backed a standalone DREAM Act. Ali Noorani, speaking for RI4A, circulated a more private message to immigration reform advocates conceding the same.⁸⁰

Forced by the strategic maneuvers of radical DREAMers to go public with their support of a standalone DREAM Act, these elites of immigration reform could not stop themselves from resorting to a tongue lashing of the meddling kids. Noorani's letter warned DREAMers that they were at "huge risk of being used by politicians." Bhargava's public response invoked the reified movement for immigration reform—referred to in FIRM's announcement just two weeks earlier as "our movement"—to try to discipline the unruly DREAMers.

Bhargava's letter responded directly to the DreamACTivist.org post. "I am moved to respond to the specific charges made against me in a recent blog post suggesting that CCC does not support the DREAM Act. I also want to make a larger point about movement ethics." Bhargava claimed that he told Senator Schumer in the June 9 meeting that FIRM and CCC supported "votes on the DREAM Act and AgJobs as separate measures to provide relief to students and farm workers" on the condition that "we can ensure the price of these important measures is not even *harsher* enforcement" and that politicians not give up on broader immigration reform. The letter then then turned to lecturing the youth who had accused him of trying to block the DREAM Act:

> It is also worth recalling some movement history; some of the *earliest* large events and actions in support of the DREAM Act were mounted by FIRM. We were for the DREAM Act before the DREAM Act was cool. Our support of this legislation, as well as for movement building strategies to empower young people in the movement, has been steadfast and unequivocal for many years. In addition to making this specific clarification, I wish to make the larger point that sectarianism is death to social justice movements. Though I believe that there is no underlying strategic disagreement in this case, those of us who share common values and principles may at times in fact have legitimate strategic differences about how to realize our goals. In such cases, movement ethics call us to seek out dialogue, listen well, assume good intent, fully understand each other's position and actively seek unity where it is possible, while maintaining the fabric of relationship when it is

not. We do not have the luxury of enmity with allies. Our commitment to these movement ethics is tested most profoundly when things are hard, and that is when our adherence to those ethics matters most.

Marisol's response on Noodlesforo was immediate and visceral: "Deepak's statement is disgusting and righteous and who the hell is he to talk about movement."[81] If the executive director of CCC thought this invocation of the history and normative orders of the movement would discipline these young undocumented activists, he badly misunderstood the moment. "The movement" could no longer be used as something to hold over and against them.

Deeds, not just words, confirmed the impact of the Schumer action. Five days after the sit-in, RI4A invited UWD to its decision-making table. Carlos Saavedra announced the invitation in a message to the UWD field:

> Finally, the United We Dream Network and NILC have been invited to be part of the management team of the Reform Immigration For America Campaign. The management team (MT) is the group of organizations that are the decision makers of the campaign, RI4A has invited us because of the pressure that they have been receiving since us (immigrant students) are not on the table for the decisions that affect our lives.[82]

Two days later, Carlos, along with Tolumo and Gaby Pacheco, attended a Senate leadership meeting with RI4A. On the same day of the meeting, Presente.org published a letter from the Trail of Dreams stating explicitly, for the first time, a demand for the immediate passage of the DREAM Act.[83] In a textbook example of the radical flank effect, as the actions of radical Noodles damaged the strategies of the CIR campaign, the leaders of the campaign made concessions but delivered them in a way that they hoped would empower the moderate leadership of UWD. It had the predictable effect of inflaming the divisions between DREAMers.

The day before this Senate leadership meeting with RI4A, the Noodles Team discussed how to hold the UWD leadership accountable for how they represented DREAMer interests. Distrust was high. Mo suggested a nonconfrontational approach on an upcoming UWD conference call:

> [T]he agenda on our end is, if after 30mins or so the [Senate leadership] meeting doesn't come up then someone will casually mention it in the context of, "and we understand there is a meeting happening tomorrow

where carlos you and trail will be attending, can we talk strategy about that meeting?" We think we need to avoid getting into a petty discussion of any sort, UWD has a lot of newer members that we need to continue to educate and work with and we don't want to turn them off in this context ... Us not being a part of this meeting tomorrow is not the end of it we think, kiran said zogby will call her with updates so we will get the info. The only part that we are iffy on is essentially how weak is the ask going to be from the peeps that are representing us.[84]

The Noodles did learn details from the meeting and not just from Zogby, but also from Craig Regelbrugge, Co-Chair of the Agriculture Coalition for Immigration Reform (ACIR). As an advocate for AgJOBs, Craig had a big interest in seeing the leading advocates of immigration reform pivot from CIR to piecemeal reform. He reported that RI4A was emphatic that it was time to pursue a piecemeal approach.[85] But the news from the meeting was not all good.

Zogby reported being disappointed because the senators were all over the place. Senator Menendez from New Jersey was still focused on CIR. Others backed DREAM but would not give up hope on CIR. Still others talked about attaching CIR to a Department of Defense bill. More hopeful was the suggestion by some of combining DREAM with AgJOBs. Reports from the meeting also mentioned that Menendez was quite angry about the inflammatory blogs being written by DREAMers.

The day after the Senate leadership meeting there was a regularly scheduled UWD "field" conference call. It provided a barometer of the competing pressures within the national DREAMer network halfway through the year. Mo sent an email to Noodlesforo with ideas about how to handle the conference call: "from noodles end of things we are going to just listen in, maybe not even announce we are there, to just hear what is said as to what happened. Not really interested in getting into it with anyone as we now have a big dc action to plan and worry about:)."[86] The message was the first mention on Noodlesforo of the next big action planned by the Noodles. Mo did not follow his own instructions for the call. Reports posted on Noodlesforo said it got out of hand. One post gave the following blow-by-blow:

> It was all going good but then Felipe [Matos] and Gaby started talking about how they reached out to Menendez staff and his staff said how upset he was about the blogs that were written. Especially the "white folks" comment.

So then there started a larger discussion about the movement. How dreamactivist are writing these blogs. Then Gaby said **"i'm not going to share these notes because you might blog it."** How Felipe is so hurt about the youth movement because it is not united anymore. Then Mo proposed to have a larger discussion about this at USSF [United States Social Forum] which he had already talked to Carlos about. Then everyone is like "no we need to have a talk about it now" Then they kept being like "you guys are not transparent, how do you expect UWD to be transparent?" blah blah blah. So then finally Mo says "This is bullshit and I'm getting off." Then Carlos gets off the call and so then Yahaira does damage control and says "let's have a meeting at USSF, for people who can't then we will have a call, I'll draft the email." Then someone says "We need to have a facilitator who is neutral."[87]

***

A month after the Arizona action, the success of the Noodles' escalating direct actions was hard to deny, even for the moderate DREAMers. RI4A was no longer blocking the DREAM Act. DREAMers were meeting directly with congressional leaders. And UWD leadership finally appeared ready to organize for a standalone DREAM Act. There was, however, no indication that the Senate or the House would put the DREAM Act up for a vote before the end of the summer. Elite allies were furious with the radical DREAMers' pressure tactics and possibly looking to cut these young undocumented activists down to size. The DREAMers themselves were divided between moderates and radicals, making united action going forward difficult, if not impossible. This division would grow deeper with the next action planned by the radicals for mid-July—an action they dubbed Noodles 2.0.

5
2010, Act II
Noodles 2.0

José Torres-Don, scratched from the DREAM 5, played a central role in Noodles 2.0. He did not take getting arrested lightly, but he felt he had little left to lose. José's college experience came to an end in the summer of 2010. He graduated with a Bachelor of Arts from the University of Texas at Austin, but his degree was meaningless in the US job market. His mom was suffering from kidney failure and could not get the necessary health care because of her immigration status. José was considering returning to Mexico with his mom, where he could legally work and she could receive medical treatment. As he considered saying goodbye to the only country he had ever really known, his fear of deportation diminished. Perhaps the most meaningful attachment jeopardized by his participation in Noodles 2.0 was his bond with ULI and its members. This campus organization—more than his course work and his social life—defined his college years in Austin. His one-year term as ULI president was coming to an end, but his love for the organization was not. The Noodles 2.0 action would sever his deep ties to the organization and its members. His painful falling out with ULI reflected a more general divide between undocumented youth activists—a divide that, by the end of the year, would split the UWD national network in two.[1]

José migrated with his family to Austin, TX, in 1991. He was four years old when he crossed the border, the youngest in a family of nine children. His family came from a small town in the Mexican state of San Luis Potosi. In an interview, he described his home, El Capulin, as "a ghost town" where "whenever you reach a certain age the route is for you to leave for the US." His family was following the same route as everybody else. His father "had been working in the US for a few years already, crossing back and forth working in Texas":

> Slowly, as my older siblings got older, they started to come. It started with one of my brothers and two of my sisters. They were in different places, 15

and 16 years old, doing domestic work, and my brothers are in construction work. It was my sister Juana, who when she came to the US, she has always, her personality has always been that she wants her family to be taken care of, she sent us stuff and messages, and she made the push that it was worth it to try to bring everyone to the US.... What surprises me is that it wasn't my father. It wasn't my dad. It wasn't my brother. It was this young girl cleaning houses.

José remembers almost nothing about his home in Mexico. He retains only hazy snippets of the way the roads looked and the dirt floor of the family house—the rest is lost to childhood amnesia. But he retains vivid, fragmented memories of the journey to the United States:

We were packing our stuff in trash bags. Putting them in the back of this old Ford truck that we had and off we went. That's the fragment I have . . . I remember just sort of going along with it. Thinking, well my mom is here, my parents they're here . . . But I definitely knew something was off, or something was wrong, that we weren't necessarily supposed to be doing this. It's the time when you, when the truck stops, and you need to get out, and it's time to run, and to go hide into a hill, and then when the guy tells us to duck when you see headlights coming from the distance . . . I felt that I'm okay, but I understood that not everything is put together for me. It sort of starts this thing within in me, that . . . my parents are the people who should take care of me and that I trust, [but they] aren't going to have everything taken care of . . . I was going to have to be grown-up. I was going to have to do things that my parents can't do. I lost that security.

The realization that parents do not control the world around them comes to all kids, one way or the other, but for José it came at such a young age and in one dramatic journey. The very moment José set foot in this country he sensed the precariousness of his situation and the limits of his parents' power to protect him. Just beyond the reach of childhood amnesia, he entered the United States and the shadow world of the undocumented immigrant, with his eyes wide open.

The family crossed into Texas near Brownsville. "But that was just the first crossing," José recounted. The "second crossing" of an internal checkpoint "was further north, at night, and scarier." This crossing remains burned into his earliest memories. It entailed walking miles through the dry brush country of South Texas to circumvent the border patrol checkpoints on the highways and byways headed north. He can remember being carried by his mom and her dropping him out of total exhaustion. "Her arms just gave way." As they walked to a designated point beyond these internal checkpoints where an uncle waited with a vehicle, the family came across another group of migrants. Among them was a woman, struggling. "To me, she sounded crazy, just sounded like someone who was not all there. Later, as I get older, when I keep remembering these things, I'm like 'mom who was that person?' and she explains to me that she and these two guys were lost and needed water." They were dehydrated and disoriented in the lethal South Texas wilderness.

After the crossing, the family settled in East Austin. They moved into a small house with their extended family. "It was entirely too many people in one house," José recalled. The family struggled to adjust to their new home. "We lived a slow-paced life in El Capulin and came to this place that, even though it is Austin and chill, it was definitely not the place that we were from. We were way over our heads." His older brothers joined their father in working construction. His older sisters worked cleaning houses with their mother. Once the family could afford it, they moved into their own house in the same neighborhood.

José and his youngest sister, Alicia, took a different path than their older siblings. They enrolled in their neighborhood elementary school, Ortega. "I liked school," José told me. "I was always very aware of where we came from [and that] I have just one job, to go to school." José said his classmates at Ortega "caught on really quick" that he was undocumented. "These kids were Chicanos, raised by Mexican grandparents, maybe, but they were second, third generation Chicanos. They look just like me, but there was this rejection. I was very scared and sensitive to it." The whole family was always acutely aware of the precariousness of being undocumented. "We didn't know anyone who got deported," José recalled, but "we knew there was no room for messing up. We kept quiet, learned how to fit in."

Alicia, two years older than José, excelled at school.[2] Success in class gained her admission to a summer camp funded by the Golfsmith Sunshine Foundation. José followed in her footsteps, working hard at school and joining the same camp. The Sunshine program guided the two siblings through their childhood education and into adolescence. During summers, the camp gave them an opportunity to leave home. During the academic year, it provided them with tutors to help with schoolwork. In time, they transitioned in the program from campers to counselors and from pupils to tutors. It provided them with a rare opportunity for undocumented kids: a job with responsibilities in a formal institutional setting.

Alicia and José both explained their fierce commitment to succeed at school as motivated by the lessons they learned from their older siblings and cousins. They wanted something different than a life of low-wage manual labor in the informal economy. Their oldest siblings joined this economy as soon as they arrived in Austin. Their slightly younger siblings received some education, enrolling in middle school and high school, but soon they, too, joined the informal economy, cutting their education short. José and Alicia appreciated the privilege handed to them as the youngest in their large family, and they seized it.

Upon completing her elementary education at Ortega, Alicia was admitted to Austin's highly competitive magnate program at Kealing Middle School. José followed her to Kealing two years later. After middle school, both gained acceptance to the Liberal Arts and Science Academy (LASA)—one of the most prestigious public high schools in Texas. With no role models, save for the mentors at Sunshine, José and Alicia followed the educational route of Austin's upper-middle-class, liberal elites.

"Kealing was a hot mess of a school," José told me in our interview. "Seventh grade sucked. I was very closed off to white folks, to white kids." Looking back, José said Kealing's teachers and administrators did not know how to handle "this brown boy from a completely different background than the rest of his classmates." He felt unsupported and unwelcomed. He turned resentful and started "to act out." "I was a bully at some point to some kids. I did not like myself. I was a little lost." He quickly learned that "when you are a brown kid the [academic] expectations are very low, and when you mess up there is no forgiveness." While feeling alienated at school, at home one of his older brothers was constantly chiding him: "Don't deny who you are." He would always say, "you're Mexican," José recalled. "He had this nationalism, that I didn't really understand, but he impressed it upon [me]." José was introduced at an early age to the emotional politics of racial, class, and national distinction in the United States.

José is a harsh judge of his younger self. He holds himself to high standards of comportment. Abruptly, in the middle of his first semester at Kealing, the one teacher he liked took leave and was replaced by a substitute. "We were really mean to this substitute," he remembered. An incident, involving a "nasty" and "inappropriate letter," addressed to the substitute and penned by José and a few fellow students, led to his dismissal from the school. José was not proud of the actions that got him in trouble, but he felt "underestimated" and "profiled" by the school administrators. When the principal was deciding how to punish him for his part in the letter incident, José remembered that he looked at his grades, thinking they would reflect that he was not a good fit with the magnet program, and remarked with surprise, "wow, you have really good grades." José felt terribly guilty that his mom was forced to come to school and meet with administrators as they decided his fate. He had dragged her into a strange world she did not know how to navigate and had shaken her confidence that he was a good child.

José was forced to move to a neighborhood middle school to finish seventh grade. His classmates at the school included several undocumented immigrants. He excelled. He impressed his teachers. He was even appointed "principal for the day" in recognition of his accomplishments. José could have stayed and graduated from the new school. He had classmates he could identify with and institutional affirmation from teachers and administrators, but he was not satisfied with the academics. The teachers at this new school "taught to the test." The work was easy and uninspiring. He also felt he had a score to settle at Kealing. He wanted to prove that "the kid they had kicked out was not me." He reapplied to Kealing and was readmitted. He recounted with satisfaction the surprise of teachers and administrators when they saw him walking the halls of the school once again.

José successfully completed middle school at Kealing and followed Alicia to LASA. In high school, it was Alicia who ran into trouble. Describing his older sister, José told me, "She doesn't step down from other people. Sometimes she rubs people the wrong way. They think she's an asshole, but she's not." She got into a series of fights with other students, and her mom decided to take her out of the magnate program and enrolled her in Anderson High.[3] (The same school the Garibay sisters had attended). José, in contrast, thrived academically and socially at LASA. He fully expected to go to college. The only question was where? HB 1403 had been in place for almost six years. Alicia, who had gone to a meeting run by Alejandra Rincón, figured out she could attend Texas state schools and was admitted to Stephen F. Austin State University. "So that made it very easy for me," José said. "Note to self, Alicia is going to college, I can too." Every student at LASA goes on to college, but the guidance and college counselors had no experience with advising undocumented students. "I would go to my counselors, and they were like I never had this problem before."

One day in the fall of his senior year, José was pulled out of class to meet with a district counselor, Angie Orosco, to talk about college. He thought, at first, "oh, these are the dynamics at LASA, right, I'm like brown, so they're taking me to talk to her." When he got to the office "there were a couple of other kids there." His friend Rosa was there. "And we're all undocumented, so it turns out." José remembered they were all surprised. "We were like 'I didn't know you were undocumented.'" Angie Orosco explained to the students how to apply to state schools under HB 1403.[4] Rosa applied to go to the University of Texas at Austin, but José wanted to get away from home. If he stayed in Austin, he would most likely have to live at home. Living at home promised to be chaotic and distracting. His mom never learned to drive but José learned to drive at fourteen. He was never going to have a license to drive, so there was no need to wait until he was of legal age. If his mom needed to go to the supermarket or to the doctors, it often fell on him to drive her. In Austin there was not just his large family, but also a much larger network of extended family and friends. His mom was the hub of this extensive network. She took in anyone who was in need. He knew that if he stayed at home his energies would be taxed by the many responsibilities always swirling around his house. "I wanted to get out of Austin. I wanted the full college experience." He decided to enroll in Texas Tech University in Lubbock.

José had a friend, Michael, from LASA already attending Texas Tech, but he did not fully anticipate how different his life would be in this large, state university hundreds of miles from home. "I had never been outside of a 30 miles radius of Austin." His parents and older siblings were afraid to drive him to Lubbock. He asked a mentor from the Golfsmith Sunshine Foundation program to drive him. José credits Texas Tech with politicizing him. "I was there long enough to get pissed off." In Austin, José bridged the worlds of his immigrant community and what he describes as "hippie Austin," but "when I get to Lubbock and see these white chicks with hair extensions, I was like how does this happen? Culturally, it was a shock. I was more used to girls in Austin being more relaxed and chill about looks, but there it's game on."

He struggled through his first semester. His academic counselor at Texas Tech was less than supportive and groused at the extra paperwork he had to do because José was an HB 1403 student. He commented more than once that HB 1403 was likely to be repealed, so José better think of a "plan B." José kept in contact with Rosa, who was fairing much better at UT-Austin. She told him about the work ULI was doing, both at the state-level to block legislation to repeal HB 1403 and at the national-level to support the DREAM Act. From Lubbock, José followed ULI's work through the organization's group emails and volunteered on its campaigns, making phone calls to state and national representatives. He decided early in this first year at Texas Tech to apply for a transfer to UT-Austin. "It was the best decision I ever made."

The following academic year he was back in Austin, living at home and taking classes at UT. He immediately became an active member of ULI. Reflecting on his college years, José said, "if anything I dedicated too much time to ULI." During the summer between his sophomore and junior year, he went to New Orleans to help in the recovery work from hurricane Katrina with the same Sunshine program that had been a fixture of his childhood. On that trip, he met a fellow UT student who lived in a housing cooperative just off campus. At the start of the fall of his second year at UT, he moved into the Taos co-operative. He loved it. He met international students, politically active anarchists, and other varieties of leftist students. The co-op had its own kind of madness, with young undergraduates binging on alcohol and drugs as they struggled with their new-found freedom from home, but it became his sanctuary from a chaotic family life at home.

At ULI, José learned at the feet of Rebecca Acuña and Julieta and Montserrat Garibay. He was deeply impressed by them and their work. "Rebecca was writing the talking points. She was super smart." José described ULI as a very cautious and conservative organization. "There were elected positions at ULI, but there was also an executive committee." This committee did not change year-to-year, which enabled Julieta and Rebecca to retain leadership even as younger cohorts of students came up through the ranks. Under the counsel of this committee, ULI did not associate or try to build alliances with radical student groups on campus. José was drawn to some of these groups, groups like !ella pelea!, an organization with a mission to advocate for "the demands of women, queer folks and people of color in our fight against budget cuts and the privatization of public education at the University of Texas Austin." But the members of ULI resisted building alliances or working with them.[5]

In 2009, at the end of his junior year, José was tapped to become president of the student organization. That summer, as the newly elected leader of ULI, under the wing of Julieta and Rebecca, he was introduced to national organizing at UWD. In June, he accompanied Julieta to the RI4A rollout in Washington and attended the UWD planning session timed with the event. He attended the DREAM graduation that summer as well, and in July, he and

Rebecca represented ULI at the UWD organizational meeting in New York City where the national network struggled to formalize its structure. He knew nothing about the emerging divide within UWD, but he was impressed by the political savvy of representatives from NYSYLC and their radicalism: "Kids get politicized in New York much quicker." Mo and Prerna skipped most of the NYC meeting, choosing instead to focus their attention on END cases. Their absence probably delayed the inevitable showdown between the increasingly radicalized José and his more conservative ULI mentors.

In the fall of 2009, as he assumed the responsibilities of president of ULI, national DREAMer activism was heating up. UWD was expanding in membership and resources. During the winter intersession, he traveled to the UWD convening in Minneapolis, MN, where he got his first introduction to the growing split between moderates and radicals. He recalled, in our interview, that the Chicago group, IYJL, advocated for a national strategy of "coming out" events and Julieta pushed back, arguing that the strategy was too radical for places like Texas. He met Mo for the first time. He was immediately drawn to Mo's quiet confidence and to the circle of "bad asses" around him. "Mo was very out with his sexuality," José recalled. José is also gay but at the time he was not out. Only a few friends knew. His sister Alicia knew, but the rest of his family did not. He was not out to his fellow members at ULI. "I remember Julieta once asked me [if I was gay], but she had been drinking, so I did not answer her."

José was drawn to the radical vision Mo put forth at Minneapolis, but he knew ULI would resist following the path advocated by the DREAMers from DreamACTivist.org, IYJL, and NYSYLC. He left Minneapolis thinking about ways he might work to support the more radical agenda coming from these DREAMers outside of Texas. And then, early in the spring semester, Mo called him: "Hey, I have a question for you, do you want to get arrested?" Reflecting on Mo's life-altering call, José said, "I think his strategy is to say the most crazy random stuff" just to test how far people are willing to go. "He tells me to think about it."

The call came at a difficult time. José's mom was in declining health, suffering from kidney failure. Alicia was running her to the emergency room at the city hospital whenever she was in critical need of dialysis. José said the ER doctors were telling Alicia "you guys can't keep doing this":

> She may have to go back to Mexico, and I'm getting alienated from ULI. What's the worst that can happen if I do this civil disobedience? The best that can happen is that it works and we push for the DREAM Act and it

passes ... [The] worst that can happen is that I get deported. I will already have my degree and I'll take my mom.

José said yes to Mo and suddenly found himself connected to an expanding network of radical DREAMers extending from California to Missouri, Illinois, Michigan, Florida, and New York. Slated to participate in the McCain action, the Noodles Team decided about a month before the action that community support in Texas through ULI was too weak and they scratched José from the action. But, in June, as the Noodles prepared for a larger action in Washington, DC, José got a second chance, and he took it.

(Und)Occupy the Capitol

Before the mid-June Senate leadership meeting that included UWD representatives Carlos Saavedra and Gaby Pacheco, the Noodles Team's plan for a "big DC action" was already underway. The Noodles Team was advocating more confrontational actions—led by Mo, Lizbeth, and radicals at NYSYLC— and were convinced that they had to make politicians feel the urgency of the moment with a display of the risks DREAMers were willing to take to push a vote for the DREAM Act. Under the subject line "CONFIDENTIAL," Mo described the proposed action in a June 17 message to Noodlesforo:

> Three days of action in DC. The vision for this is essentially having a few days we can coin as "occupation of DC" internally and something else more PC externally. The thinking being or the image we have in our heads is essentially having ... dreamers be all over capitol hill for a few days, dressed in full costume [i.e., graduation cap and gowns]. Everywhere reps go they see dreamers. Day 1 will be something timid, a mock graduation and lobby visits with threats of CD or escalation. Day 2 will be CD possibly with 20 or more dreamers (we have to begin prepping peeps for this now) and day 3 will be nothing but lobbying, but each office will be freaked out by seeing a dreamie in uniform walking around.

Mo added that this "is something i ran by carlos (uwd) a week or so ago and he was down for it so it is something we can get larger buy-in for sure. We just have to craft it."[6]

Carlos's blessing for the action suggested a momentary coming together of moderate and radical DREAMers on strategy. Divisions were still raw, but both sides needed each other at this moment. With RI4A and FIRM now acknowledging that CIR was dead, the moderates—led by Carlos, Gaby, Julieta, and a few others at the helm of UWD—recognized that they faced a real opportunity to pass the DREAM Act. And they could not deny that the confrontational actions of the "The Dream Is Coming" group had made this opportunity possible. Julieta, looking back on the events of the summer, said in our interview: "I think the civil disobedience actions, they helped a lot, they pushed the vote." These leaders also appreciated that radicals held considerable influence across the national network of DREAMers, possibly even enough to seize control at the next UWD convening in the fall. Julieta felt the influence of the radicals firsthand. José, the president of the campus organization she built, had become a core member of the Noodles Team.

With the DREAM Act now regularly in the news, scores of undocumented youth were, almost daily, learning about the UWD and joining the network. The Noodles Team agreed that mobilizing this growing support through UWD was essential for their last-ditch push to pass the DREAM Act. It was in their interest to work through UWD and not tear it apart. And in the early days of preparation for the DC action, the divide within UWD appeared to be healing. The radicals returned to a similarly central place within UWD that they held exactly a year earlier when they had organized the Dream Graduation. UWD's moderate leaders signaled a willingness to let them organize, in the network's name, a large action of civil disobedience to pressure Senate leadership. Their strategy of escalation appeared vindicated and was now officially sanctioned.

This coming together did not last long. In late June, as the Noodles Team planned for an official UWD conference call to talk about the Washington, DC, action, conflict reappeared along the established fault lines. Julieta Garibay reacted angrily when she found out—at a late hour and indirectly—about the "official" UWD conference call. In an email to the UWD field, she complained that the announcement for the conference call was not distributed widely enough. She asked pointedly, "To keep clarity and accountability with each other . . . is this another effort outside United We DREAM?!?" Mo brushed off her complaint about accountability, writing in response on Noodlesforo, "Nope all good. I cleared call with carlos, as well as national action, last week."[7] But all was not good.

Two days after the conference call, Mo forwarded a message from Carlos to Noodlesforo with this belittling preface: "And the saga of hurt egos continues." Carlos's message echoed Deepak Bhargava's admonishment to heed the movement ethic of avoiding sectarianism, but he added the imperative of DREAMers taking care of each other:

> Last week, we . . . encountered tensions between some United We Dream groups. In our last couple of calls the atmosphere on the phone line has been tense and thick, and many things have been said. It is okay to have differences of opinion/strategy/etc. It is okay to debate it, to challenge each other, to let each other be influenced by others in order to create a better world . . . But we at the end of the day—we either fight together or not. I think that for us in order to move forward we need transparency, accountability, leadership and most importantly responsibility . . . We have a lot of work ahead of us, we have a country to change, a base to keep energized and most importantly we have to take care of ourselves.[8]

Carlos was right to worry. Care for each other, and for self, became a casualty to the pressures of the Noodles' campaign of escalation and the conflict between DREAMers that flowed from it. As organizing raced on through the summer, the emotional toll on many activists was high.

Lingering bad feelings over past actions and real disagreements over future strategies quickly unraveled the tenuous agreement between moderates and radicals. The two sides headed into the July Washington, DC, action as divided as ever. The moderates refused to support the Noodles 2.0 proposal. They organized instead a more symbolic action aimed at President Obama. This alternative action included a teach-in called "DREAM University" and a coming-out rally in Lafayette Square in front of the White House. The radicals pushed forward with their plan for acts of civil disobedience in the offices of Senate leaders.[9]

The radicals' (und)occupy[10] action followed the template of the Tucson sit-in. "Just as in the original Noodles action," Flavia explained on the forum, "we want people to coordinate and work with their local media on a state by state basis. So if we have a CDer from KC, there should be a KC media coordinator."[11] On the first of July, Mo informed the group that the Dream Is Coming website was "updated with a dc based ticker. Let's build the buzz!"[12] They set a target of twenty arrested DREAMers for Noodles 2.0. They had started distributing civil disobedience toolkits and doing intakes of prospective participants back in early June, but they worried they might not have enough volunteers for the high-risk action. Mo sent out a call on the Fourth of July for more Noodles:

> We need some potential noodles asap. We have 20 signed up now but some are for sure going to drop off. We need to get more feelers out there and get some interested peeps to sign up. Based on turn out and the legal call today we might have to extremely alter our CD strategy, so if you have anyone that might be interested now is the time to get them registered on the intake form.[13]

Worries about the number of participants turned to concerns about a lack of funds. Twelve days before the action, Mo posted on the forum an urgent call for money. "Just wanted to send a reminder/heads up that we are in dire need of funds for the DC action. We might not be able to even use all the noodles we have available as we don't know if they can physically get to D.C., so if you are doing local fundraising please remember we need to fund this collective action as well!"[14]

Local groups came through with the resources for the travel of twenty-one DREAMers slated to be arrested, as well as for scores of supporters. The California contingent, organized by the Spicy Noodles, made a road trip across the country. They dubbed the trip the "CA DREAM freedom ride." The press release for the ride read: "*15 DREAMERs will travel for 15 days, through 15 states, and over 5,000 miles* from Los Angeles, CA, to Washington, DC, and back, to join the mass mobilization of students that will take part in the three national days of action in DC."[15] Other groups from Arizona, Texas, Illinois, and from states along the east coast made similar road trips. As hundreds of DREAMers from across the nation arrived in Washington, DC, many learned for the first time that the action had split into two distinct strategies, overlapping only with the shared DREAM Graduation. They were forced to choose sides or to try to bridge the divide.

José reached across the divide and invited Julieta Garibay to join him at the last planning meeting for the (und)occupy action. In our interview, José described the scene when Julieta came to the meeting:

> Until the very, like the day before, two days before, I told Julieta. And I was like Julieta I'm going to do this. We were already in DC. She even came with me to a prep meeting. You could already tell that the tension was, was

[laughing nervously], there was a lot of tension. People were like looking at her. And I did not understand. I was like, if I would have known, I wouldn't have invited her. It was just an uncomfortable moment. But it was from both sides.

José knew very well that there was a divide, but only at that meeting did he grasp how acrimonious it was.

The tension between Julieta and Mo, in particular, was palpable. It could not entirely be explained by their disagreement over how to resolve a classic strategic dilemma: Whether to play "naughty or nice" with their allies and politicians?[16] It had a deeper source. Mo believed Julieta represented the DREAMers who acquiesced to the leaders of "the big orgs" and their prescription of the proper role of undocumented youth in the politics of immigration reform. She was accomplished, professional, and, in his eyes, desperate to win the affirmation of these allies. She believed the organized actions of DREAMers should conform to behavior that would win and secure this affirmation. She thought all paths to legalization ran through the political leadership of these allies. In turn, Julieta believed Mo inspired a dangerous current among undocumented youth that threatened to undermine the safe spaces and protective alliances she and other DREAMers had worked so hard to build. Julieta had come to believe that Mo was ruled by the resentment he felt for any dependency on allies. He was willing to risk the futures of undocumented youth to prove DREAMer independence and to settle scores. Anger and a desire for revenge motivated his strategies. At this last preparation meeting before he was to be arrested, with Mo and Julieta in the same tension-filled room, José started to fathom the emotional depth of the moderate-radical divide. Like choosing between warring gods or ultimate values, there seemed no way to adjudicate between the very different visions of the road forward imagined by Mo and Julieta.

The day of action began with the annual DREAM Graduation at a church. Hundreds of undocumented immigrants in caps and gowns attended, with the moderates, the radicals, and the undeclared or unaware, under one roof. Just hours before the graduation, the DreamACTivist.org server went down. It did not return to full running capacity until after the events of the day. I asked many of the DREAMers I interviewed what caused the website to go down at this critical moment? Was it too much traffic? Was it hacked? I heard many conflicting accounts, including the rumor that someone within DreamACTitivist.org brought the server down on purpose.

It caused considerable confusion for the organizers of the Noodles 2.0 action. The email addresses given to their press contacts were all part of the DreamACTivist.org domain. Organizers improvised a work around and the action went forward.

According to David Bennion's blog of the day's events, after the graduation ceremony ended, twenty-one Noodles "fanned out to the offices of Senators Feinstein (D-CA), Reid (D-NV), McCain (R-AZ), Menendez (D-NJ), and Schumer (D-NY), where they began peaceful sit-ins." After short "lobbying" visits, the DREAMers from the offices of Menendez, Feinstein, and Schumer gathered in the atrium of the Hart Senate Building. There they sat down in their caps and gowns in a circle facing outward. Spread out at the center of the circle was a colorful banner that read, "Undocumented and Unafraid | DREAM Act NOW." Capitol Police quickly arrested the twelve DREAMers in the atrium. The four DREAMers in McCain's office and the five in Reid's office continued their sit-ins and waited to be arrested.[17]

In our interview, José described what happened in Reid's office. He entered the waiting room with four other DREAMers—Erika, Isabel, Nico, and Laura. Dressed in caps and gowns, they attracted a crowd of onlookers. "We take a seat. And then, we go around telling our stories, as people are crying on one end, and on another end, they are pissed off. They are trying to convince us to get up, that we are going to be arrested." Brent Wilkes, the head of LULAC's Policy and Development office in Washington, DC, was there trying to get them to call off the sit-in was. José said he thinks Julieta may have sent Brent to try to talk him out of getting arrested. Brent called Representative Luis Gutiérrez on his mobile phone and got him to speak to the group to try to convince them to call off the action. Mo and Kiran were coming in and out of the office in their efforts to coordinate the ongoing sit-ins in different parts of the building. When Brent put Gutiérrez on speakerphone, José said, "Mo saw it as a golden opportunity" and started recording the exchange on his phone. "We had no idea Brent would put Gutiérrez on the phone," he recalled. "It was a happy accident." I asked him why it was happy:

> Because we'd been screwed over by this guy in private meetings and nobody has been able to call him out, fully. And there's an opportunity there, where he sort of just loses it. He's just like, well, you guys are adults now. And, you know what to do. Oh, so now we are on our own? But better to know for real than like not.

Brent and Representative Gutiérrez did not know the conversation was being recorded.

The recording preserves a rare glimpse of radical DREAMers defying a powerful ally. It is transcribed here it in its entirety. The recording begins just as Brent puts Gutierrez on the speakerphone. He extends the phone to place it in the middle of the group sitting on the floor, and asks, "Can you hear us?" Gutiérrez replies, "I, I, I can, but . . ." He pauses, very briefly, and says, "What is the goal?"

ISABEL: To get the DREAM Act passed as soon as possible.
GUTIÉRREZ: Okay.
 [The word is drawn out. He pauses, then continues]
GUTIÉRREZ: And so, for you guys to walk away from there, what has to happen?
ISABEL: The DREAM Act has to be passed. They need to put it up for a vote and passed.
ERIKA: We know that Senator Reid has the power to put the DREAM Act in to a vote, so we are not gonna, we're gonna sit here until we make sure that he actually does that.
G: That he actually does what exactly? That he actually puts on the schedule a vote for the DREAM Act?
 Multiple DREAMers speak at once: Yes. Puts it. Yes, correct.
 [The DREAMers sound nervous as they try to find their footing under Gutiérrez's direct questioning.]
GUTIÉRREZ: What if it fails?
ISABEL: Well, we'll keep fighting for it. I mean you know one of the aids here for Mr. Reid said that a week ago this bill failed, or something, and they put it up a week later and it passed. So, we can do the same for the DREAM Act. I mean . . .
G: Ok, so . . .
ISABEL: We have to take a risk. La vida es un riesgo. Life is a risk.
G: Alright, hey, you know something, you guys are all adults. You know exactly what you are doing. And, you know, I wish the best for you.
ISABEL: Listen, uh . . .
NICO: We have Erika from Arizona. We have Laura from California. We have José from Texas. We have Isabel from Virginia, and myself from Illinois. We are from all over. We came here because this is our common goal. Youth and students from around the nation are tired of waiting for all

these, you guys just keep debating, and you guys pointing fingers, and it's the Republicans and it's, and, you know we need action. We're tired of the debates. It's time to act. We are tired of waiting. We've been undocumented for, I've been undocumented for 18 years. We have people here for 10 years, 19 years, since they were one year old. Like, we need this to happen now. And that is what we wanted to make clear when we had the rally outside your office.

G: I'm ready to get comprehensive immigration reform enacted which includes the DREAM Act. I think you all know. I mean listen, the last time we were in Washington, DREAMers came, we said we'd take their place on the line, uh, as people who would get arrested. Next time I get arrested, I suspect that that may happen, given the [inaudible], so I understand it. I understand your frustration.

BRENT WILKES: [off camera in the background] And I'm willing to take your place here to get arrested today for you.

G: I understand ... the anger and the frustration that exists with the ongoing wait and wait. I empathize and I share that with you. But I think there is movement in the Senate, number one. And I'm not quite sure your getting arrested and, um, um, and possibly deported, actually advances this. Now that's why the last time in front of the White House I got arrested along with others and the DREAMers came and left their shoes that they had walked in, um, symbolically there. And um ...

NICO: But nothing really happened that day, nothing happened, and to this day nothing has happened. And you know, Luis Gutiérrez, that's what we're trying to get across. Like we are trying to get across that we are, we have been waiting, and you guys, we keep waiting for you guys, you keep pushing the deadlines back. You guys keep, you are working in the background. And now, there's, we're ready to stand up for ourselves as undocumented youth and students. We are standing up for our communities and our families.

G: I haven't pushed a single deadline back. The president of the United States scolded me. I mean, my colleagues say I should not be out there doing what I'm doing. Don't you guys read the papers? I get criticized by Democrats!

ISABEL: We do, we appreciate. Representative, we do, and we appreciate that you support CIR, but we all know that's not gonna happen this year. And if the DREAM Act has a chance and it could be a first step to CIR, you know, let's do this [speaking through interruptions by Gutiérrez].

G: And you know, if it has a chance, it will pass.

ISABEL: And we believe with all our hearts it does have a chance and that if you all put it up for a vote that it will pass. And after that we will fight along with you for CIR, but first we need the DREAM Act. We have the bill 1749 29 uh, S729 as well. I mean I'm just so frustrated, I'm sorry but...

G: Ok, but let me finish, let me finish. Listen, I'm not your enemy.

GROUP: We know that.

G: I will continue to get people to understand the DREAM Act, to understand. And I have told people, and I met with DREAMers last week in Washington, DC, I invited all of the members of the Hispanic Congressional Caucus to come and meet. And about three of them actually said we cannot argue for it. It cannot pass in the Senate. What does that say for the rest of us? What does that say for the rest of the movement and frustration and the kinds of divisions that will cause? So, I have said, and we've made this very clear to anyone from the DREAM sponsors, if the bill comes up, uh, and if it is what we can do, and we will know if it is all we can do, then I say pass it. [Pause] We disagree with you in terms of your analysis of the present moment. You feel it can pass and that the rest will never pass. We don't believe that. We still believe, we believe that by saying that...

NICO: We're not saying it will never pass.

G: You weaken the possibility of the totality of it passing. Every time someone says the whole thing cannot pass, only part of it, it weakens us, it divides us, it confuses us, it scatters us all over the place. Uh, we once had a united movement for comprehensive immigration reform. Now we don't have a united movement, and that is causing, that is detrimental to the movement for all of us. I know women who have been in this country 25, 30 years waiting for comprehensive reform. Families are being divided every day, a thousand deportations every day, you know that and I know that.

MO: Congressman Gutiérrez, Congressman Gutiérrez...

G: We have to fight and work for all of them.

NICO: Let the youth speak, please.

MO: Congressman Gutiérrez, Congressman Gutiérrez, my name is Mohammad, I was one of the youth that was in the sit-in in Senator McCain's office, on May 17 in Arizona, as a result I've been placed in deportation proceedings, so for you to sit here and talk to these five, six youth that are sitting in this office, and to put them down, and to constantly tell them instead of supporting them, is a shame. You need to stand up for this community, this is going to continue to happen, and you need to be their ally.

G: You made this decision to do this as adults, to take this kind of actions, as adults.

NICO: Because nothing has happened.

G: As a member of this movement, as someone who has been involved in it from day one, from day one, I disagree, and if you disagree, you cannot, you cannot...

[Recording cuts off][18]

Mo posted to Noodlesforo immediately after the exchange that Gutiérrez "totally went out of his way to blame us for all the failures of cir and the movement." He called Gutiérrez's performance "shameful"[19] and uploaded his video to DreamACTivist.org, posted under the title "Rep. Gutiérrez talking down to youth and DREAM Act—Will CHC support DREAM?"

It is doubtful there is anything Gutiérrez could have said or a particular tone he could have struck that would have convinced the group to stop the action. The five of them were by that time a fused group with a collective resolve to get arrested. The now familiar charge that radical DREAMers were dividing and weakening the movement had no effect on them. Raising the possibility of deportation was another matter.

I asked José what he thought at the time about the risk of getting arrested. He said he feared he could be deported, and he suffered moments of doubt about the action even as it unfolded. Sitting on the floor of Reid's waiting room, he was surrounded by professed allies who, at turns, were offering to take his place and belittling him for the foolishness of a misguided strategy. "These people were pissed off," José recalled. "Durbin was completely turned off by [us]." Senator Durbin, the long-time champion of the DREAM Act, told reporters during the action that the DREAMers had "crossed the line from passionate advocacy to inappropriate behavior".[20]

> Durbin released a statement like immediately, saying ... what's happening right now is completely unacceptable. This is not the way things are done. And basically, sort of saying like the DREAM Act is dead. We are still doing the sit-in at that point! Shit, like, what, what did we just do?! [Laughing] And then, you know, Nico from Chicago says, "No, he has to say that. We

are gonna still sit here." And then it goes back to the group of us saying, "We are going to do this no matter what."

José described how the collective action itself generated a feeling of solidarity and power that ultimately dispelled these fears of deportation and niggling doubts about tactics and strategies:

> I'm with these people and it's an amazing sort of [long pause]. I mean it changes you once you are in such a vulnerable space. You are willing to do this, and it's sort of like, you can say, it will be the end of your stay in this country, and the life that you built, and, uh, . . . and *winning*! I was very afraid, but I also knew that I was with really amazing people, and that if this is the way that it is going to happen? I was like this is good. This is it!

For José, getting arrested was a moment of triumph. It triggered an emotional release, a liberating rupture from years of being told what he could not do because he was undocumented:

> As we were getting arrested, Isabel, you know, in Spanish, is [telling us] hold your head high. And it was an important moment to walk out of that building having your head held high and knowing that you had done the right thing.

In describing Isabel's defiant instruction to show pride as the police frog marched them out of the Capitol, José notably recalled that she delivered it in Spanish.

Sitting in a police wagon in handcuffs, doubt crept back in again: "What the hell did I just do?" But this doubt did not prevail. For José, the Noodles 2.0 action marked a transformative moment in his life as an undocumented immigrant and as a DREAMer. He was not alone in this. The Noodles actions, both 1.0 and 2.0, changed the collective identity of the DREAMer. The Noodle, the undocumented youth activist, willing to risk arrest to challenge allies, authorities, and institutions created a new kind of DREAMer. One who no longer sought to prove their worthiness by being all-American, by always playing by the rules, and by winning the affirmation of authorities and powerful allies. This new DREAMer was unapologetic for being undocumented and not afraid to talk back to authorities. They looked to fellow undocumented immigrants, not allies, for security. They found security in the power and solidarity of their defiant collective action.[21]

A few hours after the arrest of the last of the twenty-one DREAMers, Neidi reported the release of ten of the Noodles. She said the rest "will most likely be released today as well."[22] Seven more were released later that evening. Four were held overnight and released after being arraigned in court. Despite initial condemnations of the action from political allies, the Washington, DC, occupation was followed by surprising and sudden movement in the Senate.

The week after the action Senator Reid announced that the way forward for comprehensive reform was blocked and it was time to push more viable piecemeal alternatives, specifically mentioning the DREAM Act. A July 28 *Roll Call* article reported that not all Democrats were onboard:

> Rep. Luis Gutiérrez, the Illinois Democrat who chairs the Immigration Task Force for the Congressional Hispanic Caucus, said he will continue to press for passage of comprehensive immigration reform instead of "settling" on its components, although he said somewhat sarcastically that he understands why Reid may be pivoting to the DREAM Act. Reid has "like 10 kids who are going to get arrested in his office" if the DREAM Act does not pass, Gutiérrez said. "And he's got his election in Nevada. I mean put all of this in context."[23]

Gutiérrez's criticism and explanation of Reid's pivot confirmed that (und)occupy DC had worked as planned. Noodles 2.0 succeeded in driving a wedge between Gutiérrez and Senate leadership, and this gave Reid the opening to shift the legislative agenda from CIR to the DREAM Act and other piecemeal bills.

Reid's new openness to pursue narrower legislation did not end resistance from CIR advocates in Congress. Kiran told Noodlesforo that aids from the offices of Durbin and Reid were "concerned about CHC/Gutiérrez causing problems for Dream even if we have the votes." On the same thread, Lizbeth reported that "Speaker Pelosi said today at Netroots—that the CHC does not want dream to move as stand alone but as part of CIR."[24] The Noodles Team debated how the Gutiérrez video could be used as leverage. José was under great pressure to take the video down. It was ULI's connection with LULAC's Brent Wilkes that led to the Gutiérrez call. José forwarded to Noodlesforo a message from Wilkes saying that LULAC was forced to suspend all support of DREAMers unless the video was taken down:

> Unfortunately, we are in serious trouble with the Congressional Hispanic Caucus over a video that was posted on YouTube under the heading Rep. Gutiérrez Puts Down DREAM Act. I called Congressman Gutiérrez on his cell phone and I put him on speaker with the students in Senator Reid's office which included Jose Torres because I was misinformed that he might be able to talk them out of getting arrested. The Congressman is livid and is blaming LULAC because he did not agree to have the phone conversation recorded. The students have refused to take down the video even after I spoke to Jose and Mohammad personally and asked them to remove it. There was a big meeting with the Congressional Hispanic Caucus today and this was topic number one. Our reputation is being seriously damaged by this video and the students refuse to help us. Consequently we are not in a position to help you at this time nor will we be able to assist the DREAM Act students any further until this matter gets resolved. I am sorry that your group is being impacted by this but we really have to back away from assisting anyone involved with the DREAM Act at this time because of these students' refusal to take down the video. I am afraid the DREAMERs are losing a lot of support in Congress and they have made a serious tactical blunder, but I guess they will have to learn the hard way.[25]

The consensus on Noodlesforo was that making the video public was a breakthrough, not a blunder. Confrontational tactics were working. There was no reason to take the heat off.

David Bennion detailed on Noodlesforo what they were learning, on the fly, from the reactions of politicians to their confrontational tactics. "U should not be afraid to pick fights w allies like Gutiérrez, u will always win, he knows that, it's why he tried to get LULAC to threaten to sue." He added:

> If you're worried about damaging relationships with Guti, just remember how good the relationship is right now with Reid and how shitty it was 9 days ago. There are five very good reasons why that change happened, and their names are Isabel, Nico, Laura, Erika, and José.

David concluded with two suggestions of how to move forward with Gutiérrez and the CHC:

> First is to go the sit-in/arrest route. He will yell and holler and threaten and cry but so did Reid's staff when the Reid 5 were in his office and now Reid

is Dreamers' best friend. Seriously it's not about personal feelings or emotion with politicians but about cold political calculation, and no matter how much we might (or might have) liked Gutiérrez, this is true for him too. Second suggestion is to really leverage the video from Reid's office with a targeted message and promotion strategy. It's good the video is up at Dreamactivist with a transcript and statement from the Reid 5, but the video still only has 1700 views. Get it to 10,000 or 50,000 and Gutiérrez will do whatever you ask him to.

Mo agreed with David's analysis. He saw no risk in damaging the relationships with Gutiérrez: "those never existed." He suggested the Chicago group should decide how to go after Gutiérrez.

Tañia, speaking on behalf of IYJL, argued that civil disobedience was not the best course to take:

We need to target Gutiérrez. I think Chicago can take and should take leadership on this, but I am interested in suggestions as to how to do it. As expected Gutiérrez is a bit angry, well actually, very, very angry. And precisely because he is the face of CIR, we are in fact asking him to admit defeat, and refute his own position and analysis. Politicians don't do that easily . . . At this point protests, or sit ins will only make him more angry at us, which while fun, doesn't get us what we want. Open to suggestions on actions or strategies, on or off the list.

IYJL ultimately resisted calls for a Gutiérrez sit-in action, but the video stayed up on DreamACTivist.org with a link to a petition demanding the Chicago congressman and the CHC stop holding the DREAM Act back.[26]

After his arrest and release, José returned home to great turmoil. Members of ULI were alarmed by his participation in the Washington, DC, action and the controversy stirred by the Gutiérrez video. Montserrat took him out to lunch shortly after his return. He still felt very close to Montserrat. He knew she did not support his turn to civil disobedience, but he respected her nonetheless. Over lunch Montserrat expressed concern about the risks he was taking. José appreciated her concern. She made the familiar argument that acts of civil disobedience and confrontation were not strategically wise in the Texas context. José understood and respected her position, even though he disagreed. But when she warned him against following Mo's lead, he turned cold. He thought she was painting Mo's radicalism with a brush tinted with a touch of Islamophobia. When José made this point in our interview, he was quick to qualify that he might have misunderstood Montserrat, but he left the lunch meeting having lost trust in her intentions and moral compass.

When I interviewed Montserrat, she spoke of the falling out with José as the lowest moment in her years of involvement with ULI. She cared deeply for José and the end of their relationship continued to trouble her. She, too, recalled their meeting after the Washington, DC, occupation. She described their disagreement over the posting of the Gutiérrez video as the wedge that split them apart:

> We were really close. But when he started being a part of DreamActivist and Mohammad, I took it very personal . . . I mean, he came to me, and he was like I'm working with them. And I was like fine. Just be careful, be careful, and really think through what they are doing and how they are doing things. But, so we had worked a lot with different organizations, and one of the things that really broke us apart, I guess you could say, was when there was one of the sit-ins, and we had a really good relationship with LULAC, with Brent Wilkes. We had given him the number, his personal phone number, and it was, I think, with Luis Gutiérrez, the incident, they videotaped it, the whole conversation. And [DreamActivist] didn't want to take down the video from the internet. And they had asked us, you know, that this is not helping the movement, we can't be fighting like this, fine with the people that are really against us, not the people that are helping us. I had a conversation with José and just saying you know these are relationships that we have built with people. This is how we are working. This video is not going to help the movement, it is just showing that we are divided.

But she was not going to change José's mind. They now saw things quite differently. Montserrat recalled his response: "He said we need to put pressure. We need to get things happening." If this meant sacrificing ULI's ties to LULAC, so be it. She could appreciate the logic of the tactic. "He's very smart. Really, really smart, but I think, to me, it was hurtful, of course it was hurtful." His lack of loyalty to ULI and its members stung Montserrat.[27] In the context of discussing her sadness over how things ended between her and José, Montserrat expressed her regret that he had, as she saw it, fallen under Mo's influence.

Julieta shared her sister's concerns about Mo's almost Svengali power over young and impressionable DREAMers. "For 2010, [UWD] allowed [affiliates] to do direct actions," she explained in our interview:

At the same time, knowing that some of our leaders were brand new, you cannot expect, at least in my perspective, you cannot expect someone to do a sit-in, when they just got involved.

But Mo, according to Julieta, was more than willing to put these neophytes in harm's way. Julieta acknowledged the success of the actions led by Mo in 2010, but she thought his tactics unethical. She said he pushed impressionable young DREAMers into getting arrested and then walked away once he got what he wanted from them. She also questioned the legitimacy of the organizational decision process leading to the actions:

> I think the civil disobedience, yeah, they helped a lot, they pushed the vote. I agree. But, at the same time, even, from what I heard from people who have participated in those actions, is that there was never the back up. There was never like, we got your back even if you get in trouble. And I think that's the difference. And it was interesting because it was never really brought to the table of let's like do civil disobedience. It was very much like all-of-a-sudden they started doing them.[28]

As she spoke in our interview about Mo's reckless willingness to put vulnerable youth in harm's way, Julieta did not directly refer to José's involvement in the Washington, DC, occupation, but he was the first person she and Montserrat knew and cared for to fall in with Mo.

Back at home, José was also faced with his mom's deteriorating health. The family's options were limited. They could return to Mexico to find her treatment or move somewhere else in the United States where local health subsidies might make the treatment she needed affordable. Alicia, who had returned to Austin after graduating from college with a nursing degree, researched their options and convinced their mother to move to North Carolina, where she could receive outpatient dialysis. Austin and ULI no longer felt like home. After sixteen years of being tied to Texas, and three years of service to ULI, José felt cut loose.

The Republican Sympathy Campaign

Having pushed the Senate leadership to abandon CIR and open discussions on advancing piecemeal legislation, the Noodles Team turned to a national strategy of securing sixty votes for the DREAM Act. (The needed votes in the House, if the bill was allowed to come up, were never in doubt.) Success in the Senate depended on winning a few Republican votes. The radicals organized a pressure campaign to target a handful of key Republican senators in Ohio, Utah, Maine, Kentucky, and Massachusetts. DREAMers were already organized in Kentucky and Massachusetts, but they needed to recruit organizers to send to Ohio, Utah, and Maine.

Mo proposed that the central organizing tactic in each of these states should be to find DREAMers facing deportation and "to get them to go public and essentially fight as many cases, publicly, as we can." The tactic was based on past successes:

> We have never lost a public END case [i.e., a public campaign to stop a DREAMers deportation]. It is VERY difficult to piss-off anyone, even a republican, with a *good* END case. We can garner some sympathy from republicans and possibly personalize the issue for them so when it comes time for a vote they'll be in our favor.

It made for a straightforward modular ask in the key states: "Senator _____ _____, stop the deportation of _____ by supporting the DREAM Act." The challenge was to find END cases in these states.[29] Mo asked Carlos Saavedra for UWD funding to support this "Republican Sympathy Campaign." In early August, Mo told Noodlesforo that UWD would support the campaign and cover the expenses for sending organizers to the three states without DREAMer organizations. Mo told me, more than once in our interviews, that UWD never came through with the money. He saw it as a betrayal. But, more importantly, it cut short a campaign that he believed might have changed the outcome.

The radicals not only worried about the resources needed to organize in multiple states but also about finding END cases to leverage. Mo raised the possibility that they might have "to create end cases where we can't find one." He spelled out his thinking. "Find a good candidate and (as controversial as it might be) get them detained then rally around it. This might be a last step but just something to think about."[30] The suggestion introduced a radical inflection to the strategy: creating deportation cases as an instrument to push specific politicians on policy. The Noodles Team did not take this "last step" of manufacturing END cases, but in the following year, this strategy would become the controlling idea behind the escalating actions of NIYA.

José went to Utah to organize for the Republican Sympathy Campaign. He was joined by Ernesto, a DREAMer from California. In Salt Lake City, they established a DREAMer organization centered around the students at the University of Utah. José was not at sea in Salt Lake City. He was familiar with student politics and culture at a large state university in a white, conservative region. He had, after all, spent a year at Texas Tech in Lubbock. José and Ernesto followed the sympathy strategy, finding and publicizing an END case. They attracted local media attention to the case and worked to redirect this attention on the state's two Republican senators. As with most cases of social movement campaigns, it is hard to make strong claims about the causal impact of their work, but Senator Bob Bennett from Utah, a lame duck in a lame-duck session, was the sole Republican to vote for cloture for the DREAM Act on December 17. His fellow senator from Utah, Orin Hatch, abstained from the same vote, but many believe he would have voted for cloture if he knew his vote would have made a difference.

Another element of the Republican Sympathy Campaign was to publicize undocumented youth with ambitions to serve in the military. To this end, DREAMers organized an action targeting their "old friend" and war hero Senator McCain, but also directed at the handful of Republican senators still on the fence about the DREAM Act. In September, Mo traveled to Arizona to organize the action:

> We did a 23-day boot camp in front of his office. It was pretty intense for someone who doesn't care about the military. We slept outside his office in 110-degree weather. We wrapped the tent with boot-camp fabric that we bought from the fabric store. Made our own flagpole. Did some crazy patriotic shit. I'm not a fan of the military, but we had kids who were willing to die for this country and that sounds great messaging.[31]

Mo said the boot camp was his "favorite action" of 2010.[32] I was incredulous that he favored it over the two Noodles actions. Mo insisted. He loved how it turned sacred symbols of the country against the racist dispositions of nativists. The DREAM Army also proved popular across the radical-moderate divide.[33]

Back on the Hill, a bewildering frenzy of inside politics swirled around the DREAM Act. There was precious little time left before the fall recess and November elections. Schumer, angry that his long-promised comprehensive bill was declared dead by the Senate majority leader, threw cold water on the standalone approach, publicly voicing doubt that there were sixty votes for the DREAM Act. Senator Feinstein rallied support around the idea of packaging DREAM together with AgJOBs. Both pieces of legislation had enjoyed bipartisan support in past years. Joining the two held some promise of crossing the sixty-vote filibuster threshold in the Senate. AgJOBs had more Republican support than the DREAM Act, but it called for enhanced immigration enforcement measures that repelled many Democrats and advocates for immigrant rights. Mo, speaking for many DREAMers, told Noodlesforo that if a standalone DREAM Act ever came to a vote, it would ultimately attract many of the same enforcement measures present in the AgJOBS legislation. To woo Pentagon hawks, Senator Feinstein proposed adding military service to the paths toward citizenship included in the DREAM Act. Still other Democrats proposed appending DREAM to the Defense Authorization Bill. Senator Menendez and the CHC leadership behind Gutiérrez and New York Representative Lydia Velasquez backed this last option.

Republicans responded to Reid's pivot to narrower immigration legislation by claiming that there was no time before the November elections for a serious debate on the DREAM Act. They attacked Reid's support for it as nothing more than pandering to the Latino vote in his hotly contested bid for re-election in Nevada. They voiced outrage at the proposal of attaching the DREAM Act to the Defense Authorization Bill. "This is an all-time low for me being in the Senate, and that's saying something," Senator Lindsay Graham told a reporter at *Foreign Policy*. "The one area that's been kept off limits from partisan politics has been the defense of our nation."[34] Supporters countered that DREAM was related to defense because the most recent version of the act included military service as an alternative path to college for citizenship, a provision the Pentagon prized because it would bolster recruiting. The defense bill had also attached to it a measure repealing the military policy of "Don't Ask Don't Tell." Gaby Pacheco said in our interview that the Democrats knew very well that the Republicans would never vote to swallow both attachments to the defense bill. Reid nonetheless supported this CHC backed option. When I asked Mo about the September 21 vote on the defense bill with DREAM attached, he dismissed it as a "fake vote" crafted only to curry favor with Latino voters in the upcoming November elections. Democrats knew it would fail. On this point, he and Gaby agreed.

The Republicans indispensable for passage of the DREAM Act balked at voting for it as an attachment to the defense bill. After the legislative loss, Reid promised he would put the DREAM Act up again for a vote, but there was no time to do this before the midterm elections. Reid faced a tough re-election bid. A few days before voters went to the polls, he said on the Univision network he would put the DREAM Act up for vote during the lame-duck session. It was an election promise made at the last hour as he trailed in the polls, but one he would end up honoring after his surprisingly strong victory on November 2 against a national tide of anti-incumbency and Tea-Party Republican insurgency.[35]

"Petulant Children" and the "Nonprofit Industrial Complex"

The Defense Authorization vote did nothing to change the radical DREAMers view of the directors of the nonprofits and unions behind RI4A and their allies in the Democratic Party. They continued to doubt Democrats support for the DREAM Act. They now also had to contend with criticism from the Left that the DREAM Act was a bad compromise for undocumented immigrant communities because of enforcement measures and the military enlistment provision. The same day the Senate voted against cloture on the defense bill, Truthout.org posted an opinion piece authored by five DREAMers from California. Neidi Dominguez, a core member of the Noodles Team, was one of the authors. The piece sought to defend DREAMers against challenges coming from different political corners.

The opinion piece was prompted, in part, by interactions stemming from an August 19 town hall meeting held by "DREAM Team LA and OC [Orange County] DREAM Team, in collaboration with The Dream Is Coming." The meeting was organized as a forum to address "major questions and concerns" about the DREAM Act and the "strategy and tactics that undocumented youth have embraced." The organizers wanted "to create a safe space for undocumented youth and allies to talk about the shift in the DREAM Movement." It featured a panel discussion with Lizbeth Mateo and Yahaira Carrillo from the DREAM 5, along with Carlos Amador and Jorge Guitierrez, two participants in a recent fifteen-day hunger strike targeting Senator Feinstein. The authors of the Truthout.org piece reported that "more than 250 people" participated in the town hall and described the experience as exciting, overwhelming, painful, and unprecedented: "We knew that in this place we would need to conduct painful but necessary conversations."

The authors flagged the military service option of the DREAM Act as one of these difficult conversations:

> Many of the straight men who took the mic had strong critiques of the DREAM Act and its military provisions. They questioned our support for an admittedly less-than perfect piece of legislation. Each time, the panelists responded candidly to questions as well as concerns about the DREAM Act and our movement. This experience was uplifting as well as frustrating for us. We did not want to silence anyone in that space, nor did we dismiss anyone's critiques or comments, but we left that space feeling like it was necessary for us once again as UNDOCUMENTED AND UNAFRAID activists to put forward our responses and reactions to these critiques, with the purpose of creating dialogue in order to move forward.

They felt compelled to respond to "the attitudes of privilege and self-righteousness that we believe fuel the opposition to our movement."

The authors challenged these attitudes and defended what they described as "a shift in the DREAMer movement" toward autonomy and escalation by and for undocumented youth:

> Our so-called allies need to realize that they are not undocumented and, as such, do not have the right to say what undocumented youth need or want. Our progressive allies insist in imposing their paternalistic stand to oppose the DREAM Act and tell us that this is not the "right" choice for us to acquire "legal" status in this country. We wonder: Who are they to decide for us?

They raised particular concerns about allies working for the "Nonprofit Industrial Complex." They described this complex as "a network of politicians, the elite, foundations and social justice organizations" modeled "after capitalist structures instead of challenging them." They argued that this network works to "control social movements and dissent" and masks "corporate greed and exploitation." The authors rejected the Complex's models for organizing and celebrated the recent move by undocumented youth to cut ties with nonprofit organizations and operate "as donation-only and volunteer-based organized groups." They ended the piece with a note of confidence and a rallying call:

We are building the DREAM Movement action-by-action, city-by-city, and campus-by-campus. In the spirit of the Freedom Rights and Chicano movements of the 1960s, we have decided to put our bodies and lives on the line. Repeatedly, undocumented youth have risked the threat of physical violence, incarceration, and deportation by engaging in acts of non-violent direct action in order to push the immigrant rights movement forward. We must look to Yahaira, Mo, and Lizbeth, the students who staged a sit-in in McCain's office. We must look to the "Trail of Dreams": Felipe, Gaby, Carlos, and Juan. We must look to DREAM Team LA and Orange County DREAM Team, groups of young activists for the DREAM Act. We must look to the women and men in the DREAM movement, undocumented queer and transgender young activists with emerging ideologies that challenge the capitalist, heterosexual and misogynistic systems here in the United States.[36]

This California town hall meeting and the Truthout.org post reflected a growing confidence among radical DREAMers that escalating actions were building a new movement. This migrant rights movement challenged the immigration reform movement—a fake social movement, propped up by "so-called allies" employed in the "nonprofit industrial complex," who claimed, without right, leadership over the politics of reforming immigration. It sought to pierce the veil of "the movement" that nonprofit leaders like Bhargava and politicians like Gutiérrez repeatedly invoked to blunt the radical edge of DREAMer activism.

This DREAMer declaration of independence and indictment of the compromised politics of their nonprofit "allies" did not go unnoticed. Sally Kohn posted a scathing response on *Daily KOS*. Sally was, at the time, an occasional, unpaid political commentator for FOX News. She would soon move to fulfill a similar role at CNN and MSNBC. Before this TV work, Sally worked as a "campaign strategist" for CCC. In this capacity, she developed a new media organizing project on health care reform in rural communities. Before working at CCC, she worked at the Ford Foundation, "helping to manage more than 15 million in annual grants." If there is a nonprofit industrial complex as these undocumented youth claimed, Sally was one of its denizens.[37]

Sally's response opened with a bit of reportage: "the immigrant rights movement is in a frenzy" over the public charge made in Truthout.org by radical undocumented youth against nonprofit organizations. Sally joked as she judged them. They incredibly "turn their anger" not on the senators who voted against cloture nor on the Republican Party. "No, in the tried and true tradition of circling the wagons and shooting ourselves, the DREAM activists are attacking the mainstream immigrant rights movement." Sally then checked her reader: "Let me stop here and clarify that I do not believe unanimity in movements is a good thing." Sally did not want the reader to think her a milquetoast liberal:

> It's important that we remember there would have been no Civil Rights legislation but for Malcolm X and the Black Panthers whose relative extremism made Martin Luther King and his adherents seem more reasonable to the powers-that-be. At the same time, Malcolm and the Panthers also pushed King to be more radical—an essential force in keeping the mainstream Civil Rights movement from being dangerously co-opted by the liberal establishment. That said, there's a difference between dissent and disrespect. The DREAM activists have crossed the line.

They had stepped over the ethical line of intra-movement respect, Sally wrote, by "acting like petulant children." Sally taunted the disrespectful kids, calling into question their radical bona fides. The words of these radical DREAMers may be tough, but she found their actions "tame and uninspired." Only the Trail of Dreams impressed Sally. The actions leading to arrests in Arizona and Washington, DC, were apparently wanting in audacity.

She counterpunched that the petulant DREAMers represented at best the interests of a narrow group of undocumented immigrants on an "elite path." The "mainstream" organizations of the movement represented "low-wage workers who are struggling to make a living and support their families and were not going to be helped, immediately or ever, by a DREAM Act." She glossed a history of the DREAMers to defend these mainstream organizations:

> And yes, the immigrant rights groups being critiqued are 501(c)3s. So are lots of the groups critiquing them. But more importantly, it was these very same 501(c)3s that incubated and trained the DREAM Act students, hosted their meetings and supported their travel, provided media support and in countless other ways encouraged and facilitated the DREAMers' work.

There was truth in Sally's history, but for undocumented youth who had lived this history they knew it was a partial truth, at best.

Sally's account exaggerated the contribution of nonprofits and diminished what the DREAMers built on their own, often against the active resistance of "mainstream" organizations. She also defamed the DREAMers: they were petulant in their words about allies but tame and uninspired in their direct action against injustice. They called themselves undocumented and unafraid, but Sally told her readers to question their discipline, self-control, and even courage.

Sally's attack prompted spirited defenses from DREAMers. On his Citizen Orange blog, David Bennion featured a guest post from a DREAMer, named only as Mark. He took issue with the idea that DREAM activists represented a narrow constituency in the larger movement. He reiterated the DREAMer response to charges of selfishness: No one cared more about the struggles of undocumented parents than their children. And no one cared more about passing the DREAM Act than the parents of undocumented youth. He also took issue with her claim that DREAM activism was not only selfish but tame. He described the actions of self-sacrifice of the "DREAM 21" who risked everything in Washington, DC, in July. He concluded by addressing Sally's "petulant children" charge—which sent him, as it likely did many other readers, to the dictionary to be certain about what the scold exactly entailed. "Petulant, according to Dictionary.com," Mark wrote, means "moved to or showing sudden, impatient irritation, esp. over some trifling annoyance." The charge had no face value for two obvious reasons:

> 1) Formulating the ideas for such actions [as the DREAM 21] on their own, carefully planning out the logistics of the task, and having the guts to carry on even with such self-sacrificing consequences in return . . . that can be described with plenty of different words, but I'd have to say neither "petulant" nor "childish" could be two of them. 2) The chance to live out our dreams as documented Americans is certainly not something trivial to us, which is why we will continue to fight as if we've never known defeat.[38]

A shared outrage toward the paternalism of nonprofit elites, nicely captured in Mark's reply to Sally's petulant DREAMers article, set a combative tone for the fall meetings held by undocumented youth across the country to organize for the lame-duck session of Congress.

DREAMer In-fighting

Texas DREAMers met in Austin on October 16 to talk strategy for the last two months of the year. Hosted by ULI, the meeting centered on discussions of how undocumented Texans should represent themselves at the last national convening of UWD scheduled for the following week in Kentucky. They all understood that a push for the DREAM Act in the lame-duck session of Congress would bring national focus on undocumented youth organizing in Texas. Senator Kay Bailey Hutchison's support of the bill in 2007 made her an obvious target for the campaign to find the few Republican votes needed to win. These discussions inevitably turned to debates over tactics with the hosts from ULI coming under considerable pressure to depart from their traditional moderate approach toward politicians.

Julieta Garibay and Rebecca Acuña remained influential at ULI. They sat on an advisory board that guided the current leadership. José's participation in (und)occupy DC sent shockwaves through ULI. As a former president of the organization, he was widely respected by members. One member, Karla, described him as someone who always brought good humor to the difficult work at ULI, but after the DC action she sensed a real change. There was now a chill between José and others at ULI whenever they crossed paths. She said in our interview that he had gone from "always joking" to being "standoffish."[39] José's actions, and the more general drift toward confrontation by many DREAMers, put Julieta in a difficult situation. Her experience in Texas politics told her that confrontational tactics against "KBH" would backfire, but she sensed the growing momentum across the UWD network to "escalate." Rebecca Acuña, her best friend and long-time partner in the building of ULI, remained firmly against escalation. Rebecca thought a hunger strike targeting KBH was misguided, let alone acts of civil disobedience that might lead to arrests. Explaining her thinking in our interview, Rebecca said she advised ULI members to "let KBH sit back and play kingmaker. She didn't need to vote for the DREAM Act in 2007 and did. If you threaten her, you rile up her base and force her to do something that would not make her look weak."[40]

Pressure against ULI and the conservative approach of its veterans came principally from a new organization at the University of Texas at San Antonio, DREAM Act Now. The organization was founded in the spring of 2010 by two undocumented students, Lucy and Pam. Both were born in Mexico City and raised in the Dallas Metro area, but the similarities stopped there. Lucy's family suffered from extreme poverty in Mexico City. She recalled in our interview times when there was not enough food to eat. When she was six years old, her family crossed the border in the dead of night, evading the US Border Patrol. She grew up in working-class South Dallas. Her mom dragged her every Sunday to hours of worship at a Pentecostal church filled with Mexican families not unlike her own. She rebelled in her own quiet way by flouting the modest dress code of her church, cutting her hair short, and dying it bright colors. In 2006, when the student walkouts hit Dallas, she and her classmates joined the action only to be blocked by administrators who put the school in lockdown. When it came to academic performance, she was not so rebellious. She excelled at school and attended a magnet high school. When she was admitted to UTSA, she jumped at the opportunity to move to San Antonio, a city she associated with Chicano radicalism and the promise of personal and social freedom. She was the first in her family to go to college.[41]

Pam grew up ten miles south of Lucy's neighborhood, but her mostly white and relatively affluent suburb was a world away. Pam's parents are both college-educated, and they worked in the banking industry in Mexico City. Nonetheless, economic insecurity stalked them. Her family came to the United States on tourist visas, the "privileged way." When they arrived in Dallas in the late 1990s, her parents found stable work in decent paying jobs. They settled in the suburbs to provide their two daughters with a safe neighborhood and good schools. Within a few years, the good jobs disappeared and her parents turned to long hours of menial work to pay the bills. Pam and her older sister Karla were raised with high expectations of educational and occupational achievement. When Pam first set foot on the campus of UTSA, her older sister, Karla, was just seventy miles up the interstate at UT-Austin finishing up her pharmacy degree. Karla was single-mindedly focused on her professional ambitions and avowedly apolitical. Pam started college in San Antonio as a self-professed Republican interested in studying business and political science.[42]

Pam met Lucy by chance. She was in her second semester at UTSA when she stumbled across a meeting Lucy had organized with Benita Veliz to talk about the DREAM Act. Benita, who had addressed the 2009 DREAM Graduation in Washington, DC, was a prominent local DREAMer. Graduating high school at the age of sixteen, she received a full scholarship to attend Saint Mary's University in San Antonio.[43] On her way to work one day, she was pulled over. The traffic violation led to questions about her immigration status, and she was placed in removal proceedings. Benita stopped her own deportation with a letter she wrote to *The New York Times*. National publicity led to prosecutorial discretion for deferred action on her case.[44] When Lucy started to plan a DREAMer organization at UTSA, she leaned on Benita for advice. Lucy herself is naturally shy but has a steely resolve. In Pam, she found a fellow DREAMer with an outgoing personality and boundless energy. Just as Pam started to participate in DREAMer politics with Lucy, she was arrested, detained by ICE, and placed in deportation proceedings.

The arrest happened during spring break. Headed from San Antonio to Dallas for a statewide DREAMer meeting, Pam stopped in Austin for an evening of fun at the SXSW music festival. It was Saint Patrick's Day. Waiting at a bus stop with her friends for a shuttle to ferry them to a music venue, a cop aggressively moved the overflowing crowd off the street and back up onto the sidewalk. Pam reacted angrily to what seemed to her to be an abuse of authority. She spoke back to the cop and was arrested.

Pam called her sister, Karla, from jail at three in the morning. It went to voice mail before she could answer. The message left was an automated recording asking if she would accept a call from the Travis County Jail. Disoriented and confused, it took some time for Karla to piece together what was happening. She knew her sister was in town for SXSW. She went to the website for the jail and searched for her name in the database of inmates in custody. She found Pam's name and "immediately knew it was really bad news." Not knowing what to do, she called her parents. They, too, were at a loss. Karla was due at work for an early morning rotation at a hospital—one of the very last steps in her long path to the completion of a pharmacy degree at UT. In a most excruciating decision, she decided to go to work that morning to avoid jeopardizing her degree. She worked that day, checking her phone constantly and not knowing Pam's fate.

The Travis County Sheriff under the federal 287(g) program routinely shared information about inmates in the jail with ICE. In Pam's case, this led to ICE placing an immigration hold on her. The next day, after a court arraignment for a minor charge, she was transferred to ICE custody and detained at the T. Don Hutto Detention Center in Taylor, TX, thirty miles northeast of the county jail. As Karla and her family anguished over what to do, Pam's friends, plugged into the Texas DREAMer network, contacted Barbara Heyns, the director of the immigration law clinic at the University of Texas. Barbara immediately set to work to get Pam released.

Pam and Karla both reacted to this traumatic event by throwing themselves into tireless advocacy for the DREAM Act. But their shared commitment led to very different forms of activism. In May, after she graduated from the pharmacy program at UT, Karla devoted all her energies to working with ULI. For Pam, her arrest and detention at Hutto deepened her fledgling involvement with Lucy at UTSA. For Karla, Pam's detention heightened her fears of deportation and shaped a cautious disposition toward activism. In Julieta, she found a close friend and companion who believed DREAMer advocacy should always work to keep undocumented youth safe. ULI provided her with a safe space for political engagement and a support group with ties to powerful allies. Pam's response was very different.

Having been outed as undocumented in the riskiest way possible, Pam decided "I am already on the radar screen of ICE," so "I might as well push as hard as I can." She found in Lucy a quiet but resolute companion who wanted to push a more defiant, rebellious line of action. In Felipe Vargas, they discovered an activist who saw movement spaces as incubators for collective attacks on power holders, the very opposite of the safe spaces ULI sought to build and protect. Felipe saw in Lucy and Pam radical DREAMers who could execute Mo's Republican Sympathy Campaign in Texas.

At the end of the summer, following months of DREAMer advocacy that included involvement in the Trail of Dreams, the McCain sit-in, and the Washington, DC, occupation, Felipe Vargas returned to his hometown of San Antonio to help take care of his mom, who was battling cancer. Back home, he reached out to Pam and Lucy through their DREAM Act Now! organization. Felipe offered Pam and Lucy a wealth of experience in organizing and a direct connection to the radical DREAMers at The Dream Is Coming. They also found in Felipe a person deeply mistrusted by the leaders of ULI.

Julieta Garibay first met Felipe Vargas in 2005 in Philadelphia, PA, at an NCLR convention. They shared a panel on organizing undocumented youth with Carlos Saavedra and Walter Barrientos. Over the next five years, they crossed paths at CCC, NILC, and UWD meetings. They did not like each other. To Felipe, Julieta and ULI represented the wing of UWD that was closest to the allies running the nonprofits. She had a longstanding relationship with Josh Bernstein at NILC and spoke at the roll-out of RI4A. She had also tried to stop José's participation in Noodles 2.0. To Julieta, Felipe was an interloper who spoke of radicalism, revolution, and confrontational tactics, asking DREAMers to run risks that he, as a citizen, did not face. Although he was from Texas, he had no history with DREAMers in the state. He became involved in organizing undocumented youth as a graduate student in Indiana. He appeared to her too eager to join whatever the latest hot action was. More importantly, Felipe was closely identified with the radicalism that Julieta associated with Mo and Lizbeth.

At the Austin meeting, the members of the UTSA organization took a radical posture in discussions of how to influence KBH. Julieta suspected Felipe was behind the new organization and their talk of escalation. She publicly confronted Felipe at the meeting. Several people I interviewed remembered their tense public argument. They fought over the familiar issues dividing UWD: strategic differences over what lines of action were called for, and opposing characterizations of the immigrant rights movement and the role of "allies" and the nonprofits in it. This conflict between two veterans of DREAMer activism was predictable. More surprising was the rift that emerged between activists who had only just joined the struggle.

A week later, the sisters, Karla and Pam, squared off in a breakout session for Texas DREAMers at the convening of UWD in Kentucky. Karla recalled that Pam forcefully argued for a sustained hunger strike and even acts of civil disobedience to pressure KBH. Karla challenged her sister, contending that these pressure tactics would be met with forceful resistance in the conservative political context of Texas and boomerang on DREAMers. She also warned that these actions could jeopardize the health of activists and lead to detentions and deportations. Unlike Julieta and Felipe, Pam and Karla did not know much about the yawning breach between undocumented youth at the national level. They were relatively new to DREAM activism. This was their first UWD convening. They may not even have appreciated how closely their dispute mirrored a divide that was tearing UWD apart. The Kentucky convening made clear that this divide was now running wide and deep through DREAMer activism, splitting undocumented youth in every place they organized across the country, breaking apart longstanding friendships between people with years of shared work on the DREAM Act, like José and Julieta, and even putting siblings at odds.

In Kentucky, UWD implemented, for the first time, organizational rules for self-governance. Delegates participated in an open election to fill positions on the board of directors and the coordinating committee. The established UWD leadership hoped this election would settle disputes about transparency and accountability within the network. The rules of governance opened three new positions on the board of directors to election. The terms of established board members—Walter Barrientos, Mattias Ramos, Cristina Jimenez, Julieta Garibay, José Luis Marantes, and Josh Bernstein—were slated to continue. The rules governing the election declared public campaigning for these positions out of bounds. The moderates did not stand to lose majority control of the board no matter the result of the election, but this prohibition may have reflected moderate DREAMers' anxiety of the popular influence of The Dream Is Coming leaders.

When the ballots were counted, to the surprise of many, Felipe Vargas had won the most votes. Mo was tickled in our interview when retelling how UWD leaders announced the results. They initially reacted thinking the lead vote getter was Felipe Matos of the Trail of Dreams. They were visibly discomfited, Mo recalled, when they realized that the winner was in fact Vargas not Matos. Another notable outcome of the election was the lack of undocumented immigrants elected to the board. All three new members were citizen allies. And the key paid staff positions, such as the position of national coordinator held by Carlos Saavedra, remained open only to citizens. Months later, after the dust had settled from the failed push to pass the DREAM Act in the Senate, the UWD board moved to strip Felipe Vargas of his position. The board cited a raft of issues to justify the action, but procedurally the most important would be the charge that there had been an organized campaign to elect him.

When we asked Mo about this, his response was cheeky. He said Felipe Vargas's election was "our parting gift" to UWD. His talent for making trouble would consume energy and resources in an organization the radicals had given up on. That said, Mo and Lizbeth continued to work through UWD as a vehicle to reach and mobilize undocumented youth new to DREAM activism. The organization was already dead to them but burying it before the votes in the lame-duck session of Congress made no sense. And Mo and Lizbeth still relished the battle with the moderates over the hearts and minds of UWD's expanding constituency. For others on the Noodles Team, the struggle with UWD leadership and its patrons was taking a heavy toll. Marisol said in our interview that she dropped out of the struggle ahead of the Kentucky meeting. For five long years, she had committed herself almost wholly to organizing and empowering undocumented youth. She had been as instrumental as anyone in building the UWD network, but now she was worn out by a year of intensifying disputes with its leadership. She said candidly in the interview that she "broke down" in the fall and had to "step away." She applied to graduate school and enrolled at the University of Michigan. She would never again take an active role in DREAMer activism, but in Ann Arbor, MI, she shared an apartment with Mo and he retained her counsel. Almost seven years after the events, Mo still referred to her as the "puppet master" of the DREAMer insurgency.[45]

The Lame-Duck Session

The midterm elections sent a seismic shockwave through the Democratic Party. The Republicans recaptured a majority in the House of Representatives, gaining sixty-three seats, the largest gain for any midterm election since the 1930s. The Republicans also gained six seats in the Senate, leaving the Democrats with a razor thin advantage. It was obvious to all that immigration reform, comprehensive or piecemeal, would be on hold indefinitely once the new Congress opened session in 2011. In the wake of these elections, advocates for immigration reform finally coalesced around passing the DREAM Act in the lame-duck session.

DREAMers who had failed to see eye-to-eye on past strategies came together for a final push. In Texas, for example, the DREAMers at ULI set aside their differences with Pam and Lucy and joined the UTSA hunger strike to increase pressure on KBH—a hunger strike that lasted for more than forty days. In my interviews, DREAMers from both sides talked about this moment of coming together as genuine. In this flush of solidarity, Lizbeth Mateo called Gaby Pacheco to ask her to take the lead in a sit-in at Senator McCain's Washington, DC, office.

Lizbeth told Gaby that her arrest would energize undocumented youth across the nation and flood senators with calls and emails demanding her release and the passage of the DREAM Act. Mo and Lizbeth planned for five others to be arrested along with Gaby. They recruited another big name in DREAMer circles, Jorge Gutiérrez, who had been featured in the documentary "Papers." Hoping to draw on popular interest in the DREAM Army action, they included two DREAMers who wanted to serve in the military. Noemi and Alma filled out the group. Mo and Lizbeth considered Gaby the lynchpin to the action. "We told her flat out, from the get-go," Mo said, "all we need from you is just for you to be in jail, so that all these people go crazy: 'oh my God you got Gaby Pacheco.' And we can generate a shit ton of calls."[46]

Gaby understood the strategy and agreed to the action, at least at first. She said, in retrospect, "I practically got brainwashed to do it":

> They contacted me and I had a nice long, lengthy conversation with Lizbeth. It was maybe like two hours, and she was saying how committed they were to the movement and how they knew how committed I was. It was this whole organizing or like the psychological thing. And you know this is where we had this whole conversation about suicide.

According to Gaby, in talking about how committed she and Mo were to the movement, Lizbeth said they were ready to amplify any DREAMer suicides that might occur to advance political goals. "That kind of freaked me out a little. But, at the end of the day, I was also like, you have to put your life on the line. So, I come to DC."[47] Gaby said that almost immediately after saying yes to Lizbeth, she started to regret the decision. "I'm feeling really weird about this action. This is not going to work. The media doesn't care about [sit-ins] anymore. They're not going to come." She doubted the effectiveness of yet another sit-in and feared the personal consequences of getting arrested. She worried about what an arrest might mean for her dream of becoming an educator.

Gaby voiced her doubts about the soundness of the action with the other participants:

I come up to DC and I'm there and they're going through the preparation for the action. And I'm just sitting there. And I tell the people there, look "I have to be honest with you. I don't think this is the right thing to do. And I feel like the reason why I'm being asked to do this is because I did the Trail and when I do things the media comes." And then people got offended [laughs], and they were like "What the hell! Who do you think you are?"

Gaby recalled that Jorge, in particular, took her to task. "He said, 'I've been a part of Papers,' dada dada dada, 'if you think you're the only one with media exposure'":

And they put me against practically a wall. And they start telling me how I can't be selfish. And I'm being selfish. And I have to do this for the movement. And the movement needs me and think of all the people. And I'm like "oh, okay." And, so I say, "Fine, whatever, for the movement."

She reluctantly went forward with the plans.

The next day, November 17, the six DREAMers gathered in the waiting room of McCain's Washington, DC, office. The senator refused to talk to them, but they did catch him trying to exit through a side entrance. They chased after him asking him why he would not give them "the chance to serve the country like he did." McCain is reported to have said in return, "Good, go serve," as he jumped into an elevator. Gaby described the action as unraveling when the media did not show up to cover the sit-in, "as I predicted." She said the entire group started to doubt the action. The six kicked everyone else out of the waiting room as they deliberated on what to do. The discussion was tense. The group, according to Gaby, came to an agreement that she and Ivan should leave the sit-in before the arrests and act as spokespersons for the group.[48] She remembered Mo exploding when he realized what was happening. "Mo is like, 'no fucking way, no fucking way, she's not going to get arrested.'"

Mo's interpretation of what transpired differed in important ways, but his account accorded with Gaby's in its details. From his perspective, the sole aim of the action was to get Gaby arrested, and she clearly understood this. When Mo realized that the group was changing the plan and that Gaby was opting out, he believed she had manipulated the others and the outcome. They agree he called her either a "manipulative bitch" or "manipulating bitch" when she walked out of McCain's office. After the arrest of remaining DREAMers, Gaby approached Mo. She held Noemi's glasses and was trying to give them to Mo for him to safeguard until she got out of jail. He was so angry he would not look at her. She reached out to grab his arm to get him to pay attention when, according to Gaby, Mo took a swipe at her. He did not make contact. When I asked Mo about this interaction, he responded, "how did I become this evil character in this movement? I swung at her? No way."

There were other serious charges the moderates made against the radicals. Gaby said in our interview that shortly after his fight with Mo, she met with Julieta, José Luis Marantes, and Carlos Saavedra to talk about publicly exposing the dangerous behavior of "Mo and company." They discussed how the radicals had exploited young, impressionable DREAMers in San Antonio, TX, dangerously risking their health in a prolonged hunger strike, and how Felipe had harassed Julieta at Texas meetings of DREAMers. On the flipside, the radicals charged the moderates of withholding funding from UWD sanctioned actions, like the Republican Sympathy Campaign, just to weaken their influence. They also charged the moderates of using libelous talk about exploiting suicides to undermine NDLON's support of The Dream Is Coming. Sorting out fact from fiction in these charges is not easy and ultimately less significant than an underlying reality. The divide was now deeply personal and beyond repair.

Mo and Lizbeth approached Carlos Saavedra to plan how to follow-up on the Washington, DC, McCain action. They wanted Carlos to focus UWD's material resources to increase the pressure on targeted senators. They envisioned a series of actions along the lines of what was developing in San

Antonio, TX, with the hunger strike and a planned sit-in at KBH offices, and in Utah, Maine, Ohio, and Massachusetts where activists were using END cases to pressure Republican senators. But the fallout from the McCain action made it impossible for the two sides to work together ever again.

Mo was bitter, but he saw it coming. A day before the McCain action, Mo wrote an angry email under the subject line, "This movement is in need of a cleansing and a fresh start":

> For the past two years we have been fighting what you would think was a campaign for the dream act but it really wasn't. For the past two years we have been fighting a campaign to get allies on our side, for folks not to refer to us as "those selfish kids" who do not care about their families . . . You tell us we have no chance without you, that we will continue to suffer and live in fear if we do not have you looking out for us and protecting us, but the reality is that **we will never win with you.** Our situation has only worsened under your leadership and there are no signs that it will be changing. But you forget, we can force it to change, we can force YOU to change. We are no longer afraid and you cannot and will not hold us down any longer.[49]

He ended the email with a threat: "Some of you will stay but most of you have to go." The email stayed in his outbox, unsent, but Mo would try to make good on the threat in 2011.

Three days after the McCain action, Carlos Saavedra announced UWD's final campaign of the year. He circulated the plan in a memo entitled, "In Service to America and the American Dream." The memo obliquely referenced the sit-in:

> This week Gaby Pacheco asked Senator McCain if he would allow her to serve in the military by passing the Dream Act, the Senator replied, "You want to serve? Then 'go serve.'" So the Dreamers will do just that. They will live up to the American tradition of service. Will America live up to its tradition by allowing these dreamers to serve fully, by becoming Americans?

The campaign called for three phases. First, DREAMers would set up food banks outside the home offices of targeted senators. Second, DREAMers and allies would hold "2000 ThanksDreaming Dinners (house meetings) to have conversation about what thanksgiving means to you? And what does it mean to be American?" Third, as senators returned to Washington, DC, after the holiday, the campaign called for "1000 Dreamers and supporters to donate blood . . . outside of senatorial offices." The memo described the "theory of change" behind this "unified" strategy":

> We will show people in target states that immigrant students (and their community) contribute and serve, so that we generate public support and impact public opinion, thereby setting up a moral dilemma for the Congressmen either to vote against these "good citizens," or to vote for the DREAM Act.[50]

The memo reminded the radicals of an earlier "empty" symbolic campaign sponsored by UWD: "Don't Deport Dora." The campaign had called on people to sign a petition to stop the deportation of the beloved cartoon character. It set a deadline for her deportation and a target for the number of signatures needed to stop her removal. Mo said they had to set back the date of Dora the Explorer's "fake deportation" multiple times, because of a lack of signatures.[51]

The two sides soldiered through to the end of the year following their different strategies. Carrying out lobbying visits, they walked the same halls of Congress, not speaking to each other. The House passed the DREAM Act on December 8, but it was just a tease. The real struggle was always in the Senate. On December 18, the DREAM Act fell five votes short of the sixty needed for cloture in the Senate. When the votes were tallied, DREAMers from the two camps sat on opposite sides of the gallery, devastated and divided.

6
2011

NIYA and the Bad Dreamers

On January 4, 2011, a group of undocumented youth organizations and leading DREAMer activists sent an email to the "field team" of United We Dream. The first lines of the message read: "We, the undersigned, would like to announce the end of our affiliation with the United We Dream Network. Effective immediately please remove our organizations from UWD mailing/field lists." The signatories included the following organizations: NYSYLC, DreamACTivist.org, IYJL, NC Dream Team, DreamACTivist Virginia, One Michigan, and DreamACTivist Pennsylvania. A half-dozen individuals also signed on to the letter, including the leaders and/or co-founders of DREAM Team LA, Kansas-Missouri DREAM Alliance, Inland Empire Dream Team, and Student Immigrant Movement, MA. The letter offered an apology to fellow undocumented activists for not communicating earlier their growing mistrust of UWD leadership. "Some of us tried, on several occasions, to bring these issues forward in a manner that would hold the UWDN together, but ultimately nothing happened." The frenetic pace of the 2010 campaign left little time to articulate and circulate these concerns. Now, however, "with no relief via legislation in sight," the authors thought it time to pause, reflect, share what they learned from the past two years of struggle, and to explain their decision to formally separate from the network.

It was a long farewell letter detailing the authors' past commitment and contributions to UWD. It highlighted the part NYSYLC played in helping secure funding for the formation of UWD, the contributions of DreamACTivist.org to the original board, and the role of IYJL, NYSLYC, and Virginia DreamACTivist members on the national coordinating committee. The authors expressed regret about their withdrawal but wrote that they could no longer ignore that UWD leadership simply "did not share their vision of what a grassroots organizing model looks like."

The letter cited many critical flaws in the constitution and mistakes in the operation of the network, but one overarching sin accounted for most of these: The leaders of UWD were more beholden to their nonprofit patrons than to undocumented youth, and this fealty to elite allies explained the network's unwillingness to push early enough and hard enough for a standalone DREAM Act:

> Over the course of the last two years, we have learned that the leadership of this Network, **those who serve on its board and are paid staff members**, were some of our biggest obstacles to winning the DREAM Act in 2010. While we risked our lives and families for this movement, they placed substantial roadblocks in our path, despite their stated mission to empower undocumented youth.

The letter stopped just short of blaming the leadership for the failure of the DREAM Act.

The authors justified their withdrawal from the network with an account of a handful of the most egregious derelictions of duty committed by UWD leadership during the 2010 campaign. They cited a general failure of accountability by the formal decision-making bodies of the organization and a complete lack of transparency in the work of the board and paid staff. Of the board's eight members, only two were undocumented. Three members did not represent any "youth-led organization." The board never shared notes or minutes of its meetings. Decisions to hire paid staff were never made public, let alone opened up to the input of UWD's putative base:

> Jose Luis Marantes was suddenly hired as a consultant when his contract with the Center for Community Change ended. His hiring was not made public until after it was final. His actual job description, workplan and accountability measures have also not been shared with affiliates. There is no review process for current staff. The National Coordinator [Carlos Saavedra], who is paid $45,000 per year, is not subject to performance evaluations or adjustments to pay based on performance.

The letter charged that this lack of transparency and accountability functioned to hide the leadership's refusal to challenge its nonprofit patrons who were actively working against passage of the DREAM Act:

> Neither SEIU nor CCC supported the DREAM Act as a stand-alone bill until almost the end of the campaign (and, in fact, there is evidence

that both organizations worked behind the scenes to stop a stand-alone DREAM Act from moving forward when it had its best chance of passage), yet staff from both organizations were allowed to be on the founding board of UWD, suggesting a serious conflict of interest or even an attempt to bridle grassroots activists.

The letter pointed to the events in June of 2010 as evidence supporting this most serious charge:

[A]fter the NYSYLC exposed RI4A for stalling on the DREAM Act and failing to represent undocumented youth, UWD was offered two seats to the RI4A management table. Carlos Saavedra unilaterally took the seat on behalf of UWD membership but to date he has yet to even once share any notes or details from meetings.

It described leadership's allocation of funds as further proof of the network's control by these outside forces.

The letter detailed how UWD used its budget to reward friends compliant with the CIR agenda and to choke-off the challenge of independent activism by undocumented youth. Funds earmarked to train undocumented youth to target undecided Republican senators went to the wrong places or disappeared altogether. It claimed UWD gave $5,000 for a training to "Student Immigrant Movement (Carlos Saavedra's own group) from Massachusetts, a state already well-organized and with 9/10 of its members of congress sponsors of the DREAM Act," but it allocated next to nothing for organizing in Maine with its two undecided senators:

After an almost two-hour call, Saavedra would not budge on changing the figures, saying that "it is bad relationship-building with the SIM group to change a promise now." ... Eventually, to make up for the lack of any work being done in Maine, an additional $1,000 had to be spent to send two organizers to Maine.

Organizing in other critical states, such as Utah, received no funding at all.

Poor judgment in the distribution of funds exposed another serious problem: UWD leadership failed to support emerging and active DREAMer organizations. The letter cited as evidence the decision to hold a national field meeting in Minnesota at the start of the year. The local organization rewarded with hosting the meeting was a weak advocate for DREAMers. "[It] questioned whether the campaign should even be pushing for the DREAM Act," whereas active DREAMer organizations in critical swing states had to fight just to get invited to this and subsequent field meetings. For the March 2010 field meeting in North Carolina, the NC Dream Team was told there was no space or resources for them to attend the gathering in their own backyard. When UWD leaders were questioned about decisions to deny material support to these organizations, they deflected with: "What have they done for dream in the last six months?" and "I have heard they are too much into the CIR vs. DREAM drama."

This failure to seed the organic growth of the UWD network, the letter argued, revealed that the leadership fundamentally misunderstood the national landscape of DREAMer activism. It was out of touch with undocumented youth mobilizations already underway and lacked vision as to where material support could best be used:

> The UWD website describes the southeast as having "little to no social justice infrastructure." This demonstrates a clear misunderstanding of the region—where within living memory, the civil rights movement made its most profound gains. We simply cannot tolerate a leadership which is ignorant to the nature of our movement in any region let alone the southeast!

More damning was the authors' claim that this failure could not be chalked up to simple ignorance. It betrayed a sinister motive. They contended that UWD leadership actively worked to "stall the growth" of the network because it wanted to block emerging mobilizations of undocumented youth that threatened to challenge their nonprofit patrons:

> A newly formed group in California asked three different ways to attend the UWD Field Meeting in Kentucky, pledging to fundraise the cost of transportation themselves. Carlos Saavedra, Matias Ramos, and Jose Luis Marantes all rejected them. Instead UWD invited and paid for CHIRLA to attend.

The letter referenced UWD's attempts to incapacitate the UTSA hunger strike as another example of this active effort to undermine emergent mobilizations.

UWD leadership failed to seed or support activism across the network—both where youth were already showing initiative and where senators and congresspersons were still undecided on the DREAM Act—because it never developed "a strategy to win." It promoted empty symbolic gestures that chewed up resources and time that should have been spent on actions in the home states of undecided politicians. UWD failed to back the escalation of direct actions first spearheaded by The Dream is Coming in May. The letter expressed surprise and dismay at the actual response of UWD leadership to the Tucson sit-in:

> We expected . . . a call to action and serious escalation. Instead, in an effort to show the "moral crisis" we are facing in this country, UWD leadership decided it was time to launch an effort to "stop Dora the Explorer's deportation." It failed even in that capacity—Dora's campaign picked up no steam and she was deported on the Fourth of July!

Leadership not only ignored the call to escalate, but it actively warned groups not to work with those calling for escalation.

The authors ended by saying that they did not plan to release the letter to the public because they did not want to "*damage the capacity of any of our organizations, UWD etc.*," but the serious nature of their charges and the tone in which the letter delivered them communicated another intent. The authors were settling accounts with UWD's leadership and its patrons. The letter was crafted by activists who wanted to damage UWD and, more importantly, to replace it with a new network organized by and for undocumented youth.

The letter was almost exclusively backward looking. Going forward, the radicals withdrawing from UWD faced a very different political context than the one that framed past struggles and disputes. This new context obviated many of the conditions central to the grievances voiced in the letter. Differences over how to influence the national legislative process suddenly did not matter. In the new year, CIR and the DREAM Act were both political impossibilities. This harsh political reality dealt the professional advocates of immigration reform a humbling blow. Past claims to expertise by the directors of CCC, NIF, America's Voice, and RI4A now sounded risible.

The radicals posed one important forward-looking question in their farewell letter. "After ten years of fighting for DREAM, and with no relief via legislation in sight," what could undocumented youth "hope for"? Their answer: "We would at least have an authentic network for immigrant youth, led by immigrant youth." On this the radicals were united. "So now we are choosing to start over." The letter announced a provisional time and place for this new start:

> In early March we will be launching the new network, with an initial convention to take place in Indiana. We urge the remaining members of UWD to take a serious look at what has happened in the last year... If you choose to stay, we hope you fare better than us *as you stick to the network's intended mission*.[1]

Self-Instrumentalization

The new network needed resources. Its founders could expect little help from foundations and nonprofit organizations. The bruising politics of the past year left them with few friends in those quarters, and that was fine with them. They did not want the incapacitating strings attached to foundation grants and alliances with nonprofits. The leaders of the new network hoped that organizations controlled by undocumented youth would provide the needed resources and vindicate their declaration of independence from "the nonprofit industrial complex." This trust was not unfounded. Over the last year, every time the radicals actualized the coming-out call of "undocumented and unafraid" through protest and civil disobedience, undocumented youth rallied to their side. An aggressive campaign of defiant collective action could recruit undocumented youth and rally resources to the new network. It would be a taxing method of organizing, requiring the execution of a series of high-risk protests.[2]

The new political context raised the question of who or what they should target with these protests? The wins and wounds of the past two years of organizing provided some answers here. In 2010, the experience of organizing successful public campaigns to stop deportations allowed radical DREAMers to do what was previously unthinkable—engage in acts of civil disobedience leading to arrests. The END campaigns demonstrated that when placed under the pressure of a public campaign, ICE would invariably grant a stay of removal for a DREAMer. The radicals learned that within ICE, as Mo put it, "the local office doesn't give a fuck." Local agents often act recklessly in pursuit of enforcement goals. But "the DC office is political," sensitive to public pressure, and can always "override the local office."[3] This raised the tantalizing possibility that an aggressive campaign of civil disobedience might get the local and national offices working at cross-purposes. It could sow and exploit discord within this huge federal agency.

Mo took the lead in envisioning this new line of protest. In early spring, Marco Saavedra, a DREAMer about to graduate from Kenyon College, described on his blog Mo's vision of how to unsettle ICE, as a protean mix of the "prophetic" and the "reckless." Mo loves to imagine what his opponents will do in response to an unexpected action by "illegals," and how bystanders will judge their response. He loves talking with ICE and Border Patrol officers. He often charms and disarms them. He wants to get inside their heads. Are they clever? Are they curious? What do they think of "illegals like him"? He tries to anticipate how they will feel and act if an "illegal" gets an upper hand over them? These projections of his are like imaginary probes sent into the future. This is what Marco recognized as the prophetic side of the imagination. If Mo engages in prophecy, this inspiration comes from his uncanny feel for the game and its players.[4]

Mo is restless, always eager to test his hunches. He is not afraid of being wrong. When stakes are high, he does not grow risk averse. He expects to lose strategic gambits in a drawn-out struggle. If Mo's creative visions for protest are reckless, as Marco said, if he is willing to put others at risk in actions that may not work, he takes these setbacks seriously as lessons for future actions. I have heard him say as an action was going quite wrong, "well, we've learned something." Mo acknowledged in one of our interviews that some of his ideas about possible actions are reckless. He always tries them out on Lizbeth first: "She is my moral compass."[5]

When I asked him about what inspired the new line of actions targeting ICE, Mo repeated what he had said about the origins of the sit-ins of the previous year: "It all started with and goes back to deportation cases." A few of these END campaigns for DREAMers proved to have spill-over effects. The outcome of these campaigns succeeded in stopping the deportation of undocumented immigrants who were not (strictly) DREAMers. For example, the Taha campaign in the summer of 2009 won deferred action not just for him, but also for his undocumented mother. It was in this context that Prerna remembered Mo saying, "if we can stop his deportation, we can stop any deportation." And the Rigo case suggested that with enough public support, they could stop the deportation of an undocumented youth who fell outside the strict categorical distinctions drawn by the DREAM Act and the "moral standards" of the "good" DREAMer.[6] Mo sought to explore the opportunities opened by these cases. These cases suggested that the protective "halo" now firmly fixed around DREAMers might be extended as defense for a wider circle of undocumented immigrants.

He started thinking of ways to reproduce the spillover effect in some END cases through a wider orbit of DREAMer activism. Toward the end of 2010, the Noodles Team sought to leverage END campaigns to pressure key Republican senators to support the DREAM Act. As they searched for these cases, Mo floated the idea that they consider "creating END cases where we can't find one. Find a good candidate and (as controversial as it might be) get them detained then rally around it."[7] The legislative goal that first prompted this idea of getting a DREAMer detained was now no longer in view, but creative adjustments of this controversial tactic of self-instrumentalization to the political reality of 2011 brought surprising new ends into view.

Mo began thinking of ways of experimenting with collective acts of DREAMer self-instrumentalization to reproduce on a larger scale the spillover effects of earlier END cases. This provided the creative spark for an audacious strategy of using DREAMers as bait to draw ICE into enforcement actions that could then be blocked and rolled back. Political scientist Luisa Heredia captured the logic behind this tactical innovation: radical DREAMers "leveraged their liminal legal and valorized social status to successfully move into and out of the state's enforcement apparatus."[8] Publicizing these protests and how DREAMers could move in and out ICE custody would expose the limits of the federal agency enforcement powers to a wider population of undocumented immigrants. By using DREAMers, in effect as object lessons in the defanging of ICE, Mo hoped to enlist a wider orbit of undocumented youth, including those who never imagined themselves as DREAMers or un-deportable. In the next iteration of protests, these new recruits pressed into defiant action would become object lessons for a still wider population of undocumented immigrants. These escalating iterations of civil disobedience would thereby reach out to educate and empower an ever-widening circle of undocumented immigrants. Their very success would provide proof of a radically new concept: If undocumented immigrants come out of the shadows in organized action, ICE cannot deport them. In this fashion, the DREAMer's halo could be expanded to encompass, protect, and empower more-and-more undocumented immigrants. The founders of the new network memorialized this guiding principle as "empower, educate, and escalate."

Going South

The farewell letter to UWD mentioned a convening of the new national network in the spring in Indiana. There the network could tap a local group, organized by Felipe Vargas, willing to engage in civil disobedience. But another geographical center pulled on the founders with the gravity of history and the promise of new recruits. Their new, inchoate strategy of targeting ICE needed steely undocu-activists. Going South seemed not only a good place to lure local ICE offices, but also to find these new undocu-activists. The founders scratched plans for the Indiana convening and decided to launch the network in the South, precisely where UWD had failed to organize in the previous year's campaign. In the South, where Republicans and racist local authorities ruled, where copy-cat legislations of Arizona's SB 1070 were spreading, and where undocumented immigrants lived under increased immigration enforcement, the radicals believed they would find young activists, motivated by anger and desperation, who could drive the kind of protests they were starting to envision.

Viridiana Martinez, co-founder of NC DREAM Team, was one of the authors of the farewell letter. It was on Viri's insistence that the letter criticized UWD's failure to organize in the Southeast: "We simply cannot tolerate a leadership which is ignorant to the nature of our movement in any region let alone the southeast!" In 2010, UWD failed to include NC DREAM Team in its organizing plans. The group had not even been invited to the field office meeting held in its own state. NC DREAM Team drew support not just from the research triangle around the universities in the east, but also from the western farmlands in the shadows of the Great Smoky Mountains. Led by Viri and fellow co-founders Loida Silva and Rosario Lopez, the NC DREAM Team brought together an angry and committed core of activists with none of the nonprofit or public institutional supports available to undocumented youth in states like California, New York, Illinois, or even Texas.[9]

Independent of UWD and the Noodles, NC Dream Team launched a sustained hunger strike in the summer of 2010 targeting the Democratic senator from the state, Kay Hagan. In the fall, when José Torres-Don and Alicia Torres moved from Austin to outside of Charlotte, NC, they connected with Viri and the NC DREAM Team. José and Alicia introduced Viri to Mo and Kiran. Viri accompanied them on lobbying visits in Washington, DC, through the last months of the 2010 campaign. By the end of the year, Viri was a core member of the radical group ready to split from UWD.

Alicia described the undocumented youth she and José met in the North Carolina as being very different from the DREAMers they had worked with in Texas. As she put it in our second interview, they "really lived under enforcement." Fear was concrete and immediate in North Carolina, and the kids they met there were angry and impatient with empty promises of reforms that never came. Viri embodied this temperament. She gave it voice in fiery and stirring words. She was a force, and everyone who met her knew it.[10]

A region in the Southeast extending across parts of three states, from Charlotte west to Asheville and southeast toward Atlanta, is home to a large population of undocumented immigrants. Drawn to the region by its high demand for low-wage agricultural and industrial work, relatively low cost of living, and natural beauty, many undocumented immigrant families have settled in the region and call it home. Most of them are originally from Mexico.[11] One of many interesting findings in sociologist Alexis Silver's rich ethnographic study of immigrant youth in a rural North Carolina community is how strongly they felt attached to their small Southern hometown. They loved its sights, sounds, and pace. The DREAMers I interviewed who had lived in North Carolina and northern Georgia expressed a similar strong attachment to the region.[12]

By 2011, this attachment was being sorely tested by the increased policing of immigrants. At the national level, detention centers were expanding their capacities to hold more immigrants, and deportations were skyrocketing. The total number of deportations in 2010 was more than double the number in 2000, and more than ten times the number in 1990. At the state level, politicians were passing legislative measures to make states like North Carolina and Georgia less welcoming to and more dangerous for undocumented immigrants. At the local level, counties and municipalities were moving to empower their law enforcement agents to work as proxy immigration officers for ICE.

Undocumented youth growing up in these Southern communities experienced this ratcheting up of enforcement. Deportation was not something they just heard about in the news. They were losing people they knew, friends and family. And they could remember the safer days of their early childhood. A mounting anxiety was now attached to everyday activities and imperiled future aspirations.

Along with connections to NC DREAM Team, Mo and Marisol had built strong contacts during the 2010 DREAM Act campaign with undocumented youth living in the Atlanta area. As far back as 2008, Marisol's work with the Phoenix Fund had made her aware of the work of the Georgia Latino Alliance for Human Rights (GLAHR). Georgina Perez, who worked with GLAHR, first reached out to DreamACTivist.org in the spring of 2009. Gina came to the United States with her mother when she was two years old. The two of them had first lived in California before moving to Atlanta when Gina was just seven years old. She did well in school. After graduating from high school, she was admitted to Georgia State University. At the time of her first contact with DreamACTivist.org, Gina was juggling college, work, and political engagement. Almost a year passed before she reached out again.[13]

Just as DREAM activism exploded on the national scene in the spring of 2010, local immigration events in Georgia caught national attention. In March, Jessica Colotl, an undocumented student at Kennesaw State University, was pulled over for a traffic violation on her campus. She was arrested and turned over to ICE agents who detained her for thirty-seven days. Under political pressure, ICE eventually deferred action on Jessica's case. After her release, the Cobb County Sheriff issued a new warrant for her arrest, charging that she had lied to police officers. The sheriff's action signaled to the public that if ICE would not do its job, local law enforcement would. It was in this context that Georgina reached out again to Mo in an email:

> I just wanted to let you know what is going on here in Georgia, you probably have heard already about Jessica Colotl's case, which has gotten MAJOR NATIONAL attention. This is big for us in Georgia because no one really talks about what is going on because of repercussions, which is exactly what happened with Jessica's arrest warrant set out by Cobb County's Sherriff, who is a complete asshole; well anyway that is another story. I just wanted to let you know that I have been working for Georgia Latino Alliance for Human Rights (Marisol from NY gave me the contact information) and we have been working really hard on promoting the Dream Act. We have come a long way from a year ago, I get many calls at the office from Dreamers calling us and wanting to get involved, of course I give them all the information for DreamActivist.org. I know we have not gotten the chance to touch base and we just want to let you know that we are here and FIGHTING because Georgia is a very HOSTILE state![14]

Gina's message came as Mo and Marisol were swamped preparing for the Tucson action, but they did not forget the note. They sent Gina an intake form for DREAMers considering participation in the Washington, DC, action later that summer. She did not join Noodles 2.0 but her message from Atlanta—"we just want to let you know that we are here and FIGHTING because Georgia is a very HOSTILE state!"—was not lost.

Georgia made headlines again in the fall of 2010, when the Board of Regents of the state's university system voted to ban undocumented students from attending the state's top five public universities and prohibited them from qualifying for in-state tuition at all colleges. In January, HB 87 was introduced to the Georgia legislature: a bill modeled on SB 1070. By April, it was clear that the state legislature was poised to pass it. Georgia's new anti-immigrant policies drew the attention of the radicals. The state seemed a perfect place to convene the new national network and to stage their first acts of civil disobedience.

Gina was still working in Atlanta at GLAHR, and she became the local point person for coordinating events in Georgia. The nonprofit was "doing a lot of know your rights work," and, according to Mo, had "filing cabinets filled with A#'s." (ICE tracks every undocumented immigrant it processes by A#'s or "alien numbers.") GLAHR's files offered a rich source of active deportation cases to fight.[15] In Georgia, the new network could organize END campaigns, mobilize undocumented youth newly excluded from the state's top public universities, and organize against the imminent passage of an Arizona-style law. It could also draw on the mobilizing capacity of the NC DREAM Team in nearby communities in North Carolina.

Atlanta: The Convening of National Immigrant Youth Alliance and the Georgia 8 and the Georgia 5

On April 2, undocumented youth from the across the country convened in Atlanta to form the National Immigrant Youth Alliance (NIYA). Given their understanding of the failure of UWD, the organizers of the new alliance directly addressed the question of who they served in a consensus mission statement:

> NIYA serves undocumented youth from all walks of life and not just the typical valedictorian. There's a need to re-define what a "Dreamer" is to be more inclusive of all those young people who are not class presidents, valedictorian, star athlete so that they feel identified with NIYA and are

empowered. A real attempt to become a more integrated/multi-cultural alliance needs to be made.[16]

A post by "Angy" on DreamACTivist.org echoed the new network's rejection of being identified with the good DREAMer who grabbed headlines and populated TV news profiles:

> During the battle for the federal DREAM Act last year many of our youth felt excluded and isolated themselves from the fight. The definition of dreamer became a 4.0 GPA valedictorian student who was part of every club/team, received every award and every scholarship. Senators presented these students during their floor speeches and those were the stories shown in the media, excluding all of our other youth. Where were the stories of the LGBTQ undocumented youth? The day laborers that qualify for the DREAM Act? When did they mention the mommy and daddy youth? What about the high school and college dropouts who can still apply? Did I miss the stories of the G.E.D holders?[17]

The convening sought to establish principles of governance that would ensure against repeating UWD's failure to be inclusive of all undocumented youth.

A document circulated after the convening set down these principles. It was clear on the guiding values, but thin on practical rules:

> The purpose of this document is to outline a proposed direction for us to take in regards to maintaining current members, as well as developing and building new members. In order for The National Immigrant Youth Alliance to progress we need a membership structure which promotes constant communication, a deep relationship with the organization, and establish rapport between members and from members to each other. In order for us to succeed we really need to foster a sense of family, we need to ensure that we are building strong roots, a strong foundation locally.

Over the next two years, as NIYA activists organized a series of direct actions across the nation, these professed values would prove hard to live up to. Under the pressure of planning and executing high-risk protests, organizers compromised the principles they avowed at the Atlanta convening. These compromises stemmed, in part, from the exigencies of the actions. To protect the activists put in harm's way by the actions, and to protect the element of surprise critical to the success of these actions, their planning and execution demanded tight command and control of communication by a small number of organizers. This type of control ran counter to fostering "constant communication," "rapport," and "a sense of family" among all members. Notes taken at the Atlanta convening, however, suggest that there were internal problems in the network present at its founding that may also have led to the compromise of these principles, regardless of the exigencies of these protests.

These notes list results from a survey of participants at the NIYA convening reporting positive and negative feedback. Overall, the feedback speaks to a successful launch, but a few comments suggested that some of the painful dynamics from the previous year had not been left behind. First, according to these notes, the convening spent too much time on recent history. Some participants were "too obsessed with the past." The past haunted the new network. Many participants could not forgive or forget "the movement" that used them over the past two years. The DREAMers at UWD also haunted them. Second, some complained of attitudes and practices they described as a "dictatorship—some feel like there are certain members that get to dictate the direction of the group." This criticism echoed tension internal to the Noodles Team that surfaced after the Schumer action.[18]

Two days after the Atlanta convening, NIYA announced its existence to the public with an act of civil disobedience:

> The day started with hundreds of youth marching through Atlanta chanting "Undocumented and unafraid!" and "Education not deportation!" After presenting a petition to Georgia State University's president, eight undocumented youth occupied a street until they were arrested.[19]

The intersection they "occupied" was on the border of the campus of Georgia State University. Their public "ask" was that Georgia "drop the ban" on undocumented students at its top state universities. Just prior to the action, the undocumented youth slated to be arrested recorded videos explaining their action. Gina, in her video, promised:

> I will no longer stand and wait for someone to come and save me. I will no longer wait for others to come dictate and tell me what to do while I'm being denied access to higher education.

She was "tired of students like Jessica [Colotl] being persecuted for trying to get a basic education." Gina recounted how when Jessica's arrest became news "we became scared and many allies told us to be quiet, to take a step back." With this act of civil disobedience, Gina was serving notice that these allies were wrong. "I've come to the realization that in order for us to beat this, we have to show them that we're more unafraid than ever before." She ended the video with a warning to allies, politicians, and immigration police:

> We're not going to stand back. We're not going to be silent. We're not going to be in the shadows. We're not going to let this happen any longer. We're going to step up and fight for our communities.[20]

The action led to the arrest of seven of the eight who blocked the intersection. Two of the arrested were from North Carolina, including Viri.

Kemi, a founding member of DreamACTivist.org and the keynote speaker at the 2009 Graduation in Washington, DC, described the Georgia 8 action in a "training manual" written for a "youth empowerment summit" NIYA held in Atlanta later that same month:

> They sat down asking university presidents to refuse the ban. They sat down asking fellow undocumented youth to continue to nurture the fire within themselves. They sat down asking Georgia and the rest of the country to take a long, good stare at this festering wound. They sat down asking the Obama administration to stop deporting our youth and tearing apart our families, to become the administration that we believed had the audacity to believe in true change. They sat down in the belly of hate. And they refused to get up. They *refused.*
>
> I still have trouble explaining the intensity, the rawness, the pride, or the grounded feeling of Dignity on that day, surrounded by echoes of **Undocumented! Unafraid!** Echoes that I long to believe were loud enough, unapologetic enough to reach into the closets of those youth in Georgia and across the country who yearn to be able to come out and to say those words, but are in such hostile territory they cannot.[21]

Dulce Guerrero, a high school student and the only participant under the age of eighteen to sit down in the intersection, left the action just before the police started to make arrests.

Dulce went back to her high school fired up. She organized a walkout that same spring and forged a network of high school students willing to engage in civil disobedience. Dulce and Georgina together formed a new organization and NIYA affiliate, Georgia Undocumented Youth Alliance (GUYA). In late June, GUYA led a group of five high school students in a second act of civil disobedience, the first NIYA action to lead to the arrest of high school students. Led by Dulce, they called themselves the Georgia 5.

The core members of the new NIYA network initially planned to stay in Georgia. The state had a lot to offer. It was an easy place to find deportation cases. There were frequent ICE raids, checkpoints, and other policing methods that could be targeted by direct actions, but other nodes in the new national network were pulling organizers away.

Between the first and second Atlanta actions, Mo traveled to Indianapolis to help with an action of undocumented youth at the state capitol. He brought with him what NIYA had learned from the Georgia 8 action. "Logistically," Mo told me in our last interview, "we learned a lot in the Atlanta action." They learned how to block a busy intersection of fast-moving motor vehicles. They used what they referred to as "fake cars," cars driven by supporters, to approach the intersection from different directions and all stop at the same time to allow activists on foot to occupy the intersection and then block it by sitting down. They worked on their chanting. They learned they had to communicate better, especially with family members. Mo said "parents were freaked out" by the arrests. "We didn't talk well with them."[22]

Another critical failure was that the action did not trigger ICE involvement. "We called the local ICE office with our best racist accents" trying to get "the damn illegals detained," Mo recalled, but to no avail. In Indiana, NIYA tried again to see if an action at the state capitol could land DREAMers in ICE custody. It was the second in what would turn out to be a long series of actions that year aimed at getting DREAMers into ICE custody. All these protests failed to achieve this end, but they succeeded in attracting public attention, new recruits, and many critics.

NIYA carried out a dozen different campaigns in its first year of operation. Following the two separate actions in Atlanta and the one in Indiana, NIYA activists organized protests in San Bernardino, CA, and Los Angeles, CA; Charlotte, NC; Mobile, AL, Montgomery, AL, and Birmingham, AL; Phoenix, AZ; and Portland, OR. In some of these campaigns, they executed multiple direct actions. The goals of the actions were many and evolving.

They included pushing Obama to act independently of Congress with an executive order protecting DREAMers from deportation; widening the circle of undocu-activists willing to engage in civil disobedience by involving undocumented high school students and the parents of DREAMers; executing actions in the most anti-immigrant states in the country such as Arizona, Georgia, and Alabama; and, most importantly, reaching into the shadows of these most hostile places with the NIYA message: "Come out!"

Across these many ends, these escalating actions aimed to educate and empower undocumented immigrants with the message that if you come out with an organized community behind you, you will be safer than you are now living in the shadows. Kemi explained the lesson taught by escalating protests to NIYA's Georgia Youth Summit:

> We find ways to stay in hiding so we don't get caught by police, and when we do happen to get caught—rolling a stop sign, driving to school—it's tough love, instant deportation. But when we work through our fears and choose to buck the system and openly risk arrest, something strange happens. Police officers treat you nicely (as they're arresting you, nonetheless), ICE officers treat you differently and suddenly, under the microscope of the public eye, the PR machine of ICE and DHS decides it's a bad idea to get involved and try to deport anyone. ICE is a greater threat when you accidentally come into contact with them than when you get all up in their respective grills and tell them that you are undocumented and unafraid.[23]

NIYA activists were using DREAMers, using themselves, as an object lesson to show to other undocumented immigrants that they would be safer getting "all up in ICE's grill" than hiding in fear.

As its series of escalating actions unfolded, NIYA mobilized undocumented youth embraced by its redefinition of the DREAMer—undocumented youth who could not go to college because they lived in states that excluded them from tertiary education or because economic pressures precluded it, and who did not always play by the rules and stay out of trouble. These new activists only half-jokingly referred to themselves as "bad dreamers." Santiago Garcia-Leco, from North Carolina, whose college aspirations were blocked by anti-immigrant state laws and who "never felt like a DREAMer," was one of these new activists drawn to NIYA's escalating actions.

"I Hated Seeing Undocumented People Asking for Help ... I Hated That"

Santiago was born in 1990 in Cheren, a small town in the Mexican state of Michoacán.[24] He was the fourth child born in his family. His father was mostly absent for the first years of his life, away in the United States with his brother, Santiago's uncle, trying to make a living for the family. He came back to Cheren only occasionally for short visits. As Santi grew into a toddler, his older brothers made the transition to migrant labor in the United States, like their father and uncle before them.

Santi's mom was left to raise him alone. She struggled to provide for the two of them:

> My mom's illiterate and it was hard to find work. She cleaned houses but there weren't even enough people with money for housecleaning. The situation got really bad. We ended up sleeping by the railroad tracks and eating out of garbage. My mom felt bad. She even thought about stealing. It was really hard to communicate with my dad. It was all through letters. There were other family issues. My mom's family wasn't supporting her, because they don't like my dad. But she wouldn't tell my dad about this, because she didn't want him to worry. There were times when they would go a year without speaking together.

When Santi turned four, his mother decided it was time for them to join the family in the United States. She took him on foot through the desert and across the border.

"We were lucky," Santi said, because "my father arranged for a family friend to guide us through the crossing." He's not sure exactly where they crossed:

> I don't really remember much. I remember crossing through the desert at night because I fell on a cactus bush and I had like cactus thorns all in my but, and all these women were taking them off [laughing]. I was yelling. That's the only thing I remember. It was very intense. It is hard to remember exactly, but by four you have memories. I remember running in the dark and red and blue lights. Once we got to my dad, and meeting my dad for the first time.... I actually have a picture of me when I met my dad, when I was running up to him.

His dad was working in western North Carolina in the small town of Burnsville. Santi spent his early childhood in this rural North Carolina town.

He started elementary school in Burnsville, and spent the next fourteen years of his life struggling to stay in school:

> I loved school because . . . I think there is so much emotional stuff that goes on for families that immigrate to the US—like for my mom leaving the other siblings. My dad's parents dying and not being able to go back to see them. That led him to drinking a lot. My mom also drank a lot. So, for me, school was, you know, like this escape place where I could feel safe, where I have control over what is going on in a way. I had to fight actually, after fifth grade, with my parents, to keep going to school.

At the end of his fifth grade, the family moved to Marion, NC. His parents thought this transition to a new home marked a good time for Santi to start working for a living:

> It wasn't that they didn't want me to have an education, but for them it was more important that for me, as a man, that I know that if I needed anything in life that I had to work. I started working when I was ten years old. I worked in the fields. I did any kind of work that I could at that age . . . I had to buy my own [school] supplies. Book bag, it had to come from my money. That's how they were raised. So, they sat me down and told me, "hey you know we need help and I don't think it will be good for you to go to school anymore." And at that time, I felt like I can't let go of that, because I was scared that if I don't have school, what do I have? It was this comfort that I didn't want to let go of. So, I told them that "no, I didn't want to quit school."

Santi persuaded his parents to let him continue with school. He went on to complete middle and high school in Marion.

I asked Santi what it was like growing up undocumented in western North Carolina. I asked about the level of fear he experienced because of his immigration status during his school years. He emphasized the pernicious effects of racism on his psyche as a child over the insecurity of being undocumented:

> I think it was more about being a person of color. I think that was the biggest issue for me. And even as I got to be more active into activism, for me, it was hard to connect with being undocumented. Of course, it is all connected,

but for me I was always undocumented, and then being this gay kid, and like gay brown kid in a southern state. So, I mean, in school, I think being undocumented wasn't a big thing. I heard about it, but I didn't even know what it was when I heard my teacher say "he is here illegally." But, I think for my teachers, I don't know, but I think it was more that I was a person of color. And my family was this Mexican family in this town with very few Latinos. In downtown there were more Latinos, but we lived in the country, moved by ourselves. In school it was more about being this kid of color and feeling different. I was the only kid who was not white in my whole [elementary] school.

His immigration status appeared to him incidental to this primary danger. Racism was the source of the threats he faced as a Mexican kid in rural North Carolina.

Santi first felt the danger specific to being "here illegally" when his family became the target of violent and menacing neighbors:

Being undocumented finally hit when we moved into a trailer park and we were the first Latino family to live there. And our neighbors started shooting at our house at night. The first time it happened my dad thought it was fireworks. The second time it clicked and realized it was gunshots. They looked at the side of the trailer. My mom wouldn't let us go to the bathroom after 9PM. We had to sleep on the floor. No one could leave the house.

Santi recalled being confused by his parents' inaction:

For me, at that time, I was like why isn't my dad doing anything? Why isn't my mom doing anything? I thought it was because they don't love us. But then it hit me, that they weren't calling the cops because they were scared that if they went to the cops, and they asked them if they were legally here, they were going to get deported. And all these years of sacrifice would be lost, just like that. So, they didn't say anything.

Santi said he felt more angry than afraid. "I was so mad and then one night my dad almost got shot in the forehead. He almost got shot right here [gestures to his forehead]." His anger was directed not just at the shooter, but at his parents for their impotence. "I was so angry at them."

Santi decided to confide in his elementary teacher about the shootings. He does not remember what he expected her to do, but he was taken aback by what happened next:

> And of course, with the white-savior mentality, she went and told all the other teachers, and the teachers went and told the counselors. And then, finally, one of the counselors decided to go to the trailer park, and told the owner of the trailer park . . . and he called the cops. But they were really, really supportive, in the sense that, you know, they were like your immigration status doesn't mean anything. But this hits the spot, and the guy was finally sent to jail. But that was the time when I realized: Oh shit, this is what it means to be undocumented. This is why my parents are so afraid.

As his awareness of his vulnerability grew, so did his feeling of shame about this immigration status.

He tried furiously to bury this shame. He became angry with people and situations that threatened to surface this shame. Santi described the somatic expression of this surfacing as a burning sensation. He explained his decision to "come out" to his family as an act to counter very similar, self-destructive feelings:

> [W]hen I was 15, I told my mom that I was gay. I remember I was listening to ABBA "Dancing Queen." I don't know what got into me. I already have to carry that I'm undocumented, this dirty secret. Every time it comes up, the burning ears, the shame, it was just too much. So, I'm listening to music. I say fuck it. I have to do something. I'm killing myself. I went to my mom and she's making tortillas. I said, "Mom, I think I'm gay. No, I know I'm gay." "Okay," it got quiet. She kept making tortillas and then said, "That doesn't matter, what matters is that you are hard-working, responsible, you love your family."

It was a pivotal moment in Santi's life: Not because of his mom's reaction— her part acceptance and part dismissal of his sexuality—but because of his honesty and openness with himself:

> I think that growing up, the way that I grew up, I was very independent. I had to come to terms with what I was facing myself, even to bring it to

the table, even to my mother. When I was going up the stairs, I was just thinking, I have to be ok with this decision about being open about it. If I'm okay, it doesn't matter what my mom thinks about it. It may be hard and hurt my feelings, but if I'm ok, I can live with it. I wanted her to be okay with it, but I had already made my decision to be open with it.

Immediately after coming out to his mother, Santi felt as if "this heavy thing had been lifted." He then "came out" to all his friends at school.

Santi always loved school, but during his junior year the weight of being undocumented crushed this love:

Everybody was talking about scholarships and what colleges they wanted to go to . . . I spoke to my counselor and I said I want to go to this school and she said "you can't go because you don't have a social security number." When she told me that my ears, I remember, got so red, so embarrassed, so ashamed, so embarrassing.

In a flash, his will, his work ethic, his smarts, all his academic accomplishments, suddenly did not matter. "And I just gave up. I didn't go that whole year. I think I went to 40 days." Santi had wanted to go to University of North Carolina, Chapel Hill. "I felt I could because I was working so hard. I had good grades, not perfect but I knew if I worked hard I could make it." The counselor's words crushed him. "Just the way that counselor spoke to me, it was just, you know 'we'll try to work something out,' but it was really just a 'no.'"

The disappointment derailed his junior year. He fell into a deep funk, but as he entered his last year of high school, he pulled out of the depression:

I have that dropout drama. I decide that if this is going to be my last year of school, I'm going to make it the best year possible. I love writing, so I stacked-up on classes. I was taking eight classes a semester. I took sixteen classes my senior year. After school, I would go to another school. I want to take more writing classes, anything I can take for free, now!

He worked hard and made up all the missed credits of his junior year:

It was the best year of my life. I was so focused. There was no time to be sad. I was so focused about school. But when it came to graduate, the last month, all the same feelings, all the excitement was finally coming down, and I got sad, all my friends are going to school and I can't.

He fell again into a funk. "I didn't want to walk the stage. I told my parents. But they were like 'no, you even fought us to do this.'" They could not convince him. Santi explained that he did not want to give the white administrators and teachers the satisfaction of seeing it all end for this "brown" kid. "When the principal hands me the paper, it's like thank you and now it's over. I didn't want to give them that. I didn't walk."

With high school over, Santi looked for a job. "You have to have money," after all, he said in our interview, but "what killed me was what all these white people expected of me." And more than anything, "I didn't want to give them this satisfaction." Santi punctuated this last statement with "fuck that," then laughed, flashed a guilty look because we are conducting the interview in a church, and then blew a kiss to the cross hanging on the wall to our left. So, to find work Santi decided to move away from home. "I thought I'd move to the biggest city around, so I moved to Asheville. I didn't want to be too far from my younger siblings. I have a really strong relationship with my younger siblings."

It was in Asheville that Santi was drawn, somewhat reluctantly, into the world of undocumented activists:

> One day, out of nowhere, someone invites me to go to a meeting about immigration. Oh my god, why do I want to go to a meeting about immigration. It was an old friend from Marion. He was like "I'm involved in this stuff about the DREAM Act. The DREAM Act would help people like us who weren't born here but were brought as kids." He was the one who told me I should go to this meeting, "we need more people to come."

Santi's friend prodded him to get involved. "I didn't want to go. The first two times he invited me, I didn't go. The third time, I did. I said why not. This was the summer of 2010." Santi was almost completely unaware of the actions DREAMers were taking across the nation. Growing up in Burnsville and Marion, he heard and saw next to nothing of immigrant mobilizations. And now, in Asheville, he had this very small window onto local activities.

He was not initially impressed by what he saw, but the idea of undocumented youth taking public actions to call attention to their immigration status was intriguing enough to keep him involved. "[I] start doing more flyer-ing and doing outreach to folks." The same friend from Marion, who invited him to the first meeting, "tells me something about that there are kids 'coming out' who are publicly saying they are undocumented." The idea struck Santi as ludicrous. "I'm just like 'why are they doing that? Why are they proud of something that is so shameful?' That was my mentality back then. But, then I was still curious. I wanted to see what it was all about."

I pressed Santi in our interview to explain his early misgivings and why he got further involved given his initial aversion:

> I don't know. I think that, in a sense, I was, it was my own thing about being ashamed. I wanted them to feel ashamed too. I wanted them to realize that this was something that they had to be ashamed of and not feel proud and not feel that they had a right. Because I was still with that mentality, you know, you're undocumented, you do not have a right.

Santi was repelled, yet intrigued. His reaction to the interactions between allies and undocumented youth at the meetings he attended contributed to his unsettling ambivalence. "Just seeing all these white folks, you know, talking to these kids about this. I hated that. I hated that."

Santi expressed, repeatedly, his disdain for feeling beholden to "allies." He referred, for example, to his third-grade teacher who intervened when his neighbor was shooting at his family's mobile home with kindness and gratitude, but also as acting "with the white-savior mentality." Allies at these meetings evoked similar feelings:

> I grew up in all these spaces where, you know, where people of color were always clinging on to white folks for help. And I hated that feeling. And I also hated being in this room with these kids complaining and embarrassing [themselves in front of] these white people . . . But then at the same time I was still curious. If this [DREAM Act] passes, I'd be able to go to school. And I wouldn't have to pay out-of-state tuition.

Self-interest and an almost grotesque fascination with the disturbing emotions stirred by the interactions between undocumented youth and allies kept Santi going to the meetings. And he slowly got more involved.

A local Asheville group, Jovenes por un Sueno, organized the meetings. The group was funded by a nonprofit organization within the RI4A network.

It was housed in a community center named the Nuestro Centro. Weeks into his growing involvement with the group, Santi met the co-founders of NC DREAM Team:

> Over that summer there were the three women who were doing the hunger strike in North Carolina. The coordinators for these meetings, somehow, they were in touch with them, and they brought them over to speak to us.

Santi was still struggling with his disdain for what he saw as the temperament shaping DREAMer activism:

> The mentality that we had was, or in the folks that I was included with, was this very victim mentality—like "poor us," you know, "we've had to go through all this and now we can't go to school"—that very mindset, that I had. And I didn't like it. I didn't like for us to be very, like, "please do this for me," in a very polite way. I hated it.

But Loida, Rosario, and Viri left him with an entirely different impression:

> They weren't asking nicely for it. They were demanding it. They were demanding that their senator support the DREAM Act. And for me that was very curious. And it was something different, and, also, they were on a thirteen-day hunger strike.

He immediately felt that their approach was something he could get behind, without shame:

> I was so intrigued by their work. I wanted to, you know, learn more about it. I didn't tell them, of course, but I was impressed by the way they were approaching, asking for this thing. Because at that time, and for me myself, I didn't know much about politics. But I was [thinking] how is it going to work by just asking, by just passing flyers, and signing little cards? It just didn't sit well with me. But when I met these women, I was like maybe that's the way to go with it. Maybe that's the key to actually [passing] the DREAM Act.

A couple months later, Loida moved to Asheville to go to college. Santi reached out to her, and they became close friends.

Loida introduced Santi to the more confrontational activism of The Dream Is Coming:

> [S]he was talking to me about all these kids that were doing, that had done, an action in Arizona. And I was just hearing about it, and it was so exciting. Of course, at first, my mentality was how can you come out publicly and say you are undocumented. But when she was telling me that the other woman who she had done the hunger strike with, Viridiana, that she had come out at a conference saying she was undocumented in front of so many people that didn't want her to come out, it was just so exciting. And, I felt, for the first time in my life, that I was excited about being undocumented.

Recall how Prerna Lal talked about why so many undocumented kids identify with the DREAMer character, even if "it is so fictional." Prerna said that identifying with the DREAMer character "makes them feel special and wanted in a society that doesn't want them." It could be "the one enabling thing in your life," she said. How could you "blame anyone for having that feeling," for wanting to identify with the image and share in some of the affirmation showered on the DREAMer character? Compare that sentiment to how the defiant, radical DREAMers made Santi feel. The contrasts and parallels are striking.

Santi could never identify with the good DREAMer image. He did not see himself in it. He never expected nor wanted that type of affirmation. "Fuck that!" Of the authorities in his life, the administrators and teachers, Santi knew "what all of these white people expected of" him, of this gay, brown, Mexican kid growing up in the South. He even knew what the well-intended, third-grade teacher with her "white-savior mentality" expected of him. And it "killed" him. But, when he learned about the radical DREAMers and their defiant actions, being undocumented—something that had always made him burn with shame—suddenly thrilled him. He could identify with them. He wanted to see himself in them. Wouldn't it just kill all those white people and their expectations?

Santi and Loida were together in Asheville, NC, in December when the Senate voted on the DREAM Act. They watched it on TV. "We cried. This is the end of the world. Little did we know that kids in DC were saying what is our next step?" Despite the crushing disappointment, Santi and Loida continued organizing. "Loida was definitely my window into everything." It was through Loida that Santi started to follow Viri's work with the new

NIYA network. "The first civil disobedience that happened in the South, in Georgia . . . that was the big, my big wakeup call." If not for Viri's involvement in the Atlanta action, Santi might not have been aware of it:

> For me it was finally, damn, you know these kids are willing to risk arrest and they're willing to say they are undocumented in front of cops and they're going to be arrested and they might get deported. Me and Loida were scared . . . Oh my god what if they get deported, what's going to happen. We were watching this and keeping up with Viri, and then when it happened and they got released, for me, it was just this unbelievable thing. Just a few years back, I was so scared of telling the cops about what was happening at home, because I was undocumented. My parents had that fear. They were growing old with that, the years were passing by and still with that fear. And then you have these kids, that [were] so in your face and they were demanding something. They were saying that they were undocumented in front of so many cops . . . This is something I want to be part of.

Inspired by the NIYA action, Santi started to work more directly with the NC DREAM Team.

A month after the first Atlanta action, Santi traveled with members of the NC DREAM Team to Arlington, VA, to attend the "Turning the Tide" conference. The conference was sponsored by faith organizations, but it brought together many of the usual suspects in the nonprofit immigration field. Gaby Pacheco addressed the conference:

> And she was talking about how it was important to have strong allies, and it was important to build good allies, and to trust what our allies are telling us. And I walked out. I just walked out. I couldn't take it. And then Mohammad followed me. And he was like "why did you walk out?" And I told him, "I just don't like her like that." I didn't know Mohammad at this point. I didn't even know the work he had done.

It was not, however, the first time Santi had heard Gaby speak.

A little more than a year before, the Trail of Dreams made a stop near his home in Marion, and he heard Gaby speak. He knew next to nothing about immigration politics at the time. He remembered that someone asked her, "what could they do to help?" And she replied with "something about buying t-shirts and following her on her fan page." It turned him off. This experience was important to Santi, because it was *his* own impression of moderate DREAMer activism before he fell into orbit of the NIYA activists and learned of their history with Gaby Pacheco and the Trail of Dreams.

Santi's disdain for Gaby's talk made an impression on Mo. He asked Santi to come meet other NIYA members at the conference. "And I follow, and there are all these, you know, all the outcast kids talking 'this is a shitty conference, they want to brainwash us, they want to speak for us,'... ah, okay!" The "outcast kids" included: "Mohammad, it was Gina, she participated in the first CD in Georgia, it was Adam, I forget his last name. I remember those three, and, of course, Viridiana was there."

Santi learned from Viri about how NIYA emerged in reaction to the events of the previous year:

[S]he started to explain everything to me. Finally, I saw that there were kids, part of the national work, who did not agree with Gaby, with the mentality. And I say Gaby, because if you were a kid in a small town, you would see her. She was the face... And I was like *what*! All this was going on and I had no idea. And I had no idea. I wanted to get involved.

Santi explained his attraction to the NIYA kids was connected to his visceral dislike for the "good" DREAMer, the "face of the movement," with their straight A's "sucking up to the allies" and asking, "please," for support. "Because you know, even at that time," when Gaby came through his part of North Carolina:

I started drinking when I was thirteen. I started partying and doing drugs when I was very, very young. And that was an image that they didn't want to portray and that's the image that they didn't want to represent. And also, my siblings, that didn't have a chance to go to school, that had to do landscape work, those images, were not... the youth that the DREAM Act [was] to benefit.

Before the encounter with "the outcast kids" in Arlington, Santi felt he "wasn't the Dreamer. That was a big thing. I felt like I couldn't share my story. I didn't feel connected. But Viridiana was, 'no, stories like yours need to be heard.'" Later that summer, at a rally organized by the NC DREAM Team, he "came out" about his immigration status. It was liberating, but Santi recalled thinking at the time, he wanted more: "Let's see what the folks in Georgia experienced." Toward the end of the summer, Viri proposed to the members of the NC DREAM Team that they organize with NIYA a civil disobedience action in Charlotte. Santi jumped at the opportunity.

Charlotte, September 12

Following the actions in Atlanta, GA, and Indianapolis, IN, NIYA worked with DREAMers in Southern California on two actions: one in San Bernardino on July 12 and another in Los Angeles on August 23. In all these actions, local and national goals mixed. The San Bernardino action was, in part, a response to the police at California State University, San Bernardino, cooperating with ICE. The Charlotte, NC, action was similar in that it targeted a college and local police cooperation with ICE. Across the local contexts, NIYA saw the actions as part of their national mission to educate and empower undocumented immigrants. A few months into the NIYA escalation, Mo said it was clear that they were succeeding with part of the mission. With every action, with every DREAMer jailed, Mo said NIYA recruited increasing numbers of undocumented youth to "participate in getting the jailed out. And as they made the calls to politicians demanding their release, they learned how it worked, they learned how to play ICE."[25] The actions, as intended, became object lessons and proof of concept for new recruits like Santi. But all these NIYA actions were also running into the same problem.

These acts of civil disobedience led to arrests, but the activists were not actually getting into ICE custody. The full object-lesson they hoped for included getting ICE to detain DREAMers and open deportation proceedings on them, so they could show undocumented immigrants how to organize a pressure campaign to get someone out of detention and to stop their deportation proceedings. It was becoming clear that ICE wanted no part in detaining undocumented youth arrested for acts of civil disobedience. The Indiana action led to arrests but not ICE detention. The two California actions had the same outcome. Even the second one, carried out in the offices of ICE located within the Los Angeles County Jail, did not result in immigration detention. As *activists* they were, in Mo's words, "too safe." In one regard, that was the educational point of the actions, but they wanted to push the instruction further and make *this point* sitting inside ICE's deportation machine. They wanted to show that even when in immigrant detention centers, facing orders of immediate removal, they could save themselves.

With the Charlotte, NC, action, Santi recalled, "we wanted to motivate people not to be afraid. Fear was real back then. We wanted to say to our community that the more public you are, the safer you are." Getting arrested served to broadcast this advisory statement, but the full NIYA lesson plan called for getting detained by ICE and then organizing communities to stop the deportation of the activists. This second step was being thwarted. In Charlotte, NC DREAM Team and NIYA tried again, hoping that this time an action in a county that had just joined the federal 287(g) program might meet a different outcome.

Santi described the different messages they sought to send with the civil disobedience: "For all our actions there is an internal message and then the message you give everyone." The "outside" message focused on North Carolina's policy for enrollment in state colleges and universities, local police cooperation with ICE, and the state's leading Democratic politician. The protest was staged at a major intersection near Central Piedmont Community College to call attention to a degrading education policy that made undocumented immigrants wait until all citizens had signed up for classes before they could enroll. Santi described the policy as designed to remind us of our "back-of-the-bus" status. In addition, Charlotte is in Mecklenburg County, at the time one of the few counties in the state with a 287(g) program, empowering local police to enforce immigration laws. Police arrests might automatically trigger ICE holds. Senator Kay Hagan (D-NC), who voted against the DREAM Act in 2010, was another target. And finally, NIYA, working with the NC DREAM Team, was looking ahead to the 2012 Democratic National Convention to be hosted in Charlotte.

Marco Saavedra, an undocumented activist who had been working with Mo on deportation cases in Ohio, joined NIYA for the Charlotte action. It was his first act of civil disobedience. This is how Marco explained the last component to the action's message:

> A reason they wanted to plan the civil disobedience was because Charlotte was going to host the Democratic National Convention in a year, 2012. And they wanted to have these open cases. I mean, I think it was kind of witty, they wanted us DREAMers facing deportation as the convening was going to come to town, so as to show you still have all these DREAMers facing deportation with these open cases in this very county.[26]

If everything went perfectly, this action of civil disobedience would lead to arrests and deportation proceedings.

The action centered around blocking a large intersection. The plan was for seven people to get arrested, but, according to Santi, the action went a little off the rails:

> We were sitting right there in front of the community college. There was a big intersection, too big actually. It was too big. My sisters almost got run over because . . . the cars were so mad. "You illegals, why are you doing this. We have to go to work. It's late." But yeah it was crazy, there was so much traffic.

The reaction of the police to the seven sitting in the intersection did not go as planned:

> I think we really pissed off the cops. They were really, really mad. They were telling Mohammad to back off. And he wouldn't. He wanted to see where they were taking us. And the cop finally got pissed. He was like "ok, your going in with them." They did that to him and to two others that weren't supposed to be arrested.

Mo getting arrested unnerved both the NIYA activists arrested with him and those organizing on the outside. The plan was for Mo to coordinate the work on the outside. If the arrested were taken into ICE custody, Mo would lead the public campaign to stop their deportations and secure their release from detention. Now Mo, the activist with the most experience in stopping deportations, was inside with the rest of them.

The ten arrested were not all held together in the local jail. Santi, after being booked, was separated from the others:

> They separated us because there were so many of us . . . And when that happened, I was a little bit scared that they will no longer see us as a group. And, the way they did treat me was like they thought I was just another person, you know, that had found myself stuck in a 287g county.

This was scary, but also the goal. Santi started to believe he might succeed where past actions had failed and get into ICE custody:

> I think that the best thing was being processed, and knowing how it worked. Immigration was already there. And for me it was the first time

encountering immigration, an immigration agent. When I was there, when I did the interview, I was shaking. I might get deported. What did I get myself into? But . . . the whole point was that we wanted to end up with immigration.

When the interview wrapped up, "they told me that in 30 minutes you are going to be transferred to Georgia to a detention center, because you are not a US citizen and you are not giving us information that you have ties to the country." Santi was scared and started having second thoughts. He wondered if he should try to stop or slow down the process. He was given a form to sign:

> I was shaking and I was like wait a minute was this supposed to happen? Should I take it? But at that time, I was like, I think this is what we wanted. So, I just signed it. They were so set that they were going to send me to the immigration detention center, and the load was like 30 minutes away, and they were going to be able to take me that same day. I was just sitting there, and when the folks outside heard about this, they were freaking out. They were like this has never happened.

It is in these moments that Mo's confidence proves indispensable. He steadies those around him, reiterates the plan, and adjusts calmly to events on the ground. But Mo was inside with the arrested.

On the outside, the NIYA activists were struggling to adjust to Mo's absence. Santi's call came first. He spoke with Felipe Vargas and told him that he was about to be sent to immigration detention. Santi described the call:

> I knew that Felipe was nervous. But I didn't know why he was nervous. "We are going to get you out. We are doing everything we can. Just stay strong." Yeah, I'm fine. I was nervous, but I was now feeling more nervous because I was hearing him nervousness on the phone.

The anxiety was short lived:

> Because there was so much publicity around us, and like people knew about us, and they were making calls and signing petitions, by the next day, I was released. It was so quick.

All ten arrested in the Charlotte action were released within a few days, no one got further than county jail.

Santi was simultaneously relieved and disappointed. For a long anxious moment, he thought he might succeed where others before had failed. Although he did not get into ICE custody, Santi did not consider the action a failure. He and others just like him had learned a valuable lesson:

> Man, it's so easy to get in and get out, for us. For other people who were not so involved, it was so important that they saw, oh these kids, undocumented kids, got arrested and then they were released. And, on the next day on the news to hear, oh they just got released. That was a big thing for us.

Getting arrested also changed Santi in a deep, personal way. He had jumped at the opportunity to join the Charlotte action because he wanted to experience what "the folks in Georgia experienced." When he first heard of the purpose behind the Atlanta action, Santi said: "It felt, it felt true. I wanted to do that, I wanted to, for myself." The experience did not disappoint. It was everything he had hoped for and more:

> It is this sort of moment of liberation. I imagine it as like a baptism... I mean, just as you are sitting there, and you see all these people they're supporting you, and you're afraid that they're going to arrest you, though you know it worked [in the past], you still don't know if it is going to work this time. So, I was still afraid. Because even before that, just driving, I was afraid. Every time I saw a cop, I was afraid. Every single time my dad would drive, I was afraid that he wouldn't come home... So, for me, to do that, I think that personally it... was like I wasn't afraid anymore.

Santi was not alone in describing the action as transformative. Alicia Torres, also arrested in the Charlotte action, said she went into it with fear, "fear I had carried for years." The action lifted this burden. "When I was released from jail, I felt bullet-proof!"[27]

Marco Saavedra turned to poetry and religion to do justice to the force of the experience:

> i remember the first night in jail, we both cried, first me, then he, and i asked him: "why don't we go to paradise tomorrow." he didn't answer, the question

was too absurd. i thought of mexico, maybe southern france . . . but really i was thinkin' of christ on the cross telling the crucified criminal adjacent to him: "today you will be in paradise." absurd, as well, i suppose. what i mean by this is that behind the horror is the glory, that one can be free while imprisoned, and that slow sullen tears sometimes drift into the light.

Charlotte was also Marco's first act of civil disobedience. In the months to come, he would spend many weeks behind bars. Civil disobedience would carry him not only to jail, but to ICE detention, and across the border with Mexico. In the same blog entry describing his first night in jail, Marco described the NIYA philosophy of civil disobedience as construction in defiance of destructive injustice: "We build our castles for tomorrow—strong as we know how—and stand within them, free within ourselves."[28]

The Charlotte civil disobedience not only forged the personal transformation of jailed activists, but it also sowed the seeds of a new tactic in the NIYA repertoire of protest. While Mo and Marco sat in jail, there was literally, not just figuratively, a condemned prisoner "adjacent" to them: Javier had been stopped by police, allegedly for a broken license plate light. Unable to produce papers, the police arrested him, and ICE put an immigration hold on him. Mo and Marco started working to stop his deportation right there as they sat together in jail. NIYA activists had already worked hundreds of deportation cases, but Javier's case was the first they started working "from the inside." Until this point, DREAMers had been trying to get into deportation proceedings to show the community that they could stop their *own* deportations, but the Charlotte action suggested that once in ICE custody activists could stop the deportations of others from the inside. But how to get inside?

Catching ICE in Alabama

Changed by his Charlotte baptism, Santi was looking for more of the same empowerment. Alabama had just passed HB 56—an enhanced version of Arizona's SB 1070:

Mohammad invited me to, he said, "hey, do you want to go to Alabama." I was like "yeah I want to do this. I feel like we need to do this." So, I quit my job, and I went down to Alabama. And it was just me and him for a few days.

They went down to do some reconnaissance, a lead team soon to be followed by scores of NIYA activists:

> For me it was the best experience, organizing wise. I mean it was like starting from the bottom. And it gave me this real vision of all these other organizations and all these conversations that Mohammad and Viridiana had, it was the first time I experienced them for myself.

NIYA did not have an affiliated organization or established contacts with undocumented youth in Alabama. Earlier actions in Georgia, Indiana, California, and North Carolina were organized with members of the network already embedded in the local communities. To make matters more difficult, local nonprofits immediately attacked NIYA organizers as interlopers.

"As we got there," Santi recalled, "I get this call" from a person working for a local organization:

> The first thing that came out of his mouth was "are you with DreamACTivist and NIYA or with UWD?" I told them that . . . my organization is with NIYA. So, he's like, "OK, so let's try to meet some time." I was like that's weird. Little did I know that all these organizations were mad at us. They called us outsiders and that we didn't know what was going on in Alabama. But I mean our argument has always been that it doesn't matter where you are. What happens to an undocumented person in Alabama is going to happen to an undocumented person in North Carolina. I mean all these policies, all these laws, already exist, they just don't have a big fancy name like HB 56. These organizations were feeling very territorial and it was funny because an organization that was mad at us had actually asked me, earlier, to go down there and work with them. I was still an outsider, but that was okay?

Santi described how they started organizing by embedding themselves in an undocumented community:

> We lived in a trailer park for three months. We lived with the community. We saw the experiences that they lived. We heard their stories. It was just so great. We just started from the bottom. We started working with families. Felipe was doing his trainings in our trailer. Kids, after school, would come [to these training]. It was very beautiful grassroots work.

Without connections to a local DREAMer organization or networks, they were forced to forge connections from scratch:

> It was my first exposure to this kind of work. And I was feeling like this is the kind of work we should be doing. At the same time, it was bittersweet, because I was like why is all this work not being done by all these other organizations that are getting the money to do it. And then, at the same time, it was like well they shouldn't even exist because they don't even know the experience that we have. They don't know like the family Martel, they don't know their experiences. They don't listen to their experiences, and they don't let those experiences lead the work.

I asked Santi how many people came down for the Alabama actions. "From NIYA? I think in the hundreds, like a hundred and something, yeah, people in Alabama." They came from across the national network. In the trailer park where Santi stayed, "we had people from Pennsylvania, DreamACTivist Penn. We had members from NC DREAM Team also come down. We had Nico from Chicago, IYJL."

The communities they worked to mobilize with were under attack. The people they met were gripped with fear. And these NIYA kids were asking them to think of participating in acts of civil disobedience. Looking back, Santi said, "We were crazy":

> We would go to trailer parks. We would go to schools. To all these places, just talking to folks. And the biggest thing that people were afraid of was this law. They were afraid that if they said they were undocumented they could get deported right on the spot. So, for us, that called for the need of a CD, of course. We wanted to demonstrate that the very thing you are afraid of is not going to happen and the notion that the more public you are the safer you are, just that core belief.

Their work succeeded in spreading this core belief:

> It was really, really great. Just in the CD, one of the girls in the trailer park, she was 17 at the time, she had never heard of, about people being undocumented and coming out unafraid. She had never had any kind of exposure to any kind of organizing, but she was one of the first who was like "I

want to do it. I want to participate. I want to participate in this action." And I think that for me that was so big. Seeing someone who didn't know us, but trusted us and trusted the message that we were carrying.

This trust extended beyond the Alabama youth:

> It was also the very first time that parents were participating in CDs. So that was a big thing. Because I think at that time, the way that I was seeing the work that we were doing was creating this bridge. Seeing how much power us as DREAMers had. How much power we had in our hands and at the same time, you know, how can we share that power with our parents.

Getting parental involvement in civil disobedience actions was one of two new strategies in the Alabama campaign. Undocumented immigrants who could never fit in the categorical distinctions drawn for inclusion in the DREAM Act joined their children in getting arrested. Tañia Unzueta enlisted her father, a veteran organizer in Chicago, to join the campaign. He led other parents in this new step of parental involvement.

The other strategic advance in Alabama was devising a new way to get into ICE detention. The strategy came to be called "the silent action." Among the first activists to arrive in Alabama were Jonathan Perez and Isaac Barrera from California. They had been arrested in the summer action in San Bernardino.[29] They drove to Alabama with Lizbeth Mateo. Isaac and Jonathan would be the first NIYA activists to "break into" ICE detention. They may have gotten lucky because they arrived early. Other NIYA activists would try again in the days to follow as the Alabama campaign continued, but once the news got out about Jonathan and Isaac, local ICE agents were wise to what they were doing. But Jonathan and Isaac were also very cagey. As Mo said, "it's hard to be rude"—especially to scary authorities—but Jonathan and Isaac were good at it. Their silent action was a command performance of the "bad dreamer."

On November 18, Jonathan walked into a Border Patrol office in Mobile, AL, to get detained. What happened next was captured in an undercover NIYA video and posted on the internet.[30] Before Jonathan leaves his car to enter the building, his compatriot, Isaac, asks him if he has any "last words?" Jonathan replies, "Let's take this ICE out!" He enters the Border Patrol office. His phone is in his breast pocket, the camera lens peeping out of the pocket and filming. A woman in civilian clothing greets him with a skeptical, "Can I help you?"

JONATHAN: What is this?
WOMAN: Border Patrol.
J: Oh shit! [Long pause] Yeah, we're lost.
WOMAN: Okay, um, where you trying to go?
J: Mobile [He mispronounces Mobile with an exaggerated ending of *bile*, as in stomach bile.]
WOMAN: Where?
J: Mo-*bile*.
WOMAN: Okay. Hang on one second.

The woman looks confused or maybe in disbelief and beats a hasty retreat, leaving the lobby using her card key to access some back offices.

Twenty seconds later, but it feels like an eternity, a man in civilian clothes walks in with a John Wayne swagger. He is followed by another man dressed in a green Border Patrol uniform with a gold badge on his chest and a gun on his belt, his step less confident than his partner's. The man with no uniform addresses Jonathan with, "Hey, what's going on hoss?" (You can't make this stuff up.) What follows is a brilliant theatrical performance of activist jiu-jitsu:

JONATHAN: Huh?
MAN-IN-CIVVIES: How you doing?
J: I'm doing good.
M-IN-C: Can we help you with something?
J: Yeah, you know what, I'm actually not lost, I'm just kind-of pissed off. What are y'all doing here?
M-IN-C: What are we doing here?
J: Uh, hun.
M-IN-C: Doing a job.
J: What's your job?
M-IN-C: Doing a job. Why?
JONATHAN: What's your job?
M-IN-C: To enforce immigration laws.
J: That's what you do?
M-IN-C: Yeah.

MAN-IN-UNIFORM [SPEAKS UP FOR THE FIRST TIME]: That's what we do. [Pause] What can we help you with?
J: So y'all are deporting people.
M-IN-C: We don't deport people. Judges do that.
J: You all take 'em there, right?
M-IN-U: It is our mission to protect the border.

He sounds a little unsure of himself, as if self-conscious of the absurdity of border protection in Alabama. There is a long pause, and then the man in civvies, as if compensating for his partner's timidity, challenges Jonathan: "What's it to you?"

J: I'm undocumented too?
M-IN-C: You're what?
J: I'm illegal too?
M-IN-C: Oh, you're illegal. [Nodding his head]
J: You think I should be deported too?
M-IN-C: I don't know. Why don't you show us some ID?

He extends his hand and walks to Jonathan's side blocking him from the exit door. Jonathan is about to get detained.

M-IN-C: Let's see what you got for ID.

The camera is fixed on the man in uniform as, off-camera, Jonathan pulls out his ID and gives it to the man in civvies. Then, back on camera, the man in civvies hands the ID to the man in uniform. He looks at it for a few seconds, and then turning it over in his hands addresses Jonathan:

M-IN-U: So how did you get to the United States?
J: Cross the border.

Jonathan's delivery of this line is pure deadpan humor:

M-IN-U: When did you do that?
J: Long time ago [is that a chuckle from Jonathan?]
M-IN-U: You have any other ID with you?
J: No, not with me?

The video cuts out at this point, but shortly thereafter, Isaac, bringing coffee from IHOP, joins Jonathan and the men of Border Patrol. Jonathan and Isaac are rewarded for their performance with a trip to the Basile Detention Center in Louisiana.

A NIYA press release on November 20 announced the success of the action and explained its purpose:

> We know many of you think it's crazy but why not? Immigration thinks it has some power over our communities, they think they can hold us hostage with the threat of detention. So why not take the power away from them and let them know we can go to detention on our own terms. If we take the fear card away from them then what do they have to hold over us? What would it look like the next time a bill like HB56 were proposed and the community was actually willing to stand up to the racist legislators?

On closer inspection, this is not really a press release. It is not addressing the press, nor the authorities, nor allies, but "us"—fellow undocumented immigrants. And the sheer audacity of its claim—"we can go to detention on our own terms"—reads like a threat:

> So far we've been able to show you that if you are undocumented and organized you are safe from deportation. Obama memo or not, if you are a part of a larger community then you are safe from deportation. What immigration authorities are banking on is your fear; you need to be afraid of them therefore they can rule your life. Are you really going to play into their hands? By not coming out you are playing into their hand. They are banking on the fact that you will be afraid of them. If you challenge the system, it will fall apart. The power of civil disobedience is that we go against the norm. We change the power dynamics and show that we are the ones to dictate our futures. We are the ones in control. It isn't that the cops are arresting us; we are allowing for the cops to arrest us and on our own terms. It isn't that ICE has the option to detain us; we are dictating whether we allow for them to detain us or not. We are the ones in control, regardless of what the authorities think. Once we take the power back from them then we can start to win. That is what we do with civil disobedience. We can organize inside and out.[31]

The action realized the audacious vision that NIYA activists could use themselves, as DREAMers, to catch ICE and then push back on its violence from inside of the deportation machine.

Once Isaac and Jonathan succeeded in getting into ICE detention, NIYA activists went to work on securing their release. Marco said in our interview that "what was really strong about [the Mobile action] was that it had happened before even DACA had been announced. They were just trusting organizers to get them kicked out [of the Basile Detention Center in Louisiana]." It took an anxious week before pressure from NIYA secured their release.

Jonathan and Isaac demonstrated that NIYA could get into detention centers on their own terms. Marco said NIYA had not set up the organizational capacity to use this opportunity to work cases from the inside. The Basile Detention Center was not an easy place to find immigrant detainees, because it was housed inside a larger jail with only a fraction of its beds reserved for inmates under ICE's custody. Mo goes so far as to not call the action an infiltration. He maintains that the point of this silent action was first and foremost to show that undocu-activists could get in and out of detention.

Alabama was NIYA's largest campaign to date. In addition to the silent action, activists carried out civil disobedience actions in Montgomery and Birmingham that led to multiple arrests of undocumented youth and their parents. NIYA organizers struggled to communicate with and support all the jailed activists and their loved ones. There were heated disputes over the use of money donated for bail bonds, and, more importantly, over whether the wishes of some of the arrested had been heeded by organizers on the outside. With the number of participants, the involvement of parents in civil disobedience, and the success of the silent action, Alabama was a signal achievement in NIYA's mission of escalation—a high watermark. It also marked the beginning of open divisions within NIYA that would lead to damaging defections from the alliance.

7
2012 and 2013
Infiltrators and Coyotes

NIYA continued organizing civil disobedience actions into the spring of 2012. On March 20, NIYA worked in Phoenix, AZ, with Erika Andiola, a leader of the Arizona DREAM Coalition and a participant in the 2010 (und) occupy action in Washington, DC, to stage an action with undocumented high school students. Six students blocked the intersection of W. Cheery Lynn Rd. and N. 75th Ave, right outside of their school, Trevor G. Browne High School. The group included students as young as sixteen. Video posted to the Topo YouTube channel captured the emotional intensity and careful choreography of the protest.[1] The chants are tight and rhythmic. The timing and coordination of the collective action is precise. The poise of the teenagers in the face of Sheriff Arpaio's officers is remarkable. The optics are powerful.

In Phoenix, NIYA not only confronted Arpaio's officers, but also harsh criticism from local nonprofits decrying the "recklessness" of getting minors arrested. Local groups voiced outrage that interlopers would manipulate impressionable kids to engage in dangerous actions. These criticisms were not new. GLAHR repudiated NIYA's actions in Atlanta, GA. The San Bernardino, CA, and Charlotte, NC, actions came under attack from fellow DREAMers and "allies." After Alabama, charges that NIYA activists were interlopers who descend on a community to create a spectacle of undocumented protesters getting arrested, and then move on, leaving local groups to handle the legal fallout for participants, grew louder. Accusations spread, through DREAMer circles and beyond, that NIYA was diverting the money it raised to bond protestors out of jail to fund its escalating direct actions. But the attacks in Phoenix reached new levels of volume and vitriol.

Somos America, a coalition of immigrant rights groups in Arizona, circulated a press release repudiating the action. It included a letter from a teacher at Trevor Browne High School claiming that the students involved in the action had been manipulated:

Dream Activist Mohammed Abdullah [sic] came [from] Michigan, from the outside, albeit with good intentions but irresponsible in its execution. Following the chaotic arrests of the Dreamers, Mohammed Abdullah posted a fundraising plea on his website asking for donations to liberate the Dreamers from jail. I opposed any activity where the safety of the Dreamers was unnecessarily put at-risk. What was the goal of this protest? To stop Joe Arpaio? Community Leaders, local organizations, and the US Department of Justice, are all currently attending to the abuses of Joe Arpaio, so why endanger minor high school children? I want to make it clear that I'm not against youthful civic participation in our community, but I don't appreciate outsiders coming to Arizona in a sneaky way to agitate our Dreamers... Our youth need proper guidance in order for them to positively engage in our community. High school students are vulnerable and sensitive and perhaps a little lost, especially in Arizona's current political climate.[2]

Carmen Cornejo, a longstanding DREAMer ally who worked with Erika at Arizona DREAM Act Coalition, amplified the criticism in a Facebook post. "I'm truly saddened for today's civil disobedience event. There are several things wrong about it." She made the now familiar charge that NIYA activists were interlopers. "[The action] was never brought for discussion to the Arizona DREAM Act Coalition where most of the protesters participate. Initiating this event coming from the outside is an act of disrespect." She questioned if it had a higher purpose than grabbing headlines. "I do not completely disagree [with] civil disobedience as tool but I do not know what is the real intention of the protest short of getting Arpaio angry." She addressed her post directly to Mohammad:

> I have no problem if some older dreamers choose to follow you for a civil disobedience rally but I resent the fact of having minors participating in this. I think we must respect their youth and not block any possible opportunities they may have. We collectively have a responsibility to protect the High School students. I thought there was an internal agreement that the people protesting would always be college graduates.

She ended the letter on a more personal note:

> I felt disrespected since I was never properly informed of the action even [though] you and I communicated previously to your visit. You purposely

hid the real intentions of your trip. As you may know, I have been working for the DREAM Act way before there was an ADAC, Dreamactivist, etc. . . . I think I deserve a little consideration. I do not want all my work and the work of others to be even questioned. Genie Z and I are the only persons working successfully stopping detention and deportations of DREAM Act students in the Phoenix metro area with the help of great lawyers and allies. We cannot invest time and resources helping people who got themselves into trouble following a poorly planned event.[3]

In an email to fellow NIYA members, Jonathan Perez provided a forceful, point for point, rejection of Carmen's letter. Two of his counterpoints tightly framed NIYA's disregard for its critics and their preferred form of advocacy. The first counterpoint, quoting Carmen and then countering, read:

"As you may know, I have been working for the DREAM Act way before there was an ADAC, Dreamactivist, etc."* [thats why it took so long to even get close telling us to remain in the shadows]*

And the second:

"I thought there was an internal agreement that the people protesting would always be college graduates." *[oh no she didn't, . . . was this United We Dream? anyway fuck that shit, ive gotten arrested twice and in detention but if it was up to you, i would not be allowed to be part of that life changing experience OH HELLZ NAH, this is going back to the "good" immigrant "bad" immigrant argument. Frankly i am a #baddreamer and seriously college graduates are not gonna lead this movement for long, the ones who will lead it are the ones who don't make it that far. I'm so digusted by this I might drop out of community college again]*[4]

When the six high school students walked free from jail, NIYA considered the purpose of the action to be crystal clear and the risks taken vindicated. The other undocumented students at Trevor Browne High School, some of whom had told the six they would get deported, got to see them return to school, feeling freer than the day before their arrest. And there was nothing Sherriff Joe Arpaio, his officers, or ICE could do to stop this newfound freedom.[5]

The Phoenix action marked a year of almost continuous campaigns of civil disobedience. NIYA activists had demonstrated that they could organize in any immigrant community in the United States. They could recruit undocumented youth anywhere to risk arrest, train them for civil disobedience, compel the police to arrest them, and then get them released. NIYA activists had become adepts in the practice of a new undocumented protest liturgy, and they were capturing the attention of local migrant rights activists everywhere. A NIYA action in Portland literally took over the city's May 1 demonstration. It had become almost too easy. In Mo's words, they were now almost "too safe."

OFA Sit-ins and DACA

That same spring, in a departure from the actions organized to empower local communities, NIYA pivoted back to pressuring national politicians for policy change. In late April, Senator Marco Rubio announced a compromise DREAM Act. News reports suggested he was in dialogue with the presidential campaign of Mitt Romney. Having survived the Republican primaries, Romney appeared poised to soften his immigration positions as his campaign eyed the Latino vote for the general election. NIYA organizers thought it an opportune time to directly pressure the Obama administration on protecting DREAMers.

To this end, NIYA hit on a clever inflection of its sit-in protests. Starting first in Colorado, undocumented youth staged a sit-in the Denver campaign office of Obama for America (OFA).[6] Sit-ins at OFA offices then followed in other swing states: in Ohio and North Carolina, as well as in cities such as Atlanta, Salt Lake City, and Oakland. In these OFA sit-ins, NIYA activists wearing their caps and gowns sat down in the middle of the campaign offices. They asked people showing up to volunteer, "Why is Obama deporting DREAMers?" NIYA threatened to expand these actions to other campaign offices unless Obama issued "an executive order to stop the deportation of DREAM Act-eligible youth." With a nod to the Occupy Wall Street movement, NIYA activists called the actions (und)occupations.

Two weeks into the OFA (und)occupations, President Obama announced an executive order, Deferred Action for Childhood Arrivals (DACA), which provided DREAMers with protection from deportation and with work benefits.[7] Some Washington, DC, insiders credited the NIYA actions with forcing Obama's hand. For years, he had argued that he did not have the constitutional power to sign such an order. Prerna Lal, in our interview, said she was told by White House staffers that the (und)occupations unsettled the Obama administration and, at minimum, accelerated the timing of the executive order. If the order was inevitable, the administration did not want to sign it in the spring. They would have preferred to wait until later in the year for greater electoral effect in the presidential campaign.

Marco Saavedra told me he did not believe the executive order was a direct response to the OFA sit-ins, but credited Mo for genius timing:

> What was so savvy was that Mo anticipated DACA coming and took the opportunity to directly attack Obama. It set to rest any idea that targeting Obama, turning the pressure up on him, could backfire.[8]

Immigrant rights groups had largely resisted attacking Democrats and the president. They focused their energy instead on Republicans at the national and the local levels. The OFA actions broke this resistance. For the next two years, Obama would face increasing pressure from immigrant rights activists until his signing of the Deferred Action for Parental Accountability (DAPA)—an executive order extending DACA-like protections to the undocumented parents of citizen children.

With the announcement of the passage of DACA, Josh Hoyt, the director of ICIR, advised NIYA to declare victory and take its foot off the civil disobedience accelerator. Josh wrote Mo, "I would own the victory, say Obama did it because of your occupation, and keep your powder dry so you can revisit the strategy if you need it again." He warned against continuing the occupations after the DACA memo, quoting Saul Alinsky: "A strategy that drags on is a drag."[9] NIYA did call off the (und)occupations, but with their most audacious actions still to come, Obama would stay in their crosshairs.

NIYA Ascendant?

Just prior to the OFA actions, NIYA drafted a report for potential funders touting its accomplishments. The report, an account of NIYA's first year of work, described an ascendant network. It listed twenty-five undocumented organizations affiliated with the alliance. These affiliates were organized in seventeen different states. It also reported engaged individual members from fourteen other states. The report described seven NIYA projects: Youth Empowerment Summits (YES), Education Not Deportation (END), Secure Your Own Community (SYOC), UndocuHealth.org (a crisis hotline staffed by mental health volunteers), UndocuQueer.org (a book project), UndocuShow (a call-in show and podcast), and UndocuArrest. Some of these projects were more aspirational than fully operative, but four had established records of accomplishments.

Starting with Atlanta, GA, NIYA organized fourteen YES trainings in different parts of the county. These trainings engaged a total of 475 individuals and launched eight new local organizations. The report announced trainings pending in three states where the alliance had yet to establish a presence: Nevada, New Mexico, and Iowa. END campaigns were at the center of NIYA's work, as they had been for DreamACTivist.org: "Our member organizations have organized around 87 deportation cases with an overall success rate of just over 85%." According to the report, NIYA's END cases differed from the work of other organizations aimed to stop deportations, "because we work on criminal cases publicly, with the intent of winning them in an effort to create precedent for who is actually a 'good immigrant.'" The SYOC program sought to establish a clearinghouse of information gathered from the END cases. It distributed online intake forms for undocumented immigrants seeking to fight deportation and provided trainings for local community organizations seeking to begin their own END campaigns. "We have spent over $35,000 in advocacy tools (online database), educational material and trainings for fighting deportation cases."

UndocuArrest, the last project listed in the report, was the name NIYA gave to its civil disobedience work. The report claimed that in ten different NIYA protests more than seventy undocumented immigrants risked arrest and deportation. "To date we have spent $54,000 on civil disobedience actions. $27,000 of which has been allocated to bail funds, with the remaining money allocated to civil disobedience trainings as well as action development." The report cited "tentative" upcoming actions "scheduled across the nation," but did not suggest the form they would take. The report concluded with an overall view of its expenditures. "Currently, as NIYA, we have raised over $120,000, all of which has been allocated to our current programs. We anticipate our expenses through the fiscal year 2013 to be upwards of $280,000, including newly hired staff positions as well as an extensive training and leadership development program."[10]

NIYA was approaching UWD's scale in affiliated organizations, if not budget. In its one-year record of actions, it could fairly claim to have well surpassed the rival DREAMer network in the scale and scope of its work. With DACA following immediately on the heels of the OFA sit-ins, NIYA could also plausibly claim to have achieved more of an impact on immigration policy in one year than UWD and its nonprofits sponsors had achieved over the past three or four years of advocacy.

Despite this impressive record, there were signs that the NIYA network was in trouble. To expand the reach of its work, the alliance needed more funding than it could raise from member organizations and individual supporters. In a reversal of its founding philosophy, to go it alone, it started to look for foundations and nonprofit organizations willing to support its work. Even as other migrant rights organizations started to carry out work modeled on its UndocuArrest program, NIYA's difficult reputation scared away all funders. And cut off from this funding, NIYA started to lose core activists to better-funded organizations starting to do similar work.

Right around this one-year mark, Tañia Unzueta left NIYA to go work with NDLON, and IYJL's affiliation with NIYA came to an acrimonious end. The split stemmed from conflicts that surfaced during the Alabama action. With these defections, NIYA took a big hit to its organizing capacity. IYJL was one of the most influential DREAMer organizations in the nation. Respect for NIYA's leadership within undocumented activist circles took a hit with the Chicago group's departure.

On the other hand, Tañia's departure reflected the growing influence of NIYA's strategy of resistance with other migrant rights organizations. Although it came under attack from many "allies" for its confrontational and risky tactics, NIYA's methods were gaining respect in the form of imitation. Tañia and other members left NIYA for better-funded organizations, like NDLON, who recruited them in part to put the radical DREAMer toolkit to work for their own campaigns. Mo recalled that as Tañia prepared to leave, Chris Newman, legal counsel for NDLON, reached out to him to talk about enlisting her to adapt some of NIYA's tactics for a new campaign they were launching:

[He] says, "hey, I just want to tell you we are starting the #Not1More Deportation campaign, because of what you guys have done." . . . That pissed us off. They are coopting the work that no one will support, and they will fuck it up. Then they enlist Tañia on Undocubus.[11]

He felt, at the time, abandoned. Speaking five years after Tañia left to go work with NDLON, he was still bitter.

In all three interviews, Mo never claimed to be blameless in the defections NIYA suffered in 2012. When I asked why the alliance started to lose core members, he offered some reasons outside of his control, but he also took personal responsibility. He acknowledged that his drive to tightly control the plan and execution of NIYA actions made him very difficult to work with. On the many clashes he had with other strong-minded activists during these actions, Mo said, "I was such a drama queen back then." But it was more than intra-organizational drama. The defections started to mount precisely as NIYA made yet another move to escalate.[12]

The loss of Tañia and other core members, whether they were pushed away by internal conflicts or pulled away by opportunities offered by better-funded organizations, undoubtedly weakened NIYA's organizational capacity and membership support. These push and pull forces do not, however, fully explain why this seemingly ascendant organization collapsed within two years. NIYA retained dedicated members equal to the task ahead of executing a new series of escalating actions. Over the next year, through the travails of living on the road; couch surfing from one place to the next; living on Raman noodles; and spending time in jail, detention, and endless court proceedings, these remaining members carried to success NIYA's most *demanding* campaigns yet.

The defections in 2012, although not fatal, were nonetheless a sign of a serious problem: the physical and emotional toll of the confrontational and risky forms of protest demanded by NIYA's path of escalation. This stress of escalation contributed to these defections, and the actions still to come would prove even more taxing. NIYA's escalating actions, which hinged on the self-instrumentalization of DREAMers and the emotional cost of using themselves and their bodies as tools to challenge authorities and inspire others, possibly more than any other factor, threatened the future viability of the organization. Of course, escalation through DREAMer self-instrumentalization was responsible for NIYA's dramatic success over its first year of operation. NIYA's last two campaigns would call on undocu-activists to "pimp" themselves once again as DREAMers, but with these two innovations, the costs of self-instrumentalization proved higher than in past actions—maybe too high.

Of the many creative forms of protest to spin out of Mo's prophetic and reckless imagination, the visions directing NIYA's final campaigns were the most audacious yet: infiltrating detention centers to stop removal procedures at the very last possible moment and crossing borders to undo deportations that had already been carried out. Marco Saavedra, more than any other NIYA activist, experienced the full power of these new twists to NIYA's self-instrumentalizing activism. Marco may also have suffered more than any other from their full emotional toll. Marco's course of activism—rising rapidly to ecstatic heights of engagement and then collapsing almost as dramatically in emotional exhaustion and self-doubt—was similar to the trajectory of NIYA's collective actions after the spring of 2012. His experiences illuminate the dynamics leading to NIYA's greatest accomplishments and dramatic collapse.

"For It Is Counter-Hegemonic To Be Counter-Intuitive"

Marco's involvement in DREAM Act politics started in the summer of 2010. He took part in the NYSYLC hunger strike outside of Schumer's office, although he was not a formal member of the group. He did not go to high school or college in his hometown of New York City, and so he did not know the CUNY students leading NYSYLC. He had spent much of the previous decade hundreds of miles from his home attending classes on the idyllic, rural campuses of a prestigious boarding school and a selective liberal arts college. It was an improbable education for a kid born into rural poverty in Oaxaca and raised in Washington Heights.

Marco wrote in his undergraduate sociology thesis: "My family had been farmers for millennia—ever since first setting foot on this continent. We had settled in a small village (*San Miguel Ahuhuititlan*) located in the rugged southern state of Oaxaca where the *Sierra Madre Sur* and *Sierra Madre Oaxaca*, the unconnected southern spine of the Rocky Mountains, unite." His ancestors lived there through the rise and fall of the Spanish empire and one hundred years of Mexican independence. "What finally made us flee north was the start of a new era—unfair and unbalanced neoliberal trade agreements between Mexico and its richer neighbors destroyed our ability to sustain ourselves."[13] Marco was three years old when he crossed the US border around Nogales with his father, mother, older sister, and an aunt. His father had made the trip a number of times before. "Back in '93," Marco told me, "it was pretty easy to get over the border in Nogales."[14] It would not be the last time he crossed the international border cutting through that desert town.

His family settled in Washington Heights, NY. They were one of a small number of Mexican families living in this upper Manhattan neighborhood. Their neighbors were "predominantly Dominican folks." His family's social connections were limited to a tight circle—mostly made up of the families of aunts and uncles who had made the same trip from Oaxaca and the families they met at their small Pentecostal church. Marco's father worked pumping gas in New Jersey and delivering produce to local restaurants. His mother cleaned the halls of a nearby Catholic girl's school.

Marco went to Juan Pablo Duarte Elementary School or PS 123. It was located right across the street from his apartment building. "The school," Marco explained, was "named after one the founding fathers of the Dominican Republic," reflecting the strong Dominican character of the neighborhood. For middle school, Marco tested into a magnet program at the Mot Hall School in Harlem. I asked him if he was good at school, and Marco's reply was characteristically modest: "A little bit, yeah. I think I barely made the cutoff."

At Mott Hall, he gained admission to a special program called "Prep for Prep." The program, he explained, "prepared inner-city students for private day or boarding schools." Marco added, sheepishly, "again, barely, I made the cutoff." After a year in the program, he was admitted to Deerfield Academy, a prestigious boarding school in western Massachusetts. Marco described Deerfield as a "conservative stronghold" and a "surreal place" that made him "feel so out of place." I asked Marco if he had wanted to go to boarding school, or if the decision was made for him:

> I had few friends from middle school. We were also a close-knit family, and my parents were a little bit overprotective when we were growing up. So, I was kind of excited to go to boarding school. But, at the same time, I didn't have a frame of reference of what boarding school or public high school were. I mean, I had a pretty good guess, . . . but we had been kind of like geared into this fourteen-month preparatory component that would end up in boarding school, so it almost seemed like unquestionable.

The experience at Deerfield was at first alienating, but he adjusted to it:

> I made friends that I still stay in touch with. I feel like it is one of those things when you are living it, I mean, I think when I was . . . sixteen, I did not have a sense of the world or even of myself, to realize what everything

meant. Like, why every building was named Koch, after David Koch? Now it makes me more uneasy. I mean, the type of student that boarding schools prepare, basically everyone, it's a safe bet, that most everyone, if you had to guess what they are doing now, they are probably all bankers. I liked the experience, and at the same time, when you are undergoing it, what is the alternative?

Marco did well academically at Deerfield, but he was disappointed with himself for not taking full advantage of the intellectual opportunities offered.

With the help of college counselors, both at Prep for Prep and Deerfield, he learned about a unique opportunity to study at Kenyon College:

Kenyon has been providing financial aid for undocumented students for a while. They're not too public about it, but now its public. They've been public with my story and stuff. But, yeah, I mean they were really hush about it, but we knew that they did because the CEO of Prep for Prep, that got me into boarding school, she sits on the Board of Trustees for Kenyon College, so she knew that they provided it.

As he prepared to leave Deerfield for Kenyon College, he did not know what he wanted to study in college. Marco laughed as he remembered telling people he "wanted to study economics in college." His real passion was for art but that seemed an impossible and forbidden pursuit. "Maybe it's the whole immigrant conflict of you want to make money for your parents."

His intellectual pursuits started to broaden literally on the day of his graduation from Deerfield Academy:

I remember after high school everyone goes to senior parties. It's pretty unhealthy, cuz like, there's nothing more unhealthy than 18 year-old rich kids whose parents give you a keg. It's pretty sad, from what I heard, but I guess I kind-of wanted to go. But instead, my parents drove up in our huge van that we use for the transport of produce, and we just went back home.

His classmates drove off to graduation parties of excess feted by their rich parents, and he with his parents in the family's delivery truck headed southbound on I-91 back home to Washington Heights. "And on the ride home," maybe wishing he was with his rich classmates doing damage to his health,

Marco decided, "I might as well just start reading. And I started reading Elie Wiesel's *Night* for the first time." Marco felt he had "underused" his high school education. To atone for this, he dedicated himself to reading that summer a series of fourteen books he should have read at Deerfield. *Night* was the first in the series and he started it with boarding school disappearing in the rearview mirror of the delivery truck.

During our interview, Marco tried to remember the books in the series and the logic of their selection. "I think that's when I read Kafka's *The Metamorphosis*, coupled with *The Plague*, and just some really dark stuff." Searching his memory for more books, "*Beloved* was on the list," he reflected, it felt "good to get these different frames of references." Richard Wright's *Native Son* was another book he remembered reading. Reflecting on the selection, Marco said, "I just wanted to take myself more seriously, but I think I was also freaking out about what would happen next."

His intellectual turn deepened, and his frames of reference expanded at Kenyon. He became an admirer of the literary work and social criticism of James Baldwin. He read the works of W. E. B DuBois and chose sociology as his major. He painted and fell in love with poetry.

He wrote his undergraduate honor's thesis on DREAMer activism. Reflecting his lyrical approach to social science, its title read, "Undocumented & Unafraid: A So[ul]cial History of the Student Immigrant Movement."[15] Research for this thesis came from his first-hand experiences observing the movement in the spring and summer of 2010. Students at Kenyon are encouraged to pursue study abroad for their junior year. Because of his immigration status, Marco could not leave the United States. As an alternative, he did an internship in Washington, DC, with Sojourners—an evangelical social justice group—and spent a visiting semester of course work at Georgetown University. His goal for the spring semester and summer away from Kenyon was to take a closer look at church-based immigrant rights work. Marco was and remains deeply religious—although the nature of his faith has changed considerably over the years. His stay in Washington, DC, coincided with the pivotal DREAMer actions of that year.

He went to the first screening of *Papers* in Washington, DC. He attended a closed-door event for undocumented youth to greet the trekkers from the Trail of Dreams as they arrived in Georgetown and were met by members of NYSYLC who had walked from New York to join them. He went to hear a talk by Matias Ramos at Georgetown and was introduced to him after the event. He joined fellow New York DREAMers at NYSYLC in their hunger strike outside the offices of Senator Schumer. He also met Mo that summer. Marco did not take an active role in the planning of any of the actions that year, but he had a front row seat for many of them. He was not privy to insider talk about a growing split within UWD, but he told me that even from his vantage point "the divide was pretty easy to see."

He returned to Kenyon in the fall for his senior year to write his thesis. He continued to follow DREAMer events online and through social media. When he finished his finals for the fall semester, he drove with friends to Washington, DC, to be there for the final vote in the Senate. They arrived—a few hours after the votes were tallied—to disappointment. I asked Marco about how the failed vote affected him. He said he was not "personally crushed," as so many other DREAMers were. Marco "more and more wanted to just make art," and he did not see his future as tied to being able to gain legal employment or a path to citizenship.

He graduated from Kenyon in the spring of 2011 and started an internship with a faith-based social justice group in Ohio:

> It's taken a lot of names, but I guess at that point, I was supposed to be hired by Cincinnati Faith and Justice. It's kind of a more evangelical, well it was a traditional church-based organizing structure, but their goal was to outreach to evangelical folks. I think it has now morphed into this larger vision of the Evangelical Immigration Table—definitely more tailored to conservative evangelicals.

Just north of Cincinnati, OH, in Butler County, Sheriff Rick Jones was becoming notorious for his zealous immigration enforcement. According to Marco, "he was one of the few sheriffs that implemented 287g in the country." Working at Cincinnati Faith and Justice, Marco contributed to a campaign to stop the deportation of a DREAMer named Julio, who had been detained in Butler County. Julio's case, Marco said, "exposed [me] to a lot more family members and community members that [were going] through the same thing." He wanted Cincinnati Faith and Justice to build on Julio's case and take on more deportation cases in Butler County:

> But I was, we were, receiving a lot of push back . . . from our superiors. Because they wanted to control a lot of the messaging and wanted to use

this one example [Julio's case] to build their immigration base, but not really take on more deportation cases.

Marco was forced to look elsewhere for help to take on the cases from Butler County that Cincinnati Faith and Justice would not touch.

"I started talking to Mohammad at that point." Marco sought advice from others too, "some UWD folks" and other groups. "They were all really slow to respond and Mo is just always eager to take on cases and respond with this is what you can do." With Mo's help, Marco started working independently on other deportations in Ohio. He was quickly drawn to Mo's broader vision of how to challenge immigration enforcement. When NIYA and NC DREAM Team started to plan for their Charlotte, NC, action, Marco wanted in.

Marco's family was not happy with his activist turn. His mom and sister took a bus to Charlotte to try to intervene. They made a dramatic entrance in the middle of a final preparation meeting for the action. They angrily confronted Mo, accusing him of having manipulated Marco. They told Mo that they held him responsible for Marco's safety. Their intervention did not stop Marco from going ahead with the action. He was by then already deeply devoted to NIYA's philosophy of escalation.

Marco captured the originality and bruising moral force of Mo's imagination unlike anyone else I interviewed. His co-authored book with Steve Pavey, *Shadow then Light*, memorialized in word and pictures the fruits of this imagination. The book quotes Baldwin from *Nothing Personal*: "One discovers the light in darkness. That is what darkness is for." And for almost two years, Mo's vision of activism offered Marco a quest for light that sent him deep into the dark shadows of carceral America.[16]

In a spring 2012 blog, after the Charlotte and Alabama actions, Marco described Mo's improvisations on civil disobedience as conveying a "prophetic" and "reckless" message for undocumented communities:

Abdhollahi's critique of institutions and ineffectual and patronizing processes & philosophies ushered in a new paradigm of thought, and more: demonstrated to other undocumented youth the liberating effect of owning our status & utilizing it as a moral force. In effect, this multiplied the potential for empowerment. All else of the programs he engaged (and helped form) hinge on this idea: Come Out. Come Out: You must forbear; forbear you must (Faust).

For it is counter-hegemonic to be counter-intuitive:

> When they damn us to hide: we come out.
> When they tell us to follow: we lead.
> When they mire us in bureaucracy: we organize.
> When they tell us it is not possible: we imagine.
> When we are told to stop: We fight.

But even at the rapturous heights of his new commitment to the practical philosophies that ushered from Mo's counterintuitive imagination, Marco betrayed a doubt that it asked too much:

> Perhaps what Mr. Abdhollahi means is more than what he can do. In other words: he has almost unfeasibly ensured new patterns of thought & a new beat for undocumented youth (and the greater undocumented community) to walk in:
> Undocumented. Unashamed. Undocumented. Unafraid. Undocumented. Unapologetic.[17]

Since the departure of Prerna, the radical DREAMers had lacked someone who could give voice to the creative genius of their new activism and explain its meaning. With Marco, NIYA had its bard. But he was more than just that.

By 2012, Marco, working alongside José Torres-Don, directed most of NIYA's END campaigns. He understood what it took to stop a deportation, and he knew what made for a good END case. He was adept at identifying the legal details in a case that increased or diminished the chances of winning a stay of removal. He was also good at reading whether a detained person and their family would commit to what was needed of them to carry out a public campaign. Marco made for an almost perfect infiltrator.

The BTC Infiltration

Jonathan Perez and Isaac Barrera had shown in Alabama that NIYA could get into detention centers. Mo and Lizbeth now started to strategize a way to expose the indiscriminate nature of ICE enforcement by using detention centers as places to find and work END cases. With each new month, the number of people detained and deported by ICE was breaking historical records. The Obama administration insisted that ICE was exercising discretion in the operation of this formidable machinery for detaining and deporting immigrants. Official memos from current and previous ICE directors provided guidelines to the agency's field offices for the exercise of "prosecutorial discretion" in the furtherance of enforcement priorities. A June 2011 memo from Director John Morton updated these guidelines, clearly instructing ICE agents that, in order to prioritize the removal of felons and individuals that pose a serious threat to public safety, they should exercise discretion in the prosecution of immigrants who posed no public risk. The Obama administration contended that the tens of thousands of immigrants detained and deported each month reflected these priorities. If ICE was following the principles guiding prosecutorial discretion, law-abiding undocumented immigrants should not be taking up space in detention centers, and no one who qualified for DACA should be languishing in an immigration jail.[18] The scores of END cases NIYA had worked on over the past year suggested the truth was quite otherwise. Independent studies of deportation cases from across the country also suggested that a large share, if not a majority, of removals were of non-felons.[19]

Mo and Lizbeth knew detentions centers were filled with immigrants with deportation cases that could be stopped by public pressure campaigns—the kind of cases that the Obama administration claimed ICE was not targeting for removal. The problem was finding them. Once in detention, immigrants are cut off from their families, their support networks, and even legal counsel. Held in ICE-controlled facilities, family and friends are afraid to visit. Inmates are often effectively denied access to phone calls because of exorbitant pricing on calls from the centers; this also restricts their access to legal counsel. As they languish there, shut off from the outside world, ICE officers hound them to sign voluntary deportation orders. Detention centers are the black holes of the shadow-world of immigration enforcement. Once someone enters, the presumption by loved ones on the outside is that they are lost.[20] In the past, NIYA activists had to rely on family and friends to bring individual cases to them. The process was slow and painstaking. Breaking into detention centers, as Jonathan and Isaac had done, opened a radical, new approach.

NIYA had been arguing that the surest way to avoid detention and deportation was to move into the public light. Come out of the shadows, make your status public, tell your story, then your community can protect you, and ICE cannot touch you. From shadow to light, as Marco and Steve Pavey's book framed it. ICE is a raptor in the dark, but out of the shadows, NIYA aimed to show it could harass ICE like crows on an owl in the daylight. If NIYA activists could break into these black holes of mass detention, they could not only expose the administration's lies about its enforcement priorities, but they could find in these carceral spaces hundreds of winnable END cases, all gathered for them by ICE itself. The same number of cases that it had taken NIYA activists all of the previous year to find might be found in one infiltration. ICE's detention centers could be used against the agency by turning them into organizing spaces. Infiltrations could, as Marco said in a video recorded moments before he infiltrated the Broward County Transitional Center (BTC) in Florida, "flip the organizing narrative." The aim was to "walk into detention centers, organize, and walk out."[21] It was an ingenious plan of "political jiu-jitsu."[22]

Marco told me he was not scared as he prepared to infiltrate the BTC detention center, because he did not think it would work. He figured if he succeeded in getting arrested, immigration officers would pull his file, see he was a DREAMer, and release him. But he was wrong. On July 11, just as Jonathan and Isaac had done in Mobile, Marco walked into a Border Patrol office in Fort Lauderdale, FL. NIYA secretly recorded the audio of the interaction.[23]

This is how it unfolded. Marco tells a Border Patrol officer that he has not heard from a friend for days and fears he has been detained. The officer asks if his friend is an "illegal alien." Marco does not answer directly but replies that they crossed the border together from Mexico into Arizona:

OFFICER: Does he have papers?
MARCO: No.
OFFICER: How old were you when you crossed?
MARCO: Fifteen.
OFFICER: Do you have papers?
MARCO: No. Just this ID.
OFFICER: Do you go to school?
MARCO: No, just work here in Fort Lauderdale.
OFFICER: You know I have to arrest you?
MARCO: Oh?

It was only when he was being processed that Marco started to get scared. The officers saw that he had a prior arrest in North Carolina (from the civil disobedience action in Charlotte), and they figured his would be an expedited removal case. Marco said in our interview that "fortunately the North Carolina case had been closed," blocking his expedited removal, and he was sent to the men's section of BTC as ICE officers worked on an order for his removal. Nine days later, on July 20, Viridiana Martinez was detained at the Port of the Everglades. She was sent to the women's section of BTC. A month after Obama's signing of the DACA memo, NIYA had two DREAMers in ICE custody at the same privately run detention center.

Inside, Marco and Viri turned to gathering information on removal cases. It took Marco a little time to adjust and get to work. The "boredom gets to you," he said. "You miss clean socks." But organizing on the inside proved quite easy. In an immigrant detention center, all the undocumented are already out. They have nothing to hide. There is no risk in going public with their case. The worst has already happened. And they are already "organized" by the very confines of the jail. Marco described life in detention this way: "Inside it was pretty safe—excessive church going. There is so much church going in there. It's crazy like, the chapel's full every period, even outside in the courtyard."

Marco's personal religiosity helped him tap these religious networks, and he started doing intakes by the score. He would ask his fellow inmates when and how they came to the United States; why were they detained; if they were DREAM Act eligible; if they had US citizen children; if they had a criminal record; if they had a case for asylum or a U-visa;[24] if they had loved ones who depended on them for survival, such as ill or disabled family members; if they had a lawyer; who was on the outside waiting for them; and would these loved ones be willing to take public actions to pressure authorities on their behalf? Marco later wrote of these men he met in detention:

> I loved the men, because they first loved me. Theirs was a faith unseen, how you trust a 22-year-old who tells you to tell your family to tell a youth to tell the country your hardest truth is beyond me.[25]

Marco, a religious virtuoso, was practicing a new faith learned from NIYA: own your status, bear witness, and wield it as an organizing and disruptive moral force.

As Marco gathered this information in the men's section of BTC, Viri did the same in the women's section. All the information they gathered was shared with the NIYA base camp, where a half-dozen organizers worked around the clock to stop as many deportations as possible. The most difficult task was sneaking signed waiver forms out of the detention center from each detainee authorizing NIYA organizers access to private information on the legal charges they faced. NIYA organizers contacted family members and asked them if they would be willing to go public to fight for the release of their loved one. Would they start a petition? Hold news conferences? Pressure local politicians? In short, would they help launch a public campaign to stop the deportation?

The base camp organizers compiled all the information fed to them by Marco and Viri in a spreadsheet. In total, Marco and Viri met with over two hundred detainees and did 188 documented intakes (not all intakes provided the complete information they hoped for). The detained came from twenty-six different countries of origin. More than two-thirds of the detained came from four countries: El Salvador, Guatemala, Honduras, and Mexico.[26] Of the 170 intakes with relatively complete information, sixty had no criminal record, roughly one in three. Most of these detainees without criminal records were detained after being stopped by law enforcement in a motor vehicle. Out of the 170 cases, ninety-three were initially detained for legally spurious reasons or after one of the following minor infractions: driving without a license, a moving or traffic violation, riding in a car stopped for a violation and failing to present some form of identification, or being caught-up in an investigation or raid targeting someone other than themselves. Out of the 170, eleven were DREAMers (i.e., they would qualify for the DREAM Act), at least ten had good grounds for a U-visa, at least twenty-four had grounds for asylum or temporary protective status, forty-five were parents of children with US citizenship, and at least twenty-five had no legal representation or were the clear victims of legal malpractice. In short, the majority deserved consideration for prosecutorial discretion and deferred action according to the Morton memo and the DACA executive order.[27] BTC was filled with the kind of immigrants that fell outside of the Obama administration's stated enforcement priorities. Out of these cases, NIYA launched ninety-four online petitions. Marco estimates that at least forty deportations were stopped by their efforts. Mo estimates more than seventy were stopped.

Once Marco and Viri finished their intakes and fed all the information to the base camp, NIYA released to the press that it had two infiltrators inside BTC.[28] Almost immediately, Marco and Viri were released, or better put, kicked out. Viri described the release in a talk at the University of New Mexico. She was escorted without explanation from the women's section through "a side door" and brought to the front of the center where authorities do intakes. Viri did not know what was happening. "They had guards all around me like I was some big time criminal or something. I was like what's wrong with you people? What are you afraid of?" Marco had also just been separated from the other detainees, but she did not yet know this when she witnessed an amazing scene. She saw scores of men in their orange jump suites amassing outside the intake center. They were saying, "we want to see Marco?" Then the men began to chant and pump their fists in the air:

> "Marco! Marco!" And we are talking like five hundred, six hundred immigrant detainees, like "Marco! Marco!," all male. It was crazy. I was just like, "what am I in a movie? What have they done to Marco? What's going on?" I didn't see Marco. And then they forced them into the courtyard, and they started chanting: "Free at last! Free at last."

The removal of Marco, without explanation as to where he was being taken, had triggered a mass demonstration in the men's section. Marco was then brought into the intake center, joining Viri. They were told, "your ride is here," and were "literally kicked out . . . told to go to the other side of the fence."[29] Viri and Marco had walked into detention, organized the release of scores of detainees, and now they walked out, free.

Marco and Viri's exploits gained widespread media coverage. The Spanish-language media paid the most attention. Univision and Telemundo brought news of their actions to millions of Spanish-speaking viewers. Marco and Viri appeared on *Democracy Now* and their actions were also the subject of a long story in *American Prospect* and a radio segment on "This American Life." Seven years later, the film director, Alex Rivera released a feature length documentary/docu-drama of the action. It debuted at the Sundance Film Festival and SXSW.

Coyote Dreamers

The BTC action in Florida is the best known of a half-dozen NIYA infiltrations. It was also the most successful in terms of the number of deportations the action stopped. From the very beginning it had proved difficult for NIYA activists to infiltrate detention centers. The DACA order and news of the BTC infiltration altered ICE practices at the field level, making it still more difficult. In the late summer of 2012, NIYA activists broke numerous traffic laws across the Southeast trying to get into detention, but with little success. They did manage to carry out three more infiltrations over the next year. Creative strategies to solve the problem of getting into detention led to the next, and last, audacious move in the NIYA escalation: the border crossing actions of the #BringThemHome campaign.

One of the last successful infiltrations before the #BringThemHome campaign was executed by Claudia Muñoz. To get detained, Claudia drove a car onto a bridge in Michigan that crossed into Canada. She stopped her car just before the border crossing and waited for border patrol to detain her.[30] Mo had come up with this idea of using border crossings as a method of forcing ICE to detain undocumented activists. But he soon saw an expanded purpose to a border crossing action: a dramatic way to call attention to the fate of deported DREAMers and to assert a claim for their right to return.

Well before the BTC infiltration, Mo floated the idea past two lawyers: What if he, and maybe a few other NIYA members, crossed into Mexico and then crossed back? He characterized the action as the next step in NIYA's escalation. Margo Cowan, the Arizona lawyer who helped the Noodles with the Tucson action, thought it a very risky idea that could end poorly for the border crossers. She suggested returning to the drawing-board for the next step in escalation. David Bennion was more sanguine. He grasped immediately that the action could force Customs and Border Protection (CBP) officials to place activists directly into immigration custody, and he started to work out the legal means to ensure that the border crossers could not be just turned away at the port of entry. He emphasized that the selection of participants would require attention to their legal cases for asylum or humanitarian parole[31]

Mo raised the idea with Marco before an OFA action in Ohio:

Maybe I should have been suspicious from the get go. He was like, "I was thinking about pushing the envelope on deportation and using my own story of being gay from Iran. What if I went to Mexico, and came back asking for asylum? And then he was like, what if a group of people do that?"[32]

Marco said the idea went "dormant for a while, but I guess he floated that idea around with other people." Mo approached Viri with the idea. Santiago said he also talked with Mo about participating in the action.

Lizbeth remembered him raising the idea when they were working together in Florida at the BTC base camp. She appreciated the disruptive power of such an action. She also saw it as a chance for her to realize long-held dream to return to Mexico and to visit family. She argued against Mo participating in the border crossing. She thought NIYA needed him on the outside to organize the release of the participants from detention. "People call Mo a dictator, but he makes sure things get done," Lizbeth told me, and that is "what you want when you are sitting in jail."[33]

Mo approached Marco again with the idea in early 2013. Marco had his doubts, but he emphasized in our interview that he "believed in the action." Like Lizbeth, he connected with the audacity of a border crossing protest carried out by undocumented activists. But he also told me he had no illusions about why Mo wanted him to be involved in it:

> He really wanted people that he could use that had, since he had burnt bridges everywhere in the movement, that had connections. He wanted to use me, because I have a lot of faith connections, and I was still seen as pretty favorable in terms of people outside of NIYA.[34]

Marco agreed to participate. LuLu Martinez, a DREAMer with considerable organizing experience in Chicago and a history of working with IYJL, agreed to join the action, too. Lizbeth was already committed. A few other NIYA members at first agreed to take part, but backed out as the action drew near.

Marco suffered second thoughts, too. At a very late hour, after Lizbeth and LuLu had already crossed over into Mexico, he seriously considered backing out:

> I called [Mo] and I was like "I don't know if I want to do it"—the night before I was supposed to leave. Again, I tried to find other excuses, and then I was like, "why don't you do it Mo?" I guess that's what everyone was telling me, just why doesn't Mo do it? And he was just like "I need to be on this side because I don't trust people to do it, to make the calls." And so, I guess, I swallowed it because Liz had left and so had LuLu.[35]

The three DREAMers who crossed over from the US side—Marco, Lizbeth, and LuLu—were joined on the Mexican side of Nogales by six DREAMers who, for various reasons, found themselves back in Mexico and now wanted to return home.

NIYA found these DREAMers in Mexico through informal networks, connections made through their deportation work, and through posts on Facebook. They used Facebook to solicit intakes from those who wanted to return to the United States and might be willing to participate in the action. Most of the DREAMers who wanted to participate were not ready in time for the July action. Some of these would, however, join the second and third border-crossing actions. The first action was rushed, in part because Lizbeth was scheduled to start law school at the end of the summer and she wanted the action to happen early enough to ensure her release in time for the start of the academic year.

The group met for a few days before the action in a migrant shelter in Nogales, Mexico. There they prepared for the border crossing and what they expected would be a few weeks in detention after the crossing. Benito Deal, a US citizen and NIYA ally who had worked with the BTC base camp, coordinated a training in the shelter to prepare them action.[36] The plan was for the nine to present themselves at the border and ask for entry into the US under humanitarian parole. If that did not work, they would ask for asylum. Once across and detained, NIYA would work on their cases as they did most deportation cases. They would mobilize community support and pressure politicians to demand that ICE release the DREAMers.

On July 22, 2013, the DREAM 9, as they were called, walked from the migrant shelter to the pedestrian crossing that joins the two Nogales. On Twitter, Mo described the action as the work of "legal coyotes." All nine DREAMers were taken into custody and transferred to a detention center in Eloy, AZ, run by the Corrections Corporation of America (CCA). Eloy made the BTC look like a country club. The facility was a prison designed to punish its inmates. Detainees only got one hour outside in the yard—and in the Arizona summer heat it offered no respite from the prison walls. Inside, the DREAM 9 started to organize fellow detainees. They distributed a NIYA phone number for inmates to call if they wanted help fighting their deportation. LuLu and Maria Ines were punished for these actions and placed in solitary confinement—or what CCA officials referred to as "administrative segregation." In her second day of solitary confinement, Maria Ines was placed on a suicide watch.

Marco described the Eloy detention as much more stressful than the BTC infiltration:

> In Florida, I was there covertly for two weeks, and on the last week, it was within four days of being announced, [that] we were kicked out . . . it just

felt everything was moving in the right direction. But from Eloy it was like we are going to have the big bang at the beginning of the action, right, and, ever since then, every day that gets added like you're gonna lose hope. You don't know exactly what is going on on the outside.[37]

The DREAM 9 were not granted humanitarian parole. During their first week of detention at Eloy they all received "credible fear interviews" with asylum officers as a preliminary evaluation of the merits of their asylum claims. All nine passed this "credible fear" threshold, but they were not immediately released after the interviews. NIYA activists worked the media and hounded pro-immigrant politicians to pressure the Obama administration for their release. Some of these encounters with politicians turned ugly. With LuLu's participation, attention naturally turned again to Representative Gutiérrez. He was slow to support the DREAM 9, prompting NIYA to organize a sit-in with LuLu's mother in his Chicago, IL, office.[38] He responded angrily to the pressure and criticized NIYA's tactics in the DREAM 9, but he released a letter with fellow Congress member, Jared Polis, addressed to President Obama, calling for the release of the DREAM 9. Four days later, thirty-four Democratic members of Congress signed a similar letter addressed to Obama calling for their release.[39]

Prominent immigrant rights advocates strongly criticized the action. The most vocal among them, the former president of American Immigration Lawyers Association, David Leopold, called the action a "political stunt." Leopold questioned whether the members of the DREAM 9 had legitimate asylum claims. He charged NIYA activists with "being flippant about U.S. law and U.S. policy and putting their own personal interests ahead of millions and millions of others who are so desperately waiting for Congress to do something on immigration reform." Mo fired back in the press that David Leopold had no right to criticize the action of undocumented immigrants fighting for families torn apart by deportation: "He shouldn't be speaking in the first place. Unfortunately, it's not his place to say that this action goes too far because he is not undocumented."[40] Other immigration lawyers questioned the actions opportunistic use of asylum laws and openly worried that it might have a broad impact on how future refugee cases would be handled by asylum officers and immigration judges.

From the far right, *Breitbart* ran profiles on the leaders of NIYA and DreamACTivist.org, using screen shots from their social media accounts and undisclosed internal DHS documents as its sources, casting them as dangerous radicals in a growing anti-white, open borders movement.[41] Picking up on these *Breitbart* stories, immigration rights bloggers Susan Pai and Blase Garcia decried the dangerous impact of NIYA radicalism, triggering a social media storm.[42]

The public attacks on the action were withering and for some of the DREAM 9, anxiously waiting for release from Eloy, they were emotionally devastating. LuLu, Marco, and Maria all reported feeling hurt and abandoned by the public criticism from allies. In our interview, Lizbeth did not report such misgivings. Marco had anticipated these attacks and placed responsibility on NIYA leaders for their unwillingness to heal divisions with potential supporters of the action.

Before leaving for Mexico, he sent an email to the NIYA core members suggesting an apology be sent to organizations whose support they might need to help bring the DREAM 9 safely home:

> I've been speaking recently with possible supporters of the upcoming action & a reservation folks have raised has been the unhealthy rapport NIYA has kept with other orgs. I think this can be amended by some sort of public apology/ declaration—here's is my suggestion & I hope it is considered & responded to by folks on this list as I am currently enroute to Mexico & I think coming out & saying this maturely could help the action & put myself (& i think other participants) at greater peace.

Responses to Marco's call for an "apology/declaration" were mixed. Some backed it. Others responded that these "orgs" had more to apologize for than NIYA. Mo, uncharacteristically, admitted some fault in handling interactions with other organizations. He thanked Marco for the suggestion and asked everyone to focus on making the upcoming action a success.[43] It is not clear what efforts, if any, were made to repair relations with potential supporters before and during the DREAM 9 action.

Despite the attacks on the action by allies and opponents, the DREAM 9 were released from Eloy on August 7, freed to pursue their asylum cases. Marco flew home. A few months later, after a long silence, he sent a short message to the NIYA core asking to be removed from their email list, ending his affiliation with the alliance. When I interviewed Marco, almost exactly one year after the DREAM 9, I asked him if he still believed in the action. "I feel like yes and no. I describe it as very Faustian. We gave up a lot, to gain a lot. I still believe in the idea."[44]

Maria Hinojosa, during a program on the DREAM 9 produced by NPR's *Latino USA* that first aired in October of 2015, asked LuLu and Maria a similar question. "Was it worth it?" LuLu replied, with some hesitation and equivocation, that it was. She added, however, that the action convinced her of how "unhealthy organizing" can be and said the action marked the end of her personal involvement in activism. Maria, who by her own account was traumatized by her detention in Eloy, also answered yes. "Everything I have right now would not have existed if I would have not made that decision of going back." Maria Hinojosa pressed her on the answer, given how painful the action was for her:

MARIA HINOJOSA: Is there a part of you that thinks back and says how could NIYA have done that, how could they have involved you, a kid essentially, who didn't know a whole lot?
MARIA INES: I don't blame them. We were all kids. And we did what we thought was right. If I had los huevos that Mohammad had to do that, I think I would have done that too.[45]

As difficult as the action and detention was for Maria, it did not deter her brother, Alberto, and her mother and father, from following her lead and participating in the later actions of the #BringThemHome campaign.

Lizbeth and Mo viewed the DREAM 9 action as a success. They rejected outside criticism and did not share in the misgivings of some of the participants. NIYA's core members, now considerably smaller in number, moved to organize a still larger border crossing in late September: the DREAM 30. In that action, no NIYA activists crossed over to Mexico to join the DREAMers seeking re-entry. In the end, thirty-four people joined this second round of the #BringThemHome campaign—the four late additions included parents accompanying minors. To the surprise of NIYA organizers, these parents and their children were released into the United States almost immediately after the crossing. The rest of the DREAM 30 were sent to El Paso, TX, and detained in a jail run by ICE. Unlike the DREAM 9, not everyone in this second action won release into the United States. Four were deported after their credible fear interviews. These deportations dealt a harsh blow to a group that had fused in training sessions in Nuevo Laredo and weeks together in detention. The rest, including Maria's brother Alberto, were set free in the United States to pursue their asylum cases. NIYA claimed success and pushed ahead with round three, the Reform 150, in the spring of 2014.

The legal strategy for the third action was to leverage US citizens and DREAMer children to bring deported parents back home. The surprising immediate release of parents crossing with minors in the DREAM 30 action fueled optimism for this next round of the #BringThemHome campaign. NIYA sought to cross dozens of families along with a group of individual DREAMers. It was a big gamble and logistically more difficult than the DREAM 9 and DREAM 30 actions. The plan called for 150 participants to gather in Tijuana for trainings before the crossing. Organizers struggled to find a location to house all the participants. These large Tijuana trainings were chaotic compared to the preparations in Nogales, and even those in Nuevo Laredo. Just before the crossing, the lead citizen-ally organizer suffered a metal breakdown. The initial plans of crossing everyone at once were scratched, and only the DREAMers in Reform 150 group crossed on the scheduled day. The younger children accompanied by their parents crossed two days later. More than half of the Reform 150, possibly as many as three-fourths, gained access to the United States. The parents of Alberto and Maria Ines gained access. The husband of one of the DREAM 9, gained release but only after an excruciatingly long detention. One of the members of the Dream 30, who was deported in that earlier action, gained access on his second try with the Reform 150. The cost of these victories were high: in terms of the time participants spent in detention, the bond payments they paid for their release, and the many who were deported back to Mexico and incurred multiyear bans on reentry. NIYA did not survive the Reform 150 action. Before the action was over, the alliance was broken. It had carried out its last protest.

NIYA had unwittingly run headlong into the heart of a controversy that would reshape political debates around immigration for years to follow: the rights of refugees and asylum seekers attempting to cross the southern border. At the start of 2013, Mo, Lizbeth, Marco, and other NIYA activists could not have anticipated that their work and the plight of refugees would become so intertwined. Some immigration lawyers had raised a concern about the impact of the DREAM 9 legal strategy for asylum law, but no one anticipated the events to come. The waves of unaccompanied minors and families from Central America had only just started to register when NIYA organized the first crossing in the #BringThemHome campaign, and few predicted that these waves of migration would continue coming, ever faster and larger, for years to come. As I write this in the summer of 2019, the numbers of migrants presenting themselves at the southern border asking for asylum protection—just as the participants of the #BringThemHome campaign did—continue to grow to unprecedented levels.

***

NIYA unraveled just as a collective "NIYA-fication" of (im)migrant rights organizations was taking hold. NDLON's #Not1More campaign, for example, was turning to civil disobedience to stop ICE buses loaded with deportees. UWD, at its fall 2013 convening, voted to authorize participation in civil disobedience. UWD members went to the border in 2014 at the height of the first unaccompanied minors "border crisis" to get arrested. Immigrant groups across America turned to civil disobedience to stop police cooperation with ICE. In Austin, TX, for example, undocumented immigrants explicitly followed NIYA's UndocuArrest project to attack the Travis County Sheriff's cooperation with ICE. Following NIYA's SYOC trainings, local organizations across the nation stepped up efforts to fight deportation cases. And the directors of large nonprofits in the immigration field started to demand that Obama use his executive orders to provide immigrants with relief from the ever-rising number of deportations. For years they had resisted attacking the president, and now they referred to him as the Deporter-in-Chief. In November 2014, Obama bowed to the pressure. Once again, he did what he had previously said the Constitution did not allow, and he announced his Deferred Action for Parental Accountability (DAPA) order to expand protection to the undocumented parents of children with US citizenship.

Conclusion

On the Mysteries of Movements and Radicalization

I first interviewed Mohammad Abdollahi two months after the DREAM 9 crossed the border in Nogales, AZ, and a few days before the DREAM 30 crossed at Laredo, TX. From that moment on, I wanted to understand how NIYA activists came to imagine that they could bring deported DREAMers back into the United States. This book attempts to explain how they dared to do this, how they imagined they could become coyote DREAMers. I thought then that these border crossings, along with the NIYA infiltrations and undocu-arrest campaigns, represented the radical edge of a dynamic social movement. I still hold this to be true. After years of research, I am also convinced that how this network of activists managed to carry out an escalating series of defiant and risky forms of protest holds general insights for understanding the radicalization of social movements.

I want to extract and highlight these insights in this final chapter. But even now, after years of reconstructing a historical narrative of the protests choreographed by these undocumented activists, I am balked by a question that puzzled me from the start. If this is a history of movement radicalization, *who radicalized what?* The straightforward answer—a faction of DREAMers radicalized the US (im)migrant rights movement—is not wrong, but it does mislead.

The protagonists at the center of this story of movement radicalization contest the very meaning and significance of the DREAMers and the social movement they supposedly radicalized. In the preface to this book, I described how Mo rejected as nonsensical an interview question about how DREAMer activism fits within the wider movement for (im)migrant rights. He insisted there was no such movement. In that same interview, he also distanced himself from the DREAMer identity, referring to himself as an "illegal" and repudiating his own DREAMer coming-out story. Prerna Lal, possibly the first activist to inspire a temperament and practice that we might term DREAMer radicalization, insisted she never felt like a DREAMer and referred to the identity as "so fictional."

Again, *who exactly radicalized what?* The name and character of the collective actor and the movement, their very meaning, are hotly contested precisely by those who can rightfully claim agency over radicalizing protests for migrant rights. Adding to this confusion, my empirical analysis of this movement radicalization reveals that the subject and object of the historical narrative emerged first as phantoms of sort, as mutually and recursively implicated reifications. In this narrative mystery, the subject exists through its effects and the object through its agency.

I take some comfort that giants of sociology found a similar sort of mystery in explaining the origins and effects of complex social phenomena. Take, for example, Émile Durkheim's classic study of elementary forms of religion. Durkheim reveals the source of the totem's religious force to be none other than the transporting emotional power of the collective gathering of the totemic clan. The totem's sacred power emanates from the "collective effervescence" unleashed by the corporeal co-presence of the clan members. But this transporting emotional experience is only made possible because the sacred totem seizes and holds the collective attention of the gathered. The collective effervescence depends on the symbolic mediation of the sacred object. The fount of the symbol's religious power flows, mysteriously, through its effects. The totem's divine force emanates from the collective emotions it calls forth. Durkheim explains that "because the religious force is none other than the collective and anonymous force of the clan and because that force can only be conceived of in the form of the totem, the totemic emblem, is, so to speak, the visible body of the god." The force of religion that binds the clan flows through the phantom objectivity of the totem, through a powerfully real reification.[1]

Or take, for example, Pierre Bourdieu's account of the origins of state authority. The state, he writes, "exists through its effects and through the collective belief in its effects, which lies at the origin of these effects." In tracing the state historically back to the earliest encounters with it, Bourdieu shows that you cannot separate out when and where it first "acts" from when and where it is first "invoked" by officials as already existing. In the beginning, the state "exists essentially because people believe it exists." Bourdieu refers to this as a "kind of sleight of hand that the social world constantly produces," and adds that it also "makes life very hard for the sociologist." The state, like Durkheim's elementary religion, is "a well-founded illusion" or a "mysterious reality." Something very similar to what Georg Lukacs theorized as a social logic of fetishisms (in)forms the origin of the state: the logic always involves an unconscious convolution of cause and effect.[2]

This same kind of sleight of hand makes it difficult to fix who radicalized what in the struggle for migrant rights. Tracking cause and effects is hard because the subject and object in the social process, "the DREAMers" and "the movement," are both "well-founded illusions"—"mysterious realities." Asking *who* radicalized *what* presents an almost intractable puzzle because you cannot fix the who or the what at the kicking-off point of the symbolic-interactive process of radicalization. And the creative moments of radicalization in this process flow from interactions between these phantom objects—collective actors and movement, both mysterious in their origins and reality—convoluting cause and effect. And here's the rub for explaining radicalization: the fight over the meaning and character of these mysterious realities, the DREAMer and the movement, the contention generated by the very activists called to struggle by or for or against these reifications, inspires the creative process radicalizing protests and contouring the social movement. Almost a half-century ago, Alain Touraine argued that what a social movement is cannot be separated from the effort to articulate its cultural challenge to society.[3] I would add to this that intra-movement struggles to articulate the mystery of a movement and its purpose animate the very protests defining the contours of that movement and its challenge to society.

Happily, once into the narrative flow of historical events of this symbolic-interactive process of radicalization and movement, these "theological" questions lift—somewhat. By tracing the activists' struggles to articulate what the movement is, we see its contours in the very actions they imagine and execute. The choreography of protest turns clarifying, and concrete lessons about radicalization appear. And yet mystifying reifications reappear at every radically new move in this choreography.

What were the key moments in the process of radicalization across this narrative? The agent of radicalization, the radical DREAMer, appears definitively in 2010 with collective acts of civil disobedience. But this is already well into the narrative: almost a full decade after proposed federal legislation and successful state legislation created a juridico-political categorical distinction judging some undocumented youth as worthy of differential treatment from other unauthorized immigrants. Media reports gradually filled in this categorical distinction with stories of the exceptional DREAM Act student. Nonprofit professionals and advocates for immigration reform managed the publicity of these students, curating their public character.

Gradually undocumented youth recognized that the categorical distinction drawn in the federal and state versions of the DREAM Act joined them together by shared educational and political interests. Recall Rebecca Acuña's thrill in 2003 when she found out from her college newspaper that there were other students enrolled at her university under the Texas DREAM Act: "Oh my god, it's *a thing*. It's not just me." Well before she knew of the existence of organizations supporting undocumented youth, an abstract categorical distinction had created a social fact that linked Rebecca's fate to others in her school. It took years, however, for undocumented youth linked by this abstraction to identify as DREAMers. The promise of legislation and media publicity of the DREAM Act student did not automatically give rise to a collective identity, let alone collective agency. That required, at least in part, organizing.

With the help of nonprofit organizations, undocumented students on college campuses formed support and advocacy organizations. Off campus, undocumented youth came together through Web 2.0 sites. The protests of 2006 raised the promise of a mass social movement, and they inspired many of these emerging activists to be more public with their status. When they dared to "come out" with their stories—first online and then on campuses—the DREAMer crystallized as a salient collective identity. It is at this point that the term, DREAMer, appears in the media and in the communications of undocumented youth. Nearly a decade after the legal abstraction was first drawn, the DREAMer became a collective subject with something like a will and agency, no longer just a legal categorical distinction or a victim story in the media. Only the DREAMer, by coming out, could bring the DREAMer to life—a moment of mysterious reality with its convolution of cause and effect, and a radicalizing moment too. Not surprisingly, the new identity is controversial, its meaning and significance fought over, not the least of which by the very people now starting to call themselves DREAMers.

At this point, the well-founded illusion of the DREAMer begins to have real effects on both the experiences of undocumented youth and "the movement" for immigration reform led by the nonprofit organizations that had first framed and publicized the character of DREAM Act students. Recall Frank Sharry's retrospective account of this effect on the opinion pages of *The Washington Post*. He asked, "How did we build an immigrant movement?" His answer: "To most Americans, undocumented immigrants were unknown and invisible. To some, they represented a menace. But then, just a few years ago, Dreamers—who take their name from the Dream

Act . . .—started to come out as 'undocumented and unafraid.'"[4] DREAMers did not just take their name from the act. The productive power of rational-legal political institutions, the categorical distinctions drawn in federal and state bills, went a long way to making them subjects. And so did the work of the nonprofit organizations championing the DREAM Act and the immigration reform movement. From Sharry's perspective, the DREAMers were both the cause and the effect of this movement.

Most historical and sociological accounts of the rationalized state-making of political subjects seem to end badly for the subjects—probably because the state's productive power tends to make them, as Michel Foucault theorized, "docile and useful." There is reason to believe that the directors of the big nonprofits of the immigration field and their allied politicians—elites like Frank Sharry, Ali Noorani, Deepak Bhargava, and politicians like Luis Gutiérrez—trusted the DREAMers would be useful for the "movement" they sought to lead, and docile to its ends.

Prerna and Mohammad's work on DreamACTivist.org first amplified the call to come out. They then imagined ways to radicalize the now out-and-proud DREAMer. They wanted to dash any expectations that DREAMers would stick to the passive role of the innocent victim, abide by the rules, and follow the lead of the nonprofit professionals and their "movement" for immigration reform. Prerna and Mo were never overly identified with the good DREAMer image and quickly devised ways of bending this fetishized character to new ends.

Prerna was the first to deploy the public reputation of the DREAMer to challenge the nonprofit professionals coordinating and directing the political work of undocumented youth. She resented how they benefited from the uncompensated labor of undocumented youth. She wanted to break their control over DREAMers. She advocated that undocumented youth exploit the public influence of the DREAMer image to win independence from the nonprofit advocates of immigration reform, telling fellow undocumented youth at UWD that it was time to "whore ourselves out to the media" to cut the incapacitating strings of the nonprofits and fight for "our" interests.

Following Prerna's inspiration, Mo devised the first protest declaring DREAMer independence: the sit-in at Senator McCain's Tucson, AZ, offices in May 2010. This action was made possible by DreamACTivist.org's public campaigns organized in 2009 to stop the deportation of DREAMers. From their success, Mo realized that the DREAMer was, in effect, un-deportable. DREAMers had such a hold on public sympathy that Democratic politicians, and even some Republicans, could not afford to be seen as indifferent when it came to their deportation. Luisa Heredia beautifully captured the new strategy: The "exceptionality" of the good DREAMer could now be "leveraged" by undocumented youth to fight hard and outside of the rules that had always straitjacketed DREAMers. The un-deportable DREAMers could now use acts of civil disobedience to pressure advocates and politicians of immigration reform to abandon their ill-fated policy goal of CIR and prioritize a standalone DREAM Act. A more radical DREAMer was emerging from this self-instrumentalization of the good DREAMer character. Some DREAMers were thrilled by the new radical image, while others feared it jeopardized the DREAMers' public status and the protection it offered.

The professionals and politicians of immigration reform responded to these acts of civil disobedience by invoking the mysterious realities of the movement and the DREAMer. They invoked the moral expectations associated with the good DREAMer to try to push the radicals back into line. Lizbeth Mateo recalled how directors at CHIRLA would preach to DREAMers that it was selfish and a betrayal of their parents to advocate for the DREAM Act over CIR. This emotional manipulation was exemplified for her in the "creepy" stranger sent by CHIRLA to check in on her at the UWD convening and to make sure she was sticking to the CIR line. She could not shake the memory of him sidling up to her, unannounced and unwelcomed, declaring, "Aren't they being selfish!?"

Deepak Bhargava, reacting to the public charges made by the Noodles that he was working behind the scenes to block the DREAM Act, reminded DREAMers of their origins in the movement and the ethical imperatives they owed to it:

> We were for the DREAM Act before the DREAM Act was cool. Our support of this legislation, as well as for movement building strategies to empower young people in the movement, has been steadfast and unequivocal for many years . . . We do not have the luxury of enmity with allies. Our commitment to these movement ethics is tested most profoundly when things are hard, and that is when our adherence to those ethics matters most.

He warned ominously, "sectarianism is the death of movements." Representative Luis Gutiérrez challenged the Noodles occupying Senator Reid's office with a similar pedantic charge: "Every time someone says the whole thing cannot pass, only part of it, it weakens us, it divides us, it confuses us, it scatters us all over the place. [W]e once had a united movement for comprehensive immigration reform. Now we don't have a united movement." Sally Kohn labeled the radical DREAMers "petulant children" for disrespecting their allies and crossing the movement that made them. But in the hands of the radicals, moral courage and independence—not obedience and fealty—now defined the DREAMer. They no longer looked for affirmation or permission from professional allies. And they had unmasked the movement the allies invoked to bring the radical DREAMers to heel—it was a fake movement manufactured by a nonprofit industrial complex.

The radicals saw through this reified movement to a new one. Their announcement in Truthout.org in the fall of 2010 declared: "We are building the DREAM Movement action-by-action, city-by-city, and campus-by-campus . . . . we have decided to put our bodies and lives on the line."[5] By year's end, undocumented youth had weaponized the DREAMer and turned this powerful public character against their erstwhile patrons. It was a Frankenstein story of sorts. The DREAMer, the cause and effect of the immigration reform movement, was now leading a new movement for and by undocumented immigrants. Movement radicalization and reification intertwined once again.

Not all DREAMers followed the radicals. Many thought the confrontational approach of the Noodles was counterproductive. Rebecca Acuña expressed this when she told Texas DREAMers that pressure tactics against Senator Kay Bailey Hutchinson would backfire. Many remained closely identified with the good DREAMer character, making it hard for them to engage in actions that placed this public reputation at risk. Recall when asked by *The Washington Post* if she would participate in the act of civil disobedience planned by allies to mark the end of the Trail of Dreams, Gaby Pacheco said: "We don't want to do anything to make us seem radical . . . We want to show our love and all our passion and our desire to stay in the country." Moderates feared that breaking the law, even in the form of a moral act of civil disobedience, could undermine not just the public influence of the DREAMer image but also the protection it afforded them.[6] Some attacked the Arizona 5 for the sit-in action at McCain's office because their law-breaking actions threatened this good image. Later acts of civil disobedience and defiance by NIYA activists were met with similar, albeit more angry criticisms.

Moderate DREAMers did not want to jeopardize the support they received from powerful allies. They had close and longstanding associations with leaders of nonprofit organizations that they did not want to sacrifice. Julieta

Garibay spoke for many moderates who stayed with UWD when she said to a reporter at the end of 2010, "we can't do it by ourselves." Many of the radicals came to DREAM Act activism through online organizing. Unlike campus organizers, their online activism developed independently from nonprofit organizations. This may explain why it was easier for Mo and Prerna to defy the authority of the professional leaders of immigration reform, but it cannot account for all radicals. Lizbeth and José Torres-Don led prominent campus organizations with strong ties to nonprofit organizations, yet they willingly sacrificed these associations when they led acts of civil disobedience.

It was not just differences over what law-breaking actions might mean for the DREAMer image and powerful alliances that divided the moderate and radical camps. The risks and rewards of civil disobedience also split the camps. There were some who could muster the confidence or courage to engage in civil disobedience and some who could not. It took remarkable courage to pull off the NIYA escalation. This courage was fortified, for some, by anger. Radicals cultivated their anger and used it to chase off the paralyzing feelings of fear endemic in the communities of undocumented immigrants. Anger was a North Star for some radicals. It guided the defiance of Mo and Lizbeth.

Although it provided formidable fuel, anger alone did not propel radical protest. Equally powerful yet more joyful emotions inspired those who pushed through the fears stirred by defiant protests. The joys of defiance were closed off to DREAMers who could not get themselves to take the risks of protest. They did not feel its liberating power from fear and its solidary effects. Veterans of NIYA protests felt "bulletproof." They felt un-deportable. The transformative emotional experiences of civil disobedience widened the gulf between radical and moderate DREAMers. The "baptism" of civil disobedience, as Marco Saavedra described it, cemented the sectarian divide.

A shared disdain for the inherent constraints of the good DREAMer image united the radicals. It motivated and inspired their escalation of authority-challenging protests. They saw proof of this limitation in the timidity of UWD's official campaigns. The moderates leading that organization were too attached to the safe spaces they had built on campuses and their protective alliances with powerful citizens to effectively challenge the authorities and institutions victimizing immigrants. The radicals developed a critical analysis of "the DREAMer narrative." They saw it as the product of rationalized norms that referred to no one real—the perverse creation of the original categorical distinction drawn by the DREAM Act separating a fictional innocent and an Americanized undocumented kid from "illegals." Jonathan Perez said, if he had stuck to this narrative, as he believed the moderates at UWD wanted undocumented youth to do, he would have been denied "the life changing experience" of getting arrested twice and going to detention. "OH HELLZ NAH.... i am a #baddreamer."

The radical DREAMers who formed NIYA never forgot the wounds of 2010. NIYA activists delighted in pulling off confrontational actions that their moderate counterparts did not dare to even imagine and that triggered apoplectic criticism from citizen allies. Gaby Pacheco said in our interview in 2013, "you can't imagine what they've done. It would blow your mind!" At the center of these mind-blowing actions was the NIYA strategy of DREAMer self-instrumentalization. Their creative and high-stakes exploitations of DREAMers, of themselves, in ever escalating protests betrayed real feelings of aggression, and even some cruel joy, directed toward the good DREAMer. As moderates attacked them for how their escalating protests threatened to undermine the DREAMer image, radicals pushed back with still more defiant actions and risky exploitations of the privilege of the DREAMer. They wanted to shock and scandalize the moderates, and they did.

Alicia Torres told me, after a training for Round 3 of #BringThemHome, that NIYA activists renounced the privilege that came with the DREAMer status, but they were willing to "pimp" it to defend undocumented immigrants who enjoyed no such privilege. Radicalization was in part the unfolding of a struggle shaped by DREAMers exploiting and subverting their own public character as a DREAMer—using the image of the good immigrant kid who followed the rules and sought affirmation from authorities to tap the radical affordances made possible by this image to challenge authorities. The NIYA radicals freely used the DREAMer character, but they no longer identified with it. They played with the social and moral distance between their new radical activist identifications and the DREAMer identity to conceive of actions of self-instrumentalization that a self-identified or over-identified DREAMer could never imagine. They devised creative ways of pimping the DREAMer for strategic advantages in their struggle against the forces of state violence.

The best place to exploit the DREAMers' exceptionality, NIYA activists concluded, was in places where things were hardest for immigrants, and where local authorities and local ICE offices could be expected to take the bait. This "reckless" and "prophetic" imagination led NIYA activists south to Georgia, North Carolina, and Alabama. Precisely the places UWD refused to organize in 2010. The movement they had left behind still weighed on them. The creative new protests of the NIYA escalation carried that mark. They aimed to shock, provoke, and expose that "fake" movement. In the south, NIYA was buoyed by undocumented youth with very different experiences of immigration enforcement than the college DREAMers who organized and led UWD. These new recruits sharpened the radical DREAMer's anger. They imagined audacious actions that those less comfortable with acting out of anger could not envision. Santiago Garcia-Leco, raised in North Carolina, living in a trailer park where a racist neighbor would take pot shots at his family home, never felt like a DREAMer, never looked to his teachers or administrators for affirmation, never expected or wanted any help from white people. "Fuck that!" When he saw news of the NIYA arrests in Atlanta, GA, he remembered wanting some of "what the folks in Georgia experienced!"

Direct actions centering on the self-instrumentalization of the DREAMer brought surprising new ends into view, sparking imaginative projections into future possibilities and creative new forms of protest. The comparatively safe legislative struggle for the DREAM Act in 2010 gave way to three years of fighting directly against the violence of ICE. With each creative escalation in protest, NIYA activists put distance between themselves and the good DREAMer character, but they never forgot that it was the DREAMer that made the run possible. Getting a DREAMer detained or having them self-deport to protect and empower other undocumented immigrants became more than a strategy. It was a new choreography of protest shaping a movement qualitatively different than the one that created and was created by the original DREAMer.

There is certainly more than one social psychological approach to action theory to explain the creativity inspiring this choreography of protest and its contouring of a movement. I find Hans Joas's pragmatist twist to Cornelius Castoriades's psychoanalytic view of the imagination most illuminating. "To do something" new, Castoriades argued, "to do a book, to make a child, a revolution, or just doing as such," requires "projecting oneself into a future situation which is opened up on all sides to the unknown."[7] Fear inhibits such projections. When we are fearful of the future, when we feel deeply insecure about our situation going forward, we cannot project creatively into it. We are more likely to run away from this situation or balk at it. Creative imagination is an emotional and cognitive *act* of will. To project imaginatively into an uncertain future requires a feel for the present situation and an anticipation of how the projection might interact with future situations. The texture of the feel of the present situation provides traction for the projection forward, it shapes the action's arc into the new situation bounded by the unknown. How this projection plays out depends on this situation, bound on all sides by the unknown, but once the projection starts to play out, the uncertain future situation solidifies in ways providing a feel for further projection.

A social movement is shaped, in no small part, by the imaginary projections of its champions. And it is sustained and advanced only through continuously new projections. Propelled by this imaginative process, fresh projections of social movement inevitably push against the hardenings of past projections. For the leaders of DreamACTivist.org, the Noodles Team, and NIYA, each new line of strategy, each new form of collective action, held an older imaginary end within it. The know-how behind each new projected action was always fragmentary, but it contained past experiences and projections leveraged for a different purpose or end. Each successful action opened their imagination to unforeseen possibilities and new lines of actions. In this pragmatic way, across a sequence of innovating actions, radical DREAMers came to make and remake themselves by instrumentalizing and leveraging reified projections of the DREAMer and the movement. They pulled off this continuous re-imagining only through carrying out actions that used these same reifications to push into and against an uncertain and dangerous future.

This choreography of protest was both scary and exhilarating. As their open-ended actions projected into uncertainty, they described the experience as a noetic figure of meaning and feeling. The first coming-out actions had this feel of projection. In time, however, coming out became a sort of confession that disciplined undocumented youth more than it launched them into gambits of self-determination against a hostile future. Implicitly, and even explicitly, radical DREAMers undermined these earlier coming out stories, and even recanted the DREAMer identity itself. The radicals pushed against this image of the DREAMer—as a reified remnant of past liberation—to reimagine themselves as "bad dreamers," as infiltrators, and finally as coyote DREAMers.

There were heavy costs to the creativity of NIYA's escalating actions. It reached its apotheosis with the border-crossing actions. In 2013, with its membership diminished by defections and weakened by internal divisions, NIYA launched one last creative move. Its core activists tricked themselves into believing they could do something that went well beyond the confines of the socio-political order of the nation they had grown to hate. Riding the reckless yet prophetic imagination that inspired escalation, trusting the genius behind their audacious choreography of past protests, they projected themselves as coyote DREAMers, capable of subverting the ultimate line of their social distinction and exclusion: the nation's territorial border. [8] Their choreography of past protest and the movement it shaped made this last step imaginable, and possibly even sensible. In the CCA jail in Eloy, AZ, with its isolation cells used to confine and punish those who dared to dissent, this dance of DREAMer self-instrumentalization may have met its painful limit. Even when done freely and to yourself, pimping hurts. The costs to NIYA's creative escalation ran too high to sustain. Was it a step too far? Or the first step in a new movement, struggling to say its name?

Acknowledgments

Laura Barberena and I launched this research project together. Laura contacted the first sample of activists we interviewed. We planned to coauthor this book, but my slow pace in making progress and the demands of Laura's career dashed these hopes. I could never have written this book without Laura's collaboration. Most of the ideas in this book emerged in discussion with her, many are as much hers as mine.

I also owe a great debt to Hortencia Jiménez. Research I did with Hortencia and Laura on the 2006 walkouts sparked my interest in the activism of undocumented youth. Hortencia also pulled me directly into migrant rights activism, recruiting me to work on the board of the Austin Immigrant Right Coalition in 2009.

This book would not have been possible if not for all the activists who agreed to be interviewed. Montserrat and Julieta Garibay were most gracious with their time. I am so grateful for their openness to discuss difficult moments of UWD and ULI's internal struggles. Through these long interviews, I know Montserrat sensed that my research was drawn to the work of the radicals, and yet she was so generous and frank with her memories of events and interactions.

I owe a huge debt to Mohammad Abdollahi. Mo sat through three long interviews. He also helped me gain access to NIYA campaigns in 2013 and 2014, allowing my observation of the DREAM 30 action and the DREAM 150 action. Mo also gave me access to a DREAMActivist.org/NIYA archive of Google group messages from 2009 to 2011.

Without Mo's help, I doubt Lizbeth Mateo or Prerna Lal would have sat for long interviews. Without Felipe Vargas, it is unlikely I would have been able to interview Mo. Felipe was also instrumental in arranging my interview with Marisol Ramos and at least a dozen others. As I describe in the Preface to this book, my 2012 interview with Felipe was a fateful encounter. Felipe and Steve Pavey shared audio and visual data captured by the NIYA media team, including the cover image used for this book.

Alicia Torres, Claudia Muñoz, and Santiago Garcia-Leco also deserve special thanks for their generosity in sitting for multiple interviews and allowing me to observe them at work on NIYA's #BringThemHome campaign. Along with Felipe and Mo, I have stayed in contact with them since the disbanding of NIYA. Claudia and Alicia pulled me into the work of Austin's Grassroots Leadership, where I now serve as co-chair of the board. Santiago provided comments on the NIYA chapters in this book. He is now a colleague with whom I discuss and debate sociological theories on social movements.

Three invitations to give talks about my research propelled work on this book. Thanks to Daniel Ritter for his invitation to speak to the Department of Sociology at Stockholm University in 2017. Vanessa Barker's comments after that talk comparing contentious politics over immigration in the US and Sweden made a great impression on my work. I am also grateful for Benjamin Bunk and Susanne Maurer's invitation in that same year to present at the Max Weber Centre for Advanced Cultural and Social Studies at the University of Erfurt. At that talk, Andreas Pettenkofer pushed me to sharpen my analysis of the power and irresistibility of reifying movements. And just before COVID-19 shut down most public events, Adrian Popan invited me to give a talk at the University of West Alabama. The presentation I crafted for that talk and the feedback I received from UWA faculty and students helped me crystallize the overall argument.

Finally, James Jasper, Felipe Vargas, Christine Williams, and Noah Hanser-Young read drafts of the book and provided invaluable comments. Their support and guidance helped me through difficult times when I doubted the merits of this project and despaired about finishing it. Noah also pulled together the index for the book.

APPENDIX

Methods and Data

The research for this book is based on fifty-seven interviews with activists involved in fighting for the DREAM Act and (im)migrant rights. Most of the people I interviewed had or once had an irregular immigration status. A small number of interviews were with US citizens who were never undocumented. This sample of interviews started with students from the University of Texas at San Antonio (UTSA) and the University of Texas at Austin (UT-Austin). These first contacts came from an earlier study of the 2006 high school walkouts I did with my colleagues Laura Barbarena and Hortencia Jiménez.[1] Some of the high school students interviewed for that study went on to DREAMer activism in college. By following them, Laura Barbarena made contact with members of DREAM Act Now! at UTSA. These UTSA interviews led us to Felipe Vargas, who connected us to DreamACTivist.org and NIYA members. At UT-Austin, I was fortunate to have Montserrat Garibay as a student in my graduate social movement course. She connected me with former ULI members and important national leaders at UWD. The greater representation of "radical DREAMers" in this sample reflects the substantive and theoretical focus of this book.

I have used the full names of leading activists in the public events chronicled in this book. Not one of the DREAMers I interviewed asked for anonymity, but in the case of those whose identities were not revealed by media reports of public events, I have used first names or pseudonyms.

Another source of data comes from emails and documents shared with me by activists I interviewed and messages sent to two different Google groups. The first of these groups was set up to facilitate communication between members of the UWD committees established in 2009. It remained very active for the duration of that year and tapered off in 2010. The other important Google group, Noodlesforo, was set up in the spring of 2010 in preparation for the Arizona action. Activity on the group was high for much of the year but tapered off after the Noodles 2.0 action.

I gained access to messages from these Google groups through a PDF file compiled from DreamActivist.org/NIYA electronic archives. The file is a scraping of messages, a cut-and-paste of what appears to be most messages sent to the two Google groups. Messages are missing from these archives, but these omissions appear to be accidental lapses in the mechanical scraping of the messages. I used messages from these groups, along with media accounts, to supplement the interviews and their accounts of DREAMer protests.

Another important primary source of research comes from observing NIYA activists at work during the last year of that organization's operation. Starting in September 2013 with the DREAM 30 border crossing, and then continuing with the EL Paso, TX, detention center infiltration in the winter and the Reform 150 border crossing action in the spring of 2014. NIYA dissolved after the Tijuana action, but former members continued their activism. Over the next decade, I stayed in close contact with Mohammad Abdollahi, Claudia Muñoz, and Alicia Torres and followed their continuing work.

Notes

Preface

1. See Dose of Tequila (2013). The title of Dose of Tequila's article comes from a heated exchange between Mohammad Abdollahi and an advocate for immigration reform posted on Facebook. The article includes a screenshot of the post. It reads: "Fuck off. Go suck united we dreams dick if you wanna support someone. Yall are delusional. You take the illegal community back 20 pegs. Been organizing 3 years to counter your bullshit and could care less what you think you can contribute. What a joke."
2. Rep. Luis Gutiérrez's (DEM-IL) 2013 "report" posted online about Mohammad Abdollahi is a good example of the "substance" behind these attacks. See http://Gutiérrez.house.gov/sites/Gutiérrez.house.gov/files/documents/NIYA.pdf [last accessed 3/22/17].
3. This Washington, DC, McCain sit-in is not to be confused with the earlier and more widely known sit-in at McCain's Tucson, AZ, office in May of the same year.
4. Interview with Gaby Pacheco, August 16, 2013, San Antonio, TX.
5. Interview with Felipe Vargas, July 26, 2012, San Antonio, TX.
6. Interview with Mohammad Abdollahi, September 18, 2013, San Antonio, TX.
7. Laura Barberena and I spent three days at the shelter observing the group prepare for the crossing and interviewing participants.
8. Signs of this movement included NDLON's #Not1More campaign which started to heat up in 2013, shaped in no small part by undocu-activist and former NIYA member Tañia Unzueta. The campaign captured national attention by blocking the path of buses filled with ICE detainees headed for the Mexican border for removal. At roughly the same time, United We Dream, the moderate DREAMer counterpart to NIYA, was losing patience with the politics of immigration reform on the Hill and started planning acts of civil disobedience.

Introduction

1. Contentious politics is the preferred term in McAdam, Tarrow, and Tilly (2001). Challenger is term used in Amenta (2006).
2. Although he does not use the term reification, this point is made very clear in Tilly (2004). A similar claim is articulated in Melucci (1989).
3. For a loose agreement on the value of this sociological definition of movements amongst scholars see Gahr and Young (2014), Melucci (1996), and Tilly (2004).

4. Note this movement "survey" was taken in the winter of 2018–2019. This "analytical" view of the social movement for migrant rights roughly accords with the analysis of Bloemraad and Voss (2020).
5. NIYA was not formed until 2011, but I use it here anachronistically as a shorthand label for a network of radical DREAMers that went by various names from 2009 to 2014.
6. See Polletta (2006).
7. See Sennett (1981, x–xi) and Touraine (1981).
8. This book's focus on the importance of internal struggles to social movement dynamics adds to a small but growing sociological literature on conflict within movements that includes Bernstein (1997), Polletta (2006), Ghaziani (2008), Gould (2009), and Perkins (2022). In particular, it builds on Francesca Polletta's analysis of the importance of the "spontaneous movement" narrative of the 1960s student sit-ins to the Civil Rights Movement.
9. See the Appendix of this text on methods and data for a longer discussion of the sources used for this research.

Chapter 1

1. Interview with Gaby Pacheco, August 16, 2013, San Antonio, TX.
2. See McCarthy and Zald (1977) for the original articulation of their "resource mobilization theory, and see McCarthy and Zald (1987 [1973], 374, 384) for the professional view of radical activism.
3. On top-down social movement manufacturing, see Walker (2014) and Zald and Lounsbury (2010).
4. For a summary of the original 2001 bill see https://www.congress.gov/bill/107th-congress/senate-bill/1291 [last accessed April 1, 2016]. In later iterations of the DREAM Act, volunteering for military service was added to educational achievement as grounds for eligibility. This breakdown of eligibility is drawn from the sociologist and education scholar Rincón's (2008) overview of the DREAM Act. Unlike some histories, Rincón correctly highlights the educational priority in these benefits and protections. NILC was clearly building on the victory in *Plyler vs. Doe*.
5. For a history of NILC, see Drake and Wheeler (1992). More recent NILC financials are drawn from IRS 990 forms for 2000 to 2004.
6. This history of the Ford Foundation's role in the creation of a nonprofit "immigration field" is drawn from Korten (2009, ch. 5). For Sutton and Morris quotes, see pages 94 and 95.
7. For grant amounts to NIF and NILC (NCIR) in the 1980s, see the *Annual Reports* of the Ford Foundation (1982, 1983, 1984). For the role of Vice Chair Jay Mazur from International Ladies Garment Workers Union in NIF, see National Immigrant, Refugee & Citizenship Forum (1984). Under Mazur's leadership, the ILGWU merged with the Amalgamated Clothing and Textile Workers of America to form the Union of Needletrades, Industrial and Textile Employees (UNITE) in 1995.

NOTES 269

8. This discussion of the nativist Right is drawn primarily from Gonzales (2014, ch. 1).
9. Jessica Vaughan (2006) made the term popular in a report for CIS supporting the policy changes proposed in HR 4437. Although first articulated as a justification for HR 4437, the logic of the argument was used to defend earlier pieces of legislation similar to HR 4437, like California's Prop. 187 in 1994. See Ira Melhman and Dan Stein's articulation of FAIR's defense of Prop. 187 in Jost (1995).
10. Quoted in Zolberg (2008, 411).
11. For a detailed account of the intended and actual effects of PRWORA from a restrictionist perspective, see Borjas (2002).
12. Wheatley (2017) provides an excellent review of the provisions in IIRIRA and their inauguration of a long period of "crimmigration." Also, for the forgotten role of Democrats in passing AEDPA and IIRRIRA and the effects of these laws, see JayGR's (2008) blog post on *Daily Kos*.
13. Titled "Limitations of eligibility for preferential treatment of aliens not lawfully present on basis of residence for higher education benefits," Section 505 reads "(a) IN GENERAL: Notwithstanding any other provision of law, an alien who is not lawfully present in the United States shall not be eligible on the basis of residence within a State (or a political subdivision) for any postsecondary education benefit unless a citizen or national of the United States is eligible for such a benefit (in no less an amount duration and scope) with regard to whether the citizen on national is such a resident' (IIRIRA, Title V, 505(a)). For a discussion that this does not constitute a "flat bar" on undocumented students because of the modifier "unless" and how states like Texas exploited this to pass in-state tuition laws, see Rincón (2008, 61).
14. This is the compelling argument made by Massey, Durand, and Malone (2003).
15. See Eschbach, Hagan, and Rodriguez (2001) and Dunn (2009).
16. For a close look at one of these new immigrant communities in North Carolina, see Silver (2018).
17. See Korten (2009, ch. 6) for an account of Soros's funding of the field. It should be noted that Korten's book was sponsored by the CCC and its forward was co-authored by CCC's director, Deepak Bhargava.
18. Zolberg (2008, 20).
19. See https://www.ice.gov/factsheets/287g [last accessed March 2, 2015].
20. S.1291 and HR 1918 in 2001; S.1515 and HR 1684 in 2003; S.2075 and HR 5131 in 2005.
21. On this point, see Nichols (2013) excellent discussion of the origins and development of the DREAM Act.
22. HB 1403 in Texas and AB 540 in California. See Rincón (2008) for a history of the development of these state-level policies.
23. In a LexisNexis search of the terms "Dream Act" and "immigration" in English language newspapers in the United States from 2002 through 2004, I counted at least forty different DREAMer stories, many of them appearing multiple times in print, following this form.
24. Quoted in a *Los Angeles Times* article, see Mena (2004).
25. McMahon (2002).

26. For early reports on the Cairo case see Flores (2002) and Davidson (2002). For the original quote, see "Testimony of the Honorable Orrin Hatch," June 20, 2002, https://www.judiciary.senate.gov/imo/media/doc/hatch_statement_06_20_02.pdf [accessed March 2, 2015].
27. Riley (2002).
28. Riley (2003).
29. Wall (2004).
30. See Lueke (2005) for an early media report of Marie's legal peril.
31. Meyerson (2005).
32. See Piven (2004, 135–136) for a brief description of CCC.
33. Delgado (1986).
34. For the CCC/FIRM timeline, see https://www.communitychange.org/real-power/immigration-timeline/ [last accessed February 12, 2016].
35. See Foundation Center (2016) for top recipients of 2006. For an organization with no history of working with migrants, CCC's appearance on the list was rather sudden. The years 2006 to 2010, when CCC had its greatest total grant revenue, correspond with the years it received large grant totals to work in the nonprofit immigration field. For CCC revenue data for the decade, see its IRS 990 forms. Over these same five years—2006 to 2010—CCC received $6,435,000 in grants from the Ford Foundation alone. CCC's yearly grant revenues for the decade peaked in 2008 at $17,728,535. At the time, its executive director, Deepak Bhargava, was paid over two hundred thousand dollars a year. CCC enjoys access to the political elites of the Democratic Party.
36. It was not a period completely lacking in collective action. The Immigrant Worker's Freedom Ride organized by SEIU, UNITE, HERE, and the AFL-CIO's bused nine hundred immigrants across the country in the spring of 2003. Some scholars claim the freedom rides helped lay the foundation for the massive mobilizations in the spring of 2006. The lead organizer, Maria Elena Durazo, president of HERE, claimed it was the start of a movement. The causal claim is tenuous. A more likely causal relationship is that the freedom rides help lay the foundation for FIRM and a stronger policy linkage between elites directing organized labor and the directors of nonprofits in the immigration field. On the freedom rides and their relation to 2006, see Shaw (2011). In my interview with Marisol Ramos (February 13, 2017, McAllen, TX), who was co-founder of the New York DREAMer organization NYSYLC and worked with NYIC and CCC in 2005, she describes the 2003 freedom rides as an important precursor to the coalition of organizations brought together in FIRM (see the discussion in Chapter 2 of this text). The freedom rides included a prescient act of civil disobedience at the internal border patrol checkpoint outside of El Paso when the riders refused to show identification and were briefly detained before pressure from politicians secured their release. For the formal launch of FIRM, see Center for Community Change (2004).
37. On the relationship between these state-level nonprofits and CCC and foundations, see Korten (2009, 111).
38. Torres (2004).

39. See Davidson (2004) for the *Deseret News* article, Ustinova (2004) for *The Philadelphia Inquirer*'s coverage, and Sheridan (2004) for *The Washington Post* report. On Marie Gonzalez's role in the events, see Hoover (2004).
40. See Center for Community Change (2004a, 2004b)
41. See Hoover (2004) and NYIC Media Advisory on FIRM website for June 2005 referencing "We Are Marie Campaign" archived here, http://archive.justingrady.com/FIRM/wearemarie/downloads/nyic_advisory_063005.pdf [last accessed June 26, 2017]. Also see Center for Community Change (2005).
42. Gonzalez (2005, B7).
43. See Center for Community Change (2006).
44. See Barberena, Jiménez, and Young (2014) for an account on the spontaneity of the marches and walkouts and their relationship to formal organizations. In this article, we do not suggest that there was no organized resistance to HR 4437 before the mass rallies and that these efforts did not contribute to events. Immigrant, social justice, humanitarian, labor, religious, and Latino organizations opposed HR 4437 immediately after its passage. Community-based organizations, churches, and the Spanish language media provided organizational support and education for small anti-HR 4437 rallies in the winter, but these organized efforts cannot explain the earthquake of March 2006. For an excellent overview of the events, see Bloemraad, Voss, and Lee (2011).
45. For CCC's account of its role in the events of 2006 see its immigration timeline on its website, see https://www.communitychange.org/real-power/immigration-timeline/.
46. For a revealing account of the sequence of organizational support, see Diaz and Rodriguez (2007). Jesse Diaz and Javier Rodriguez were lead organizers of the March 25 Coalition that pulled off the massive Los Angeles demonstration. They make clear that organized labor (SEIU and the UFW), as well as the large nonprofits, were clearly uneasy riders in the bandwagon, scrambling to react after the initial mass mobilizations.
47. See Center for Community Change (2006a)
48. Campo-Flores (2006, 35).
49. "Crucial and hidden role" is a direct quote from CCC's own account, see https://www.communitychange.org/real-power/immigration-timeline/. The "cornerstone" claim comes from FIRM's website at https://www.firmaction.org/about [last accessed June 2, 2022]. The clearest statements of the nonprofit immigrant field seeding the movement come from Part III of Korten (2009). Most likely written in 2007 and 2008, the book was sponsored by CCC and, as per Acknowledgments, Deepak Bhargava helped with the selection of cases. See Korten (2009, xxii) for the "full-fledged social movement" claim, and Korten (2009, 120–121) for general claims about building the infrastructure and national communication network for the movement.
50. See the Gabe Gonzalez video posted for 2007 on the CCC timeline for a statement of the inevitability of the movement winning, https://communitychange.org/real-power/immigration-timeline/. For a nice critique of this sentiment, see Gonzales (2014, ch. 2).
51. The 2006 push for comprehensive reform failed as a strong nativist reaction made itself felt in the offices of Republican and Democratic politicians. Later in the year,

NILC pressed its political allies on the Hill to put forward the DREAM Act once again. It gained some bipartisan support, but it, too, failed.
52. Cardenas (2006).

Chapter 2

1. This section is based primarily on four interviews: Julieta Garibay, May 18, 2013, Austin, TX; Rebecca Acuña, August 23, 2013, Austin, TX; Montserrat Garibay, December 11, 2013, Austin, TX; and Alejandra Rincón, August 19, 2016, San Francisco, CA.
2. This discussion of advocacy for in-state tuition in Texas draws from my interview with Alejandra Rincón (August 19, 2016, San Francisco, CA), and from Rincón's (2008) book on the undocumented immigrants and higher education.
3. Rick Norriega, quoted in Rincón (2008, 79–80).
4. Interview with Claudia Muñoz, October 10, 2013, El Paso, TX. Claudia spent the summer of 2004 in Prairie View after Alejandra pushed her family to send her. This is exactly the same time that the Garibay sisters met Alejandra. See Chapter 7 of this text for a glimpse of Claudia's work with NIYA.
5. Interview with Alejandra Rincón, August 19, 2016, San Francisco, CA.
6. Interview with Rebecca Acuña, August 23, 2013, Austin, TX.
7. The University of Texas at the time had a "top ten" rule guaranteeing admission to any student who graduated within the top ten percent of their high school graduating class.
8. Rebecca captures the reifying effect of categorical distinction drawn by HB 1403. Reification literally means thing-ification.
9. Interview with Alejandra Rincón, August 19, 2016, San Francisco, CA.
10. Interview with Montserrat Garibay, December 11, 2013, Austin, TX.
11. At the time of the interview, Rebecca worked as Communications Director for US Representative Pete Gallego from Texas's 23rd district. She would go on to become Wendy Davis's press aid for her Texas gubernatorial race in 2014.
12. Jiménez (2011) provides a detailed account of the planning for this Austin rally.
13. The following section is drawn primarily from an interview with Gaby Pacheco, August 16, 2013, San Antonio, TX. It also draws from her telling of her story at a November 2010 presentation in Washington, DC, at Busboys and Poets, sponsored by Campus Progress, see https://www.youtube.com/watch?v=WtbvjN4Uhfw [last accessed April 10, 2017], and her 2013 testimony in front of US Senate, see https://www.c-span.org/video/?c4441430/gaby-pacheco [last accessed April 18, 2017].
14. Quote from Senator Durbin's introduction to Gaby's 2013 Senate testimony.
15. A video of her address to the media is archived at https://www.youtube.com/watch?v=QDWDzHYz_6o [last accessed June 10, 2019].
16. Corina Garcia declined sitting for an interview in the fall of 2016. She said at the time she was too busy. She did not answer a follow up request in 2017.
17. Interview with Lizbeth Mateo, August 18, 2014, San Jose, CA.

18. Movimiento Estudiantil Chicano de Aztlán (MEChA) was founded at the University of California at Santa Barbara in 1969. MEChA organizations on campuses across the West and Southwest attracted undocumented youth looking for organizational support. This was not just true in California. For example, undocumented students at UT-San Antonio first came together through MEChA events (Interview with Lucy Martinez, July 26, 2013, San Antonio, TX.
19. Rich Stolz had worked for CCC for over a decade and was, at the time, the coordinator for FIRM and at the center of the push for immigration reform in Washington, DC. In 2009, he would become campaign manager for RI4A. The press conference was held at the National Press Club. The CCC press release announcing the conference listed the planned speakers as "Congressman Lincoln Diaz Balart (R-FL), Cristina Lopez, Center for Community Change/Fair Immigration Reform Movement (FIRM), Ana Avendano, AFL-CIO, Carmen Berkley, United States Student Association (USSA), Josh Bernstein, National Immigration Law Center, Reverend Thomas G. Wenski, US Conference of Catholic Bishops, Jaime Contreras, Service Employees International Union, Rodrigo, Immigrant Student, and Lizbeth, Immigrant Student." For press release, see Center for Community Change (2007); for profile of Stolz, see https://www.weareoneamerica.org/staff/rich-stolz [last accessed September 2, 2016].

Chapter 3

1. See the October 2008 draft of "YOUTH ORGANIZING FOR THE DREAM ACT: A Proposal for National Peer-to-Peer Networks." Draft shared with author by Marisol Ramos. It was first written by Marisol for the Phoenix Fund and later incorporated in UWD grant proposal.
2. Interview with Marisol Ramos, February 13, 2017, McAllen, TX.
3. Phone interview with Josh Bernstein, November 19, 2015.
4. Interview with Prerna Lal, November 11, 2015, Berkeley, CA. All quotations from Prerna in this chapter come from this interview unless otherwise indicated.
5. Both Claudia Muñoz and Marco Saavedra make this point in their interviews. Interview with Claudia Muñoz, October 10, 2013, El Paso, TX, nine to ten days into the detention of the DREAM 30; interview with Marco Saavedra, August 6, 2014, Bronx, NY.
6. One can imagine what the immigration lawyers of NILC thought of this blog post in 2009 as they worked with Prerna at UWD. Prerna's post can be found at http://prernalal.com/2009/06/uscis-priority-deport-11-year-olds/#ixzz3rCr6cRaK [accessed October 25, 2015]. An ABC news report on the Bledniak case can be found at http://abcnews.go.com/US/story?id=7795246&page=1 [accessed March 24, 2016].
7. DAP is still up and running as of April 20, 2023, see https://dreamact.info/forum/.
8. The use of "interpellation" is drawn from Althusser (1971).
9. This marvelous post, written almost a year before the UWD convening, is accompanied by an ambitious reading list that includes Chakraborty's chapter 8 in *Provincializing Europe*, Kafka's *The Trial*, Becket's *Waiting for Godot*, Blanchot's *Waiting*, Bayart's

chapter on "Global Godot" in *Global Subjects*, Bourdieu's *Pascalian Meditations*, and songs on waiting by Fugazi and Lou Reed. http://prernalal.com/2008/03/the-politics-of-waiting-asylum/#ixzz3qYZpAdc2 [accessed October 24, 2015].

10. I borrow the phrase from Auyero (2012). Prerna's insights are similar to those drawn by Auyero in his "tempography" of the waiting experiences of destitute subjects of the Argentinian state. Like Auyero's analysis, Prerna saw the "productive power" of the state in these waiting rooms. In making people wait, the state makes subjects. Unlike Auyero's account of the submissive effects, and Foucault's general theory of this type of "productive power," Prerna sees in this particular waiting room of history the making of subjects of the state that share an implicit activist disposition. In a shared recognition of the pain endured by waiting, undocumented youth can claim their worthiness not by dutifully being patient, she argues, but by making trouble. Prerna was self-consciously using Foucault's theory of productive power against Foucault's substantive view of its effect as making subjects docile and useful.

11. I interviewed Mohammad Abdollahi three different times: first on September 19, 2013, in San Antonio, TX, at Felipe Vargas' family home; again on July 22, 2016, in Mo's empty San Antonio, TX, apartment; and once again on January 14, 2017 in Nogales, AZ, at his house abutting the border wall. In this chapter, all quotations from Mo come from these interview unless otherwise indicated.

12. For this Quaker interview, see http://prernalal.com/2008/03/gay-iranian-seeks-asylum/#ixzz3qYeWHj15; for the solicitation of stories, see http://prernalal.com/2008/03/calling-all-dream-act-students-to-participate-giving-voice-to-our-dreams/#ixzz3qa7eYYsB; for blog post announcing slow release, see http://prernalal.com/2008/04/documenting-the-undocumented-part-1/#ixzz3qfQZCPMB; and for the call to "come out," see http://prernalal.com/2008/04/10-undocumented-students-are-attending-harvard/#ixzz3qfFTeONp [accessed October 25, 2015].

13. This claim does not diminish the significance or creative initiative of the coming-out action in Chicago in March 2010, organized by the undocumented youth of IYJL. Coming out in virtual space undoubtedly felt safer than coming out in physical spaces governed by others. This Chicago action is discussed in the next chapter.

14. For an excellent example of this sociological perspective, one directly informed by DREAMer activism, see Enriquez and Saguy (2015). My own research on the emergence of temperance and antislavery in antebellum America relied heavily on theories of the cultural power of transposing schemas across movement contexts. I argued that variants of the confessional schema influenced a wide array of protest repertoires that extended from as early as the temperance confessions of the 1830s to coming out in the gay and lesbian liberation demonstrations of the 1970s. (Young, 2002, 2007).

15. See Sharry (2013).

16. See Lal and Unzueta (2013).

17. I think Prerna, Tañia, and Mo's accounts present an important challenge to sociological accounts. When it comes to explaining new movements, we put too much explanatory power in the transposition of cultural schemas across contexts. Just to be clear, my past research relied heavily on this theoretical view of schemas and transposition.

I think their challenge, which comes from a more pragmatic view of creativity and agency, exposes the structural bias of theories of cultural schemas where agency is constricted as the transposition of schemas across different contexts. The work of McGarry and Jasper (2015) and Whittier (2012) may be closer in spirit to the view of these undocu-activists, and better capture the creative source of new collective identities and new lines of collective action.

18. It is Rich Stolz and not Rick Schwartz. Stolz was a long-time employee of CCC. He was coordinator of FIRM until he was tapped to become the director of the Reform Immigration for America Campaign. Chisme means gossip in Spanish. Mo claims not to speak Spanish. I once heard him say in a 2014 meeting with Irineo Mujica, a prominent organizer of the migrant caravans, "I don't speak Spanish, I only know the swear words"—and apparently at least a few other colorful terms, like chisme.

19. DreamACTivist.org is no longer up and running, but in the archives on UWD's website you can see the DreamACTivist.org imprimatur on UWD online material through much of 2010.

20. DreamACTivist.org/NIYA archived most of the correspondences of these three committees that were sent through the Google groups. They include thousands of email exchanges extending from early 2009 through 2010, with most of the exchanges falling between March and September of 2009. Marisol Ramos also shared UWD correspondences from this period. The historical narrative that follows in this chapter is drawn largely from this archive of correspondences, cited hereafter as: NIYA archive of UWD committee correspondences. Reading across these messages I count roughly twenty-five active participants in the Google groups over this period. These participants are roughly equally divided between citizen allies and DREAMers. Most, but not all, of the allies were professional advocates. Among the unpaid UWD volunteers, undocumented youth outnumbered citizen allies. The most active undocumented volunteers belonged to SWER, NYSYLC, and DreamACTivist.org. The role of the National Korean American Service & Education Consortium (NAKASEC) in the early UWD work is an important and still untold story.

21. According to a July 1, 2009 email from Matias Ramos, who attended a FIRM "pillar meeting" in March that planned the rollout of the RI4A campaign, a dozen organizations made up "the decision-making nucleus" of RI4A (see NIYA archive of UWD committee correspondences). According to Marisol Ramos, the twelve were the CCC/FIRM member organizations: CHIRLA, MIRA, ICIRR, FLIC, NYIC, CASA de Maryland, and One America/PCUN; and NIF, America's Voice, Gamaliel (a national coalition of progressive faith groups), SEIU, and AFL-CIO. A large grant from Four Freedoms Funds (FFF), a collaborative fund backed by the Ford Foundation and the Carnegie Corporation, among others, bankrolled the RI4A campaign. This precise list of twelve organizations comes from a personal correspondence with Marisol Ramos (March 14, 2017). Many of the UWD committee members were unclear about how or whether to distinguish CCC and its FIRM affiliates from the RI4A campaign, and for good reasons. The "exciting movement" quote comes from LULAC's June 2, 2009 press release announcing the campaign: Action Alert: Campaign to Reform Immigration FOR America!, https://advance-lexis-com.ezproxy.lib.utexas.edu/api/

document?collection=news&id=urn:contentItem:7VWF-4P70-Y9B9-H0SD-00000-00&context=1516831.
22. In the original draft, Prerna refers to DREAM as a "down payment" but Josh Bernstein suggests "building block" as a less provocative term. See Prerna Lal's March 10, 2009 email and Josh Bernstein's suggestions of revisions in same thread (NIYA archive of UWD committee correspondences).
23. "Puppet master" was the phrase Mo used to describe Marisol in our third interview in Nogales.
24. See Marisol Ramos's July 27, 2009 email discussing the funding history of UWD in preparation of early June UWD strategy meeting (NIYA archive of UWD committee correspondences).
25. Interview with Julieta Garibay, December 11, 2013, Austin, TX.
26. http://prernalal.com/2009/06/initial-thoughts-on-reform-immigration-for-america/#ixzz3rCpZDYLG.
27. For the article, see Tran and Lal (2009).
28. In two blog posts in early 2009, Prerna describes herself as a "Marxist-Foucauldian, radical queer womyn of color" and someone who appreciates "that queer theory—for the most part—is supposed to liberate us from essentialism, but without a preliminary conversation about our unique lives and shared experiences, there is no way to move forward." See http://prernalal.com/2009/03/732/#ixzz3r7PU93xg and http://prernalal.com/2009/03/b-i-t-c-h-a-personal-statement-on-international-womens-day/#ixzz3r7NhDfKD [accessed May 19, 2017].
29. Kyle de Beausset from Citizen Orange confirms Prerna's account in a June 18, 2009 email cited below.
30. This exchange unfolded online over the UWD Google groups; see the thread starting on June 18, 2009 (NIYA archive of UWD committee correspondences).
31. In some initial plans, Josh Bernstein was suggested as keynote speaker and José Luis Marantes as emcee. See a June 30, 2009 email for José Luis Marantes's description of the graduation (NIYA archive of UWD committee correspondences).
32. http://prernalal.com/2010/01/new-project-when-facebook-meets-daily-kos-for-color-of-change/#ixzz3rNBTqdy3 [accessed May 19, 2017].
33. See Gonzales (2014, 3) for data on rising ICE removals under Obama starting in 2009.
34. A 2000 memo from Doris Meisner, commissioner of INS, outlined the principles for prosecutorial discretion for deferring action regarding the deportation of certain "illegal aliens" to "better focus" scarce resources on enforcement "priorities." Later, "the Morton memo," issued in June 2011 by then-ICE Director John Morton, would build on the Meisner memo establishing clearer guidelines on prosecutorial discretion in immigration cases. In 2012, with DACA, Obama expanded on these principles drafting an executive order to provide deferred action to all DREAMers. In 2008 and 2009, however, when Mo started to work on deportation cases, activists were just learning how to force ICE to use its prosecutorial discretion to defer action on the deportation of DREAMers.
35. Interview with Prerna Lal, November 11, 2015; also, see Mohammad Abdollahi's February 11, 2018 email message on the outcome of the Taha case and deferred action won for parent.

36. In 2017, under the Trump regime, Mohammad Abdollahi and Dulce Guerrero presented a training on how to stop deportations in Austin. They used the Rigo case as an example of how community support and public pressure succeeded in stopping a deportation that all the legal and policy experts believed was impossible. Secure Your Own Community training at Workers Defense Project, September 30, 2017, Austin, TX. That said, this case was exceptional. Mo told me many times that DUI cases are near impossible to win.
37. Interview with Gaby Pacheco, August 16, 2013, San Antonio, TX.
38. Interview with Marisol Ramos, February 13, 2017, McAllen, TX. Marisol described these annual meetings as times when "we would hear from Papa Durbin about DREAM Act updates." Otherwise, she said, the professional advocates closed them out of policy discussions.
39. For this post, see http://prernalal.com/2010/02/reform-immigration-for-america-hits-the-iceberg-on-lgbt-immigration/ [accessed January 6, 2017].
40. Interview with Prerna Lal, November 13, 2015, Berkely, CA.
41. For this post see, http://prernalal.com/2010/01/recap-of-netroots-nation-san-francisco-event/#ixzz3rO1UIvlL [accessed April 16, 2017].

Chapter 4

1. Author's field notes from Austin Immigrant Rights Coalition (AIRC) meetings in the winter/spring of 2010. The steering committee of this Austin, TX, organization was split over how to address the problem of allotting limited resources for the different goals of showing solidarity with activists in Arizona, resisting local law enforcement's cooperation with ICE in the Travis County Jail, and supporting RI4A's CIR efforts by, among other things, sending a group to the March for America scheduled in late March.
2. Interview with Gabby Pacheco, August 15, 2013, San Antonio, TX. This chapter's account of the origins of the Trail of Dreams comes from this interview.
3. For quotation on media impact, see Pacheco (2012).
4. Interview with Mohammad Abdollahi, September 19, 2013, San Antonio, TX; Interview with Felipe Vargas, July 26, 2012, San Antonio, TX.
5. Montgomery (2010, C01).
6. Some of the key staffers, doubting the viability of CIR, that the radical DREAMers were in contact with, worked in the offices of Senator Durbin and Senator Feinstein. Interview with Lizbeth Mateo, August 18, 2014, San Jose, CA, and Interview with Mohammad Abdollahi, July 22, 2016, San Antonio.
7. The quote comes from my interview with Mohammad Abdollahi, September 19, 2013, San Antonio, TX. It is his recollection and characterization of what Josh and José Luis said on that call, not their actual words.
8. March 15, 2010 email from Carlos Saavedra: "UWD Field Update—Confidential Moving Dream Forward." Shared by Mohammad Abdollahi with author on April 22, 2016.

9. In my second interview with Mohammad Abdollahi, July 22, 2016, San Antonio, TX, he said, reflecting on the failure to pass the DREAM Act in 2010, "I think the main thing is that we ran out time."
10. Interview with Mohammad Abdollahi on September 19, 2013, San Antonio, TX.
11. Mohammad Abdollahi's April 27, 2010 email to Carlos and José Luis. Shared by Mohammad with author on April 22, 2016.
12. Interview with Lizbeth Mateo, August 18, 2014, San Jose, CA.
13. Interview with José Torres-Don, July 23, 2014, San Antonio, TX.
14. The initial proposal was outlined in a document entitled "Self Deportation Narrative." Mohammad Abdollahi shared document with author on April 22, 2016.
15. See "Self Deportation Narrative" document, fn. 14.
16. Marisol Ramos's opening message on the Google group can be found in the NIYA/DreamACTivist.org archive of Noodlesforo: cited hereafter simply as Noodlesforo. For the discussion of the origin of the Noodles name, see the April 15, 2010 message from Juan forwarding the exchange between Prerna and Flavia.
17. For estimate of the number of people working on the project, see Flavia's message on Noodlesforo, May 30, 2010.
18. The initial list of potential Noodles included DREAMers from specific states hoping to generate pressure on politicians pivotal to advancing and passing the DREAM Act: California's Senator Feinstein sat on the Senate Immigration Subcommittee and her strong support for the AgJOB Act inclined her to favor of a piecemeal approach over CIR. Chicago's Representative Gutiérrez, the author of the CIR bill in the House and a leader of the Congressional Hispanic Caucus (CHC), was a key target because he could hold up action on DREAM in the House and also influence the decision-making of the Senate Majority Leader, Harry Reid. Illinois was also home to Senator Durbin, the politician most identified with the DREAM Act. Kansas City was important because Senator McCaskill of Missouri was viewed as a potential swing vote influencing other moderate Midwestern Democrats in the Senate, and Senator Brownback of Kansas was one of a few Republicans projected as a possible supporter of the DREAM Act. Michigan's Senator Stabenow was a potential co-sponsor of the act and Representative Conyers was important for championing the act in the House as the Chair of the Judiciary Committee. In Massachusetts, Senator Brown, like Brownback, was viewed as a moderate Republican who could vote for the act. Similarly, Texas was a target because Senator Hutchinson voted for the DREAM Act in 2007 and might do so again. See the "Noodles Targets" document for this logic behind the selected participants. Mohammad Abdollahi shared document with author on April 22, 2016.
19. McCain faced a primary challenge from J. D. Hayworth, a rightwing talk show host in Arizona who loved to talk tough on immigration and paint McCain as "pro-amnesty." In the spring of 2010, the challenge was being taken seriously, see Phillips (2010).
20. See the April 6, 2010 Google chat between Mo and Marisol for the KFC ticker idea. Shared by Mohammad Abdollahi with author June 26, 2016.
21. Marisol's message on Noodlesforo, April 8, 2010.
22. Yahaira's and Flavia's messages on Noodlesforo thread, April 17, 2010.

23. Flavia's message on Noodlesforo, April 20, 2010.
24. David's response to Mo's thread on Noodlesforo, April 20, 2010.
25. Interview with Mohammad Abdollahi, July 22, 2016, San Antonio, TX.
26. Interview with Lizbeth Mateo, August 18, 2014, San Jose, CA.
27. See Yahaira's message on Noodlesforo, April 20, 2010, for original schedule, and Flavia's message on Noodlesforo, May 4, 2010, sent after the Noodles' Durbin visit in Chicago for reasons for pushing the action back to May 22.
28. Kiran's message on Noodlesforo, May 8, 2010, about Monday's visits to Brownback's, LeMieux's, Menendez's, and Durbin's offices. See also Mo's message on Noodlesforo, May 8, 2010, reporting on Friday's visits to Feinstein's, Boxer's, and Lugar's offices.
29. Mo's message on Noodlesforo, May 11, 2010, reporting on Monday's visits.
30. Noorani's message sent out on May 10 under the subject line "ri4a posture" was provided to author by Mohammad Abdollahi on June 26, 2016.
31. See Cristobal's message to Erin on Noodlesforo, May 6, 2010, about Danielle Alvarado of Arizona's No More Deaths, who they were contacting for advice about conditions on the ground in Arizona. The exchange reveals that the group did not want Carlos Saavedra to know too much about the action ahead of time. See also Mo's message on Noodlesforo, May 9, 2010, in which he raises these concerns.
32. Erin's message on Noodlesforo, May 6, 2010, relaying advice from Margo about the conditions on the ground in Arizona.
33. Kyle's message on Noodlesforo, May 11, 2010.
34. Mo's message on Noodlesforo, May 13, 2010.
35. Flavia's messages on Noodlesforo, May 14, 2010 and May 15, 2010.
36. See Tania's message on Noodlesforo, May 15, 2010, for the Chicago group's press release.
37. Alma's message on Noodlesforo, May 13, 2010.
38. See Marisol's message on Noodlesforo, May 16, 2010, for solidarity actions and the Noodles spreadsheet, "National Actions after Noodle D-Day."
39. See Mo's and Kyle's messages on Noodlesforo, May 16, 2010.
40. Felipe's message on Noodlesforo, May 16, 2010.
41. See Lizbeth's message on Noodlesforo, May 16, 2010. She reports that Mo cannot reach Julia Preston but that they have made contact with someone else at *The New York Times* who is interested in writing an editorial.
42. Rigo's message on Noodlesforo, May 17, 2010.
43. Marisol's message on Noodlesforo, May 17, 2010.
44. Mo's message on Noodlesforo, May 17, 2010.
45. Rigo's message on Noodlesforo, May 17, 2010.
46. See Flavia's message on Noodlesforo, May 17, 2010, for a copy of the press release.
47. Daniel's message on Noodlesforo, May 17, 2010; also see Daniel's message on Noodlesforo, May 18, 2010, with analytics on traffic.
48. See the Noodles Media Hit spreadsheet at https://docs.google.com/spreadsheets/d/1UyfOPhNxMSj2oh0hHR7aLouL6iuLZxtFbuuLxCjPDYk/edit?hl=en&hl=en&pli=1#gid=0 [last accessed May 19, 2017].
49. Marisol's message on Noodlesforo, May 18, 2010.

50. Juan's message on Noodlesforo, May 18, 2010.
51. Flavia's message on Noodlesforo, May 18, 2010.
52. Adam's message on Noodlesforo, May 18, 2010.
53. Azadeh's message on Noodlesforo, May 19, 2010.
54. Flavia's message on Noodlesforo, May 19, 2010, bold in the original.
55. Press release from the Noodles Team/The Dream Is Coming, May 20, 2010. See Tania's message on Noodlesforo, May 19, 2010, for a copy of the release.
56. See the Dream Team LA press release, attached to Azadeh's message on Noodlesforo, May 20, 2010.
57. "Courage in Arizona" (2010, 26).
58. Preston (2010, 15).
59. Interview with Mohammad Abdollahi, September 19, 2013, San Antonio, TX.
60. See Flavia's message on Noodlesforo, May 17, 2010, for a copy of the press release.
61. Kiran's and Marisol's messages on Noodlesforo, May 19, 2010.
62. Interview with Julieta Garibay, May 18, 2013, Austin, TX. Julieta spoke candidly about how being kept in the dark made her feel disrespected.
63. RI4A email blast, May 18, 2010, "Reform Immigration For America To Begin Sustained Campaign of Civil Disobedience"; see Marisol's message on Noodlesforo, May 20, 2010.
64. See Marisol's message on Noodlesforo, May 27, 2010, for a forwarded FIRM statement, bold text in the original.
65. Carlos's message to the United We Dream Field, bold appears in the original, forwarded in Marisol's message on Noodlesforo, May 27, 2010.
66. Adey Fisseha, from NILC, makes this argument in her May 22, 2010 email to Marisol and Carlos, message forwarded to Noodlesforo, May 27, 2010.
67. Mo's message on Noodlesforo, June 2, 2010.
68. Tania's message on Noodlesforo, June 2, 2010.
69. Marisol's message on Noodlesforo, June 2, 2010.
70. Kiran's message on Noodlesforo, June 10, 2010.
71. DreamACTivist.org's post, June 10, 2010, shared with author by Mohammad Abdollahi on April 22, 2016.
72. See messages on Noodlesforo, June 10, 2010, reporting that allies were getting angry calls and hate mail from DREAMers.
73. Tania's message on Noodlesforo, June 10, 2010.
74. Mo's message on Noodlesforo, June 10, 2010.
75. For the NDLON account balance, see Neidi's message on Noodlesforo, June 25, 2010.
76. Neidi's message on Noodlesforo, June 10, 2010.
77. Lizbeth's message on Noodlesforo, June 11, 2010.
78. For NYSYLC press release: see "Open Letter on the Thursday, June 10, 2010 Actions of the New York State Youth Leadership Council" at https://www.nysylc.org/2010/06/open-letter-on-the-thursday-june-10-2010-actions-of-the-new-york-state-youth-leadership-council/ [last accessed December 14, 2016]. Also, see Marisol's message on Noodlesforo, June 14, 2010, for a copy of the open letter.
79. Personal communication with author, December 14, 2016.

80. Copies of the statements from Sharry, Noorani, and Bhargava were shared on the Noodlesforo. See Rigo's message on Noodlesforo, June 10, 2010; for Sharry's letter, see https://americasvoice.org/blog/open_letter_to_dream_activists_from_frank_sharry [last accessed November 12, 2017]; see Marisol's message on Noodlesforo, June 11, 2010, forwarding of Marissa Graciosa's blast of the Deepak Bhargava's official CCC/FIRM response; see Kyle's message on Noodlesforo, June 11, 2010, for Ali Noorani's more private statement to immigrant reform advocates.
81. Marisol's message on Noodlesforo, June 11, 2010.
82. Carlos's message, forwarded in Cyndi's message, on Noodlesforo, June 15, 2010.
83. See Kiran's message on Noodlesforo, June 17, 2010, for a forwarded Presente/Trail of Dreams letter.
84. Mo's message on Noodlesforo, June 16, 2010.
85. Marisol's message on Noodlesforo, June 17, 2010, forwarded Craig's report.
86. Mo's message on Noodlesforo, June 17, 2010.
87. Priscila's message on Noodlesforo, June 18, 2010. USSF was scheduled to open in Detroit in five days—June 22–26.

Chapter 5

1. The following biographical account comes from an interview with José Torres-Don, July 23, 2014, San Antonio, TX.
2. Interviews with Alicia Torres, December 15, 2016, Austin, TX; and May 24, 2018, Austin, TX.
3. Alicia enrolled a few years after Julieta graduated from the same school (see Chapter 2 of this text).
4. Angie Orosco was Alejandra Rincón's replacement at the Austin Independent School District.
5. For this mission statement for !ella pelea!, see https://ellapelea.wordpress.com/tag/ut-austin/ [accessed 10/25/15].
6. Mo's message on Noodlesforo, June 17, 2010.
7. See Rigo's message on Noodlesforo, June 17, 2010, with a forwarded message from Julieta. See also, Mo's message on Noodlesforo, June 21, 2010.
8. Mo's message on Noodlesforo, June 23, 2010, with forwarded message from Carlos.
9. See Levin (2010) for coverage on the moderates' alternative action.
10. The term (und)occupy is used anachronistically here. The term was first used by radical DREAMers in 2012 to describe the NIYA occupation of Obama for America campaign offices, after the Occupy Wall Street events of 2011. That said, this is how Mo first described the idea of the Washington, DC, action on the Noodlesforo: "The vision for this is essentially having a few days we can coin as 'occupation of DC.'" See Mo's email on Noodlesforo, June 17, 2010.
11. Flavia's message on Noodlesforo, June 29, 2010.
12. Mo's message on Noodlesforo, July 1, 2010.

13. Mo's message on Noodlesforo, July 4, 2010.
14. Mo's message on Noodlesforo, July 8, 10.
15. For the press release, see Nancy's message on Noodlesforo, July 9, 2010.
16. On this classic strategic dilemma, one faced by actors or players across various social arenas, see Jasper (2006).
17. The most detailed account of the action can be found in David Bennion's blog on Citizen Orange, http://www.citizenorange.com/orange/2010/07/dream-act-21-arrested-on-capit.html [last accessed July 10, 2017].
18. For the video, see http://www.youtube.com/watch?v=GzW2IamxXlg [last accessed July 17, 2017].
19. Mo's message about the Gutiérrez video on Noodlesforo, July 24, 2010.
20. For the Durbin quotation from the day of the action, see Rosenthal (2010).
21. Nichols (2014) makes a similar point in his excellent history of the DREAMers.
22. Neidi's message on Noodlesforo, July 20, 2010.
23. See Stanton and Bendery (2010).
24. See messages from Kiran and Lizbeth on Noodlesforo, July 25, 2010.
25. See José's message on Noodlesforo, July 25, 2010; and the email from José on July 28, 2010, to Mo with the forwarded message from Brent Wilkes.
26. See David's message on Noodlesforo, July 29, 2010, and Tania's response, July 29, 2010.
27. Interview with Montserrat Garibay, December 12, 2013, Austin, TX.
28. Interview with Julieta Garibay, May 18, 2013, Austin, TX. Julieta's analysis of the 2010 actions is clearly informed by the longer sequence of direct actions organized by Mo extending to 2013, and not just the Noodles actions.
29. See Mo's message on Noodlesforo, August 2, 2010, and the attached document titled "Republican Sympathy Campaign."
30. Mo's message on Noodlesforo, August 2, 2010.
31. Interview with Mohammad Abdollahi, September 19, 2013, San Antonio, TX.
32. Interview with Mohammad Abdollahi, January 1, 2017, Nogales, AZ.
33. Interview with Campos, August 23, 2013, Austin, TX. Loren, who succeeded José as ULI president in the fall of 2010, talked about how he was particularly interested in organizing a DREAM army action in Texas to pressure Senator Hutchison.
34. Quoted in "Reid's DREAM Rider" (2010, A10).
35. See Zehr (2010) on Reid's promise.
36. Zamorano et al. (2010).
37. For biographical details on Sally Kohn's professional experience, see *Politico*'s "The Arena" profile at http://www.politico.com/arena/bio/sally_kohn_.html [last accessed August 11, 2017]. See Kohn (2010) for *Daily Kos* article.
38. See Mark's guest post on David Bennion's blog at http://www.citizenorange.com/orange/2010/10/dreamer-responds-to-petulant-c.html [last accessed August 12, 2017].
39. Interview with Karla, August 7, 2013, Austin, TX.
40. Interview with Rebecca Acuña, August 23, 2013, Austin, TX.
41. Interview with Lucy, July 26, 2013, San Antonio, TX.
42. Interview with Pam, June 23, 2013, San Antonio, TX.
43. Interview with Benita Veliz, October 22, 2012, San Antonio, TX.

44. See Downes (2009) for an opinion editorial on Benita's deportation proceedings.
45. Interview with Mohammad Abdollahi, January 1, 2017, Nogales, AZ.
46. Interview with Mohammad Abdollhi, September 19, 2013, San Antonio, TX.
47. Interview with Gaby Pacheco, August 16, 2013, San Antonio, TX.
48. For media accounts of this second McCain sit in, see Hing (2010), Carcamo (2010), and Zapor (2010). Also see Gaby's address to the media after the event, telling DREAMers to "wake up" and call legislators, "let this be the last time that we put our lives on the line": https://www.youtube.com/watch?v=QDWDzHYz_60 [last accessed January 8, 2018].
49. Mo shared the email with this author, June 26, 2016 correspondence.
50. See "In Service to America and the American Dream," circulated by email on November 20, 2010, to the "Core Team" by Carlos Saavedra. Mo and Lizbeth shared email with this author, see December 15, 2016 correspondence.
51. Interview with Mohammad Abdollahi, January 15, 2017, Nogales, AZ.

Chapter 6

1. This farewell latter was shared with author by Claudia Muñoz, see correspondence after the interview with Claudia Muñoz, July 6, 2014, Bronx, NY.
2. Jasper (2004) provides an excellent theoretical discussion of precisely the organizational/resource dilemma and tradeoffs the new network faced.
3. Interview with Mohammad Abdollahi, September 19, 2013, San Antonio, TX.
4. Here are two examples from author's field notes: First, we are in Nogales, AZ, January 2017, just days before Trump's inauguration. Mo lives in a house almost literally abutting the wall that divides the AZ side from the MX side of Nogales. We leave his house. Mo is driving with a suspended license. I'm in the passenger seat. We are headed north to Tucson. As we get out of Nogales, we hit a Border Patrol checkpoint. We are waved to a stop. Mo carries his papers from his deportation proceeding. It is how he gets through these checkpoints scattered all over the southern highways of the border states. Mo starts chatting with the Border Patrol officer. Mo gently reaches toward his neck and touches his scarf—it looks like a green camouflaged keffiyeh. The officer does not flinch, stepback, or even look askance, at the gentle touch. Mo asks him if it is standard issue? Is it regulation? The officer laughs. Says something that I can't here and then protests that its cold out. He glances at Mo's papers, pays them no mind. He already knows Mo, and he is not interested. He doesn't ask me the standard question asked at all the checkpoints: "Are you a US citizen?" After a short chat, he waves us on. Second example: El Paso in the fall of 2013, outside of the ICE detention center near the airport. There is small gathering of protestors calling for the release of the DREAM 30 and a handful of journalists and cameraman covering the event. Mo and Claudia Muñoz have been doing interviews with the journalists for the last half-hour. There is lull, I watch Mo walk toward the entrance gate to the detention center. He walks up to the passenger side window of a car arriving at the gate. Two agents are inside. The one on his side lowers the window. Mo has flyers for the ongoing

demonstration. He greets them with a smile. He offers them a flyer. The agent asks Mo if he is with the 30? Mo says yes, and starts asking about the conditions inside. Are all the beds filled? Mostly asylum seekers? He asks them what trailer in the complex houses the offices of the asylum officers? The agent appears to be answering freely at first and then stops himself. He says, "hey, why do you want to know? Are you trying to trick me?" Mo laughs: "No, no, no." The conversation continues for a bit more. Through it all, Mo is sporting his black t-shirt with "undocumented" written in white letters across his chest. For Marco's description of Mo's vision, see "On Mohammad Abdollahi," posted April 17, 2012, https://undocumentedohio.wordpress.com/2012/04/17/on-mr-mohammad-abdollahi/.
5. Interview with Mohammad Abdollahi, January 15, 2017, Nogales, AZ.
6. See Chapter 3 of this text for a discussion of these cases.
7. See Mo's message on Noodlesforo, August 2, 2010; also see Chapter 5 of this text for a discussion of this strategy in the Republican Sympathy campaign.
8. See Heredia (2015, 79).
9. Interview with Viridiana Martinez, October 1, 2017, Austin, TX.
10. Interview with Alicia Torres, May 24, 2018, Austin, TX.
11. Estimates of the population of unauthorized immigrants are hard to make and the source of much disagreement and controversy. That said, DHS and Pew reports suggest that by 2011, Georgia and North Carolina each had as large or larger populations of undocumented immigrants than Arizona, and equal to or near the size of populations in Illinois and New Jersey. Compared with Florida and Northeastern states, Mexican immigrants constituted a larger share of undocumented populations in Georgia and North Carolina. For DHS estimates, see https://www.dhs.gov/sites/default/files/publications/ois_ill_pe_2012_2.pdf; and for Pew estimates, see https://www.pewresearch.org/wp-content/uploads/sites/5/reports/133.pdf.
12. Silver's (2018) wonderful book captures the changing federal, state, and local enforcement pressures that undocumented kids in rural North Carolina had to negotiate from the mid-2000s to just after Obama's DACA order in 2012. Silver demonstrates how undocumented youth drew support from their local high school, teachers, soccer teams, community organizations, and, most of all, friends and families to survive wave after wave of enforcement enhancements. The undocumented youth Alicia met in North Carolina could have jumped from the pages of Silver's study. The four interviews I did with DREAMers who gew up in or spent significant time in North Carolina or Georgia—Alicia, Jose, Santiago, and Brandon—along with more informal conversations with Dulce, Brandol, and Jonathan, echoed the shared sentiment described in Silver's book.
13. See Georgina Perez Regional Rep Application Form submitted to DreamACTivist.org in April 2009 and correspondence between Mohammad Abdollahi and Georgina Perez, October 16, 2009.
14. Message from Georgina Perez to Mohammad Abdollahi, May 16, 2010.
15. Interview with Mohammad Abdollahi, January 15, 2017, Nogales, AZ.
16. National Immigration Youth Alliance founding document (DreamActivist.org/NIYA archive).

17. An excerpt of the Angy post was archived on Prerna Lal's blog, see http://prernalal.com/2011/06/deconstructing-the-dreamer-status/.
18. NOTES—National Immigrant Youth Alliance, April 2 and 3, 2011 (DreamActivist.org/NIYA archive).
19. See Harlah (2011) for this description of the protest.
20. For Gina's video, see https://www.youtube.com/watch?v=mTeh1m0qiEU [last accessed April 2, 2017].
21. Georgia Undocumented Youth Alliance Youth Empowerment Summit (YES training), April 30, 2011 (DreamActivist.org/NIYA archive).
22. Interview with Mohammad Abdollahi, January 15, 2017, Nogales, AZ.
23. Georgia Undocumented Youth Alliance Youth Empowerment Summit (YES training), April 30, 2011 (DreamActivist.org/NIYA archive).
24. The following biographical account is drawn from an interview with Santiago Garcia-Leco, December 18, 2013, El Paso, TX.
25. Interview with Mohammad Abdollahi, January 15, 2017, Nogales, AZ.
26. Interview with Marco Saavedra, July 6, 2014, Bronx, NY.
27. Interview with Alicia Torres, Austin, May 21, 2018, Austin TX
28. "On Mohammad Abdollahi" by Marco Saavedra, posted April 12, 2012, https://undocumentedohio.wordpress.com/page/7/ [last accessed January 11, 2018].
29. Jonathan Perez first used the term "silent action" to describe the Mobile action. See the Jonathan Perez and Isaac Barrera panel presentation during the Art Media Immigration symposium at the University of New Mexico, November 9, 2012, https://www.youtube.com/watch?v=4ct6lMyFWfM [last accessed January 11, 2018].
30. You can see the video of the Isaac and Jonathan's silent action at https://www.youtube.com/watch?v=iA54ErBfZ8E [last accessed January 11, 2018].
31. The NIYA press release is published in Pavey and Saavedra (2012).

Chapter 7

1. Erik Sanchez's report for Topo can be seen at https://www.youtube.com/watch?v=-sIEa-m-j3o [last accessed August 6, 2016].
2. See the email from Jose F. to NIYA core members, March 21, 2012, with a copy of the press release from Somos America with the teacher's letter (DreamACTivist.org/NIYA archive).
3. José Torres-Don's email, March 20, 2012, shared the Carmen Conejo's Facebook post to NIYA core members (DreamACTivist.org/NIYA archive).
4. See Jonathan Perez's email, March 21, 2012, for this response Carmen Conejo's Facebook post (DreamACTivist.org/NIYA archive).
5. Conversation with Felipe Vargas and Mohmmad Abdollahi, January 18, 2017, Nogales, AZ.
6. See the NC DREAM Team blog entry recounting the Denver action at https://ncdreamteam.wordpress.com/2012/06/05/undocumented-youth-in-den

ver-sit-in-at-ofa-denver-office/. See also an email from Kiran Savage-Sangwan to NIYA members, June 6, 2012 (DreamACTivist.org/NIYA archive).
7. Preston and Cushman Jr. (2012).
8. Interview with Marco Saavedra, July 6, 2014, Bronx, NY.
9. Email exchange between Joshua Hoyt and Mohammad Abdollahi, June 15, 2012 (DreamACTivist.org/NIYA archive).
10. The National Immigrant Youth Alliance Unbound Packet, May 2012. (DreamACTivist.org/NIYA archive).
11. Interview with Mohammad Abdollahi, January 14, 2017, Nogales, AZ.
12. Interview with Mohammad Abdollahi, January 14, 2017, Nogales, AZ.
13. Saavedra (2011, 3–4).
14. The following biographical account comes from my interview with Marco Saavedra, July 6, 2014, Bronx, NY.
15. Saavedra (2011).
16. Pavey and Saavedra (2012).
17. "On Mohammad Abdollahi," posted April 17, 2012, https://undocumentedohio.wordpress.com/2012/04/17/on-mr-mohammad-abdollahi/.
18. For the precise "guidance" Obama's director of ICE, John Morton, issued to field offices and special agents a memo regarding the exercise of prosecutorial discretion in furtherance of priorities, see the June 2011 Morton memo at https://www.ice.gov/doclib/secure-communities/pdf/prosecutorial-discretion-memo.pdf.
19. For one important study released shortly before the NIYA infiltrations, see AILA (2011), "Immigration Enforcement Off Target: Minor Offenses with Major Consequences," https://www.aila.org/File/Related/11081609.pdf.
20. For studies on the growing system of immigrant detention centers and the conditions under which detainees are held, see Romero Jr. (2018), Meissner et al. (2013), National Immigrant Justice Center and Detention Watch Network (2015), ACLU (2014).
21. Quoted from video of Marco Saavedra's infiltration, posted by DreamACTivist.org, https://www.youtube.com/watch?v=QPqEuTop41g [last accessed May 15, 2018].
22. The phrase "political jiu-jitsu" comes from Sharp (1972, ch. 13). See Muñoz and Young (2017) for an earlier version of the following analysis of NIYA infiltrations.
23. For audio, see the video of Marco Saavedra's infiltration, posted by DreamACTivist.org, https://www.youtube.com/watch?v=QPqEuTop41g [last accessed May 15, 2018].
24. U-visas are granted persons who have been victims of a crime committed in the United States and have cooperated with authorities in the investigation of the crime. The Victims of Trafficking and Violence Protection Act of 2000 created the U-visa.
25. Quoted in Pavey and Saavedra (2012).
26. There are ten missing data points for nationality. Out of the 176 cases with complete data, fifty-six came from Mexico, thirty-five from Honduras, twenty-six from Guatemala, and twelve from El Salvador. Detainees from the Dominican Republic were the next most numerous, numbering eight.
27. The "Morton memo" refers to the memorandum issued in June 2011 by then ICE Director John Morton on prosecutorial discretion in immigration cases. The memo can be found at https://www.ice.gov/doclib/secure-communities/pdf/prosecutorial-discretion-memo.pdf.

28. For NIYA's public announcement of the infiltration, see http://theniya.org/for-immediate-release-marco-saavedra-niyas-second-implanted-activist-has-been-detained-in-broward-since-july-11-niya/ [last accessed May 15, 2018].
29. Panel discussion at the Art Media Immigration symposium at the University of New Mexico, November 9, 2012. Interview with Viridiana Martinez, October 1, 2017, Austin, TX.
30. Interview with Claudia Muñoz, July 6, 2014, Bronx, NY.
31. See Mohammad Abdollahi's email thread with Margo Cowan and David Bennion, June 4, 2012 (DreamACTivist.org/NIYA archive).
32. Interview with Marco Saavedra, July 6, 2014, Bronx, NY.
33. Interview with Lizbeth Mateo, August 18, 2014, San Jose, CA.
34. Interview with Marco Saavedra, July 6, 2014, Bronx, NY.
35. Interview with Marco Saavedra, July 6, 2014, Bronx, NY.
36. Interview with Benito Deal, October 10, 2013, El Paso, TX.
37. Interview with Marco Saavedra, July 6, 2014, Bronx, NY.
38. See a video of sit-in at https://www.youtube.com/watch?v=bIkiBWPEg-s [last accessed November 2, 2013].
39. See http://nbclatino.com/2013/07/31/34-house-members-sign-letter-asking-for-dream-9-release/ [last accessed November 2, 2013].
40. David Leopold and Mohammad Abdollahi, quoted in "Dream 9 Pushed It Too Far" (2013); see also Lorrente (2013) for coverage of the controversy.
41. See Stranahan (2013, 2013a, 2013b).
42. See "The Most Illogically Bizarre Immigration Reform Story We Have Ever Written" (2012) for an attempt to make sense of the social media dust-up. For the opinions of two notable online critics, see Susan Pai's September 28, 2013 blog at https://susanpai twitter.wordpress.com/2013/09/28/the-no-sovereign-borders-movement/. See also https://www.dailykos.com/blog/Dose%20of%20Tequila and Dose of Tequila (2013).
43. See Marco Saavedra's email thread to NIYA members on July 18, 2013, including Mohammad Abdollahi's response, and Marco Saavedra's reply to same thread on November 12, 2013 terminating his association (DreamACTivist.org/NIYA archive).
44. Interview with Marco Saavedra, July 6, 2014, Bronx, NY.
45. Maria Ines's response referring to Mohammad Abdollahi appears only in the original show that aired in October 2015. It was cut from the program when it was rebroadcasted in February 2017. A rebroadcast can be found at http://latinousa.org/2015/10/16/1542-the-dream-9/ [last accessed May 19, 2018].

Conclusion

1. See Durkhiem (1995, 223). The term "phantom objectivity" comes from Lukacs's (1972) classical account of reification and the commodity fetish.
2. See Bourdieu (2014, 10, 32) and Lukacs (1972).
3. Touraine (1981).

4. Sharry (2013).
5. See Zamorano et al. (2010).
6. Quoted in Montgomery (2010, C01).
7. Joas (1996, 2000). For quote, see Castoriades (1987, 87).
8. See Wagner (2010, xii): "So it is like the saying the Native Americans have: 'Coyote is the best trickster of all, because he tricks himself.'"

Appendix

1. See Barberena, Jiménez, and Young (2014) for the methodology behind this earlier research on undocumented youth.

Bibliography

ACLU. 2014. "Warehoused and Forgotten." https://www.aclu.org/sites/default/files/assets/060614-aclu-car-reportonline.pdf.
Althusser, Louis. 1971. "Ideology and Ideological State Apparatuses." In *Lenin and Philosophy and Other Essays*, edited by Louis Althusser, 127–187. New York: Monthly Review Press.
Amenta, Edwin. 2006. *When Movements Matter: The Townsend Plan and the Rise of Social Security*. Princeton, NY: Princeton University Press.
Anderson, Benedict R. 1991. *Imagined Communities: Reflections on the Origin and Spread of Nationalism*. London: Verso.
Auyero, Javier. 2012. *Patients of the State: The Politics of Waiting in Argentina*. Durham, NC: Duke University Press.
Barberena, Laura, Hortencia Jiménez, and Michael P. Young. 2014. "'It Just Happened': Telescoping Anxiety, Defiance, and Emergent Collective Behavior in the 2006 Student Walkouts." *Social Problems* 61, no. 1: 42–60.
Bernstein, Mary. 1997. "Celebration and Suppression: The Strategic Uses of Identity by the Lesbian and Gay Movement." *American Journal of Sociology* 103, no. 3: 531–565.
Bloemraad, Irene, and Kim Voss. 2020. "Movement or Moment? Lessons from the Pro-immigrant Movement in the United States and Contemporary Challenges." *Journal of Ethnic and Migration Studies* 46, no. 4: 683–704.
Bloemraad, Irene, Kim Voss, and Taeku Lee. 2011. "The Protests of 2006: What Were They, How Do We Understand Them, Where Do We Go?" In *Rallying for Immigrant Rights*, edited by Kim Voss and Irene Bloemraad, 3–43. Berkeley: University of California Press.
Borjas, George J. 2002. "The Impact of Welfare Reform on Immigrant Welfare Use." Report for the Center of Immigration Studies. Washington, DC: Center of Immigration Studies. http://cis.org/sites/cis.org/files/articles/2002/borjas.pdf.
Bourdieu, Pierre. 2014. *On the State: Lectures at the Collège de France, 1989–1992*. Edited by Patrick Champagne, Remi Lenoir, Frank Poupeau, and Marie-Christine Rivière. Translated by David Fernbach. Malden, MA: Polity Press.
Campo-Flores, Arian. 2006. "The Next Step in a Very Long March: The Immigration Debate Spurs Bids for Citizenship." *Newsweek*, May 22, 35. https://advance-lexis-com.ezproxy.lib.utexas.edu/api/document?collection=news&id=urn:contentItem:4JYK-VJS0-TX2J-238H-00000-00&context=1516831.
Canham, Matt. 2010. "Hatch, Bennett to Vote No on Immigrant Dream Act." *Salt Lake Tribune*, September 15.
Carcamo, Cindy. 2010. "Immigration Activists Rally from O.C. to D.C." *Orange County Register*, November 17. http://www.ocregister.com/news/bill-276453-countryyears.html?nstrack=sid:832242|met:102|cat:2986969|order:1.
Cardenas, Jose. 2006. "Young Immigrants Raise Voices, and Hopes." *St. Petersburg Times*, May 13, 1A.

Castoriadis, Cornelius. 1987. *The Imaginary Institution of Society*. Cambridge, MA: MIT Press.
Center for Community Change. 2004. "Sen. Kennedy, Rep. Gutierrez, AFL-CIO, NAACP, NCLR to Join New Immigration Coalition to Press for Comprehensive Immigration Reform." Press Release, July 14. https://advance-lexis-com.ezproxy.lib.utexas.edu/api/document?collection=news&id=urn:contentItem:4CVT-TB80-0007-21JS-00000-00&context=1516831.
Center for Community Change. 2004a. "Immigrants Lobby for Comprehensive Immigration Reform; Politicians Lobby for their Vote." Press Release, September 21. https://advance-lexis-com.ezproxy.lib.utexas.edu/api/document?collection=news&id=urn:contentItem:4DCH-T1R0-0007-20Y6-00000-00&context=1516831.
Center for Community Change. 2004b. "Congressman, National Leaders Fast to Pressure Congress, Administration to Act on DREAM." Press Release, September 24. https://advance-lexis-com.ezproxy.lib.utexas.edu/api/document?collection=news&id=urn:contentItem:4DD5-PHY0-0007-2195-00000-00&context=1516831.
Center for Community Change. 2005. "Latina 'Woman of the Year' Spends Final Days Before Deportation Lobbying Congressional Leaders, Homeland Security." Press Release, June 28. https://advance-lexis-com.ezproxy.lib.utexas.edu/api/document?collection=news&id=urn:contentItem:4GH8-6G00-TWP4-7212-00000-00&context=1516831.
Center for Community Change. 2006. "Youth Being Mobilized Around Immigration Debate: Trainings Build Capacity, Enable Students to Advocate for Access to Higher Education." Press Release, February 20. https://advance-lexis-com.ezproxy.lib.utexas.edu/api/document?collection=news&id=urn:contentItem:4J9T-FKX0-TWP4-72H8-00000-00&context=1516831.
Center for Community Change. 2006a. "America's Immigrant Youth Converge on Congress, Lobby for Their Families Future, Share Powerful Stories of Separation." Press Release, May 24. https://advance-lexis-com.ezproxy.lib.utexas.edu/api/document?collection=news&id=urn:contentItem:4K1M-K5W0-TWP4-71XV-00000-00&context=1516831.
Center for Community Change. 2007. United for DREAM Act, Immigrant Students and Allies Speak out in Favor of Legislation. Press Release, September 18. https://advance-lexis-com.ezproxy.lib.utexas.edu/api/document?collection=news&id=urn:contentItem:4PPD-HKV0-TWP4-719M-00000-00&context=1516831.
"Courage in Arizona." 2010. *The New York Times*, May 20, 26. Editorial.
Davidson, Lee. 2002. "Hispanics Cheer 'DREAM.'" *Deseret Morning News*, July 14.
Davidson, Lee. 2004. "Marchers Push for Immigrant Bill." *Deseret Morning News*, April 21.
Delgado, Gary. 1986. *Organizing the Movement: The Roots and Growth of ACORN*. Philadelphia: Temple University Press.
Diaz, Jesse, and Javier Rodriguez. 2007. "A Movement of Movements? Undocumented in America." *New Left Review*, 47 (September and October): 93–106.
Dose of Tequila. 2013. "Mohammad Abdollahi: Says F Obama & Go Suck United We Dream's D." *Daily Kos*, September 8. https://www.dailykos.com/stories/2013/9/8/1237319/-Mohammad-Abdollahi-Says-F-Obama-Go-Suck-United-We-Dream-s-D.
Downes, Lawrence. 2009. "Editorial Observer: Don't Deport Benita Veliz." *The New York Times*, March 28. http://www.nytimes.com/2009/03/28/opinion/28sat4.html.
Drake, Susan, and Charles Wheeler. 1992. "History of the National Immigration Law Center." *Clearing House Review* 26, no. 1: 88–95.

"Dream 9 Pushed It Too Far, According to Immigration. Lawyer." 2013. *Huffington Post*, July 27. [Originally published on VOXXI as "Immigration Lawyer: The Nine Dreamers Pushed It Too Far.] https://www.huffingtonpost.com/2013/07/27/dream-9-imigration-lawyer_n_3663516.html.

Dunn, Timothy. 2009. *Blockading the Border and Human Rights: The El Paso Operation that Remade Immigration Enforcement*. Austin: University of Texas Press.

Durkhiem, Émile. 1995 [1912]. *The Elementary Forms of Religion Religious Life*. Translated by Karen E. Fields. New York: Free Press.

Enriquez, Laura E., and Abigail C. Saguy. 2015. "Coming Out of the Shadows: Harnessing a Cultural Schema to Advance the Undocumented Immigrant Youth Movement." *American Journal of Cultural Sociology* 4, no. 1: 107–130.

Eschbach, Karl, Jacqueline Hagan, and Nestor Rodriguez. 2001. "Causes and Trends in Migrant Deaths Along the Mexico–US Border, 1985–1998." Working Paper. Houston, TX: Center for Immigration Research.

Flores, Angel. 2002. "Latino-favored Bills Offer Hope to Immigrants." *The Rebel Yell*, August 1.

Ford Foundation. 1982–1984. *Annual Report*. New York: Ford Foundation.

Foundation Center. 2016 "Top Recipients for Grants from FC 1000 Foundations for Immigrants and Refugees, 2006."

Gahr, Joshua, and Michael P. Young. 2014. "Evangelicals and Emergent Moral Protest." *Mobilization: An International Quarterly* 19, no. 2: 185–208.

Ghaziani, Amin. 2008. *The Dividends of Dissent: How Conflict and Culture Work in Lesbian and Gay Marches on Washington*. Chicago: University of Chicago.

Gonzales, Alfonso. 2014. *Reform without Justice: Latino Migrant Politics and the Homeland Security State*. New York: Oxford University Press.

Gonzalez, Marie. 2005. "Thank You for Letting Me Stay in the U.S." *St. Louis Post-Dispatch*, July 18, B7.

Gould, Deborah B. 2009. *Moving Politics: Emotion and ACT UP's Fight against AIDS*. Chicago: University of Chicago Press.

Harlah, Kosta. 2011. "8 Undocumented Youth Arrested in Georgia as Hundreds March to Protest Education Ban." *Fight Back!News*, April 7. http://www.fightbacknews.org/2011/4/7/8-undocumented-youth-arrested-georgia-hundreds-march-protest-education-ban.

Herszonshorn, David M. 2010. "Senators Vote to Block Debate on Military Bill." *New York Times*, September 22, 1.

Heredia, Luisa Laura. 2015. "Of Radicals and DREAMers: Harnessing Exceptionality to Challenge Immigration Control." *Association of Mexican American Educators Journal* 9, no. 3: 74–85.

Hing, Julianne. 2010. "McCain Runs Away from DREAMers as Reid Vows Senate Vote: But he can't run too far." *Color Lines*, November 18. https://www.colorlines.com/articles/mccain-runs-away-dreamers-reid-vows-senate-vote.

Hoover, Eric. 2004. "Immigrant Students Ask for a Chance at College." *Chronicle for Higher Education*, April 3, 1.

INCITE! Women of Color Against Violence, editors. 2007. *The Revolution Will Not Be Funded: Beyond the Non-profit Industrial Complex*. Cambridge, MA: South End Press.

Jasper, James M. 2004. "A Strategic Approach to Collective Action." *Mobilization* 9: 1–16.

Jasper, James M. 2006. *Getting Your Way: Strategic Dilemma is Real Life*. Chicago: University of Chicago Press.

292 BIBLIOGRAPHY

JayGR. 2008. "AEDP, IIRIRA, the 1990's and the Clintons (A Betrayal of Democratic Values)." *Daily Kos*, February 3. http://www.dailykos.com/story/2008/2/3/449127/-.

Jiménez, Hortencia. 2011. "The Start of a New Era? Examining the Austin Immigrant Rights Coalition (AIRC) and Experiences of Latinas." PhD diss., University of Texas at Austin.

Joas, Hans. 1996. *The Creativity of Action*. Chicago: University of Chicago Press

Joas, Hans. 2000. *The Genesis of Values*. Chicago: University of Chicago Press.

Jost, Kenneth. 1995. "Cracking Down on Immigration: Should Government Benefits and Services Be Cut Off." *CQ Reports* 5, no. 5. http://library.cqpress.com/cqresearcher/document.php?id=cqresrre1995020300.

Kohn, Sally. 2010. DREAM Act Students Causing a Nightmare. *Daily Kos* October 12. https://www.dailykos.com/stories/2010/10/12/909688/-

Korten, Alicia Epstein. 2009. *Change Philanthropy: Candid Stories of Foundations Maximizing Results through Social Justice*. San Francisco: Jossey-Bass.

Lal, Prerna, and Tañia Unzueta. 2013. "How Queer Undocumented Youth Built the Immigrant Rights Movement." *Huffington Post*, March 28. https://www.huffpost.com/entry/how-queer-undocumented_b_2973670.

Levin, John-Clark. 2010. "Young Illegals Out Themselves, Daring to be Deported, Civil Disobedience by Students Adds a New Twist to the Immigration Debate." *The Wall Street Journal*, July 31. https://www.wsj.com/articles/SB10001424052748703578104575397180097418638.

Llorente, Elizabeth. 2003. "Undocumented Immigrant Activists Elicit Divisions Among Advocates." *Fox News*, July 29. http://www.foxnews.com/politics/2013/07/29/undocumented-immigrant-activists-elicit-divisions-among-advocates.html.

Lueke, Jacob. 2005. "Young Immigrant Pins Hopes on Congress." *St. Louis Post-Dispatch*, February 15, B02.

Lukacs, Georg. 1972. *History and Class Consciousness*. Cambridge, MA: MIT Press.

McAdam, Doug, Sidney Tarrow, and Charles Tilly. 2001. *Dynamics of Contention*. New York: Cambridge University Press.

McCarthy, John D., and Mayer N. Zald. 1977. "Resource Mobilization and Social Movements: A Partial Theory." *American Journal of Sociology* 82, no. 6: 1212–1241.

McCarthy, John D., and Mayer N. Zald. 1987 [1973]. "The Trend in Social Movements in America: Professionalization and Resource Mobilization." In *Social Movements in an Organizational Society: Collected Essays*, edited by John D. McCarthy and Mayer N. Zald, 337–391. New Brunswick, NJ: Transaction Publishers.

McGarry, Aidan, and James M. Jasper. 2015. *The Identity Dilemma: Social Movements and Collective Identity*. Philadelphia: Temple University Press.

McMahon, Susan. 2002. "Illegal Immigrants' Dream: Residency, Then College." *Lowell Sun*, July 17.

Massey, Douglas S., Jorge Durand, and Nolan J. Malone. 2003. *Beyond Smoke and Mirrors: Mexican Immigration in an Era of Economic Integration*. New York: Russell Sage Foundation.

Meissner, Doris, Donald M. Kerwin, Muzaffar Chishti, and Claire Bergeron. 2013. *Immigration Enforcement in the United States: The Rise of a Formidable Machinery*. Washington, DC: Migration Policy Institute.

Meyerson, Harold. 2005. "A Deportation Tragedy." *Washington Post*, June 29, Editorial, A21.

Melucci, Alberto. 1989. *Nomads of the Present: Social Movements and Individual Needs in Contemporary Society*. London: Hutchinson Radius.

Melucci, Alberto. 1996. *Challenging Codes: Collective Action in the Information Age*. New York: Cambridge University.

Mena, Jennifer. 2004. "'Dream Act' Offers Hope for Immigrant Students." *Los Angeles Times*, September 19. https://www.latimes.com/archives/la-xpm-2004-sep-19-me-immigrad19-story.html.

Montgomery, David. 2010. "Trail of Dream students walk 1,500 miles to bring immigration message to Washington." *Washington Post*, May 1, C01.

Muñoz, Claudia and Michael P. Young. 2017. "Turning Detention Centers Inside Out: The Case of the National Immigrant Youth Alliance." In *Challenging Immigration Detention* edited by Matthew Flynn and Michael Flynn. London: Edward Elgar Publisher. Pp. 101–119.

National Immigrant Justice Center and Detention Watch Network. 2015. "Lives in Peril: How Ineffective Inspections Make ICE Complicit in Immigration Detention Abuse." http://immigrantjustice.org/sites/immigrantjustice.org/files/THR-Inspections-FOIA-Report-October-2015-FINAL.pdf.

National Immigrant, Refugee, and Citizenship Forum. 1984. *Forum Information Bulletin* (March 19). Washington, DC: National Immigrant, Refugee, and Citizenship Forum.

Nichols, Walter J. 2013. *The DREAMers: How the Undocumented Youth Movement Transformed the Immigrant Rights Debate*. Stanford, CA: Stanford University Press.

Pacheco, Gaby. 2012. "Trail of Dreams." In *Beautiful Trouble*, edited by Andrew Boyd and Dave Oswald Mitchell, 384–386. New York: O/R Books.

Pavey, Steve, and Marco Saavedra. 2012. *Shadows then Light*. Lexington, KY: One Horizon Institute.

Perez, Jonathan, Jorge Gutiérrez, Nancy Meza, and Neidi Dominguez Zamorano. 2010. "DREAM Movement: Challenges with the Social Justice Elite's Military Option Arguments and the Immigration Reform 'Leaders.'" *Truthout.org*. https://truthout.org/articles/dream-movement-challenges-with-the-social-justice-elites-military-option-arguments-and-the-immigration-reform-leaders/

Perkins, Tracy E. 2022. *Evolution of a Movement: Four Decades of California Environmental Justice Activism*. Oakland: University of California Press.

Phillips, Michael M. 2010. "McCain Feeling Primary Heat from His Right Flank." *The Wall Street Journal*, February 4. https://www.wsj.com/articles/SB10001424052748704343104575033181531964738.

Piven, Frances Fox. 2004. "Center for Community Change." In *Poverty in the United States: An Encyclopedia of History, Politics, and Policy*, edited by Gwendolyn Mink and Alice O'Connor, 135–136. Santa Barbara, CA: ABC-CLIO.

Polletta, Francesca. 2006. *It Was Like A Fever*. Chicago: University of Chicago Press.

Preston, Julia. 2010. "Illegal Immigrant Students Protest at McCain Office." *The New York Times*, May 18, 15.

Preston, Julia, and John H. Cushman Jr. 2012. "Obama to Permit Young Migrants to Remain in U.S." *New York Times*, June 15.

"Reid's DREAM Rider." 2010. *Investor's Business Daily*, September 16, A10.

Riley, Michael. 2002. "Immigrants Shut Out of Colleges, Children of Undocumented Workers Must Pay Out-of-State Tuition." *The Denver Post*, August 11.

Riley, Michael. 2003. "A Stop by Police Ends an All-American Life for Two Brothers Who Grew Up in the U.S. Illegally. Amid Outrage from Family and Their Hometown, the Brothers Now Struggle to Build New Lives in Mexico. Deportation Kills Dream." *The Denver Post*, November 14, A01.

Rincón, Alejandra. 2008. *Undocumented Immigrants and Higher Education*. El Paso: LFB Scholarly Publishing LLC.
Romero Jr., Luis Antonio. 2018. "Immigrant Families and Detention." Unpublished diss., University of Texas.
Rosenthal, Brian. 2010. "Wednesday UCI Grad Arrested in D.C. Protest." *Orange County Register*, July 21.
Saavedra, Marco. 2011. "Undocumented & Unafraid: A So[ul]cial History of the Student Immigrant Movement." Sociology senior thesis, Kenyon College.
Sennett, Richard. 1981. "Forward." In *The Voice and the Eye: An Analysis of Social Movements*, edited by Alain Touraine, ix–xi. New York: Cambridge University Press.
Shaw, Randy. 2011. "Building the Labor–Clergy–Immigrant Alliance." In *Rallying for Immigrant Rights*, edited by Kim Voss and Irene Bloemraad, chapter 4. Berkeley: University of California Press.
Santon, John, and Jennifer Bendery. 2010. "Reid Narrows Goals for Immigration This Year." *Roll Call*, July 28.
Sharp, Gene. 1972. *The Politics of Non-Violent Action: Part Three: The Dynamics of Nonviolent Action*. Boston: Porter Sargent.
Sharry, Frank. 2013. "How Did We Build an Immigrant Movement? We Learned from Gay Rights Advocates." *Washington Post*, March 22.
Sheridan, Mary Beth. 2004. "Students Rally for Tuition Benefit; Many Undocumented Youths Say They Can't Afford Out-of-State College Rates." *Washington Post*, April 21, B02.
Silver, Alexis M. 2018. *Shifting Boundaries: Immigrant Youth Negotiating National, State, and Small-Town Politics*. Stanford, CA: Stanford University Press.
Stanton, John and Jennifer Bendery. 2010. "Reid narrows goals for immigration this year." *Roll Call*, July 28.
Stranahan, Lee. 2013. "Illegal Alien Activist Claims Employment by Restaurant Group." *Breitbart*, August 8. https://www.breitbart.com/politics/2013/08/08/illegal-alien-activist-claims-to-have-been-employed-by-restaurant-organizing-group/.
Stranahan, Lee. 2013a. "'Dreamer' Website Teaches Illegal Immigrants 'How To Lie Successfully.'" *Breitbart*, September 5. https://www.breitbart.com/politics/2013/09/05/dreamer-website-teaches-illegal-immigrants-how-to-lie-successfully/.
Stranahan, Lee. 2013b. "'Dreamer' Immigration Activist Tweeted About Killing, Eating 'White Invaders.'" *Breitbart*, September 6. http://www.breitbart.com/big-government/2013/09/06/dreamer-immigration-activist-tweets-about-killing-roasting-eating-white-invaders/.
"The Most Illogically Bizarre Immigration Reform Story We Have Ever Written." 2012. *Latino Rebels*, September 10. https://www.latinorebels.com/2013/09/10/the-most-illogically-bizarre-immigration-reform-story-we-have-ever-written/.
Tilly, Charles. 1999. *Durable Inequality*. Berkeley: University of California Press.
Tilly, Charles. 2004. *Social Movements, 1776–2004*. Boulder, CO: Paradigm Publishers.
Torres, Josue. 2004. "I Want to Live the American Dream." *Washington Post*, April 18.
Touraine, Alain. 1981. *The Voice and the Eye: An Analysis of Social Movements*. New York: Cambridge University Press.
Tran, Tam, and Prerna Lal. 2009. "Undocumented and Undaunted: Immigrant Youth at Work in the Nonprofit Sector." *Nonprofit Quarterly*, September 1. https://nonprofitquarterly.org/undocumented-but-undaunted-immigrant-youth-at-work-in-the-nonprofit-sector/.

Ustinova, Anastasia. 2004. "Immigrant Students Rally for Bill; A Demonstration Drew Dozens. The Measure Targets Teens Brought to the U.S. as Children." *Philadelphia Inquirer*, April 21, A05.

Vaughan, Jessica. 2006. "Attrition through Enforcement: A Cost-Effective Strategy to Shrink the Illegal Population." *Backgrounder*, April 2006, 1–16. Washington, DC: Center for Immigration Studies. http://cis.org/sites/cis.org/files/articles/2006/back406.pdf.

Voss, Kim, and Irene Bloemraad. 2011. *Rallying for Immigrant Rights*. Berkeley: University of California Press.

Wagner, Roy. 2010. *Coyote Anthropology*. Lincoln: University of Nebraska Press.

Walker, Edward T. 2014. *Grassroots for Hire: Public Affairs Consultants in American Democracy*. New York: Cambridge University Press.

Wall, Stephen. 2004. "A Future in Doubt." *San Bernardino Sun*, October 31.

Wheatley, Christine M. 2017. "Fragmented Borders: Deportation, Return, and (Non) Citizenship in the U.S.–Mexico Region." Unpublished diss., University of Texas at Austin.

Whittier, Nancy. 2012. "The Politics of Visibility: Coming Out and Individual and Collective Identity." In *Strategies for Social Change*, edited by Maney, Gregory M., Rachel V. Kutz-Flamenbaum, Deana A. Rohlinger, and Jeff Goodwin, 145–169 . Minneapolis: University of Minnesota.

Young, Michael P. 2002. "Confessional Protest: The Religious Birth of U.S. National Social Movements." *American Sociological Review* 67, no. 5: 660–688.

Young, Michael P. 2007. *Bearing Witness against Sin: The Evangelical Birth of the American Social Movement*. Chicago: University of Chicago Press.

Zald, Mayer N., and Michael Lounsbury. 2010. "The Wizards of Oz: Towards an Institutional Approach to Elites, Expertise and Command Posts." *Organization Studies* 31, no. 7: 963–996.

Zamorano, Neidi Dominguez, Jonathan Perez, Jorge Pere, Jorge Guitierrez, and Nancy Meza. "DREAM Movement: Challenges with the Social Justice Elite's Military Option Arguments and the Immigration Reform 'Leaders.'" *Truthout.org*, September 20. https://truthout.org/articles/dream-movement-challenges-with-the-social-justice-elites-military-option-arguments-and-the-immigration-reform-leaders/.

Zapor, Patricia. 2010. "Hunger Strike, Arrests, Other Lobbying Aim to Push DREAM Act Forward." *U.S. Catholic Service*, November 19. http://www.uscatholic.org/news/2010/11/hunger-strike-arrests-other-lobbying-aim-pushdream-act-forward.

Zehr, Mary Ann. 2010. "Sen. Reid Vows to Bring DREAM Act to a Vote." *Education Week*, November 10.

Zolberg, Aristide R. 2008. *A Nation by Design: Immigration Policy in the Fashioning of America*. Cambridge, MA: Harvard University Press.

Index

287(g) Program, 18, 172, 210, 234
9/11, 17–18

AB 540 (California), 59, 61, 65
Abdollahi, Mohammad, ix, 75–77
   accusations of dictatorship and manipulation, 194, 223, 243
   conflict with Gaby Pacheco, xi, 176–178
   DREAM Act lobbying 2010, 105
   END campaigns, 92–93, 94–95
   on "the movement," xii, 2–3, 82, 250
   organizing strategies, 79, 95, 162–163, 186–188, 226, 242
   organizing strengths and characteristics, 111, 187, 235
   recognition of DREAMer un-deportability, 95
   recording of Reid action, 151–155
   on Schumer action fallout, 128, 133–134
   on the Trail of Dreams, 103
   and UWD network, 84–85, 105, 106, 125, 135, 136–137, 175
Acuña, Rebecca, 41–50, 144–145, 170, 253, 256
AFL-CIO (American Federation of Labor and Congress of Industrial Organizations), 105–107
America's Voice, 14, 86, 128, 134, 185
Antiterrorism and Effective Death Penalty Act (AEDPA), 15–16
attrition through enforcement, 15, 18
Austin Immigrant Rights Coalition (AIRC), 46, 48

Barberena, Laura, ix
Barrera, Isaac, 217–220, 221–222, 236–238. *See also* Perez, Jonathan
Barrientos, Walter, 45, 70, 86, 173, 175

Bennion, David, xiv, 111, 158–159, 169, 242
Bernstein, Josh;
   as architect of DREAM Act, 7, 10, 17
   nonprofit affiliations, 14
   nonprofit involvement, 27, 29, 48–49, 63, 66, 71
   on popularity of DREAM Act, 20–21
Bhargava, Deepak, 26, 27, 32–3, 104, 107–8, 127–9, 167
   statement following Schumer action, 134, 148, 255–6
Bourdieu, Pierre, 251
Bush (George W.), 17, 59
   Bush Administration, 18, 92

California DREAM Network, 35, 57, 65, 66, 69, 97
Carrillo, Yahaira, 110, 112, 117–118, 137, 165, 167
Castoriadis, Cornelius, 259
CCC (Center for Community Change), 9, 17, 25–36
   conflict with radical dreamers, 66–67, 134–135
   failures of, 97, 185
   FIRM reaction following Tucson Action, 122–125, 134
   focus on CIR over the standalone DREAM act, 70, 106, 125, 182–183
   founding of FIRM, 26–27
   founding of RI4A, 86
   influence on moderate DREAMers, 125
   interregional meetings, 48–9, 54, 173
   mock graduations, 49
   as "parent" of undocumented youth organizations, 54, 69–70, 96–97
   and regional and state-level nonprofits, 14
   relationship with UWD network, 96–97

CCC (Center for Community Change), (*cont.*)
  social movement claims, 87–88
  United We Dream Campaign, 35, 69–71
  work with student groups, 35–36, 54, 63
Center for Immigration Studies (CIS), 15, 21
Change.org's "Ideas for Changing America Competition," 82, 84. *See also* DreamACTivist.org
CHC (Congressional Hispanic Congress), 125–126, 155, 157–159, 164
CHIRLA (Coalition for Humane Immigrant Rights of Los Angeles), 13, 65, 66, 82, 110, 184
  CIR over DREAM Act, 66–67
  conflict with DREAMers, 66–68, 97, 131-2, 255
  and FIRM, 27
  and student organizations, 35, 57, 62-4, 69
Citizen Orange blog, 82, 91, 169
Citizen's Crusade against Poverty (CCAP), 25
Clinton Administration, 15, 17, 18
Colotl, Jessica, 191, 195
Conejo, Carmen, 223–224
Corrections Corporation of America (CCA), 244, 261
Cowan, Margo, 111, 113, 118, 242
Customs and Border Protection (CBP), 242

DACA (Deferred Action for Childhood Arrivals), 221, 225–226, 228, 237, 239, 240, 241
DAPA (Deferred Action for Parental Accountability), 226, 249
Deal, Benito, x, xiii, 244
de Beausset, Kyle, 82, 90–91, 94, 114–115
Delgado, Gary, 25
Department of Homeland Security (DHS), 18, 24, 29, 109, 118, 197, 246
Dominguez, Neidi, 97–87, 130, 132–133, 157, 165
DREAM 21. *See* Noodles, 2.0
DREAM 5, 116, 119–122, 124, 129, 138, 165. *See also* McCain Tucson action

DREAM Act
  categorical distinction, 11, 19, 43, 55, 78, 187, 203, 217, 253, 258
  origin of, 7, 17
  undocumted youth first learning about, 40, 52, 59–60, 74, 76–7, 203–4
DreamACTivist.org, 77–79, 191, 215, 227, 246, 254
  Capitol occupation, 150–151, 155, 159
  DREAM Act Portal (DAP), 74, 75, 76, 77
  email list, 88, 90, 94–95, 129
  moderate-radical divide, 137, 160, 181
  Mo's use of, 95, 128–130
  and nonprofit immigration field, 84, 88, 91
  Tucson McCain Action, 117, 121, 254
DREAMer
  bad DREAMers, 76, 197
  campus DREAMers, 75, 130–131
  coming out, 43, 47, 78, 79–81, 145, 173, 186, 204, 206, 208
  divisions between, 135, 137
  early DREAMer stories, 21–24
  good DREAMer, 78, 187, 193, 206, 208
  LGBTQ DREAMers (*see* Lal, Prerna; Abdollahi, Mohammad; Torres-Don, Jose; Garcia-Leco, Santiago)
  narrative and character, 19–20, 24, 28, 34, 72, 76, 78, 90, 192–193, 206
  radical DREAMers, 73, 104, 107, 121, 130–131, 134, 146, 173, 185, 206
  reification of, 43, 80, 90, 100, 251–252, 256, 260
  un-deportability of, 95, 105, 188, 255
  (*see also* END campaigns; Abdollahi, Mohammad)
DREAMer mock graduations, 27, 49, 90–92, 96, 144, 149
The Dream is Coming, 121, 130, 147, 165, 173, 175, 179, 185, 206. *See also* Noodles
  website, 109–110, 129, 148 (*see also* Noodlesforo)
DREAM Team LA, 97–98, 121, 130, 165, 167, 181, 189
Durbin, Dick, 82, 97, 108, 112, 155, 157
Durkheim, Emile, 251

END ("Education not Deportation")
campaigns, 93, 94–5, 109, 111, 145, 162–3, 179, 186, 187–8, 192
as a part of NIYA, 227, 236–7, 238 (*see also* NIYA)

Federation for American Immigration Reform (FAIR), 15, 21
Feinstein, Diane, 112, 151, 164, 165–166
Fetishism. *See* reification
FIRM (Fair Immigration Reform Movement). *See* CCC
FLIC (Florida Immigration Coalition), 13–14, 27, 35–36, 54, 56, 69, 85, 86, 103
Ford Foundation, 12–13, 14–15, 25, 27, 33, 167
Foucault, Michel, 254
Four Freedoms Fund, 86, 98

Garcia-Leco, Santiago, 197–209, 210–213, 214–217, 242, 259
Garibay, Julieta, 36–41, 43–50, 144–5, 147, 173, 175, 257
conflict with radical DREAMers, 113, 145, 147, 149–51, 161, 170, 173–4, 178–9
and ULI, 36, 44–50, 144–5, 170, 173–4
Garibay, Montserrat, 36–38, 40, 44, 46–47, 144, 159–60
George Soros, 17
Georgia 8 action, 194–196
Georgia Latino Alliance for Human Rights (GLAHR), 190–192, 222
Gonzales, Alfonso, 14
Gonzalez, Marie, 24–25, 27–29, 32–33, 35, 49, 55. *See also* We are Marie campaign
Graciosa, Marrissa, 88, 122
Gutiérrez, Luis, 7, 99, 104, 126, 128, 151–155, 157–160, 164, 167, 176, 245, 254, 255

Hagan, Kay, 189, 210
Hatch, Orin, 7, 10, 22, 163
HB 1403 (Texas), 39–43, 45–46, 50, 142–144

HB 56 (Alabama), 214, 215
Heredia, Luisa, 188, 255
Heyns, Barbara, 173
Hoyt, Josh, 226. *See also* ICIRR
HR 4437 (US), 30, 31–32, 48
Hutchinson, Kay Bailey, 170, 174, 176, 179, 256

ICE (Immigration and Customs Enforcement), 18, 186–189, 236–237, 259
and A#'s (Alien numbers), 192
and cooperation with local law enforcement, 190–191, 209, 210, 249
detaining DREAMers, 108–109, 117–118, 172–173, 191
and increase in deportations, 236–237 (*see also* Morton Memo)
raids, 64, 196
and refusing to detain DREAMers, 196, 209
ICIRR (Illinois Coalition for Immigrant and Refugee Rights), 13–14, 27, 126, 130
IIRIRA (Illegal Immigration Reform and Immigration Responsibility Act), 15–16, 18, 19, 37–38
Immigration and Naturalization Service (INS), 16, 22
Immigration Reform and Control Act (IRCA) of 1986, 14, 16
International Ladies' Garment Workers Union (ILGWU), 13
IYJL (Immigrant Youth Justice League), 81, 95, 98, 104, 108, 110, 126, 128, 130, 145, 159, 181, 228, 243

JIFM (Jóvenes Inmigrantes por un Futuro Mejor), 36, 39, 40, 46–47, 69
Jiménez, Cristina, 70, 82, 86, 175
Joas, Hans, 259
Juli. *See* Garibay, Julieta

KBH. *See* Hutchinson, Kay Bailey
Kenyon College, 232
Kohn, Sally, 167–169, 256

Lal, Prerna, 71–75, 226, 236, 254, 257
  and conflict with nonprofit field, 80, 81–82, 83–84, 87, 88–91, 92–93, 97, 98, 99–100
  and DreamACTivist.org, 77–79, 87, 92
  on the DREAMer Character, 206, 250
  and self-instrumentalization, 90, 95
  and UWD national network, 85, 86, 94
Lara, Walter, 91, 93
Legal Aid Foundation of Los Angeles (LAFLA), 12–13
Legal Services Corporation (LSC), 11–12, 13
Leopold, David, 245
Lofgren, Zoe, 65
Lukacs, Georg, 252
LULAC (Latino Leadership Council), 42, 46, 50, 151, 157–158, 160
  Head of Policy and Development, Brent Wilkes, 151–153, 157, 160

Marantes, José Luis, 56, 85, 86, 88, 90–92, 97, 105–106, 175, 178, 182, 184
Martinez, LuLu, 243–247
Martinez, Viridiana, 189–190, 195, 205–209, 225, 239–242
Mateo, Lizbeth, 57–68, 82, 91, 96–97, 105, 165
  campus organizing, 175
  and conflict with moderate DREAMers, 175
  conflict with nonprofit field, 113, 124–125, 131–132
  DC McCain Action, 176–177
  as Mohammad Abdollahi's "moral compass," 187
  and Noodles, 108, 110, 112, 114, 117, 121, 146, 167
  and radical action, 236, 237, 243–244, 246, 247, 248
  and UWD network, 175
Matos, Felipe, 98, 102–103, 136, 175
McCain, John, 53, 110, 116–117, 163, 178, 180
McCain DC action, x, 52, 146, 151, 176, 178–179
McCain Tucson action, ix, 102, 104, 114–122, 124, 154, 173, 254, 256

McCarthy, John, 9
Mega Marchas, 32, 35, 48, 61, 74. *See also* student walkouts of 2006
Melucci, Alberto, 2, 3
Mexican American Legal Defense and Educational Fund (MALDEF), 7, 12, 13, 46, 105
militarization of the border, 16, 18
Milk, Harvey, 81
MIRA (Massachusetts Immigrant and Refugee Advocacy Coalition), 13–14, 27, 35, 45, 69, 96
Montsy. *See* Garibay, Montserrat
Morton memo, 237, 240. *See also* Immigration Customs Enforcement (ICE)
Mo. *See* Abdollahi, Mohammad
Muñoz, Claudia, 242, 263, 264, 265, 272, 273, 283, 284
myth, 3, 10, 33
  nonprofit immigration field's movement mystification, 33, 34, 124, 255 (*see also* nonprofit immigration field; reification; social movements)

National Council for La Raza (NCLR), 13, 45, 48, 173
National Day Laborer Organizing Network (NDLON), 111, 114, 130, 179, 228–229, 249
National Immigration Forum (NIF), 13, 14, 15, 86, 90, 98, 120, 125
Netroots Nation, 100, 157
Newman, Chris, 111, 228–229. *See also* National Day Laborer Organizing Network (NDLON)
New York Immigration Coalition (NYIC), 13–14, 27, 35, 45, 69, 70, 86
New York Times. See Preston, Julia
NILC (National Immigration Law Center), 14, 17, 109. *See also* Bernstein, Josh
  against stand-alone DREAM act, 125
  and conflict with Radical Dreamers, 83–84, 96–97, 105, 106
  origins of, 11–12
  as part of nonprofit immigration field, 10, 12, 13

and the UWD Network, 71, 82, 83, 85, 86, 135
and work with DREAMers, 27, 48–50, 63–64, 66
and work with state and regional nonprofits, 14
NIYA (National Immigrant Youth Alliance), 1, 2–3, 4, 6
   Alabama community organizing, 215–217
   Charlotte NC action, 209–214
   DREAM 9 action, ix, xiv, 242–248, 250
   DREAM 30 action xiv, xv, 1, 247–248, 250
   formation of, 192–194
   Georgia, 5, 195
   Georgia 8, 194–195
   infiltrations, 238–242
   influence of, 249
   OFA sit-ins, 225–226, 228
   Phoenix action, 222–225
   silent action, 217–221
nonprofit immigration field, 9
Noodles
   Divisions in Noodles Team, 126
   Noodles (members of actions), 111–117, 149, 157
   Noodles action, 110–119, 156
   Noodles Team, 110–119, 121–122, 129–130, 133, 135–137, 146–148, 162, 163, 165, 175, 188, 255–256, 260
   radical Noodles, 135
   Spicy Noodles, 114, 119, 131–132, 149
Noodles 2.0, 137–138, 148–151, 156–157, 169, 192
Noodlesforo, 109–118, 121, 123–125, 127–130, 135–137, 146–148, 155, 157–158, 162, 164
Nooran, Ali, 14, 98–99, 104, 113, 127–128, 134, 154
Noriega, Rick, 39
North American Free Trade Agreement (NAFTA), 16
NYSYLC (New York Student Leadership Conference), 27, 69, 70, 85–87, 145, 183
   radical activism, 110, 130, 126–127, 146, 181, 230, 234

Obama, Barack, 85, 104, 123, 148, 197, 225–226, 239, 245, 249
Obama administration, 92, 94, 195, 220, 225–226, 237, 240, 245
Ohno, Shuya, 90, 120, 125
Open Society Institute (OSI), 17, 27, 33
Orosco, Angie, 143

Pacheco, Gaby, 7–8, 50–56, 96, 164
   conflict with radical DREAMers, 104, 136–137, 178, 207–208, 256
   and the DC McCain action, x–xi, 52–54, 176–178, 180
   and SWER, 54–56
   and the trail of dreams, 98, 102–104, 167
   and UWD, 124, 146, 147
Pavey, Steve, xiii, 235, 237–238
Perez, Georgina, 191–192, 194–195, 196, 208
Perez, Jonathan, 217–222, 224, 236, 258. See also Barrera, Isaac
Perry, Rick, 39
Personal Responsibility and Work Opportunity Act (PROWRA), 15
Phoenix Fund (New World Foundation), 69, 70, 190
Plyler v. Doe, 12
Polletta, Francesca, 4
Post-Industrial Revolutionary Party (PRI), 17
Presente, 103, 124, 135
Preston, Julia, 114, 115, 117, 119

Quaker. See Abdollahi, Mohammad
QueerDesi. See Lal, Prerna

radical flank effect, 135
Ramos, Marisol, 69–71, 190–191
   departure from activism, 175–176
   on nonprofit immigration field, 88–89
   and Noodles, 109, 111, 115–116, 117, 121, 135
   support of Mo and Prerna, 94, 97
Ramos, Matias, 82, 85, 86, 108–109, 184, 234
Reid, Harry, 112, 151–152, 157, 164–165;

reification, 2, 251. *See also* DREAMer; social movement
RI4A (Reform Immigration for America), 86, 204
  conflict with radical DREAMers, 120, 125–134
  events, 90, 98–100
  rollout, 88–89
  singular CIR focus, 101–107, 113, 119
  and standalone DREAM Act, 105, 124, 127, 134, 136, 147, 183
  and UWD, 106–107, 124–125, 135–136
Rincón, Alejandra, 39, 40, 45, 47, 48, 142
Romney, Mitt, 225

Saavedra, Carlos, 45, 173
  conflict with radical DREAMers, 124, 127–128, 178, 182–184
  as Director of UWD, 96, 105–108, 135, 162, 175, 179
Saavedra, Marco, 187, 213, 230–236, 257
  criticism of NIYA, 246
  DREAM 9 border crossing, 242–245
  infiltration of BTC detention center, 238–241
Salas, Angelica, 26, 27, 131–132
Santi. *See* Garcia-Leco, Santiago
Savage-Sangwan, Kiran, 70, 97, 105, 121, 125, 136, 151, 157, 189
SB 1070 (Arizona), 4, 15, 101–102, 110, 199, 123, 124, 189, 192, 214
Schumer action, 127–135, 194
Schwarzenegger, Arnold, 56
Secure Communities Program, 18
Senator Menendez, 112, 136–137, 151, 164
Senator Rubio, 225
Senator Schumer, 127–128, 132–133, 134, 151, 164
Sennett, Richard, 5
Sensenbrenner Bill. *See* HR, 4437
Service Employee International Union (SEIU), 13, 14, 85, 86, 90, 91, 105–106, 182
Sharry, Frank, 14, 15, 80, 98–99, 128, 134, 254
Sheriff Arpaio, Joe, 113, 222–223, 224–225
Silver, Alexis, 190

sit-in at Senator Reid's office, 151–156, 158–159, 255–256
social movement, 1–6
  radicalization of, 249, 251, 256, 260–261
  reification of, 80, 123–24, 124, 251–252, 256, 260
state-level immigrant rights organizations. *See* CCC; CHIRLA; FLIC; ICIRR; MIRA; NILC; NYIC
Stolz, Rich, 34, 63–64, 66, 83, 107–108, 120
Student Immigrant Movement (SIM), 35, 45, 69, 181, 183, 233
Students Working for Equal Rights (SWER), 11, 35, 51, 54, 56–57, 71, 85–86, 102–103
student walkouts of 2006, 4, 31, 32, 35, 48, 61, 70, 171. *See also* Mega Marchas

Tilly, Charles, 2, 3
Torres, Alicia, 140–142, 145, 161, 189–190, 213, 258. *See also* Torres-Don, Jose
  radical action, 145–147, 149–152, 155–161, 170, 174, 189, 236, 257
Torres-Don, José, 108, 138–146, 147, 149–152, 155–161, 163, 170, 174, 189, 236, 257
Touraine, Alaine, 5, 252
The Trail of Dreams, xi, 98, 102–104, 131, 135, 168, 173, 207–208, 234, 256
Tran, Tam, 64, 68, 82, 89
Truthout.org, 165–167, 168, 256

ULI (University Leadership Initiative), 36, 44–48, 69, 143–146, 173
  congressional lame duck session push for DREAM Act, 176
  as moderate, 50, 144, 159, 170–171, 173
UNITE HERE!. *See* International Ladies' Garment Workers Union
Uniting American Families Act (UAFA), 98–99
Unzueta, Tañia, 80, 81, 108, 112, 116–119, 126, 128, 130–131, 133, 159, 217, 228–229
UWD (United We Dream) Network, 91–92, 147, 175–176
  beginnings, 85–88

conflict with radical Dreamers, 107–109, 113, 121–122, 162
Don't Deport Dora campaign, 180, 185
independent funding, 96
moderate/radical split, 105, 108, 121–122, 138, 147, 181–186, 189
moderate leadership, 135
and the nonprofit Immigration field, 97, 124, 125, 134, 173
organizational failings, 96–97
organizational self-governance, 175
radical influence on, 170
Steering Committee, 85, 86, 88, 105–107, 124, 125
for UWD Campaign. *See* CCC
UWD Convenings, 57, 71, 82–85, 85, 97, 104, 110, 144–145, 147, 170, 174, 249

Vargas, Felipe, ix, xiii, 45, 82, 173–173, 179, 189, 212, 215
Veliz, Benita, 91–92, 172
Vicente Fox, 17
Viri. *See* Martinez, Viridiana

Walker, Edward T., 10
We are Marie campaign, 24–25, 28, 29, 54–55. *See also* Gonzalez, Marie
Wilshire, 9, 119

Yanez–Correa, Ana, 46, 50

Zald, Mayer, 9
Zogby, Joe, 82, 85, 112, 127
Zolberg, Aristide, 15, 17

The manufacturer's authorised representative in the EU for product safety is Oxford
University Press España S.A. of El Parque Empresarial San Fernando de Henares,
Avenida de Castilla, 2 – 28830 Madrid (www.oup.es/en or product.safety@oup.com).
OUP España S.A. also acts as importer into Spain of products made by the manufacturer.

Printed in the USA/Agawam, MA
March 28, 2025

885041.017